THE DALAI LAMAS

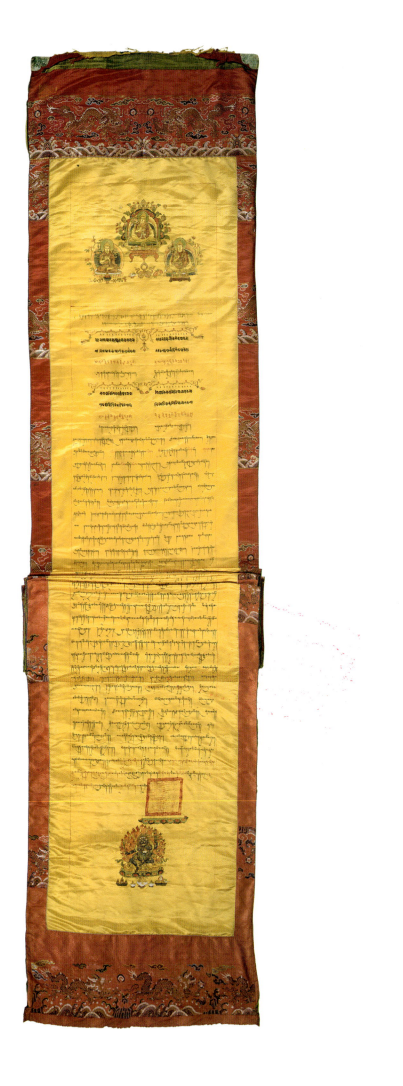

THE DALAI LAMAS
A VISUAL HISTORY

Edited by Martin Brauen

Ethnographic Museum of
the University of Zürich

in association with
SERINDIA PUBLICATIONS, Chicago

For as long as space endures
And as long as the world endures
So long I shall abide
To dispel the suffering of the World

Śāntideva, the 8th century Buddhist master
Bodhicaryāvatāra X.55

Dedicated to His Holiness, the Fourteenth Dalai Lama, who celebrates his 70th
birthday in the year this book is published, and to the Tibetan people.

Martin Brauen

First English Edition 2005
© 2005 Collective works:
Ethnographic Museum of the University of Zürich
Serindia Publications
ARNOLDSCHE Art Publishers
Authors, photographers, and image holders.

Originally published in German entitled *Die Dalai Lamas:
Tibets Reinkarnationen des Bodhisattva Avalokiteśvara*
by ARNOLDSCHE Art Publishers, Stuttgart
www.arnoldsche.com

Editor
Martin Brauen
Ethnographic Museum of the University of Zürich

English edition editors
Patrick A. McCormick
Shane Suvikapakornkul
with additional assistance from
Edwin Zehner

Translator
Janice Becker
English translations (five essays, introduction,
plate captions) © 2005 Janice Becker
for Serindia Publications

Layout and Typography
Silke Nalbach and
Karina Moschke, Stuttgart
Toby Matthews, Oxford
Shane Suvikapakornkul, Chicago

Reproduction
Repromayer, Reutlingen

Printed in Germany by
Druckhaus Beltz, Hemsbach

Library of Congress Cataloging-in-Publication Data
Dalai Lamas. English.
  The Dalai Lamas : a visual history / edited by Martin
Brauen.-- 1st
ed.
    p. cm.
  Five essays and picture entries originally written in
German and translated into English.
  "Simultaneously published in German as 'Die Dalai
Lamas' by Arnoldsche Art Publishers, Stuttgart."
  "... published in conjunction with exhibition 'Die 14 Dalai
Lamas'
... Zürich, Switzerland, August 4, 2005 to April 30, 2006."
  Includes bibliographical references and index.
  ISBN 1-932476-22-9 (hardcover : alk. paper)
    I. Brauen, Martin. II. Title.

BQ7930.D3513 2005
294.3'923'0922--dc22

2005012800

Front cover:
The Fourteenth Dalai Lama,
Photographer: Josef Vaniš, plate 244.

Back cover:
Handprints of the Thirteenth Dalai Lama,
Hanakami City Museum 花巻市博物館
plate 99.

Frontispiece:
Letter from the nine-year-old Fourteenth Dalai Lama
to his regent, as a sign of gratitude for his services and
in remembrance of a monastery a teacher of the Tenth
Dalai Lama founded. With the seal of the Fourteenth
Dalai Lama, ca. 22 m x 0.9 m, dated 9 May 1944. © John
Bigelow Taylor, New York, Collection of Jane Werner-Aye.

Insert:
Chronological chart of the Dalai Lamas and the Panchen
Lamas and their historical contexts. Illustrated with the
Ninth Dalai Lama's set of seven lineage thangkas.

ISBN 1-932476-22-9

Published by:
SERINDIA PUBLICATIONS, Inc.
PO Box 10335
Chicago, Illinois 60610
Tel: 312-664-5531
Fax: 312-664-4389
info@serindia.com
www.serindia.com

This book is printed on 100% acid-free paper
TCF-Standard.

SERINDIA
PUBLICATIONS INC.

CONTENTS

INTRODUCTION AND INTERVIEW WITH
HIS HOLINESS THE FOURTEENTH DALAI LAMA

Martin Brauen
Translated by JANICE BECKER

HOW THIS EXHIBITION AND INTERVIEW CAME ABOUT

The 14th Dalai Lama enjoys wide respect around the world. In 2002 when a German public opinion poll asked who the wisest person in the world was, 33% named the Dalai Lama, coming in far ahead of Pope John Paul II and the former president of South Africa, Nelson Mandela. The Dalai Lama is "in," but what do we actually know about him? Despite his popularity, few people know about the institution of the Dalai Lama. Who knows that only the third in the lineage was the first who received the title "Dalai Lama"? Who knows that the title "Dalai Lama" itself was awarded by a Mongolian prince? And who is aware of the roots of the concept of reincarnation?

Hardly anyone knows that of the fourteen Dalai Lamas, few have actually ruled Tibet and those who did, ruled for only a few years. Most are unaware that four Dalai Lamas barely reached maturity and their early demises remain subjects of speculation. Even fewer people know anything about the *yönchö* ཡོན་མཆོད་ [yon mchod] "patron-spiritual teacher" system, which was not invented during the period of the Dalai Lamas but only revived at that time between Mongolian tribes and Tibet and between the Chinese imperial court and Tibet. Many will be surprised to learn that some Mongolian khans and Chinese emperors maintained close ties with Dalai Lamas and were sometimes very interested in Tibetan Buddhism. The 14th Dalai Lama was not the only one forced to flee his country—two others, the 7th and the 13th, also lived in exile for a period of time. Even few Tibetans know that there were two 6th Dalai Lamas.

When I learned that His Holiness the 14th Dalai Lama would turn seventy in the summer of 2005, it suddenly occurred to me that this could be an opportunity to dedicate a book and exhibition to the phenomenon of the Dalai Lama and the 14th Dalai Lama in particular. Therefore in the summer of 2001 I traveled to Trento, where the Dalai Lama was staying for a short time, and presented my plans to him. He had nothing against it; on the contrary, he encouraged me to pursue my plans by assuring me in principle that he would come to Zürich for the opening of the exhibition in August 2005.

Thus I began my journey back into the last six hundred years of Tibetan history. I knew from the start that I did not want to make this journey alone. In Switzerland I found two eager "travel companions," Dr. Amy Heller of Nyon and Michael Henss of Zürich, both of whom are my cocurators who brought along many valuable contacts and ideas and wrote some of the captions for the exhibition and this publication. During this last year of especially intense work, others have accompanied me, in particular Dario Donati, who took on many different aspects of the project and managed them all to my complete satisfaction. He paid special attention to historical photographic material, materials on loan, and to maintaining contact with lenders. Renate Koller, who contributed valuable archival, research, and bibliographic services, accompanied me as well.

Our "travel team" also includes the many authors who kindly agreed to come on board, even though some may have come to regret their decision given their already busy schedules and many commitments. But long forgotten are the inevitable reminders to a few authors, forgotten as well are the submission deadlines missed by months. Instead, together with all the authors and other contributors, I am pleased with what we have accomplished—the first book about the Dalai Lamas both with essays by sixteen experts and with unique illustrations never before presented in this way.

Not only is our combination of text and images unique, but many of the objects shown are being published for the first time. We have the museum curators to thank for the fact that these objects could be exhibited, and also the private collectors who generously agreed to participate. My heartfelt thanks go to all these people and the many others listed on page 299 for all their friendly cooperation.

I would also like to thank the sponsors (also on p. 299) who generously contributed to this project, in contrast to others who did not want to contribute, in part out of fear of the Chinese government's reprisals. My special thanks go to Dieter Kuhn, who translated into German the essays originally contributed in English, and to Arnoldsche Art Publisher, in particular Dirk Allgaier, with whom I have now had the pleasure of producing two books in an atmosphere of great trust and understanding for my concerns. Working with him, reader Julia Vogt, and graphic designers Silke Nalback and Karina Moschke, could not have been better.

Shane Suvikapakornkul and Patrick A. McCormick played critical roles in the production of the English language edition. They ensured uniform terminology and transliteration of Tibetan terms and names, even adding original Tibetan script to the essays, and helped to clarify outstanding questions regarding the texts. Also invaluable were the services of Janice Becker, who translated the essays not written in English, applying understanding and sensitivity—a challenging task in light of the complexity and "foreignness" of many concepts and terms. My heartfelt thanks go to all three for their invaluable contributions.

THE VIEW FROM OUTSIDE

This overview of the fourteen Dalai Lamas in words and images is a lesson in Tibetan hagiography, an introduction to Tibetan religiosity, and the Tibetan history of the last six hundred years. The contributions compiled in this volume are based in no small part on original Tibetan texts. Tibetans themselves wrote these original texts representing one very special "view from within"—namely, that of a believer in a saint and even more so in a deity, manifested in the person of the Dalai Lama. Most biographies are therefore hagiographies, with all the features typical of this type of narrative—they are worshipful, admiring, reverent, idolizing, respectful, pious, devoted. They report miracles, extraordinary dreams, the prophesies of oracles, and the omniscience and benevolence of the Dalai Lamas. We can sense the reverence of these sources when reading the essays on each of the individual Dalai Lamas, even though with one exception non-Tibetans have written them. The source materials available to our authors were almost exclusively Tibetan hagiographies. "Objective" Tibetan historiography is practically unknown. Textual criticism of Tibetan texts is likewise still in its infancy.

Only with the 13th Dalai Lama do we begin to see a new perspective, however tentative and sporadic. For the first time Europeans—notably Charles Bell—came together with the Dalai Lama for extended periods of time resulting in a kind of view from the outside. As a result the Dalai Lama began to acquire "normal, human" attributes and character traits. This view from the outside, however, also widely manifests piety and reverence. As a rule the phenomenon of the Dalai Lama has rarely been subjected to subtle or nuanced analysis or criticism. This is a result of many factors, including the mystique that has surrounded the institution of the Dalai Lama for centuries, the charisma of the 13th Dalai Lama, and even more so that of the 14th Dalai Lama living today. More importantly, I believe only someone who has both insider (Tibetan) and outsider (non-Tibetan) views can provide such a critical, nuanced perspective on the man and the institution. Georges Dreyfus, who combines both, has contributed a chapter to this volume that goes beyond a traditional description of a Dalai Lama. He is a Western monk who has acquired the Tibetan title of *geshe* དགེ་བཤེས [dge bshes], yet he is also an instructor of the history of religions at an American university (see p. 298).

By the time we reach the chapter on the 5th Dalai Lama, we begin to see that the descriptions of each Dalai Lama demonstrate that their histories together form the history of Tibet over the last six hundred years. Since this history is rich and varied, yet can be quite confusing to the layperson, I have also provided a chart with the help of graphic designer Andreas Brodbeck (see folding insert).

The individual essays—even more so the chart—make clear the extent to which foreign powers and foreign interests have influenced the institution of the Dalai Lama, whether the influence is from Mongolian tribes (Tümed, Khoshod, and Dzungars), the Manchu Qing 清 emperors, or later the Russians and British. The essays also describe various attempts over the centuries to overcome the weaknesses inherent in the system of succession of the Dalai Lama. For instance, a quasi-head of government was installed over the Dalai Lama in the form of a regent, which first occurred during the period of the 5th Dalai Lama. Ever since the death of the 7th Dalai Lama, such regents received appointments to reign during the period between the death of one Dalai Lama and maturity and accession of his successor. The Manchus introduced the office of *Amban* 安班 (a Manchu delegate stationed in Lhasa; *Amban* is a Manchu-language title represented here in Chinese script) in 1720 in an attempt to stem the unrest caused by intrigues among various Mongolian tribes and their Tibetan collaborators. Around 1750, the Amban was superceded by the office of the *kashak* བཀའ་ཤག [bka' shag], a ministerial council comprised of four ministers that continues today within the Tibetan government-in-exile.

The history of the Dalai Lama also reveals much about domestic Tibetan developments. We see how a small religious group surrounding the Kadam School monk Domtön and his teacher Atiśa employed clever "inventions" and calculated political maneuvers to become a powerful religious movement. This in turn became the sole determinative power in the 17th century when the 5th Dalai Lama, together with his most important regent Sanggye Gyatso, gave this religious movement new and irrefutable legitimacy through his personal authority and by reviving older stories. The history of the Dalai Lamas also illustrates how religious and political factions repeatedly tried to seize power opportunistically, through dubious coalitions, attacks, and even murder. From the point of view of the history of religions, the study of the history of the Dalai Lamas is informative because it reveals several key features of Tibetan Buddhism: the belief in reincarnation, reverence for protective deities, and the existence of practices generally not associated with textual Buddhism, including the importance of dreams and belief in oracular prophecies, miracles, and saints appearing in miraculous stories.

Deeper study of the Dalai Lamas has revealed to me just how little we know even today about this institution of such great importance, not only to Tibet, but Mongolia and China as well. I was reminded of this again when I received a letter from Per Sørensen just as I was about to complete this introductory essay. In his letter he explained that the common translation of "dalai" as "ocean," and the resulting rendering of *Dalai Lama* as "Ocean Lama" was actually inadequate and incomplete. After providing examples to support his contention,[1] he continued, "For Mongolians, *dalai* in connection with their rulers meant something similar to the Buddhist epithet *cakravartin*, or universal king, a concept of ideal or divine rule…. While we have come to accept that Dalai Lama means 'Lama (like an) Ocean,' we should not forget that, for Mongolians, the inventors of the title, it can just as well mean 'the Universal Lama' or the 'World Lama.'"

THE PERSPECTIVE OF THE "WORLD LAMA" HIMSELF

Westerners have consistently raised the question of the origins of the system of reincarnation, in particular those of the institution of the Dalai Lama. An answer should be attempted in the introductory chapter. For Tibetan believers, however, the issue does not come up since the manifestation of the Bodhisattva[2] Avalokiteśvara in the form of the Dalai Lama or other lamas is an immutable fact not subject to question. Similarly, whether or not this system was known in India is irrelevant for the Tibetan faithful. In light of the risk that a "scientific" approach to religion such as found in this book could result in the loss of their real "essence" or at least present a distorted picture,

I defer to the words of the manifestation of the Bodhisattva Avalokiteśvara currently living among us, the 14th Dalai Lama. His is simultaneously an "insider's" voice—the voice of the *kündün* ཀུན་འདུན་ [kun 'dun] "the all-embodying," of the *kyapgön* སྐྱབས་མགོན་ [skyabs mgon] "highest protector," and of the *gyalwa* རྒྱལ་བ་ [rgyal ba] "victorious."

The following is part of an interview the Dalai Lama granted in October 2004 as part of this book project. To begin, I asked the Dalai Lama the question about the origins of the reincarnation system. As tradition requires, the Dalai Lama referred to old Buddhist legends that hold the answer:

> The basis of the…system is the theory of rebirth. This is not something unique to Buddhism but it is also there in some ancient Indian thought, Indian tradition. In India, I think, it is there even among the Hindus, but at least among the early Indian Buddhists like Dharmakīrti … [and] Vasubandhu. When [Vasubandhu] recited a text, which contained many hundred thousand verses, a pigeon was always hearing these recitations. Later this pigeon was born as Lodö Tenpa who became a great student of Vasubandhu and later wrote a commentary about the Abhidharma. So the reincarnation theory is well established in the Indian and Buddhist tradition. In India there is not only the concept of reincarnation but also a systematic process of recognizing reincarnations.

He shares the widely held opinion regarding the first use of the system of reincarnation in Tibet, which holds that the Karma School originally instituted it, although this view can no longer be considered completely correct in light of modern "scientific" investigation:

> At the time of his death, Karmapa Düsum Khyenpa clearly mentioned his rebirth would appear in such-and-such area in such and such family. So obviously the lama gave some clear instructions: "My reincarnation will appear." That mean[t] the concerned students or followers must take care.
>
> So then many lamas and their followers founded particular monasteries…In the case of India a scholar cho[se] a particular monastery and he then remain[ed] there, he bec[ame] the master of this particular monastery, but the monastery d[id] not become his personal belonging.

In Tibet the case was quite different: one great lama started with the construction of a monastery, and later this monastery became the belonging of that particular lama.

When the authentic reincarnation comes, then that monastery takes care [of the him]. So in this way the lamas' kind of estate and monastery came into existence. Then later, whether authentic or not, when there was somebody they wanted to recognize as a young lama he might become or be chosen as the reincarnation. That is also possible. In the beginning this process of selection was more genuine. One example: the 1st Dalai Lama Gendün Drup did not implicitly say that his reincarnation would come, but he indicated it, by saying that in case there [sh]ould be a rebirth of him, then one should make sure that one would not disgrace him.

Then came the 2nd Dalai Lama. He was from a young age really extraordinary, and there were very convincing indications that he was the true incarnation of the previous Dalai Lama, but their nature was completely different...so this [wa]s the start of the Dalai Lama-lineage. Then came the 3rd Dalai Lama. There was already the institution of the Drepung monastery. Drepung monastery was very big. At that time already the institution of the Karma [School] was there and maybe also that one of the female reincarnation Dorje Phakmo. I heard that her institution started at about the same time as that of the Karma [School], Düsum Khyenpa or the second Karmapa.

Archives of the Norbulingka Institute, Sidhpur, India.

The concept of a line of incarnation for the Dalai Lamas presumes the continuity between two living beings: the predecessor and his reincarnation. Since this concept often leads to misunderstandings in the west, I asked the Dalai Lama if he could address it and he replied as follows:

> Of course Buddhism accepts the existence of the continuity of a being. The Buddhist theory of "selflessness" means that there is no independent self apart from the body, because "self" or the person is designated [by] the combination of body and mind. There is a self, but there is no independent absolute self. So this is the meaning of selflessness in the context of the theory of "no-self." With respect to continuation, not only does Buddhism accept the continuity of the being, but also upholds the notion of a "beginningless" self, that is, a self with no beginning and no end until buddhahood is achieved. Any self is reborn from "beginningless[ness]" and will be reborn endlessly.

The Fourteenth Dalai Lama and the editor of this book, Martin Brauen, at the exhibition "Dreamworld Tibet" at the Ethnographic Museum of the University of Zürich, in May 2001. Photo: Hansjörg Sahli, Solothurn.

There are different kinds of reincarnations. An eminent Buddha [or] *bodhisattva* can manifest several times simultaneously, lower *bodhisattvas* reincarnate only in one person, this means once at a time. But anyone, irrespective [of whether they are] a *bodhisattva* or an ordinary person, is reborn from "beginningless[ness]" and will be born endlessly. Continuity is always there and will always be there, due to karma. Now, at one stage, if you develop a certain spiritual realization, then the birth through karma will cease. Then with willpower you can choose your rebirth. This type of rebirth we call reincarnation.

Today *tülku*—unfortunately—[has] become almost like the designation of a certain status, a social status. So, among these *tülkus*, some may have that sort of quality, the possibility to choose their rebirth, some not.

Anyway, whether a person has the designation "*tülku*" or not, those individuals who [have] already developed certain inner qualities, seek their rebirth according to their wish. So this one

calls "reincarnation." In this case too, it is the same being, it is the continuation of the same being. I think the basis of the misunderstanding about continuity is [that] there is continuation, yet momentarily it changes. A continuity, which momentarily is not changing, that kind of continuity is not there. The misunderstanding consists in the fact that some mix up conventional conditioned continuity with independent continuity.

One example: This paper lying here was produced some months ago. Since from the start of the paper up to now there is continuity/continuation. It is continuously there, but it is momentarily changing.

Let's look again at this table. On the table there is absence of—say—[a] flower. There is no flower on the table. So the absence of [the] flower is existing here. Yesterday there was also an absence of [a] flower. Today there is an absence of flowers. So that continuity is not changing.

One can see two kinds of continuity: one is as we were explaining with the reincarnation, that there is a conditioned conventional continuity. So this kind of impermanent conditioned continuity is there. But on another level of existence there is something for which you may use the word continuity or not, for example the absence of flower. Because there is no flower here, the mere absence or negation of [the] flower is there today, will be there tomorrow, will forever be there. This is not changing.

The continuity of non-existence is not changing. But the other continuity is momentarily changing. So from the beginningless time continuation is there, but it is momentarily changing. To come back to the reincarnation: As a being who changes his clothes is still the same person, equally it is the same being even if it changes the body.

Until now we have seen one type of reincarnation, those on a high level who are able to change the body according to their own wish. There is also an other type of reincarnation system, which is described in the stories of the past lamas: When a lama, a spiritual master, passes away, in order to carry on his work, one of his disciples may choose someone as the "reincarnation" of the master to carry on the teacher's work. In this case this is also reincarnation, but in the form of a separate individual. In the case of the Dalai Lamas from the 1st to the 7th, most probably these beings shared a single lineage starting from one individual. The 2nd Dalai Lama clearly mentioned that due to his karma he would come back five times, so that means up to the 7th Dalai

Lama. We also know that the 1st Dalai Lama was a manifestation of the Bodhisattva Avalokiteśvara. This is very clear. The 5th Dalai Lama, on the other hand, was (also) considered as a manifestation of the Bodhisattva Mañjuśrī.[3]

At about the same time when the 1st Dalai Lama was alive, one Karmapa, and a senior Drigung Lama were also considered to be manifestations of Avalokiteśvara. This means that there can be (simultaneously) several manifestations of one and the same source. And it is also possible that one person is reincarnated in several bodies, in one case I heard in five different bodies, in other words: five reincarnations from one source. So you see, there is a variety of reincarnations: Sometimes several reincarnations, sometimes only one, sometimes the reincarnation is the same person, and in other cases someone as his or her representative.

The world is unlimited, infinite. So a reincarnation is not bound to one place, but is sometimes here, sometimes there. Take for instance Buddha. At certain periods he appeared on this planet, but at other times his reincarnations may be at some other planets, in some other universes, and he may still be there.

In my own case: At the time of my death, when I feel that I am no [longer] useful on this planet, then I will pray that I will be reborn to be of use. I always pray, "as long as space remains and as long as sentient beings' suffering remains, may I remain to dispel their suffering." So I pray that I am born somewhere where I will be useful. A *bodhisattva* is always reborn again; he never makes a break, never disappears. He has to provide good services among the human beings, animals, insects, any living being. This is his *bodhisattva* vow.

Each Dalai Lama had a distinct personality with his own character and own achievements. If one believes in the tradition of Dalai Lamas, then the life of each must have had a deeper meaning or a deeper purpose. So I asked the Dalai Lama how he views the significance or purpose of the lives of his predecessors. To put it another way, what was the contribution of each Dalai Lama, both in the political and in the spiritual realm?

My view is that the first four Dalai Lamas provided some ground work for the 5th Dalai Lama. The 1st Dalai Lama received teachings from Tsongkhapa for a short period, and he also received teachings from many other lamas. On instructions of Lama Tsongkhapa, and particularly of Jetsün Sherap Sengge, he established the Tashilhünpo Monastery. Herewith in the Tsang area his influence was well established. Then the 2nd Dalai Lama [Gendün Gyatso], apparently due to some bad relations with the abbot of Tashilhünpo Monastery, Panchen Yeshe Tsemo, a student of the 1st Dalai Lama—as a result of these bad relations, the second Dalai Lama eventually went to central Tibet, to Lhasa. At that time the Drepung abbot, the main master of Drepung Monastery, had gotten some clear indications in his dreams, and based on these he invited the reincarnation of Gendün Drup to Drepung. Gendün Drup studied there in Drepung…[and] became the important lama of Drepung Monastery. And later he became the main throne holder (the main lama) of this monastery. And he also became the throne holder of the Sera Monastery. In this way he established some sort of power base—not in a negative sense or political sense—in the Lhasa area. Then he personally undertook…construction in southern Tibet (Chökhorgyal) and he also initiated the veneration of the famous lake, the Lhamo Lhatso. Further he also acted as an abbot in the Dhakpo Dratsang. And he established a very good monastery in southern Tibet, Ngari Dratsang. The described events clearly show that Gendün Gyatso, who was considered later as the 2nd Dalai Lama, established his influence in southern Tibet and southeast Tibet.

Then came the 3rd Dalai Lama, who got the name of "Dalai Lama" as the first one. He became strong in the Chamdo area and in Mongolia, in the later part of his life, where he also died. So now the Buddhism of Tsongkhapa was influential in the Tsang area, in central Tibet, in the south, southeast, and in Kham and Mongolia.

The 4th Dalai Lama was born as a member of a Mongolian chieftain. He was not very scholarly and he already passed away at a young age. So the reincarnation of the 3rd Dalai Lama, who had brought the Lama Tsongkhapa Buddhism to Mongolia, was born in a Mongolian chiefdom—[that] made the ties with Mongolia still closer.

Then came the 5th Dalai Lama. With the help of the Mongolians he became the head of the Tibetans, so he got the temporal power of [all of] Tibet. The 6th Dalai Lama was not successful, and he also died quite young. I feel the 5th Dalai Lama seemed to have something like a "master plan." His reincarnation, the 6th Dalai Lama, was quite a remarkable man. In some biographies of other lamas, there are accounts of some [of the] remarkable qualities of the 6th Dalai Lama. When he gave up his monkhood,

The Nobel Peace Prize medallion presented to the Fourteenth Dalai Lama, "the religious and political leader of the Tibetan people," on 10 December 1989 in Oslo.

so it seems, he deliberately did it. He wanted to establish the Dalai Lama institution in the same way as the Sakya institution. This means he wanted to introduce a hereditary system of succession, but he died unsuccessfully.

Then came the 7th Dalai Lama. In the political field he failed. Therefore he fully concentrated on the dharma, which was only of the Yellow Hat sect [Geluk School], so not non-sectarian. The 8th Dalai Lama was not that sort of personality; he did not make much contribution. The biography of the 9th Dalai Lama—although he died very early, at nine—was remarkable. If he would have survived, I think he certainly would have become like the 2nd Dalai Lama....Then the 10th, 11th, and 12th all died before [age] twenty-five. Then only the 13th Dalai Lama lived for a longer period and was more successful. So up to the 5th it seems there was a plan, an intention; after [the] 5th I think the original plan was disturbed. Then the 13th Dalai Lama once more tried to start some sort of "master plan," but he also failed.

While the Dalai Lama gave no appearance of doubting the concept of reincarnation, at several points he intimated that he

was not comfortable with some aspects of the way Tibetans treat the system. In particular, he criticized the many reincarnation lineages and lineages of descent that have come into being while he has been in exile. What does he think about that issue today?

In the early sixties, on one occasion, I think it was during the meeting with heads of religious schools, I [stat]ed some historical facts. It is important to keep the recognition and the lineage of some of these lamas who are historically authentic and based in Tibetan history. But besides that it is of no use to have too many reincarnations. Each reincarnation establishes [a] small institution. So this is not necessary. This is what I [stat]ed. At that time, the late Lukhangwa [former Prime Minister] once told me that my thinking [wa]s not good because he fe[lt that] in Tibet, particularly in the Kham area, in each monastery there is a reincarnated lama, so the institution of reincarnated lamas is very influential in the society. Therefore, he said, if we stop this system, if we do not accept or recognize it, that [instead] each monastery chooses his own reincarnated lama, this may not be helpful.

My view is still that there are too many reincarnations. Of course each group of students of a previous *geshe* or lama has the right to choose, when there is a clear indication, but as far as a monastery institution is concerned it should not recognize *tülkus*. Just treat [them] as ordinary monks.... But until now, in many cases if one has money—enough money—then one gets *tülku* recognition from the monastery. This almost is like buying [the position] with money.

And finally the unavoidable question of his own successor. Could the 14th Dalai Lama imagine being incarnated as a woman or even as a Westerner?

Yes, this is possible. Now here I made it very clear, as early as 1969, whether the Dalai Lama institution should continue or not is up to the Tibetan people. In case the majority of the Tibetan people want to keep this institution, then the next question is how to carry on the succession.... There are some possibilities, like the principle of seniority. I could appoint some senior or well-known lama, theoretically speaking. Another possibility: After my death some senior lama [c]ould be appointed, like

Presentation of the Nobel Peace Prize to the Fourteenth Dalai Lama because "in his struggle for the liberation of Tibet [he] has consistently opposed the use of violence," 10 December 1989.

in the case of the Pope. Or one could keep the institution of the Dalai Lamas, but the successor would not be found in the previous way, but with some new method. This is also possible. But in case the Tibetan people want to follow the previous way or system, then I made it very clear: if I die today, and most Tibetan people want to have another incarnation, in that case I [will] die in a foreign country as a refugee with a certain purpose. Because that purpose is not yet fulfilled, therefore my incarnation logically will appear outside Tibet.

Then the next question, male or female. As far as Tibet is concerned most probably [they] will prefer a male incarnation. But now the Dalai Lama is not only for the Tibetans but also for people who have new interest [in] Buddhism. So according to the new reality, if a female reincarnation would be more useful to the larger following, then a female reincarnation is very possible. Then I usually say in half-joke, not only a female, but also a very beautiful female, who [can] be more influential.

May she be reborn in a free Tibet!

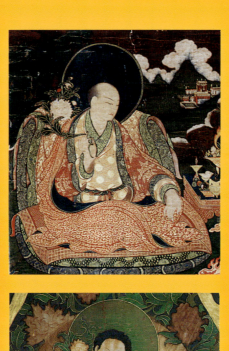

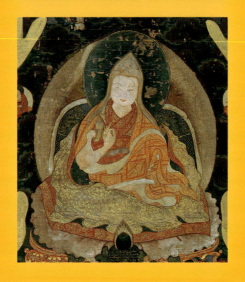

THE DALAI LAMAS
AND THE ORIGINS OF REINCARNATE LAMAS

Leonard W. J. van der Kuijp

Two interconnected images appear in the mind's eye when Tibet and Tibetan Buddhism are brought up—the Dalai Lama and the system of reincarnation of lamas and teachers, both lay and monastic. This essay discusses both from a historical perspective by traversing the grounds of Tibetan history as well as Tibetan biographical, autobiographical, and historical literature. What follows is based on what is considered historical fact, and serves to provide a guide to the pertinent features of the lives of the Dalai Lamas from the 1st Dalai Lama, Gendün Drup དགེ་འདུན་གྲུབ་ [dge 'dun grub] (1391–1474) to the current 14th Dalai Lama, Tenzin Gyatso བསྟན་འཛིན་རྒྱ་མཚོ་ [bstan 'dzin rgya mtsho] (b. 1935). The origin of the institution of the Dalai Lama is closely connected to the "invention of tradition."[1] The remarks that will be made about the origin of the institution of the Dalai Lama are admittedly speculative, in particular the idea that the men heading this institution are reincarnations of the Bodhisattva Avalokiteśvara who was himself the embodiment of the enlightened compassion ensuing upon buddhahood. Ever greater numbers of treasures have been emerging from the extraordinarily rich literary storehouse of Tibetan culture in recent years. Many previously unknown wood-block printed texts and very old, handwritten manuscripts have started to reappear. Only further investigation of these texts will prove whether the following remarks have any validity and are more than probable hypotheses. Such investigation may lead to unanticipated insights into their narrative structures and ideological projects. This means that reading through them, we should always be aware of the historical, political, and religious contexts in which they were written.

ALTAN KHAN'S LEGACY

The title "Dalai Lama" derives from a longer expression that first appears in 1578. Altan Khan (1507–1582), ruler of the Tümed Mongols (Tib. *sokpo* སོག་པོ་ [sog po]), gave Sönam Gyatso བསོད་ནམས་རྒྱ་མཚོ་ [bsod nams rgya mtsho] (1543–1588) the title *ta lai'i bla ma vajradhara* during a series of meetings that began on 19 June 1578 in Cabciyal, in present-day Qinghai 青海 Province, China. The Mongol word *dalai* indicates something vast, expansive, or universal, and therefore commonly denotes "ocean," even though such a large body of water probably fell beyond the experience of the average Mongol. Mongol *dalai* corre-

sponds to Tibetan *gyatsho* རྒྱ་མཚོ་ [rgya mtsho], the usual equivalent of Sanskrit *sāgara*, all "ocean."

It has become increasingly clear that much Tibetan literature has suffered at the hands of its editors. Sometimes the changes made in a piece of writing are due to careless oversights, other times they are intentional and reflect the editor's own agenda. Provided that the text has not been tampered with—and there is no real guarantee that it has not—the earliest Tibetan historical account of the meeting between Altan Khan and Sönam Gyatso is that found in Mipham Chökyi Gyatso's མི་ཕམ་ཆོས་ཀྱི་རྒྱ་མཚོ་ [mi pham chos kyi rgya mtsho] 1596 biography of Maitri Döndrup Gyaltsen དོན་གྲུབ་རྒྱལ་མཚན་ [don grub rgyal mtshan] (1527–1587) of Bökhar. The meeting was also recorded in the biography of Sönam Gyatso, which the 5th Dalai Lama, Ngawang Lopsang Gyatso ངག་དབང་བློ་བཟང་རྒྱ་མཚོ་ [ngag dbang blo bzang rgya mtsho] (1617–1682), almost completed in 1646. This biography and its later companion volume, his 1652 biography of his immediate predecessor, the 4th Dalai Lama, Yönten Gyatso ཡོན་ཏན་རྒྱ་མཚོ་ [yon tan rgya mtsho] (1589–1616), soon became quite influential because the author was, after all, the 5th Dalai Lama. He had these texts printed quickly, thereby ensuring a wider circulation than if only handwritten copies had been available. His large autobiography records that he edited the first work and wrote the second while en route to Beijing, to the Qing 清 court of the young Emperor Shunzhi 順治 (1638–1661).

This trip took him through largely Mongol populations, which was no coincidence because the 4th Dalai Lama himself had not been an ethnic Tibetan but rather Tümed Mongol. Yönten Gyatso was in fact Altan Khan's great-grandson. Both texts are as much biographies as they form part of a political and sociological complex in which the 5th Dalai Lama seeks to establish the theological inevitability and legitimacy of his office, himself, and his institution as the rightful ruler of Tibet, in addition to emphasizing his metaphysical ties to the ruling house of Altan Khan. This was a project he had started with his 1643 chronicle of Tibetan political history. These works display his keen awareness of the power of the "right" language and he was indeed a great master in shaping public opinion. The fact that he is often called "the Great Fifth" testifies to his political savvy and organizational skills and those of his immediate entourage. With him also began the so-called "Bodhisattva-cratic" governance of Tibet.

Turning to the Mongols, we find that Altan Khan's anonymous biography in verse, which cannot have been earlier than 1607, records the meeting between Altan Khan and the 3rd Dalai Lama. This work should hold particular authority for no other reason than that the author explicitly states that he bases this narrative on an earlier work by Sarmai (alias Uran Tanggharigh Dayun Kiya), a member of the party the Khan had dispatched in 1574 to invite Sönam Gyatso to Mongolia. The 5th Dalai Lama writes that the Khan had given Sönam Gyatso the title *ta la'i bla ma vajradhara*, although the full Mongol title[2] found in this work is longer.

Shortly after his birth, Sönam Gyatso was recognized as the reincarnation of Gendün Gyatso དགེ་འདུན་རྒྱ་མཚོ [dge 'dun rgya mtsho] (1475–1542). The latter was the second *Zimkhang Okma* གཟིམས་ཁང་འོག་མ [gzims khang 'og ma] "Lower Residence" reincarnate lama of Drepung monastery and consequently later also came to be known as the 2nd Dalai Lama. During his lifetime, Drepung became the largest and probably most influential Geluk institution, which traced its origins back to Tsongkhapa Lopsang Drakpa ཙོང་ཁ་པ་བློ་བཟང་གྲགས་པ [tsong kha pa blo bzang grags pa] (1357–1419) and his immediate disciples. Gendün Gyatso's residence there was the Ganden Phodrang, which had originally served as the residence where the Phakmodru ཕག་མོ་གྲུ [phag mo gru] rulers stayed when they visited the monastery. The Ganden Phodrang had been called the "Dokhang Ngönpo" རྡོ་ཁང་སྔོན་པོ [rdo khang sngon po] "Blue Stone House" until the Phakmodru ruler, Ngawang Trashi ངག་དབང་བཀྲ་ཤིས [ngag dbang bkra shis] (r. 1499–1564), donated it to Gendün Gyatso. Gendün Gyatso himself had already been recognized as the reincarnation of Gendün Drup, one of Tsongkhapa's last students and founder of Tashilhünpo in 1447.[3] Gendün Drup in turn was posthumously recognized both as the first "Lower Residence" reincarnate lama and as the 1st Dalai Lama.

Hierarchs of other traditions in Tibetan Buddhism gave Sönam Gyatso respect commensurate with his ranking as one of many reincarnate lamas populating the Tibetan religious landscape. Contemporaneous sources such as the biographies of hierarchs from the Karma sect of the Kagyü, those of the 5th Karmapa Shamar Könchok Yenlak ཞྭ་དམར་དཀོན་མཆོག་ཡན་ལག [zhwa dmar dKon mchog yan lag] (1525–1583) and the 10th Karmapa Shanak Wangchuk Dorje ཞྭ་ནག་དབང་ཕྱུག་རྡོ་རྗེ [zhwa nag dbang phyug rdo rje] (1556–1603), simply make reference to him as the "(supreme) incarnation of Drepung," or the *chöje* ཆོས་རྗེ [chos rje] "religious lord of Drepung." Maitri Döndrup's biographer often follows the same practice, at one point calling Sönam Gyatso the reincarnation of both Avalokiteśvara and Domtön Gyalwe Jungne འབྲོམ་སྟོན་རྒྱལ་བའི་འབུང་གནས [’brom ston rgyal ba'i 'bung gnas] (1005–1064), a motif we will return to below.

REENACTMENT OF AN OLDER RELATIONSHIP

Both the earliest Tibetan and the earliest available Mongol accounts of the meeting between Altan Khan and Sönam Gyatso display many similarities. Absent from both, however, is an acknowledgement that the two were consciously reenacting a much earlier relationship that had existed between the Mongol emperor Khubilai Khan (r. 1260–1294), who inaugurated the Yuan 元 dynasty in 1276, and Phakpa Lodrö Gyaltsen འཕགས་པ་བློ་གྲོས་རྒྱལ་མཚན [’phags pa blo gros rgyal mtshan] (1235–1280), Tibetan hierarch of the Sakya School. Later narratives do explicitly record that each recognized the other as the reincarnation of these earlier men. The 5th Dalai Lama writes in his biography of Sönam Gyatso that when the latter taught the six-syllable prayer of Avalokiteśvara to Altan Khan and his entourage, the Khan said:

> In the past, when the monastery of Phakpa Shingkun འཕགས་པ་ཤིང་ཀུན [’phags pa shing kun][4] was constructed, I was Sechen Gyalpo [= Khubilai Khan] and you were Lama Phakpa. You consecrated the monastery ...

This suggests that Altan Khan had been Khubilai in a previous life while Sönam Gyatso had been Phakpa. It is likely no coincidence that Phakpa and his personal possessions appear in the 5th Dalai Lama's autobiography with unusual frequency. The 5th Dalai Lama cites several sources he used in his study of Sönam Gyatso, including a complete biography Kharnak Lotsāwa Jampel Dorje མཁར་ནག་ལོ་ཙཱ་བ་འཇམ་དཔལ་རྡོ་རྗེ [mkhar nag lo tsā ba 'jam dpal rdo rje] had written. While this work has not come down to us, a large fragment of Kharnak Lotsāwa's manuscript on the development of the Geluk School has. Here Kharnak Lotsāwa treats Sönam Gyatso and his journey to Qinghai in a surprisingly perfunctory manner. After the Khan had invited Sönam Gyatso to visit him, Kharnak Lotsāwa writes:

1 The Third Dalai Lama, surrounded by Domtön (upper center) and scenes probably at the court of a North Indian ruler. Thangka, Tibet, 18th century, 86 x 54 cm, Schleiper Collection, Brussels. 2 Phakpa, a previous incarnation of the Dalai Lama. Thangka, Tibet, 70 x 45 cm, Collection of Mrs. and Mr. L. Solomon, Paris.

Sönam Gyatso set out northwards in the Year of the Tiger [1578]. At that time, the Tibetanized Mongol chief Karmapel [karma dpal] paid him obeisance with respect and worship, including gifts. Then in the Year of the Earthhare [1579], at the age of thirty-six Sönam Gyatso met with Athen Gyalpo ཨ་ཐན་རྒྱལ་པོ [a than rgyal po] (ie, Altan Khan) in Tshokha མཚོ་ཁ [mtsho kha]. He sated all the Mongols by teaching Buddhism to establish them in virtue. Then he went to Palden Chökhorling དཔལ་ལྡན་ཆོས་འཁོར་གླིང [dpal ldan chos 'khor gling] Monastery [which he founded with Altan Khan] and then went down to Chamdo in Kham...

Whatever the merits of identifying Altan Khan with Khubilai, tradition has never problematized Phakpa's incorporation into the reincarnations of the Dalai Lamas. As addressed later, this is a result of the specific role tradition has assigned Avalokiteśvara. For political and religious reasons, the Sakya School, particularly members of the ruling family at Sakya Monastery who were distant relations of Phakpa, were understandably disinclined to recognize Sönam Gyatso as a reincarnation of their ancestor. Moreover, the School held the opinion that Phakpa was an emanation—not reincarnation—of Mañjuśrī, the symbol of enlightened wisdom. The School held this position in recognition of Phakpa's learning. In fact, from quite early on, the School also held that Sachen Künga Nyingpo ས་ཆེན་ཀུན་དགའ་སྙིང་པོ [sa chen kun dga' snying po] (1092–1158), Phakpa's great-grandfather and the School's first

3 Sachen Künga Nyingpo, a previous incarnation of the Dalai Lama, surrounded by Hevajra (upper left), Birvapa (upper right) and Gur Gönpo (lower right). Thangka, Tibet, mid-18th century, Folkens Museum Etnografiska, Stockholm, Inv. No.: 1935.50.965.

patriarch, was a reincarnation of Avalokiteśvara. Yet in none of the writings from this School do we find Phakpa referred to as a reincarnation of Sachen.

We should keep in mind that when Altan Khan initially granted Sönam Gyatso the title "Dalai Lama," it was a relatively minor and by no means unique event despite that from the 17th century onward it came to play a significant role in Tibetan political and religious history starting with the 5th Dalai Lama. There is evidence that at least one other hierarch, Gyalwa Künga Trashi རྒྱལ་བ་ཀུན་དགའ་བཀྲ་ཤིས་ [rgyal ba kun dga' bkra shis] (1536–1605), of the Kagyü School and 16th abbot of Taklung, also enjoyed the patronage of the Khan, though perhaps not on the same scale as that with Sönam Gyatso. Gyalwa Künga Trashi's biography reports that he travelled twice to regions where the Tümed Mongols lived. The first trip was from 1578 to 1581, the second from 1589 to 1593. During that first trip the Khan gave Gyalwa Künga Trashi the title *depzhin shekpa* དེ་བཞིན་གཤེགས་པ་ [de bzhin gshegs pa], a *thamka* ཐམ་ཀ་ [tham ka] seal forged from eighty-five *sang* སྲང་ [srang] pieces, a *jasa* འཇའ་ས་ ['ja' sa] edict, and thousands of pieces of silver. Gyalwa Künga Trashi and the Khan met once more in the fall of 1578, on which occasion the Khan made him an offering of a large container made from fifteen hundred pieces of silver. The Khan no doubt made this offering in consideration of the various Buddhist teachings Gyalwa Künga Trashi had conferred.

A DOUBLE-EDGED SWORD DECISION

The reasons for the Geluk School's incredible success in their missionary work among the Mongols remain to be investigated. Probably one reason was that Sönam Gyatso was an incarnate lama while Gyalwa Künga Trashi was not. Part of the explanation would surely include the doings of Palden Gyatso, Sönam Gyatso's financial secretary, who was entrusted with the task of finding his late master's reincarnation. He rejected Könchok Rinchen དགོན་མཆོག་རིན་ཆེན་ [dkon mchog rin chen] (1590–1655)[5] as the primary and only Tibetan candidate for Sönam Gyatso's subsequent reincarnation. After some deliberation, he chose instead Yönten Gyatso, an ineffectual and rather tragic figure whose main claim to fame was being the Khan's great-grandson. Palden Gyatso and his decision are open to some skepticism and we may question his motives. The decision turned out to be a double-edged sword: on the one hand, it was a master stroke ensuring the allegiance of a large segment—but by no means all—of the Mongol tribal federations to the institution of the Dalai Lama and the its associated *labrang* བླ་བྲང་ [bla brang], or "*corporation*." The *labrang* was the repository of the economic resources of the institution of which incarnate lamas formed a transient part. His decision also ensured that the patronage with these Mongols continued as did the economic success of the *labrang*. The downside was that his decision brought the intertribal conflicts between the different Mongol groups to Tibet, a development which had disastrous consequences for the future of the country as a sovereign entity. Matters came to a head in 1720 when the Qing Emperor Kangxi 康熙 (1654–1722) stationed his military in Tibet to protect it from the Dzungar Mongols' political and military ambitions.

Yönten Gyatso's successor, the 5th Dalai Lama, was a towering figure. With him began the Ganden Phodrang governance of Tibet. Many of the best aspects of the institution of the Dalai Lama were due to his skills and those of his right-hand men, the *desi* སྡེ་སྲིད་ [sde srid] "rulers," the most ambitious and influential among them being Sönam Chöphel བསོད་ནམས་ཆོས་འཕེལ་ [bsod nams chos 'phel] (d. 1657) and Sanggye Gyatso སངས་རྒྱས་རྒྱ་མཚོ་ [sangs rgyas rgya mtsho] (1653–1705). Compared with Yönten Gyatso, the 6th and 12th Dalai Lamas fell short in their learning, political acumen, and sheer pleasure in wielding power. The 6th Dalai Lama, Tsangyang Gyatso ཚངས་དབྱངས་རྒྱ་མཚོ་ [tshangs dbyangs rgya mtsho] (1683–?1706), was very much disinclined to play the expected role of his office and rather more inclined to live up to the "Tsangyang" of his name, meaning "pure sonority." Despite having been novitiated, he wore his hair long, and lived the life of a poet and artist. Several collections of poems have been attributed to him. In 1705, he was deposed. Although he likely died around 1706, there is a long narrative—probably apocryphal—of his later years and the life he led as a wandering *yogi*.

The 7th Dalai Lama, Kalsang Gyatso སྐལ་བཟང་རྒྱ་མཚོ་ [skal bzang rgya mtsho] (1708–1757), was not formally installed until 1720. During his reign, a formal governing cabinet with him as head was established and lasted until 1959, although the landed nobility ultimately thwarted his rule. For similar reasons the 8th to 12th Dalai Lamas played rather negligible roles in the rule of Tibet. The 9th through 12th were also at the mercy of a succession of regents, their political ambitions and inter-

ests, and those of their families. None of these Dalai Lamas lived beyond twenty-one and it is likely their untimely deaths resulted from foul play.

The 13th Dalai Lama, Thupten Gyatso (1876–1933), represents a radical break with this sequence, not least because of his contact with the world beyond Tibet. Having been in exile once in Mongolia and once in British India, he sought to introduce unprecedented political and social innovations. He even unilaterally declared Tibet an independent state. Ultimately, however, his policies proved ineffective against the resistance the conservative clergy brought to bear against them. He was the most important successor of the 5th Dalai Lama and so it is little wonder that the *stūpa* containing his remains at the Potala is second only to that of the Great Fifth in terms of size, ornamentation, and splendor.

The present 14th Dalai Lama has been a potent force and rallying point for the Tibetans ever since China claimed sovereignty over Tibet in the 1950s. Going into exile in India in 1959 and headquartered in Dharamśālā, a small Indian town nestled in the Himalayan foothills, he has become increasingly present on the international scene and is a much-sought public speaker on both religious and non-religious subjects. In 1989 the Nobel committee awarded him their Peace Prize partly in recognition of his insistence that the "Tibet question" be resolved through peaceful means.

SIGNIFICANCE OF ATIŚA

How did the institution of the Dalai Lama and the idea that he was a reincarnation of Avalokiteśvara begin and gain potency? What meanings are attached to Avalokiteśvara for Tibetan self-understanding? To answer these questions in brief we must go back in Tibetan history to at least the 11th century, when the Bengali Buddhist monk Atiśa (ca. 982–1054) and his party finally reached the Tibetan Plateau in the early summer of 1042. Their arduous journey had taken them through the sweltering plains of northern India to what is now the Terāī of southern Nepāl. The Terāī abruptly transforms upwards into the Himālaya foothills which steadily rise for those on foot or horseback. Almost without warning the foothills give way to the lush and fertile Kāṭhmāṇḍū Valley, into which Atiśa led his group. There the small, determined group stayed for about a year, after which they set out for the Tibetan highlands.

4 The Fifth Dalai Lama, the "Great Fifth," with Buddha Amitābha in the upper middle and around him scenes of his visionary experiences. The painting is part of a set of thangkas and was likely commissioned during the period of Sanggye Gyatso's regency. Thangka, Central Tibet, late 17th /early 18th century, 94 x 64 cm, Potala, Lhasa.   **5** The Thirteenth Dalai Lama. Miniature painting (see plate 92). **6** The Fourteenth Dalai Lama, surrounded by the three kings and (lower left) possibly Nyetri Tsenpo, with inscription. Thangka, Tibet, 20th century, 42 x 32 cm, Collection of Harald Bechteler, Tutzing. >>>

Atiśa made the trek at the invitation of and with the financial support of Jangchup Ö བྱང་ཆུབ་འོད་ [byang chub 'od] (984–1078), ruler of Guge, a remote region of far western cultural Tibet.[6] Yet he and his followers felt no sense of urgency to travel on to Guge. Crossing into the Tibetan frontier at Nagarkoṭ (Tib. Balpo Dzong), they stayed about a year at the residence of the group leader, the Sanskritist and translator Naktso Lotsāwa Tsülthrim Gyalwa ནག་ཚོ་ལོ་ཙཱ་བ་ཚུལ་ཁྲིམས་རྒྱལ་བ་ [nag tsho lo tsā ba tshul khrims rgyal ba] (1011–c.1068), in Mangyül, Gungdang. Atiśa spent most of the rest of his life in Tibet, but through his activities and those of the body of disciples he attracted, he was able to found the Kadam བཀའ་གདམས་ [bka' gdams] School of Tibetan Buddhism. This term derives from Atiśa's disciplines taking the gyalwe-ka རྒྱལ་བའི་བཀའ་ [rgyal ba'i bka'] "word of the Buddha" and

Atiśa's *dam-ngak* གདམས་ངག [*gdams* ngag] "oral instructions" as functionally equivalent. Hence ka + dam, and we find the term *kadampa* "of or having to do with the Kadam" already attested in the early second half of the 11th century.

The Kadam School likely originated from a sense of community, both intellectual and spiritual-meditative, that grew out of the absolute authority members invested in their master's teachings. This is not to say that it was a unified or monolithic entity. All the earliest sources on the tradition describe with refreshing candor the tensions, conflicts, and outright pettiness among its founding members, even while Atiśa was still alive. These sources depict in brutal and eloquent detail the jealousies and competitions for the master's favors that filled the days of many of his disciples. Yet it was Atiśa's charisma and authority that held these men together. His teachings, encapsulated in written texts, formed the ultimate basis and authority from which the ideology of the Dalai Lama evolved conceptually until it crystallized into the institution of the Dalai Lama with its concrete, bodily manifestations starting from Sönam Gyatso.

This process was a local development, one that likely had its origins in a branch of the *Dom* (alt. *Drom*) འབྲོམ ['brom] clan, among whom Domtön Gyalwe Jungne was a member. Clan membership and self-identification with a clan, although remaining strong thoughout the Tibetan cultural area as manifest in the majority of Tibetan biographical and autobiographical literature which takes pains to trace both patrilineal and matrilineal clans and sub-clan affiliations of its subjects, gradually erodes in importance as they were slowly supplanted by Indic Buddhist social and religious concepts.

Naktso Lotsāwa journeyed to Northern India at his king's behest to invite Atiśa back to Tibet. He wrote a sketch of his journey, which although has not come down to us, a significant portion is found in the *Biography and Itinerary of the Lord Atiśa: A Source of Religion Written by Domtön Gyalwe Jungne*. Many crucial portions of this work have been written in the first-person singular and detail Naktso's travels into the subcontinent to invite Atiśa to come to Tibet, which both support the hypothesis that much of the text was in fact an autobiography. Yet we find that it has in fact come to be attributed to Domtön, who appears in different guises as Naktso's helper. It is clear that Domtön and his guises are simply manifestations of Avalokiteśvara. In other words, Avalokiteśvara functions as a kind of "bodhisattva ex machina" taking on this role from the beginning and in every way directing the narrative. He appears, for example, in the guise of a white man when Naktso and his party arrive in Nagarkoṭ. Resting there with his party in a rented bamboo hut to shelter from the blistering heat, Naktso, "suffering from the heat and crazed by fatigue," has a vision of this white man who tells him:

> Don't sleep! Don't sleep! Get up quickly!
> Don't go to sleep! Get up now and get on the road!
> If you were to fall asleep, you will lose your precious life.
> I am the tutelary deity of all of Tibet.

The owner of the hut was in fact about to burn the hut down to kill the party for the gold he knew Naktso was carrying.

Later in the text we encounter the idea that Tibet is Avalokiteśvara's special domain. In this context "Tibet" covers the area as measured from Nagarkoṭ northwards. It is important to keep in mind that Atiśa and his disciples taught religious practices centered on Avalokiteśvara widely throughout Tibet. This reflects their mission, which was in part to spread their version of Buddhism among the many non-Buddhists populating the Tibetan cultural area at that time. Of special significance may have been the Kāśmīrī nun Lakṣmī's introduction and propagation of a special variety of Avalokiteśvara-related practice. Whereas monks in the confines of their monasteries of Tantric hermits in the wilds of the Tibetan plateaus performed many such practices, Lakṣmī made it a point to move beyond the monastery and isolated hermitage to include the laity, both male and female, in a quasi-Tantric short-term fasting practice that she structured around the Bodhisattva. We cannot underestimate the impact of this kind of grassroots Buddhism.

AVALOKITEŚVARA AND HIS REINCARNATIONS

As stated earlier, Tibetans conceive of the institution of the Dalai Lama as a set in the open-ended series of Avalokiteśvara's reincarnations. In Indian Buddhist lore, Avalokiteśvara's home is Mount Potala located in southern India, although he then came to be relocated to central Tibet. Early exponents of the Kadam School were quick to universalize him as the patron-Bodhisattva of the entire Tibetan cultural area. Textual sources suggest that one community in which this concept took hold was the area of the western Tibet governed by descendants of the imperial families whose political and ideological aspirations were, if not major players in the origin, assuredly its beneficiaries. Other communities in which this concept played an overarching role were those with some connection to Domtön. As we find in an important but at first localized corpus of Kadam literature, Atiśa recognized Domtön as Avalokiteśvara, thus legitimating the proposition that he therefore physically embodied the spirit of intelligent compassion and had done so during a number of previous incarnations.

In the final and only redaction that we have, the title of this corpus in twenty chapters is *Accounts of Rebirths of Dom Gyalwe*

7 Domtön, with hand and footprints, surrounded by Atiśa (upper center) and six saints, below them Vasubandhu (5th century) below the right hand of Domtön. The protective deities below are, left, Acala (Mi gyo ba) and, right, the Red Southwest Mahākāla with knife (Lho nub mGon po gri gug dmar po), see also plate 8. Thangka, Tibet, late 17th century, 77.5 x 50 cm, Musée national des Arts asiatiques Guimet, Paris (Gift of R. Pfister, 1939), Inv. No.: 19106.

8 Domtön, surrounded by his teacher Atiśa (upper left), the blue protective deity Acala in the tradition of the Kadam School (Migyöpa, Mi gyo ba sngon po bka' gdams lugs; upper right) and the Red Southwest Mahākāla with knife (Lho nub mGon po gri gug dmar po; lower right), a special form of Mahākāla, special protector of the teachings. The Reting Monastery, established by Domtön in 1057, can be seen at the left margin, along with the picturesque and lush junipers next to it. Thangka, Tibet, 71 x 45 cm, Ethnographic Museum of the University of Zürich, Inv. No.: 14370.

Jungne འབྲོམ་རྒྱལ་བའི་འབྱུང་གནས་ཀྱི་སྐྱེས་རབས་ ['brom rgyal ba'i 'byung gnas kyi skyes rabs]. Certainly, the phrase *"Accounts of Rebirths"* suggests the same kind authority as that of the *jātaka* tales of the previous lives of the historical Buddha. The nineteenth, and by far longest chapter, explains at considerable length the ideologies that had developed around Tibetan imperial history and imperial families. It goes on to argue that a spiritual link existed between Domtön and Songtsen Gampo སྲོང་བཙན་སྒམ་ པོ་ [srong btsan sgam po], the first king of Tibet under a centralized government, a link based on the supposition of them both being reincarnations of Avalokiteśvara. The dating of the text is problematic, especially in view of the fact that it is first extensively cited in the 15th century. Strikingly, the earliest available biographical sketches of Domtön do not suggest a connection with Avalokiteśvara, nor describe him as a reincarnation. This includes the longest sketch compiled around the mid-13th century and found in a handwritten manuscript, the *Golden Rosary of the Kadampa*.

In terms of ideology, this nineteenth chapter is intimately connected with the *Kachem Kakholma* བཀའ་ཆེམས་ཀ་ཁོལ་མ་ [bka' chems ka khol ma] *"Kakholma Testament,"* a work the king himself allegedly authored. Although in view of linguistic and other grounds, this is surely a pious fiction. A tradition current by at least the end of the 12th century held that Atiśa had retrieved an ancient manuscript of this work in Lhasa towards the end of the 1040s. One of the central arguments of the *Kakholma Testament* is the ontological equivalence of Songtsen Gampo with Avalokiteśvara. There is no reliable evidence that this equation had any precedent.

Tibetan literature of the 11th century begins to elaborate on the motif of the "Three Protectors of Tibet," in which we find equivalences drawn between three Bodhisattvas and three Tibetan rulers who according to tradition played important roles in the development of Tibetan Buddhism. They are 1) Avalokiteśvara and Songtsen Gampo; 2) Mañjuśrī and Thrisong Detsen ཁྲི་སྲོང་ལྡེ་བཙན་ [khri srong lde btsan]; and 3) Vajrapāṇi and Ralpacen རལ་པ་ཅན་ [ral pa can]. This motif appears in Kadam, Sakya, and Kagyü literature, where it designates important masters belonging to these schools. It occurs in at least two different forms in early Kadam literature. We also find these same three Bodhisattvas being equated with three of Atiśa's disciples.[7] Another schema equates them with Atiśa's three

"brother" disciples,[8] although we do not know how far back this tradition goes or its motivation.

Interestingly, we also find three "Bodhisattva Protectors" in the tradition surrounding the masters of the main corpus of Kālacakra teachings, albeit here in reverse chronological order: Avalokiteśvara and Puṇḍarīka; Mañjuśrī and Yaśas; and Vajrapāṇi and Sucandra. These three men were the rulers of the mythical kingdom of Śambhāla. The Kālacakra texts in which we find this set of three dyads of equivalence entered Tibet shortly before the middle of the 11th century. We can but wonder about the impact it had on local sensibilities. Equating Bodhisattvas with rulers was not new, neither in the Subcontinent nor in early Tibet. A text in the Tibetan Buddhist canon attributed to Vairocana and written around 800 speaks of Trisong Detsen as a Bodhisattva. The Tibetan canon also contains a supposed translation of a letter attributed to Buddhaguhya in which the author suggests that Songtsen Gampo is the reincarnation of Avalokiteśvara.

HONORING AND PRESERVING THE *DOM* PATRIMONY

The *Kakholma Testament* does not mention Domtön, for which reason I am inclined to believe that this work emerged from an environment in which Domtön, his associates, and the traditions growing out of their teachings initially had no stake. If that is the case, then we must reconcile at least two initially separate lines of argument: the first in the *Kakholma Testament* in which Songtsen Gampo is equated with Avalokiteśvara, the second in *Accounts of Rebirths* in which we find a similar scenario but with Domtön at the center.

The *Kakholma Testament* has come down to us in three different recensions of which the longest is clearly connected to the ruling house of west Tibet. I would therefore argue that the use made of the *Kakholma Testament* in the nineteenth chapter of the *Accounts of Rebirths* was to create an environment conducive to establishing Songtsen Gampo as one of Domtön's previous births. Unfortunately, there is no way to date this compendium with any certainty.

The corpus of early Kadam texts focusing on Domtön was not widely known for several centuries. Four men played essential roles in the preservation and ultimate dissemination of a major portion of the corpus: Namkha Rinchen ནམ་མཁའ་རིན་ཆེན་ [nam mkha' rin chen] (1214–1286), Zhönu Lodrö གཞོན་ནུ་བློ་གྲོས་ [gzhon

9 Four-Armed Avalokiteśvara. Bronze, gilded, Tibet, 12th/13th century, H 43 cm, W 32 cm, D 17 cm, private collection.
10 One-Thousand-Armed Avalokiteśvara, at his right side the blue Vajrapāṇi, on the left Mañjuśrī, at his feet Bhutanese monks. Thangka, Bhutan, 72 x 55 cm, Ethnographic Museum of the University of Zürich, Inv. No.: 17649. **11** Eight-Armed Avalokiteśvara. Bronze, gilded, Tibet, H 218 cm, Collection of Wereldmuseum, Rotterdam, the Netherlands, Inv. No.: 29130.

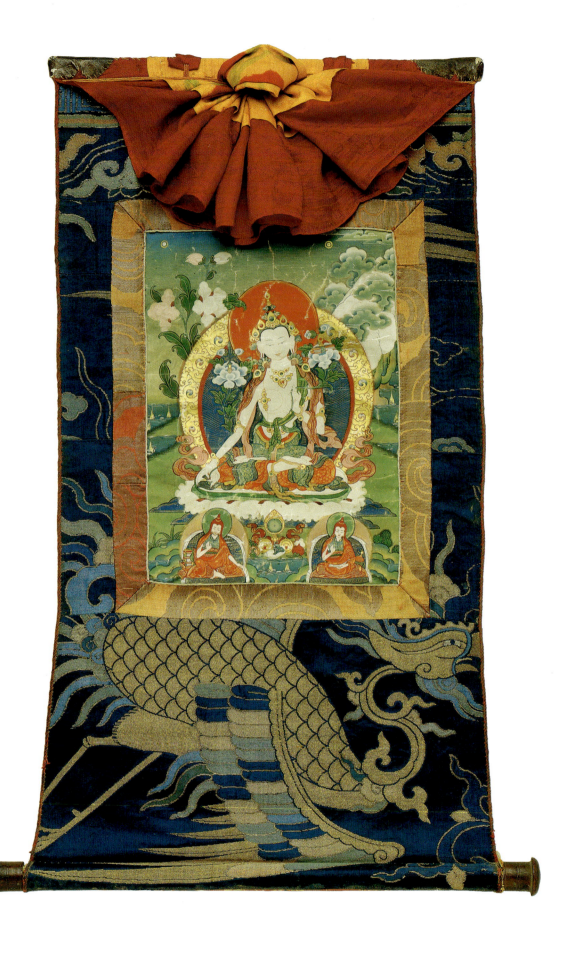

12 Mañjuśrī, with two Indian scholar-monks below. Thangka, Tibet, 28 x 21 cm, Ethnographic Museum of the University of Zürich, Inv. No.: 14421.

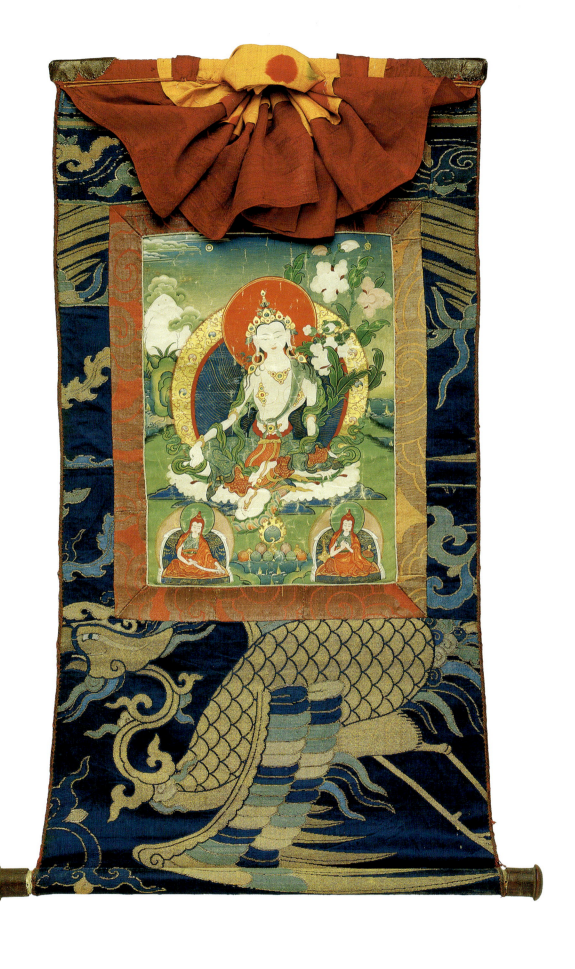

13 Two-Armed (Khasarpaṇa) Avalokiteśvara, two scholar-monks below, possibly Rinchen Sangpo on the left, Atiśa on the right. Thangka, Tibet, 28,5 x 21cm, Ethnographic Museum of the University of Zürich, Inv. No.: 14422.

nu blo gros] (1271–?), Nyima Gyaltsen ཉིམ་རྒྱལ་མཚན་ [nyi ma rgyal mtshan] (1225–1305), and Gendün Drup, posthumously recognized as the 1st Dalai Lama. All four were members of the same *Dom* clan to which Domtön belonged. This can hardly be coincidence and it is therefore likely that these men were making efforts to preserve and honor their clan patrimony, although none of these men likely imagined their activities would have such a profound impact on later events. The 5th Dalai Lama and his last regent Sanggye Gyatso were well aware of the ways in which this early Kadam literature could be used as religious propaganda. Thus it is no surprise that the 5th Dalai Lama had printing blocks of a major portion of this corpus carved.

CONCEPT OF THE *TÜLKU*

These systems of reincarnation, equivalence, and correspondence are predicated upon the metaphysics and phenomenology of reincarnation and the attendant complex concept of the *tülku* (alt. *trülku*) སྤྲུལ་སྐུ་ [sprul sku]. To put it succinctly, the *tülku* is the "earthly" manifestation of buddhahood. Through its limitless compassion and gnosis, this buddhahood generates the *tülku*, which provides a basis for the various qualities associated with the sainthood of the *bodhisattva*.[9] The idea of one Tibetan being the reincarnation of another earlier one is an important concept, though one whose origins are difficult to establish. Tibetan tradition asserts that the *tülku* phenomenon began with Karma Pakṣī (1206–1283), the second hierarch of the Karma branch of the Kagyü School. Karma Pakṣī recognized himself as the reincarnation of Düsum Khyenpa དུས་གསུམ་མཁྱེན་པ་ [dus gsum mkhyen pa] (1110–1193) and later of Avalokiteśvara, a recognition that his disciples came to embrace. There were many other Tibetan masters whose students considered them reincarnations of this Bodhisattva. We have already seen that Sachen Künga Nyingpo of the Sakya School was held to be one, while other examples include Yapsang Chökyi Mönlam གཡའ་བཟང་ཆོས་ཀྱི་སྨོན་ལམ་ [g.ya' bzang chos kyi smon lam] (1169–1233), whom the *Tho Dingma* མཐོ་མཐིང་མ་ [mtho mthing ma] "*Tho Dingma Testament*"—a work similar to the *Kakholma Testament*—prophesies as a reincarnation of Songtsen Gampo, and then Dolpopa Sherap Gyaltsen དོལ་པོ་པ་ཤེས་རབ་རྒྱལ་མཚན་ [dol po pa shes rab rgyal mtshan] (1291–1362).

Later traditions holding that the Karma reincarnations were unprecedented in history are, however, incorrect. There is

ample evidence that a number of other individuals had been considered *tülkus* during the 13th century. Although the metaphysics of the *tülku* easily allow for the possibility of an individual being the rebirth of a previous human master whose spiritual attainments—real, assumed, or self-proclaimed—served as convincing evidence of his enlightenment, it is only sporadically attested in Indian Buddhism. One example might be in Advayavajra's 11th-century commentary on Saraha's songs, where we encounter the phrase *jetsüngyi trülpeku* རྗེ་བཙུན་གྱི་ སྤྲུལ་པའི་སྐུ་ [rje btsun gyi sprul pa'i sku] "reincarnation of the holy lord."[10] In the Indo-Tibetan environment, we find clear allusions to this phenomenon in the autobiography of Throphu Lotsāwa Jampepel ཁྲོ་ཕུ་ལོ་ཙཱ་བ་བྱམས་པའི་དཔལ་ [khro phu lo tsā ba byams pa'i dpal] (1172–1236), where he refers to *tülku* Mitrayogin and *tülku* Vikhyātadeva, both Indian Buddhist masters. The earliest attestation of a Tibetan being recognized, or representing himself, as a reincarnation of another Tibetan master took place in the Kadam School in the second half of the 12th century. We

14 a–c The Three Kings: Trisong Detsen, Songsten Gampo, and Ralpacen. Bronze, chased and gilded, Tibet, ca. 1800, H between 47 and 50 cm, W ca. 35 cm, D ca. 28 cm, Collection of Veena and Peter Schnell, Zürich.

find the Tantric master Chökyi Gyalpo ཆོས་ཀྱི་རྒྱལ་པོ [chos kyi rgyal po] (1069–1144) of Könpu considering himself to be a rebirth of Naktso. We further find the Kadam master Gyer Zhönu Jungne སྒྱེར་གཞོན་ནུ་འབྱུང་གནས་ [sgyer gzhon nu 'byung gnas] recognized as the reincarnation of both a Bodhisattva as well as Ja Yülpa Chenpo བྱ་ཡུལ་པ་ཆེན་པོ་ [bya yul pa chen po], also known as Zhönnu Ö གཞོན་ནུ་འོད་ [gzhon nu 'od] (1075–1138). Zhönnu Ö figures among the most important Kadam masters of his day, one whose influence spread throughout Central Tibet and into the southern borderlands. It is in fact recorded that some two thousand monks attended his cremation.

In the 13th century, we also find the first attempts at creating a lineage of female reincarnations. Drowa Zangmo འགྲོ་བ་བཟང་མོ་ ['gro ba bzang mo] was consort to Götsangpa Gönpo Dorje རྒོད་ཚང་པ་མགོན་པོ་རྡོ་རྗེ་ [rgod tshang pa mgon po rdo rje] (1182–1258), himself regarded as the reincarnation of the Tibetan saint Milarepa. Drowa Zangmo died around 1259, after which a certain Künden Rema ཀུན་ལྡན་རས་མ་ [kun ldan ras ma] (1260–ca. 1339)

was soon recognized as her next incarnation. This lineage was short-lived, in fact ending with Künden Rema.

In summary, it appears that the concept of Avalokiteśvara as Tibet's patron-Bodhisattva first emerged in the 11th century, although his identification and association with Songtsen Gampo, first ruler of a unified Tibet, may go back earlier. A small group from the Kadam School, in spiritual allegiance with their master Domtön, elaborated on this theme in a series of texts which proposed relations of equivalence between Domtön and the Bodhisattva. They equated the site of Domtön's monastery of Reting with Mount Potala, the residence of Avalokiteśvara in south India. Finally, it appears that the Bodhisattva moved once again from Reting to Lhasa with the 5th Dalai Lama's construction of the Potala Palace.[11]

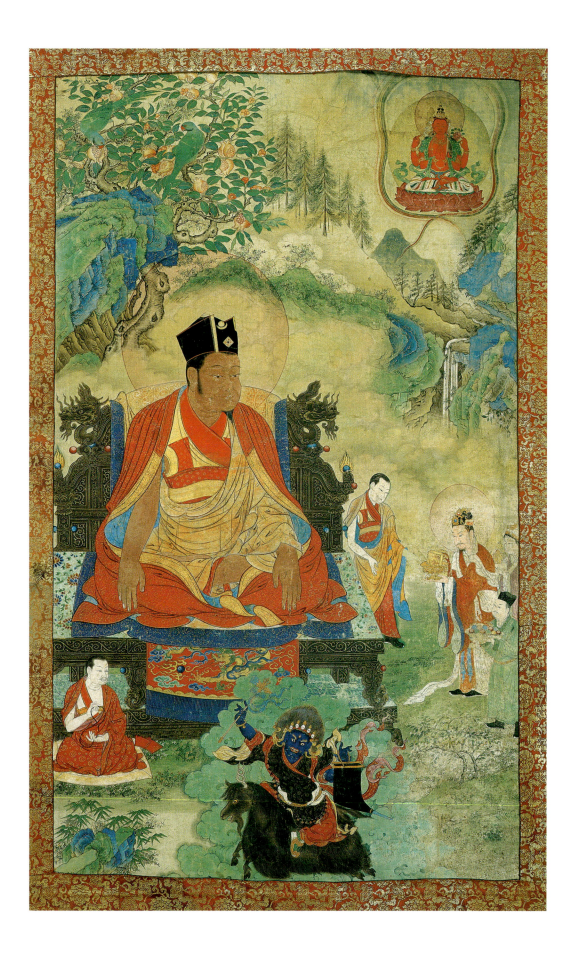

15 The Second Karmapa (Karma Pakṣi), receiving gifts and a large golden seal from Möngke, the Mongolian ruler, and his wife and a minister. This scene alludes to a meeting in China between Karma Pakṣi and the Mongolian ruler in 1255 or somewhat later. Thangka, East Tibet, early 18th century, 97 x 59 cm, Museum der Kulturen, Basel, Inv. No.: IId 13810. >>>

 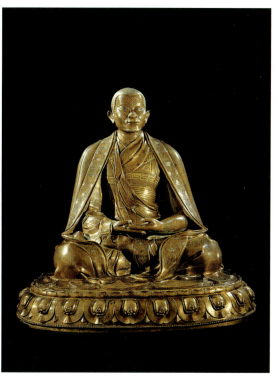

16 The Second Karmapa (Karma Pakṣi). Copper alloy, gilded, polychrome pigments, Tibet, 16th century, H 19 cm, W 14 cm, D 11 cm, Oliver Hoare Collection, London, Inv. No.: 30.　**17** The First Karmapa (Düsum Khyenpa). Bronze, inlaid with copper and silver, Tibet, 14th /15th century, H 33 cm, W 33.5 cm, D 26.5 cm, Collection of A.& J. Speelman Ltd., London.

"In general, consider the kindness of all living beings; specifically, hold a pure attitude toward Dharma practitioners. Tame (your) ego-grasping, the inner enemy." (Gendün Drup)[1]

THE FIRST DALAI LAMA GENDÜN DRUP

དགེ་འདུན་གྲུབ་

Shen Weirong 沈衛榮
Translated by JANICE BECKER

Although since the 19th century the 1st Dalai Lama, Gendün Druppa Pelzangpo དགེ་འདུན་གྲུབ་པ་དཔལ་བཟང་པོ་ [dge 'dun grub pa dpal bzang po] has been thought of as the nephew of Tsongkhapa ཙོང་ཁ་པ་ [tsong kha pa] (plates 18, 19), his personal qualities, abilities, and impact have been eclipsed by those of Tsongkhapa himself, the Great Reformer. Gendün Drup was one of Tsongkhapa's most important disciples and the founder of Tashilhünpo Monastery, the first and most important Geluk monastery in Tsang. He rendered everlasting service to the young and energetic Geluk School by acting as a *khepa* མཁས་པ་ [mkhas pa] "outstanding scholar," *tsünpa* བཙུན་པ་ [btsun pa] "man of virtue," and *zangpo* བཟང་པོ་ [bzang po] "benefactor."

It is generally accepted that Gendün Drup acquired the title Dalai Lama only posthumously as one of the two previous incarnations of Sönam Gyatso (1543–1588), to whom the Mongolian prince Altan Khan (1507–1582) gave the title in 1578. In fact, Gendün Drup was the first of the best-known line of reincarnations in Tibetan Buddhism and even during his lifetime he was recognized as the rebirth of Avalokiteśvara. Indeed, a search was made for Gendün Drup's rebirth shortly after his death. Thus Sönam Gyatso was not the "originator" of this line but rather Gendün Drup himself, who bore the title Thamce Khyenba ཐམས་ཅད་མཁྱེན་པ་ [thams cad mkhyen pa] "Omniscient," as did his immediate successor, Gendün Gyatso. Only subsequently were these first two members in the already-established line given the title Dalai Lama posthumously and thus integrated into a new series of reincarnations.

Gendün Drup was born in 1391 to a nomad family near Sakya Monastery in Tsang. His father was Gönpo Dorje and his mother Jomo Namkyi. He was the third of five children and as a young boy he was first called Pema Dorje. He is said to have come from the same Kham-area lineage as Domtön འབྲོམ་སྟོན་ ['brom ston], the founder of the Kadam School. Gendün Drup is also considered to be the rebirth of Domtön, or Avalokiteśvara. On the evening after his birth, robbers attacked his group of nomads. In the ensuing haste, his mother hid the newborn in a rock crevice before running away. A vulture protected the baby from other vultures and he remained unharmed. This vulture was an embodiment of the Four-Faced Mahākāla, which became the personal Yidam deity of Gendün Drup. Because his parents were so poor, the young Gendün Drup had to hire himself out to a neighbor to work as a shepherd wandering from village to village. His father died when he was seven. He went to Narthang, the well-known Kadam monastery in Tsang, and sought refuge with the *saṅgha* there. First he received the *genyen* དགེ་བསྙེན་ [dge bsnyen] ordination[2] from Druppa Sherap གྲུབ་པ་ཤེས་རབ་ [grub pa shes rab], the 14th abbot of Narthang and learned to write and recite under his tutelage. He could read and write in Indian languages in addition to Tibetan and Mongolian, among others, and was a good calligrapher. In 1405 at age fifteen, he was ordained as a *getsul* དགེ་ཚུལ་ [dge tshul] and given the monk's name Gendün Druppa. At age twenty in 1410 he was also ordained as a full *gelong* དགེ་སློང་ [dge slong] at Narthang.

Although while still a young man Gendün Drup had reawakened the knowledge he had accumulated in previous lives, his Tibetan biographer claims that he dedicated his life to scholarship. Gendün Drup was considered a great scholar of Narthang of the Kadam School by his contemporaries. He enjoyed an extraordinarily long life and he believed that one can never learn enough. The epithets attached to his name such as the Thamce Khyenba "Omniscient,"[3] Great Paṇḍita (Panchen), and Kapcupa དཀའ་བཅུ་པ་ [dka' bcu pa]—a special *geshe* title—demonstrate his enormous learning. Altogether, Gendün Drup received instruction, guidance, explanations, ritual texts, and the ritual instruction in various religious sects from sixty lamas throughout Tibet. The list reveals that most of his instructors were Kadam and Geluk lamas.

Apart from his long apprenticeship at Narthang Monastery, he studied in Ganden Monastery and others in Ü,[4] with the exception of Ganden all of which belonged to the Kadam School. Most of the Geluk lamas known from that period, especially Tsongkhapa and his closest disciples, taught Gendün Drup who has come to be considered one of Tsongkhapa's seven principle disciples. It is striking that we can even find names of Sakya lamas in this list of teachers.[5] This shows that on the one hand Gendün Drup was not prejudiced against other schools and became familiar with various traditions, while on the other, his close ties with the Sakya School helped spread Tsongkhapa's teachings in Tsang, a strongly Sakya-influenced area. Along with Tsongkhapa, Gendün Drup's many other teachers included Druppa Sherap and Sherap Sengge ཤེས་རབ་སེང་གེ་ [shes rab seng ge]. From the age of seven until twenty-five in 1415, Gendün Drup studied at Narthang under Druppa Sherap,

18 Tsongkhapa. Painted unfired clay with traces of gold, emblems missing, Tibet, probably made during his lifetime, 14th(?)/15th century, H 29 cm, W 23 cm, D 16.5 cm, Collection of Joachim Baader, Munich. >>>

who ordained and instructed him in most Kadam teachings and tutored him from his youth for almost twenty years. Finally he let him go to Tsongkhapa. Starting in 1415, Gendün Drup studied the complete Geluk[6] teachings both with Tsongkhapa and Tsongkhapa's master disciples for twelve years.

While tradition has generally characterized Sherap Sengge and Gendün Drup as teacher and student, in fact their relationship was more that of friends and brothers. Both came from the same area, both were ordained by the same master, and they both were among Tsongkhapa's seven primary disciples. From 1426 to 1438 Gendün Drup travelled with Sherap Sengge continuously throughout Tsang from one monastery to another. Gendün Drup and Sherap Sengge's efforts were

primarily responsible for the rapid spread of the teachings of Tsongkhapa in Tsang.

During his long years of apprenticeship, Gendün Drup particulary immersed himself in the teachings of the *vinaya* "monastic discipline" and logic.[7] At Narthang, Gendün Drup had already been introduced to the teaching of logic, which Tsongkhapa considered particularly important. He studied it again later many times with Tsongkhapa himself and his most renowned disciple, Gyaltsap Je རྒྱལ་ཚབ་རྗེ་ [rgyal tshab rje], as well as with Sherap Sengge in Ü. Gendün Drup became a renowned teacher of logic and left a series of texts on the subject. One particular tradition of the Kadam and Geluk schools is the *lamrim* "Stages of the Path," which Atiśa designed and Tsongkhapa developed and perfected. *Lamrim* refers to the complete oral instructions for *nyamlen* ཉམས་ལེན་ [nyams len] "spiritual practice."[8] Gendün Drup mastered the *lamrim* teachings under the direct guidance of Tsongkhapa himself.

According to Tibetan tradition, the impact of a great monk is evident through the manifestations of his qualities as a scholar, man of virtue, and benefactor. As a scholar, a great monk knows all objects and areas of knowledge. As a man of virtue, he follows the moral strictures of the three vows, and as a benefactor he has the zeal to be of use to others. To evaluate the life and impact of a great monk, his life must be viewed through these three fields.

First, Gendün Drup was indeed an outstanding scholar. According to the Tibetan view, a scholar's excellence should in turn be demonstrated in his ability to teach, debate, and write. Gendün Drup started teaching while he was still engaged in basic-level studies at Narthang. After becoming a monk, he turned his attention to students learning to recite and write, who called him the "Master of Writings." He began to teach officially at Sangphu གསང་ཕུ་ [gsang phu] Monastery after having been elected abbot of a college[9] there. For almost fifty years—from that point until the end of his life—he overwhelmingly dedicated himself to teaching. The significance he gave to teaching is illustrated in the prophecy of a lama[10] that Gendün Drup could live to about seventy if he meditated, but that if he taught he would not reach even sixty. But Gendün Drup did not heed this prophecy because he had resolved to spread Tsongkhapa's teachings throughout Tsang. When he was invited to Lhasa in 1450 to become abbot of Ganden Monastery, he refused the position of

20 The First Dalai Lama, surrounded by previous incarnations of the Dalai Lamas, including King Songtsen Gampo (lower right), the mystical King Lha Thothori (upper left) with holy texts and stūpas (next to him on clouds) which, as legend has it, came from the sky. Thangka, embroidery on linen, Tibet, 149 x 87 cm (with borders), Collection of the Wereldmuseum, Rotterdam, the Netherlands, Inv. No.: 29171.

head of the Geluk School. Even at an advanced age he was still travelling from monastery to monastery in Tsang in order to bestow the teachings of Tsongkhapa.

Gendün Drup was actually a *sūtra* teacher. The texts he used in his teaching included primarily the Kachen Zhi དཀའ་ཆེན་བཞི་ [dka' chen bzhi] "Four Major Difficult Texts,"[11] the Uma Riktshok Druk དབུ་མ་རིགས་ཚོགས་དྲུག [dbu ma rigs tshogs drug] "Six Texts of Madhyamaka" by Nāgājuna, the later works of Maitreya, and the six basic texts of Kadam. He made a particularly invaluable contribution by disseminating the secret teachings of Atiśa and his disciples, the Kadam Lekbam བཀའ་གདམས་གླེགས་བམ་ [bka' gdams glegs bam].

Debate is a characteristic feature of Tibetan Buddhism, with agility in disputation a special criterion for evaluating the qualities and excellence of an important personage. Apparently Gendün Drup was a master of debate and always clearly explained the opposing argument without engaging in chaotic or confused rhetoric.

He was also a very prolific writer. His collected works comprise six volumes and are among the most important texts of the first epoch of the Geluk School, along with the collected works of Tsongkhapa and his two most well-known disciples, Gyaltsap Je and Khedup Je མཁས་གྲུབ་རྗེ་ [mkhas grub rje]. His collected works primarily include numerous commentaries on the most important Buddhist texts—the *Vinaya*, *Pramāṇa*, *Abhidharma*, *Prajñāpāramitā*, and *Madhyamaka* teachings. They also include teachings about spiritual practice, instruction on meditation on deities, ritual texts, wish-fulfilling prayers, and numerous encomiums to deities and lamas. Gendün Drup began to write at age forty when he wrote a commentary on the *Madhyamakāvatāra of Candrakīrti* in 1430 at Narthang. He wrote his comprehensive commentary on the *Pramāṇavārttika* comprising three hundred folios in 1431 at Shelkar monastery. This work is one of the most important Tibetan texts on the teaching of logic and greatly contributed to the development of Tsongkhapa's teachings on the *Pramāṇavārttika*.

Among Tsongkhapa's disciples, Gendün Drup and Gyaltsap Je in particular became deeply involved with the teaching of logic. While Gyaltsap Je was more interested in semantics, Gendün Drup concentrated on textual exegesis and in 1437 he wrote a major text on the teaching of logic, Tseme Tenchö Chenpo Rikpe Gyan ཚད་མའི་བསྟན་བཅོས་ཆེན་པོ་རིགས་པའི་རྒྱན་ [tshad ma'i bstan bcos chen po rigs pa'i rgyan], based on a transcription of one of Tsongkhapa's oral teachings on the works of Künga Zangpo and Sherap Sengge. This text is representative in summarizing the most important innovations of Geluk masters' exegeses on the *Pramāṇavārttika*. Gendün Drup bequeathed two significant texts on the *vinaya* as well.[12] Based on his own two readings, Gendün Drup developed his *vinaya* instruction in Tsang.

His other two texts on the teaching of spiritual practice[13] also deserve special attention. As mentioned above, the quality of "virtue" consists of not violating the moral precepts of the three vows. The Geluk tradition expressly emphasizes compliance with the moral precepts of the three vows as the foundation of all the above qualities. Gendün Drup bore the epithet *neten* གནས་བརྟན་ [gnas brtan] (Skt. *sthavira*) "the Elder" and *duldzinpa* འདུལ་འཛིན་པ་ ['dul 'dzin pa] (Skt. *vinayadhara*) "Upholder of Discipline," which shows that he was considered virtuous.

Gendün Drup was generally known as the rebirth of Domtön (plates 7, 8) and his life and virtues were often compared to those of Domtön and measured by the way in which he dealt with the "eight temporal realities"—gain and loss, praise and criticism, fame and ridicule, and happiness and unhappiness. As a pioneer in the field of the *vinaya*, throughout his life Gendün Drup advocated the teaching of Tsongkhapa's reforms. His life was a timeless model for the high-level Tibetan monkhood. To establish Tsongkhapa's teachings in Tsang, he put aside the perfection of his own meditative practice and gave priority to teaching instead. He even twice rejected the elevated position of abbot of Ganden Monastery, the office of the head of Geluk. He instead applied even more energy to establishing Tashilhünpo in Tsang as a religious center equal in importance to Ganden Monastery in Ü. According to Tibetan tradition, "one whose learning does not impede his perfection and whose perfection does not impede his learning and who contributes to the teachings is called a 'Great Holy Man.'" This certainly applies to Gendün Drup.

According to the Mahāyāna teaching, no one should be satisfied with his or her own salvation from suffering alone. Humankind should strive to be of use to the teachings as well as to all other sentient beings. "Usefulness to others" is the purpose and primary goal of the life of a great monk or a reincarnated lama. Accordingly, a monk should unite learning, virtue, and charity in his person. A monk manifests his charity through his impact as a man of learning and virtue throughout life. His charity may consist of training disciples, building places of worship, and making sacrifices to the Three Jewels, among other examples.

When Gendün Drup was ordained as a *getsul* and received the name *Gendün Druppa Pel* at age fifteen, he added *zangpo* བཟང་པོ་ [bzang po] "benefactor" to his new name to indicate that he had wanted to become a benefactor to others from early on. He was in fact not only an outstanding man of learning and virtue, but also a significant benefactor. His biographer, Lechen Künga Gyaltsen ལས་ཆེན་ཀུན་དགའ་རྒྱལ་མཚན་ [las chen Kun dga' rgyal mtshan] compares his life story to that of the three brothers of Kadam[14] who led three very different lives. Phuchungba dedicated himself primarily to meditation and made ardent sacrifices to the Three Jewels. Chenngaba applied all his energies to building monasteries and places of worship, and Potoba devoted himself to teaching and serving the *saṅgha*. Gendün Drup chose these three very different lives as models and united the example of their impact to his own actions. Thus he trained numerous students, established Tashilhünpo Monastery, built a number of places of worship, organized the Mönlam Chenmo སྨོན་ལམ་ཆེན་མོ་ [smon lam chen mo] "Great Prayer" Festival, and served the *saṅgha*. Thus he became as invaluable to the Geluk School as these three brothers had been to the Kadam School.

One of the noblest tasks of a religious teacher is the education of students. Gendün Drup accepted this duty and made it his central focus. Because he taught from age thirty-five to eighty-five, his students were found throughout Tibet. In all he had more than sixty well-known disciples. By the end of the 15th century, not only the abbots of most Kadam and Geluk monasteries in Ü and Tsang, but those of some major Sakya monasteries in western Tsang, most of the teachers in Ngari, Ü, Tsang, and Kham—in other words, hierarchs and teachers all over Tibet—were Gendün Drup's students. This reveals how large his impact was in propagating the teachings of Tsongkhapa.

Gendün Drup's major life's work was Tashilhünpo Monastery. This became the fourth largest Geluk monastery and the first major Geluk monastery in Tsang. After Tsongkhapa himself and his disciples established the three large monasteries of Ü—Ganden (1409), Drepung (1416), and Sera (1419)—the Geluk School had established a solid basis for the religious

and secular power of Tashilhünpo. In contrast to Ü, Tsang remained more of a Sakya School area and was virgin land for the Geluk. Gendün Drup had always wanted to found a monastery in Tsang of the same stature and significance as Ganden Monastery, and so applied all his energies to that end starting in 1446. From then until his death in 1474, Tashilhünpo was the center of his life.

After his first period as a student in Ü, Gendün Drup returned to Tsang with Sherap Sengge. Both had taught primarily in the monasteries of Narthang, Jangchen བྱང་ཆེན་ [byang chen], and Tanak Rikhü རྟ་ནག་རི་ཁུད་ [rta nag ri khud]. His community of monks initially numbered about seventy disciples and was called the "great college on the southern banks"[15] because Gendün Drup and his disciples lived on the southern banks of the Tsangpo River in western Tsang but did not have any permanent settlements. As early as 1432, he had already established a first settlement for his *saṅgha* near the Nyingma School monastery, Gyang Bummoche རྒྱང་འབུམ་མོ་ཆེ་ [rgyang 'bum mo che]. The next year, 1433, he was selected as abbot of Rikhü Monastery. There he had the monastery renovated and expanded and organized the Mönlam Chenmo Festival. This resulted in the old monastery becoming a completely new Geluk monastery. In 1436 he had his own palace, the Thekchen Phodrang ཐེག་ཆེན་ཕོ་བྲང་ [theg chen pho brang], built at Jang Monastery. Because the number of his disciples at Narthang and Jang was constantly growing, it became necessary to build a palace where he could teach and occasionally retreat to meditate. The Thekchen Phodrang was an incomparable residence of its time and served as his primary living quarters for the long period before Tashilhünpo was completed.

In 1438 Gendün Drup secretly moved into the territory of Ü and thus avoided being asked to become the abbot of Narthang. In 1440 he finished his second period of study in Ü and returned to Tsang. By this time he was fifty years old and thus at the height of his powers as a man of learning and virtue. In subsequent years, he remained at Narthang and Jangchen Monastery, occasionally travelling to other sites in the western Tsang to disseminate teachings there. Even then he still very much wanted to establish his own Geluk monastery in Tsang. Fulfilling this wish initially presented difficulties—monasteries of other orders, especially Sakya and Shangpa Kagyü, succeeded in thwarting his plans. For instance, Thangtong Gyalpo ཐང་སྟོང་རྒྱལ་པོ་ [thang stong rgyal po], the legendary master of

22 The First Dalai Lama. Painted wooden statue, Tibet, 17th century, with inscription on the reverse: "In reverence to the Omniscient Gendün Drup," Beijing.   **23** The 1st Dalai Lama. Bronze, gilded, copper alloy with traces of pigments, Tibet or China, 18th century, H 25 cm, W 16 cm, D 11.5 cm, Collection of Maciej Góralski, Warsaw.

Shangpa Kagyü, openly antagonized him and more than once attempted to prevent the construction of Tashilhünpo.

But with determination, Gendün Drup ultimately succeeded despite powerful resistance. With the support of his patrons,[16] Gendün Drup had a twenty-five *zho*-high ཞོ་ [zho] statute of the Buddha Śākyamuni built in Drakmar Labrang བྲག་ དམར་བླ་བྲང་ [brag dmar bla brang] near Samdruptse བསམ་གྲུབ་རྩེ་ [bsam grub rtse] (now Shigatse). Thus began the construction of Tashilhünpo, although individual buildings were put up afterwards.[17] Construction and preparation of the images, statutes, and other religious paraphernalia continued until Gendün Drup's death. Most of the artists were Nepali, although some renowned Tibetan artists[18] also participated in furnishing the monastery.

Gendün Drup founded three *tsen nyi* མཚན་ཉིད་ [mtshan nyid] religious colleges[19] in Tashilhünpo, which were subdivided into twenty-six *mitsen* མི་ཚན་ [mi tshan], or local sections. It was also possible to study Tantrism at Tashilhünpo, although Gendün Drup was not able to establish a Tantric college. In 1449, after the summer retreats, he moved to Tashilhünpo together with his disciples to take up residence. This was the first *saṅgha* at Tashilhünpo, comprising one hundred-ten monks. By the time of his death, this number had grown to 1,500. In 1464 he gathered numerous literati from the area and prepared an edition of the Kangyur texts on Tantrism. The following year, they prepared the remaining Kangyur texts to complete the project. With that Gendün Drup's life's work was complete.

A special concern for Gendün Drup was the annual Mönlam Chenmo Festival. Tsongkhapa was the first to arrange it with the first celebration occuring in Lhasa in 1409. Gendün Drup also introduced this festival and the related worship of the Three Jewels to Tsang. He organized a seven-day Mönlam Chenmo Festival at Tashilhünpo when the statue of Maitreya was dedicated in 1463. In the first month of 1474 at the age of eighty-four, he invited 1,600 monks to Tashilhünpo and organized a twelve-day Mönlam Chenmo Festival rivalling the first Tsongkhapa had held in 1409. The number of those attending reached 10,000. Just as in Lhasa in 1409, this was the first time the Geluk School opened itself to a critical public in Tsang. The success of the festival demonstrated that the Geluk were now firmly established in Tsang. It was at this time just before his death that Gendün Drup had the greatest impact.

Gendün Drup died on the eighth day of the twelfth month of the Year of the Male Wood Horse (1474) at Tashilhünpo at age eighty-four. In 1475, the Gong Dzok དགོངས་རྫོགས་ [dgongs rdzogs] "commemoration" ceremony and Mönlam Chenmo Festival were held in his honor with more than 2,000 monks taking part. His body was temporarily preserved in his *labrang*[20] "lama's residence," and was not cremated until 1478. His relics were placed in a large *stūpa* made of pure silver and decorated with ornamentation of gold and copper.

This description of Gendün Drup's life makes clear that his religious qualities embodied the ideal holy man of the Tibetan hagiographic tradition. From the Tibetan point of view, he represented the timeless ideal of a great Buddhist monk as a model man of learning, virtue, charity, and outstanding impact. His significance to the Tibetan Buddhist society of the 14th and 15th centuries lies primarily in his propagation of Tsongkhapa's teachings and reforms in west-central Tibet, whereas Tsongkhapa and most of his disciples had been limited to Ü.

Gendün Drup, spending almost his entire life in Tsang, was overwhelmingly responsible for the propogation of Tsongkhapa's reforms. He lived in Ü only twice to advance his studies, once for ten years and again for two years. He did everything in his power to spread the teaching of the *vinaya* in Tsang and to bring new prestige to the precepts for monks, which had not been honored there. He refused the high office of head of the Geluk School and steadfastly pursued what was for him a higher goal, the establishment of Tsongkhapa's teachings in Tsang. The founding of Tashilhünpo was the final proof that thirty-nine years after its success in Ü the Geluk School had also conquered Tsang. This monastery was the symbol of its triumph in Tsang while simultaneously being a monument to its founder, Gendün Drup. That may be the reason why he was recognized after his death if not even before as the third reincarnation of Bodhisattva Avalokiteśvara in line after Songtsen Gampo, the first Tibetan king, and Domtön. It may also be why his reincarnation was found immediately after his death, the first time for a high Geluk lama. This was the beginning of the best-known and most important line of reincarnations in Tibetan history.

"As soon as I was born, I looked about timidly and found beauty in front of me, and I smiled. My mouth was turned towards the direction of Tashilhünpo and my hands were in a gesture of devotion. My body was white like crystal, emanating a very pure light. My father immediately performed a special ritual for Cakrasaṃvara." (Gendün Gyatso)

THE SECOND DALAI LAMA GENDÜN GYATSO

དགེ་འདུན་རྒྱ་མཚོ་

Amy Heller

Gendün Gyatso དགེ་འདུན་རྒྱ་མཚོ་ [dge 'dun rgya mtsho] wrote his autobiography at age forty-three in 1528,[1] by which time he had already served as abbot of three of the most important Geluk monasteries in Central Tibet. In 1512 he ascended the throne of Tashilhünpo, in 1517 the throne of Drepung, and in 1528 that of Sera. He expanded the sphere of influence of this monastic school far beyond the regions of Tashilhünpo and Lhasa, which was the location of the foremost Geluk institutions when he was born.

Through teaching actively and sending envoys to such distant regions as Guge in western Tibet and several principalities south and east of Lhasa, he greatly increased the patronage network of patrons and adherents to the Geluk teachings. During the early part of his lifetime, growing Geluk religious influence impelled Gendün Gyatso to build new temples and restore the ancient sanctuaries in Guge. He was personally responsible for founding new monasteries in the region east of Lhasa. He founded Chökhorgyal Metoktang ཆོས་འཁོར་རྒྱལ་མེ་ཏོག་ཐང་ [chos 'khor rgyal me tog thang], the "Dharmacakra See of the Victory on the Flower Meadow" on the north banks of the Tsangpo beyond Samye in 1509. This monastery came to be known as the personal monastery of the Dalai Lama lineage because it was customary for each Dalai Lama to visit it at least once during his lifetime. He founded Ngari Dratsang མངའ་རིས་གྲྭ་ཚང་ [mnga' ris grva tshang] still further east in 1541, in homage to the long-standing strong relation of patronage with the kings of Guge and to house many monks sent from there to study Geluk teachings in central Tibet.

When he wrote his autobiography at age forty-three, Gendün Gyatso was in the prime of his career as a religious master. In addition to teaching and officiating over ceremonies, he had a pronounced penchant for writing and composed rituals and many letters of spiritual exhortation to his disciples and patrons. He also wrote on religious history and composed a biography of his father who had been his principal religious teacher during his childhood and remained influential until his death in 1506. We find that both his biography and autobiography display a keen sense of the political in his life. For Gendün Gyatso, politics represented three separate areas: his role as a member of the lineage of the principal Buddhist teachers in Tibet; his participation in the complex hierarchical relations within his religious order; and teaching various princes

throughout Tibet, which was remunerated with offerings of territory and economic support. These factors interacted and led to the political legitimation of his authority throughout several regions.

This is crucial because during the lifetime of the 2nd Dalai Lama there were very troubled times in Lhasa and Shigatse—members of the Karma School had taken control of Shigatse during Gendün Drup's lifetime but as of 1480, when Gendün Gyatso was six, they led troops towards Ü in central Tibet. A period of tense retaliations from Geluk supporters ensued. In 1492, the Karma School allies invaded districts administered by Lhasa and then in 1498 occupied the region of Lhasa itself. It was only in 1517 that the Karma were finally driven out of Lhasa and the Geluk regained control there in precisely the year Gendün Gyatso assumed the abbot's throne in Drepung. In this context it is important to see how the Geluk progressively reinforced their influence in Guge where their authority was uncontested. Gendün Drup had begun cordial relations with the Guge monks and local rulers, which resulted in the king of the Guge, Lopsang Rapten ཁོ་བཟང་རབ་བརྟན་ [blo bzang rab brtan] patronizing Gendün Gyatso as the 2nd Dalai Lama, and his Queen Dondupma དོན་གྲུབ་མ་ [don grub ma] founding the Red Temple at Tsaparang. Their son continued this patronage in turn leading to the foundation of Ngari Dratsang in 1541. This patronage complemented the Geluk extension of their influence east of Lhasa through Gendün Gyatso's personal monastic foundations at Chökhorgyal and Ngari Dratsang, and his numerous letters and instructions for worship sent to local leaders.[2] In this way Gendün Gyatso consciously strengthened his patronage relationships by teaching patrons who guaranteed his economic and political security and created a support network stretching from western Tibet, Mustang in the western Himalayas, to the thresholds of Kham in eastern Tibet.[3] It is striking that he was so politically astute. As we will see, his political sense developed very early perhaps because of the opposition to the recognition of him as a rebirth, and perhaps because of the unstable regional politics in Tsang during his adolescence. This led to his searching for patronage and legitimation in the eastern districts of Ü and Guge.

His autobiography begins with salutations to Atiśa and his Tibetan disciple Domtön and to Tsongkhapa, who is revered as a substitute Buddha. It is noteworthy that Gendün Gyatso explains that he is writing his autobiography upon request, which demonstrates his awareness of himself holding a distinctive position in a lineage of Buddhist teachers. This attitude characterizes the autobiography from the beginning and shows how he had internalized both his role and its ramifications. He begins with Tashilhünpo's lamas searching for the reincarnation of Gendün Drup shortly after his death in 1474. First the lamas present auspicious offerings to a golden statue of White Tārā and then consult an oracle in Tanak not far from Shigatse renowned for his powers of clairvoyance, Lama Donyö of Tanak. Speaking for the deceased, the oracle says: "My next birth may be in China, but the Dharma is not very developed there so I do not know. Possibly I will desire to have the birth received right nearby in this region, but since I do not know precisely where my birth will be, tell the lamas to please do no harm." This message is given to the assembly of Tashilhünpo lamas, and Gendün Gyatso hears this personally from one of the main lamas of Sera at the time.

Then Gendün Gyatso explains the family history regarding the oracle, who turns out to be his very own grandfather. The family line traced its roots back several centuries earlier to the mid-8th century of king Trisong Detsen, who founded Samye monastery in 779 and proclaimed Buddhism the official religion of Tibet. At that time, a chaplain of Samye was the first recorded ancestor in Gendün Gyatso's family history. Gendün Gyatso's family line also had other illustrious ancestors tracing their origins from this chaplain at Samye.[4] Gendün Gyatso's great-grandfather first worked as secretary of a local lord, and then after developing spiritual inclinations took monastic vows under a major Kagyü teacher. In Tanak, he studied the Shangpa Kagyü tradition with several masters including a *yogin* who was a specialist in *tsha tsha*-making and divination. He specialized in rituals for the Six-Armed Mahākāla of Wisdom.

Lama Donyö Gyaltsen of Tanak was the son of Gendün Gyatso's great-grandfather and thus Gendün Gyatso's grandfather. Called "the Great Hermit," Donyö was known for his great powers of clairvoyance and knowledge of the past, present, and future and was the same lama consulted as oracle about the next birth of Gendün Drup. In addition to teachings of Shangpa Kagyü lineage, he also practiced very esoteric Nyingma teachings and studied with the Sakya teacher Namkha Naljor ནམ་མཁའ་རྣལ་འབྱོར་ [nam mkha' rnal 'byor] who was an emanation of Padampa Sanggye, a famous Indian *yogin* who had taught in Tibet. Thus Lama Donyö and his father became masters of developments in earlier, later, and intermediary traditions. He was also the founder of the monastery of Tanak, on the north side of the Tsangpo facing Shigatse.

Lama Donyö's son Künga Gyaltsen ཀུན་དགའ་རྒྱལ་མཚན་ [kun dga' rgyal mtshan] (1432–1506) was Gendün Gyatso's father. Gendün Drup, the "Omniscient" master, was the most illustrious of Künga Gyaltsen's teachers. He presided over Künga Gyalsten's novitiation ceremony at Tashilhünpo after already having visited Tanak several times during Künga Gyaltsen's childhood.[5] In addition to those of the Geluk tradition, Künga Gyaltsen also studied Shangpa, Sakya, and Nyingma traditions, as well as the family tradition of rain-making.

Gendün Gyatso introduces his biological family, their religious background, and the spiritual link between Gendün Drup and Tashilhünpo which proved crucial to his own future. When his father was forty-five in the Year of the Fire Monkey,[6] Gendün Gyatso emerged painlessly from the womb of Künga Palmo ཀུན་དགའ་དཔལ་མོ་ [kun dga' dpal mo], a spiritually inclined woman considered to be a rebirth of the *ḍākinī* and consort of Gotsangpa རྒོད་ཚང་པ་ [rgod tshang pa] (1189-1258), one of the most famous Kagyü teachers. Her status as an incarnation is not emphasized per se because by her lifetime, the Kagyü lineage from which she hailed had already recognized the rebirth of the First Karmapa in 1193, and thus incarnations were not unusual to members of the lineage. Gendün Gyatso describes his birth:

> As soon as I was born, I looked about timidly and found beauty
> in front of me, and I smiled. My mouth was turned towards
> the direction of Tashilhünpo and my hands were in a gesture
> of devotion. My body was white like crystal, emanating a very
> pure light. My father immediately performed a special ritual for
> Cakrasaṃvara.

This quote is crucial and full of religious significance—while we have the timid, human character of the young boy, we also have a spiritual linkage through the mention of white crystal, referring to Avalokiteśvara in the form of Ṣaḍakṣarī and his crystal prayer beads. Also by saying that he was facing Tashilhünpo, he is indicating the place where his predecessor, Gendün Drup, came from to be reborn in Tanak. Gendün Gyatso continues:

24 The Second Dalai Lama. Bronze, gilded, with inscription on the reverse: "The valuable omniscient Victorious Lord" Tibet, 16th century, H 24.2 cm, Tibet House, New York.

At the time of my entry into her womb, my mother dreamt that she handled many books of precious teachings and then touched her mouth. But because of the poison on the paper used to eliminate vermin, she feared that an old stomach ailment would return, but she dreamt that no harm would come. And indeed it was so. As for my father, while I was in the womb he dreamt that Gendün Drup had come to our family monastery's meditation site to meditate. Gendün called out, "You, come before me," at which point a young monk appeared and they became friends. Then the young monk was leaving, and just as he reached the door of the cave, Gendün Drup said, "I am on retreat here. For the time being, don't come up to see me."

After three days, through the liberation of meditation, he dreamt that Tārā came to invite him to Tashilhünpo to take up his monk's bowl and robe. Continuing:

At the moment of birth, just after my mother dreamed again, a voice said, "Only one son will be born to you. Give him the name 'Sanggye Pel' སངས་རྒྱས་འཕེལ་ [sangs rgyas 'phel]. This will be a sign linking him to the Buddha of the past, present and future." Thus I had this name until my ordination as a monk.[7] Also around that time, my mother dreamt of a large shrine where my father had engaged excellent painters to paint the Kālacakra maṇḍala and just then they finished the final strokes with perfection. After that, when I was about two years old, I remembered the words "tāre tuttāre" from Tārā's mantra. As there was a slight imperfection and my pronunciation was not quite correct, at first the full version [Oṃ tāre tuttāre ture svāhā] did not come. But then just after, it did.

When I was three, my mother scolded me, so I said to her, "Don't get annoyed with me or I won't stay, I'll go to Tashilhünpo. My house there is better than here. There's even molasses for me to eat there." That was the very first indication I gave of

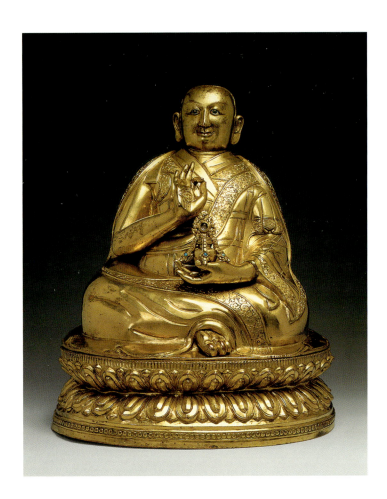

25 The Second Dalai Lama. Sheet copper, chased and gilded, with inscription on the reverse: "In reverence to the venerable omniscient Gendün Gyatso Pelzangpo," Tibet, 16th century, H 29.5 cm, Berti Aschmann foundation at the Museum Rietberg, Zürich, Inv. No.: Aschmann 141. **26** The Second Dalai Lama, surrounded by Guhyasamāja (upper left), Vajradhara (upper center) and Vaiśravaṇa (lower right). One of the monasteries may be Chökhorgyal, another may be Ngari Dratsang. Above the monasteries are two lakes, possibly Lake Lhamo Lhatso and "Gatekeeper Lake," so named in reference to Bektse. Thangka, Tibet (restored in 2004/05), 57 x 28.5 cm, Ethnographic Museum of the University of Zürich, Inv. No.: 14404.

remembering my previous birth. Also just around that time, I had made a mistake in my lessons and my mother got a bit angry. I said, "Please don't get angry with me. I have many composition teachers, so don't get angry or it will be a karmic sin." And so I started my first composition to please my mother. She was very happy because she realized that I had started composing devotional verses. And so the verses came, "Mother, may you be safe from wild dogs, and Mother, may you be safe from tigers, and Mother, may you be safe from bears, have no fear." That is what I wrote.

By then I was about five and my father was preaching away from home for the summer. He had set up some tents, and suddenly there was a giant clap of thunder. He looked inside the tent and said, "What happened?" I replied, "That sound is a resonance like the teachings of the father Lopsang Drakpa [ie, Tsongkhapa]." And immediately I intoned praise to Tsongkhapa.

Then I saw a stone shaped like Tsongkhapa, and another like Tārā. I continued with this game, piling the stones up to make a throne for the Tsongkhapa-shaped stone. Taking tiny stones, I said they were the monks in assembly around him. Except for this sort of games, I didn't care for the usual games of other children.[8]

Around this time, Gendün Gyatso developed a sense of memory, which he explains with a metaphor of a himself as a child behaving like a lama who rubs his head as if to stimulate thought:

Then once when I was alone, I touched my head rubbing it a bit and thought about knowledge. Around then my mother asked, "Well, before you were here, where did you come from?" I replied, "After my death the Chantmaster tied me with a string, and the Six-Armed Mahākāla of Wisdom came, having taken an iron boot. We became friends and I went in a black boat with a pulley rope, and I came from there. Once during that period I went to the *tuṣita*-heaven, where there were Maitreya, Atiśa, Domtön, and Tsongkhapa.

I listened to many sermons. Then, having asked what to do for the sake of all sentient beings, there appeared a lotus and two yellow petals which I had to follow for the sake of sentient beings. The petals went up to the sky and the lotus petals fell down on our family hermitage. One petal pointed in the direction of Amdo —but this was what the teacher said, I am personally not sure.

However, while I was staying at the family meditation site, one night it was cold and there was a frightening noise, which disturbed my father's sleeping position. He asked, "What happened?" A monk wearing a cotton robe and a hide hat pulled on my foot, and suddenly there was Palden Lhamo riding her mule. She came down from her mule and hit the monk with her club. She hurt the monk's hand and so rubbed it, and then suddenly they both left.

Although Gendün Gyatso does not qualify it as such, this is the earliest personal vision he describes during this lifetime. It is significant that Palden Lhamo appears, as she is one of the most important protectors of his lineage. Furthermore, the description of the help from the Mahākāla of Wisdom to reach this world is significant—according to Gendün Gyatso's biography of his father, the founder of the Shangpa Kagyü School, whose teachings his family followed, particularly revered this aspect of Mahākāla. Gendün Gyatso even calls this Mahākāla "the principal protector of the teachings of my ancestors," and describes rituals for the Mahākāla of Wisdom performed at his father's funeral to ensure him a good rebirth.[9] In a way this is the link between the biological family and the spiritual lineage of his rebirth.

As soon as Gendün Gyatso looks at his first book, the local deity appears and says that Gendün Gyatso will face some obstacles. The following day emissaries come asking questions. Gendün Gyatso writes, "I told them quite clearly, according to the memory of my previous life, my mother's name, and my own name Pema Dorje...I said this and more..." He lists other moments and finally says, "Well, there were so many signs, there is no need to write them all down. At this time in Tanak, it started to be known that the birth of Gendün Drup was in Tanak."

Thus Gendün Gyatso tells us that while he was locally recognized, the monastic community had not yet completely done so. He then describes various episodes of the process leading to the Geluk authorities completely recognizing him:

The monk Chöje Chöjor ཆོས་རྗེ་ཆོས་འབྱོར་ [chos rje chos 'byor] had a dream about the next birth and the certainty that it would be found. He had a dream about Maitreya coming to our world as well. So he wrote me a letter accompanied by various presents including incense and tea. My father started to prepare a reply, but I said I could do it myself, which I did. I thanked him for the tea and the incense and paid him respect. The presiding monk then declared that I had to meet with him. That night I dreamt of the words of the Buddha and the following morning when I woke up I was thinking about the secretary of Gendün Drup, Lama Dampa Sanggye, with whom I was friends. I went out the door just as they were blowing the conch trumpet at Shigatse fortress. Then at Sa fortress near Tanak, the local lord was having a special statue cast of the Buddha in the *bodhi āsana* position [seated in meditation touching the earth]. Just then, at the family monastery of Dorjeden in Tanak, the prayer flags all started to flutter on top of the sanctuary. Everyone was saying it was an auspicious sign and that it looked like an auspicious casting. Immediately thereafter the ritual master came and said, "The teachers who are coming will be good to you."

"Oh, who's coming?" I asked. He replied, "Gendün Drup's secretary Dampa Sanggye is coming and he will put his legs in the exact same position as the *yogin* Dampa Sanggye."

Then spontaneously I intoned the initiation to Jambala ཛམ་བ་ལ་ [dzam ba la] for the workers and all. When I took a cup of tea to drink, there was a cloth inside and I saw a *torma* on the plate which I offered to Jambala, for Jambala himself appeared. Then I intoned the words of the initiation and this made the ritual master so delighted that his faith was strengthened even to tears. Night and day there were signs including the perfect casting of Buddha image. This initiation spontaneously caused the recall and arising of visions, sometimes even of frightful ones![10]

A year later, he describes his return to Tashilhünpo:

When I was eight, I was invited to Tashilhünpo for the great tea ceremony in preparation for my ordination. When they started at the end of the evening tea, the fire was warm and I saw an emanation with two arms and a face with a frightening demeanor. There was alternate chanting and I recited all the rest. My father's disciple said, "The Great Black One is produced from the root syllable HUM," and I gave the next stanza, "She with one head, two arms, terrifying form." I continued, "These are the signs of this *dharmapāla*; she is the most special protector of all. She is my dharma protector and may She also be yours." Thus I composed a ritual for her, and asked whether they had some ink and paper ready.

Gendün Gyatso explains this episode of ritual composition by describing some of his earlier compositions:

From the time I was five or six, I had already made compositions spontaneously. At that time I saw Lhamo in a dream with her two arms holding a royal parasol and the insignia of victory. The cloth of the flags and umbrella became the wings of the *dharmapāla* who carried me into the sky where we flew to the Mountain of Potala. Once we arrived, we saw that it was a most unique mountain. It was the perfect mountain of Cakrasaṃvara—at the center was Cakrasaṃvara and I remained on one of the golden spokes there. The Gods were garbed in gold and silver taking off into the celestial realm. Our continent of Jambudvīpa was located on this precious mountain of jewels. I dreamt that I took a vow for the benefit of all the sentient beings of the continent. I declared Cakrasaṃvara would be my meditation deity. The following morning I awoke very happy and told everything to my mother. Thus arose the certainty that this vision was a sign of me having a special karmic relationship with Cakrasaṃvara as my meditation deity. Then later we went to Tashilhünpo with my father for the great tea ceremony. There was held the great assembly ... Although the monks assembled had developed great faith in me, still the presiding monks said it was not yet the appropriate time for me to take my vows. So once again I returned to Tanak Dorjedan.

When I started my lessons, I was able to learn to read and write perfectly without studying. At that time, with my father as teacher, I mastered ritual cycles for Cakrasaṃvara, Yamantaka, and special forms for the Four-Armed Mahākāla, Yama, Vaiśravana, Lhamo Makzorma, and *Dharmapāla* Bektse as well. I also learned the Shangpa and Dakpo Kagyü teachings of Mahāmudrā, the Zhije system of Padampa, and many other initiations and rituals from my great-grandfather's and grandfather's teachings.

Then when I was nine, the Guge ruler Lopsang Rapten བློ་བཟང་རབ་བརྟན་ [blo bzang rab brtan] came to Tsang[11] to visit and offered praise to Gendün Drup, to which I gave the appropriate response. His *dharmapāla* was ever-so-slightly discontent and there were visions that indicated I should make a special *torma* offering.

My father had not previously been initiated to this Four-Faced Mahākāla, but the protector's magic made the verses of the initiation audible for us and thus the protector gave us the initiation. One night later that year I composed many frightening syllables but did not write them down. Then at dawn, I instantly pronounced words to the effect that the top of the flag of victory is a wish-fulfilling jewel. Then I lit the butter lamps and my father wrote everything down. This is a description of my life before ordination.

It is fascinating to see that Gendün Gyatso's local community recognized his status and that a ruler of a distant region also recognized it specifically as a way to continue the former relation with Gendün Grup. Yet all this time, a full enthronement had not yet been authorized at Tashilhünpo. We may surmise that this long period of waiting may have contributed to Gendün Gyatso developing a sense of the complexity of political relationships within the religious hierarchy as well as a sense of secular politics.

In his father's biography, Gendün Gyatso describes a dream his father had in 1486 of Lhamo presenting him with crystal prayer beads, which Gendün Gyatso describes as evidence of extraordinary miracles happening in dreams. The crystal prayer beads are a well-known symbol of Avalokiteśvara that confirms his link with both deities.[12]

In his autobiography, Gendün Gyatso describes his recognition at last as a *getsul* དགེ་ཚུལ་ [dge tshul] "novice" at Tashilhünpo when he was between ten and eleven.[13] The initial vows of monastic ordination were at last pronounced, his hair cut, and the name Gendün Gyatso declared before an assembly of the most illustrious Geluk monks then in Tibet assembled from Lhasa and other monasteries. His education continued at Tashilhünpo and nearby Nenying Monastery གནས་རྙིང་ [gnas rnying] and sometimes at Narthang. Occasionally he returned to Tanak Dorjedan to hear teachings from his father. When he was seventeen, he was received to undergo teachings in the Nyang region around Gyantse and further south. Great belief in him and his teaching abilities came to all who had a chance to hear him. He finally learned that the long delay in being recognized and ordained was due to the animosity of certain lamas—particularly that of the Abbot of Narthang—towards his father. The abbot had said the birth of the Omniscient Gendün Drup could not come to such a man as Gendün Gyatso's father.[14]

Now all that was in the past. Guided by visions assuring a good karmic connection with Drepung monastery near Lhasa, Gendün Gyatso headed there to take his full monastic vows in 1495 at the age of almost twenty. Due to political tensions, he decided to accept invitations from patrons outside the Lhasa region, particularly those of Olkha where he founded Chökhorgyal in 1509, and was guided by visions of Lhamo during construction.[15] He presided there and as of 1512, he was also named Abbot of Tashilhünpo and travelled between these two monasteries in Ü and Tsang. In 1517, just as the Geluk regained control of Lhasa, he was promoted to Abbot of Drepung, which he assumed the same year. Thereafter he spent six months a year in Lhasa and resided in Chökhorgyal the rest of the year until his death in 1542.

Despite the fact that his biography barely discusses the sectarian conflicts of his times, Gendün Gyatso, through his travels and network of influential patrons, contributed greatly to the consolidation of the Geluk School as a political force in Tibet. Furthermore, with his historic writings, ritual compositions, and visions, he established a firm base of liturgy and ritual practices which persisted into the time of the 14th Dalai Lama.

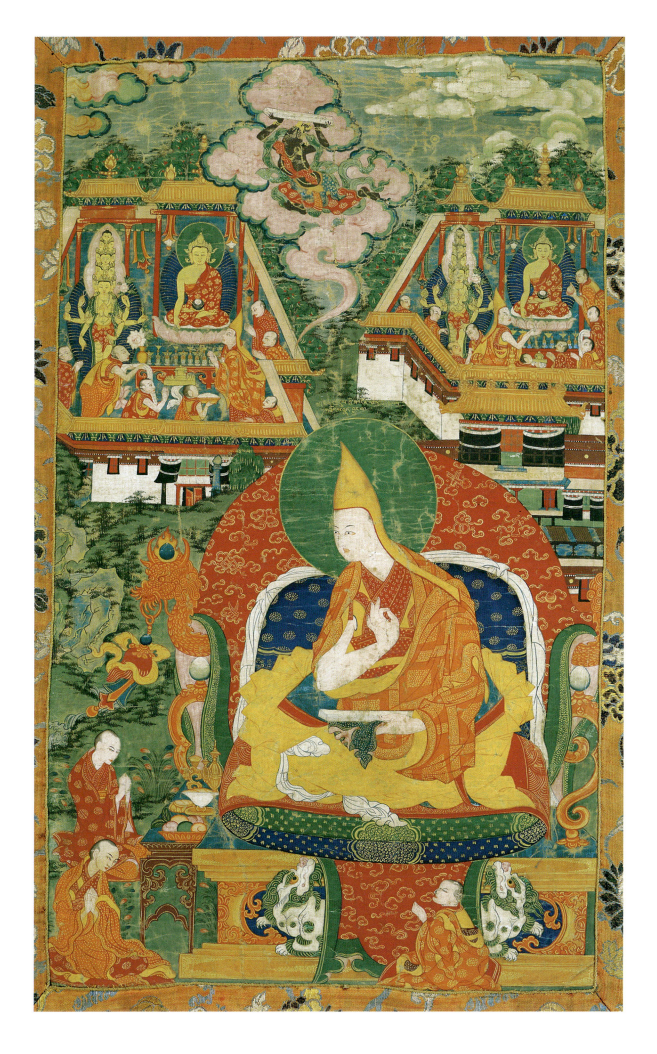

"In the past, the power of wish-fulfilling prayers brought the [Mongolian] ruler and me together. In the east, I was the spiritual teacher for the religion of the Buddha. This extremely great ruler was my patron and he showed me great honor and respect. There were always wish-fulfilling prayers to disseminate the religion in the eastern parts of the world, that gloomy land. Now that I have consented and am assisting in this work...my boon has been granted." (Sönam Gyatso)[1]

"The manifestation of the Dalai Lama, Yönten Gyatso, assumed a birth in the golden family of the Dayun Khan. Now he has spread the teaching of the Tsongkhapa everywhere among the people of Mongolia, like the sun."[20]

Karénina Kollmar-Paulenz
Translated by JANICE BECKER

1543–1588
THE THIRD DALAI LAMA, SÖNAM GYATSO
བསོད་ནམས་རྒྱ་མཚོ

On the twenty-fifth day of the first month in the Year of the Female Water-Hare (1543) in the estate of Khangsargong ཁང་གསར་གོང་ [khang gsar gong] in the region of Kyishö སྐྱིད་ཤོད་ [skyid shod] in central Tibet, a man was born whose political acumen and strategic vision would bring about the religious and political transformation of late 16th century Mongolia.[2] The 3rd Dalai Lama, Sönam Gyatso བསོད་ནམས་རྒྱ་མཚོ [bsod nams rgya mtsho], was the first to actually bear the title "Dalai Lama," which from that time onward was applied to the entire lineage of incarnations. He came from a family that maintained close ties with the Sakya School and with the ruling dynasty of Phakmo Drupa ཕག་མོ་གྲུ་པ་ [phag mo gru pa]. His father, Namgyal Drakpa རྣམ་རྒྱལ་གྲགས་པ་ [rNam rgyal grags pa], was a district official and scion of a long line of illustrious ancestors reaching back to the age of the Tibetan empire. His mother Peldzom Buthri's དཔལ་འཛོམ་བུ་ཁྲིད་ [dpal 'dzom bu khrid] family also had close ties to the Phakmo Drupa dynasty. His maternal grandfather, Wangchuk Rinpoche དབང་ཕྱུག་རིན་པོ་ཆེ་ [dbang phyug rin po che], was a renowned Tantric master in the service of the royal household. These familial political ties would prove very useful to Sönam Gyatso's ambitions.

The primary source on the life of the 3rd Dalai Lama is a biography his famous successor, the Great Fifth, wrote some one hundred years later. The Fifth based his work on a series of earlier biographies, some of which the Third's contemporaries had written shortly after his death in 1588. Since none of those contemporaneous biographies has survived, our main source is thus the Fifth's version. When approaching the life of the 3rd Dalai Lama, we should briefly consider the main features of the Tibetan biography, or *namthar*. The term *nampa tharpa* རྣམ་པ་ཐར་པ་ [rnam pa thar pa] literally means "complete liberation." Tibetan biographies start from the assumption that their protagonists have achieved Buddhahood—complete liberation—and that their biographies should illustrate their exemplary lives and inspire others to emulate them.

Because of their hagiographic subject matter, Western scholarship has often underestimated Tibetan biographies as historical sources. Despite this subject matter, however, they often describe with detailed precision major events in the life of their protagonists and provide a wealth of contemporaneous detail. As is common for this genre, the biography of the 3rd Dalai Lama begins with an account of his mother's dreams during her pregnancy which anticipated the birth of a Bodhisattva. Auspicious dreams, other signs, and wonders accompanied the boy's birth. Yet despite these auspicious signs, his parents feared that something untoward was going to happen since their other children had all died an early death. To avert the potential danger, they gave him the milk of a white nanny goat. The biography thus says that the boy received the name Ranusi Chöpal Zangpo ར་ནུ་སྲི་ཆོད་དཔལ་བཟང་པོ་ [ra nu sri chod dpal bzang po], "happy one protected by goat's milk."

Even as a young child, Sönam Gyatso showed unusual spiritual abilities, commonplace in the lives of Tibetan holy persons. Consequently as early as 1545, two years after his birth, rumors that the boy was the rebirth of the 2nd Dalai Lama[3] had already started spreading. In 1546 the rulers of the House of Nedong སྣེའུ་གདོང་ [sne'u gdong] officially recognized and installed him on the throne in Drepung. Shortly thereafter he took the *upāsaka* vow before Panchen Sönam Drakpa བསོད་ནམས་གྲགས་པ་ [bsod nams grags pa],[4] his predecessor Gendün Gyatso's most accomplished disciple and from whom he received the monastic name, Sönam Gyatso Pelzangpo Tanpe Nyima Chok Thamce Lenampar Gyalwa བསོད་ནམས་རྒྱ་མཚོ་དཔལ་བཟང་པོ་བསྟན་པའི་ཉི་མ་ཕྱོགས་ཐམས་ཅད་ལས་རྣམ་པར་རྒྱལ་བ་ [bsod nams rgya mtsho dpal bzang po bstan pa'i nyi ma phyogs thams cad las rnam par rgyal ba], abbreviated as Sönam Gyatso.

He then began to study under many teachers, starting with Sönam Drakpa himself. In addition to studying Mahāyāna Buddhist texts intensively, he also concentrated on initiation in the Tantric meditation cycles, including those for Gönpo Chakdrukpa མགོན་པོ་ཕྱག་དྲུག་པ་ [mgon po phyag drug pa] "Six-Armed Mahākāla" and for Palden Lhamo དཔལ་ལྡན་ལྷ་མོ་ [dpal ldan lha mo].[5] Meanwhile, he also began to travel extensively, visiting monasteries near and far. In 1556 alone his visits included Olkha འོལ་ཁ་ ['ol kha], Chökhorgyal ཆོས་འཁོར་རྒྱལ་ [chos 'khor rgyal], Chonggye འཕྱོང་རྒྱས་ ['phyong rgyas], Tsethang རྩེས་ཐང་ [rtses thang], Nedong སྣེའུ་གདོང་ [sne'u gdong], Samye བསམ་ཡས་ [bsam yas], and Kyishö སྐྱིད་ཤོད་ [skyid shod], all in central Tibet. He nurtured a particularly close relationship with Chökhorgyal Monastery, which the 2nd Dalai Lama had founded in the vicinity of the "Lake of Visions." At times in reading his biography, the years of his youth appear

29 The Third Dalai Lama, with scenes from his biography.
Thangka, West Tibet / Guge, 2nd half of the 16th century, 123.2
x 93.3 cm, private collection. >>>

[mkhas grub dge legs dpal bzang po], served as *upadhyāya* "instructor" and the current occupant, Gendün Tenpa Dargye དགེ་ འདུན་བསྟན་པ་དར་རྒྱས་ [dge 'dun bstan pa dar rgyas], as *ācārya* "teacher," while Shangge Phel Chögye ཤངས་དགེ་འཕེལ་ཆོས་རྗེ་ [shangs dge 'phel chos rje] and Sönam Pelzang བསོད་ནམས་དཔལ་བཟང་ [bsod nams dpal bzang] acted as *sangtön* གསང་སྟོན་ [gsang ston] "secret teacher" and *dügowa* དུས་གོ་བ་ [dus go ba] "observer."[7]

Sönam Gyatso proved a tireless advocate of the Geluk School. He not only taught ceaselessly in central Tibet and the surrounding areas but also established a series of monasteries. In 1568 he founded a personal "house temple," *Dratshang Phende Lekshaling* གྲ་ཚང་ཕན་བདེ་ལེགས་བཤད་གླིང་ [grva tshang phan bde legs bshad gling], which would later be integrated into the west wing of the Potala during the era of the 5th Dalai Lama. Serving as the Dalai Lamas' private monastery ever since, today the temple is better known as the Namgyal རྣམ་རྒྱལ་ [rnam rgyal] Monastery.[8]

In addition to his efforts in consolidating the Geluk School in Tibet, Sönam Gyatso is known for beginning Tibetan Buddhist missionary work among the Mongolian peoples. Through his initiative the Mongols[9] have been avid disciples of the Geluk School since the first half of the 17th century. He was also largely responsible for the expansion of the sphere of influence of Tibetan Buddhism as far as the lower Volga starting in the late 16th century. This in turn formed a cultural identity based on a Buddhism common to both Tibetan and Mongolian society in the early modern period.

Let us look at the circumstances leading to the famous meeting between Altan Khan, the most important Mongol prince of his time, and the hierarch of the Geluk School. As early as 1558 at age fifteen, Sönam Gyatso had already visited the northern border region of Tibet at the request of a Hor prince.[10] As his biography notes, he arranged that the Hor "gave up evil and became virtuous."[11] He also demonstrated his interest in Tibet's border regions, considered "uncivilized" in part because their inhabitants were not Buddhist, when he established monasteries there, such as Lithang and Kumbum. On his way to Mongolia in 1577, he stopped to rest at a small monastery that Rinchen Tsöndrü Gyaltsen རིན་ཆེན་ བརྩོན་འགྲུས་རྒྱལ་མཚན་ [rin chen brtson 'grus rgyal mtshan], a hermit monk, had founded in 1560 near Kökönor where a white sandalwood tree had grown after Tsongkhapa's birth. Sönam Gyatso asked the monk to build a larger monastery on the

28 Seal of the Third Dalai Lama.

to have been spent going back and forth between Drepung and Chökhorgyal constantly.

From early on Sönam Gyatso developed relationships with the royal houses of his time. For example, in 1554 he received a joint invitation from the King of Guge, Jikten Wangchuk Pekarle འཇིག་རྟེན་དབང་ཕྱུག་པད་དཀར་ལྡེ་ ['jig rten dbang phyug pad dkar lde] and his spiritual teacher, Panchen Shānti-pa, to propagate the teachings of the Buddha in Ngari[6] "for the benefit of all sentient beings." Apparently he did not accept that invitation, although he did the one he received in 1558 from the ruler of Phakmo Drupa to come to his residence in Nedong. By 1559, the young Sönam Gyatso had become the ruler's personal teacher, an office that he would hold until the ruler's death in 1564. This appointment also contributed greatly to his reputation in political and religious circles. In the Year of the Water Mouse (1552), he became the abbot of Drepung and six years later in 1558 of Sera also.

On the day of the full moon in the fourth month in the Year of the Male Wood Rat (1564), Sönam Gyatso was ordained a full monk. For the ceremony, the previous occupant of the throne of Ganden, Khedrup Gelek Palzangpo མཁས་གྲུབ་དགེ་ལེགས་དཔལ་བཟང་པོ་

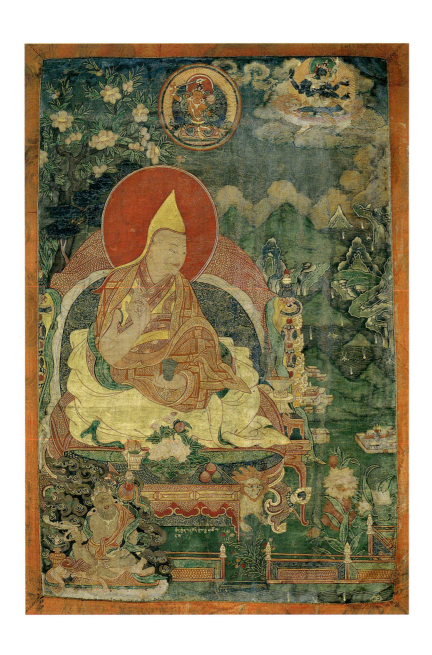

30 The Third Dalai Lama, surrounded by (among others) Mañjuśrī (upper center) and Brāhmaṇarūpa-Mahākāla (lower left). Thangka, Tibet (restored 2004/05), 57 x 39 cm, Ethnographic Museum of the University of Zürich, Inv. No.: 14405. **Detail of 30** Brāhmaṇarūpa-Mahākāla (Bramzug; mgon po bram gzugs), not shown here in the usual form of a gaunt old man. Symbols associated with him are recognizable, however, including the bone trumpet, staff, skull bowl, golden vase, and knife, swords, and prayer beads, while trident is missing.

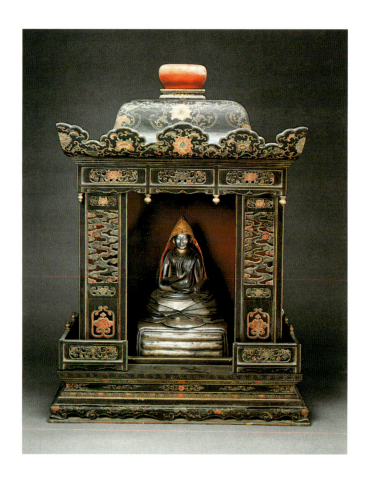

31 The Third Dalai Lama. Silver statue in black lacquer shrine, Tibet, shrine dated to 1779, figure certainly of earlier date, Beijing, Forbidden City, Yuhuage Temple (1755), built by Emperor Qianlong as the main esoteric Buddhist temple of the Imperial Palace.

site, which in 1583 was consecrated as Kumbum Jampaling སྐུ་འབུམ་བྱམས་པ་གླིང་ [sku 'bum byams pa gling]. Kumbum became one of the Geluk School's most important monasteries, housing more than 3,000 monks, and which became the subject of a monograph Wilhelm Filchner wrote in the 1930s.

At the start of the 1570s, Altan Khan sent a delegation of Mongols to central Tibet. Tibetan sources do not give an exact date for their arrival in Drepung, but a Mongolian source gives the year as 1574.[12] Sönam Gyatso initially made no effort to receive them and so the Mongol ruler sent a second delegation arriving in 1577. Sönam Gyatso now finally began the long journey to Mongolia, to Thekchen Chökhorling ཐེག་ཆེན་ཆོས་འཁོར་གླིང་ [theg chen chos 'khor gling] (Mong. Cabciyal)[13] Monastery. He arrived on the fifteenth day of the fifth Hor month of 1578.

When they met, Sönam Gyatso and Altan Khan entered into a *yönchö* ཡོན་མཆོད་ [yon mchod][14] relationship, thus recreating the relationship[15] from the 13th century between Khubilai Khan, founder of the Yuan 元 Dynasty in China, and Phakpa འཕགས་པ་ ['phags pa], head of the Sakya School. The *yönchö* is the rela-

tionship between a secular patron and a spiritual teacher. The patron makes a *wang-yön* དབང་ཡོན་ [dbang yon] "ritual payment" to the teacher for imparting a religious initiation. The *wang-yön* may take the form of goods, money, or other objects, or even military protection and aid. Following custom, Altan Khan and Sönam Gyatso exhanged titles of honor. The Khan awarded Sönam Gyatso the Mongolian title *ghaikhamsigh vcir-a dar-a say-in cogh-tu buyan-tu dalai* meaning "wonderful Vajradhara, good, brilliant, commendable ocean," shortened to "dalai lama," or "ocean lama." This abbreviation, since applied to the entire line of incarnations, is often interpreted as "lama whose wisdom is as large as the ocean."[16] This title, however, derives from *dalai-yin khan* "Ocean Khan," found in Mongolian sources as far back as the 13th century. Sönam Gyatso in turn bestowed the title *Chökyi Gyalpo Lhetshangpa Chenpo* ཆོས་ཀྱི་རྒྱལ་པོ་ལྷའི་ཚངས་པ་ཆེན་པོ་ [chos kyi rgyal po lha'i tshangs pa chen po] "Dharmarāja, Great Brahmā of the gods" on Altan Khan. Sönam Gyatso also awarded titles to a few other Mongolian princes, thus entering into *yönchö* relationships with them as well.

32 The Third Dalai Lama. Bronze, Tibet, 17. century, with inscription on the obverse, H 16 cm, The State Hermitage Museum, St. Petersburg, Inv. No.: U-985. **33** The Third Dalai Lama. Bronze, gilded, with inscription on the reverse: "This is a likeness of Sönam Gyatso, the omniscient sublime Buddha incarnation in his 42nd year," Tibet, H 17 cm, W 14.4 cm, D 12 cm, Musées Royaux d'Art et d'Histoire, Brussels, Inv. No.: Ver. 41.

Three months later, the Ming 明 emperor Wanli 萬曆 (1563–1620) sent Sönam Gyatso an invitation to come to Beijing. He did not accept and instead returned to Tibet. On his way back, he founded Chökhorling Monastery in Lithang in 1580. Later in 1583, a year after Altan Khan's death, the Dalai Lama once again embarked on a trip to Mongolia, this time at the invitation of Altan Khan's son, Dügüreng Sengge. While passing through Kumbum he founded a new college there. Sönam Gyatso spent the remaining years of his life almost exclusively in Mongolia. At the invitation of Secen Khung-tayiji, he spent a great deal of time with the Ordos Mongols between 1583 and 1584[17] converting them to Buddhism. In 1584 he travelled again to Kökekhota (present-day Hohehot) where he stayed until 1587. While there in 1585 he met Abadai Khan of Khalkha, who would found the first monastery in the Khalkha region in present-day Outer Mongolia a few years later, the Erdeni-juu near the old Mongolian capital Karakorum. In 1586 Sönam Gyatso consecrated the statue of Jobo at the Yeke-juu Temple in Kökekhota.

The next year he received an invitation to travel to Kharacin to propagate his teachings there. There on the morning of the twenty-sixth day of the black month in the Year of the Earth Mouse (1588), he finally died. His *namthar* does not mention a cause of death or where he died. In contrast, the Mongolian *Erdeni tunumal* records that "the manifestation of mortality showed itself"[18] to the Dalai Lama on the shores of Lake Jighasutai. While initially there was talk of transferring his remains to Tibet, in the end he was buried in Mongolia in a *stūpa* built north of the Yeke-juu Temple in Kökekhota.[19]

The 3rd Dalai Lama, the first Geluk hierarch to bear the title of Dalai Lama, did not bequeath a voluminous written corpus. His *Collected Works* comprise only one volume with a total of forty-two generally short entries, many of them encomia and short ritual texts. Given his many travels, he did not have time for the literary life that many Dalai Lamas after him would develop. Instead, we can describe him as a foremost missionary and traveller among the historical Dalai Lamas.

1589–1616
THE FOURTH DALAI LAMA, YÖNTEN GYATSO
THE ONLY NON-TIBETAN DALAI LAMA
ཡོན་ཏན་རྒྱ་མཚོ

When the 3rd Dalai Lama unexpectedly died in Mongolia in 1588, he left behind an uncertain legacy for the Geluk School. Although following generations could inherit the *yönchö* relationship he had entered into with a number of Mongolian princes, most importantly Altan Khan, he had still not ensured permanent Mongolian loyalty. If the Geluk wanted to consolidate their dominance among rival Tibetan Buddhist schools in Mongolia, they would need a charismatic person to succeed the 3rd Dalai Lama.

Viewed against this political and religious backdrop, the Geluk made an inspired political move in discovering the fourth incarnation of the Dalai Lama in a royal Mongolian son in Altan Khan's line. A Mongolian as the 4th Dalai Lama formed a link between Tibet and Mongolia from then onward. Tibetans had long viewed the Mongols as militarily superior but "uncivilized" because they were not Buddhists, but now they were part of a common Buddhist culture bound up with the Geluk ever since this high spiritual dignitary had been born among their ranks.

Yönten Gyatso ཡོན་ཏན་རྒྱ་མཚོ [yon tan rgya mtsho], the 4th Dalai Lama, was born to the royal Tümed Mongol, Sümbür Secen Cügükür and his wife, Bighcogh Bikiji, in the White Month of the Year of the Ox (January 1589).[21] Yönten Gyatso's father was the oldest son of Sengge Dügüreng Khan, himself son of and successor to Altan Khan. His mother traced her lineage directly to Khabutu Khasar, brother of Chingghis Khan. For the Mongols, the 4th Dalai Lama was doubly legitimate: first, as scion in direct lineage of the Mongol ruling family and second, as the rebirth of the 3rd Dalai Lama. Thus Yönten Gyatso was qualified to exercise both temporal and spiritual power over the Mongols. Yönten Gyatso spent the first years of his life in his home country, probably around Caghan Naghur (also Naghui) in Ulanchab-Amiyagh in what is today Inner Mongolia.[22] In 1591 Namudai Secen Khan, grandson of Altan Khan and then ruler of the Tümed Mongols, visited and celebrated the Mönlam Chenmo Festival together with him. Just one year later, the ruler visited again and invited him to Kökekhota, where he had Yönten Gyatso enthroned at Erdeni-juu Temple.

The Tibetan *saṅgha,* however, would not officially recognize the young Dalai Lama for almost another decade. In 1600 the Mongolians sent a deputation comprising both high priests—including the famous translator Siregetü Güsi Corji—and nobles to Lhasa to request that young Yönten Gyatso be recognized officially as the rebirth of the 3rd Dalai Lama. They invited a Tibetan delegation to Mongolia to confirm through tests that the new Dalai Lama was legitimate and to invite him to Lhasa, where he was to receive his spiritual training. Normally it would have been the Ganden Thri Rinpoche's task to accompany the young Dalai Lama from his home to Lhasa, but this time the extremely aged Thri Rinpoche, Peljor Gyatso དཔལ་འབྱོར་རྒྱ་མཚོ [dpal 'byor rgya mtsho] assigned the deceased Dalai Lama's treasurer Gushri Palden Gyatso གུ་ཤྲི་དཔལ་ལྡན་རྒྱ་མཚོ [gu shrī dpal ldan rgya mtsho] to accompany Yönten Gyatso to Lhasa. A group of lamas from various Lhasa monasteries journeyed to Mongolia, where they subjected Yönten Gyatso to the usual tests. He passed them all. The group then finally took him back to Lhasa in 1602, where the Ganden Thri Rinpoche, Zurpa Sanggye Rinchen ཟུར་པ་སངས་རྒྱས་རིན་ཆེན་ [zur pa sangs rgyas rin chen], novitiated him at the Jokhang.[23]

The 4th Dalai Lama never returned to his homeland. Like his predecessor, he began to travel, especially in Tsang where he had accepted an invitation from Tashilhünpo. Yet compared with the time of the 3rd Dalai Lama, the political situation had now changed. Their alliance with the Mongols had given the Geluk School domestic strength that the nobles of Tsang and others closely associated with rival schools resisted. But if we accept the story in his *namthar,* the young Dalai Lama remained aloof from the politics[24] of the time and left them to his officials and dignitaries. Daily political events did in fact influence how Yönten Gyatso spent his time. When the ruler of Tsang came to Lhasa for a Geluk initiation, the clerics refused him, saying that he was an enemy of Geluk teachings. It was no accident that Yöntsen Gyatso immediately repaired to Samye, to the relative security outside Lhasa.

Yönten Gyatso took vows as a full monk in 1614, just two years before his premature death. At the time he was studying with the major teachers of his time, including the Panchen Lama, the Thri Rinpoche Sanggye Rinchen, and Zimkhang Gong-tülku གཟིམས་ཁང་གོང་སྤྲུལ་སྐུ་ [gzims khang gong sprul sku]. His *namthar* tells us that a delegation from the Chinese emperor arrived in Lhasa in 1616 with a title of honor and expensive gifts for the young Dalai Lama. The Ming annals do not, however, mention this deputation. Central Tibet was also on the brink of civil war—the ruler of Tsang had been expanding his sphere of influence continuously towards central Tibet, having conquered Kyishö in 1616. Nedong, once powerful under the 3rd Dalai Lama, also surrendered to him. Under these circumstances, the Geluk's Mongol allies proved their salvation. The Mongols gathered their troops and showed their military force in Tibet under the leadership of two of the eastern Tibetan Prince Kholoche's sons. This convinced the princes of Tsang to forego their plan to conquer central Tibet.

In the middle of these power plays, the Dalai Lama died in the twelfth month in the Year of the Fire Dragon (1616) at age twenty-seven. The cause of death is not clear. His *namthar* cites no unnatural circumstances around his death, although this is not unexpected because normally a spiritual master's death was meant to be a demonstration of his enlightenment for others and not a matter of foul play. Yönten Gyatso's ashes were put in a *stūpa* in the vicinity of Drepung. Like the 3rd Dalai Lama, Yönten Gyatso also left only a small oeuvre of writings compiled in one volume. Yönten Gyatso remained the only non-Tibetan Dalai Lama to sit on the lion's throne at Ganden Phodrang དགའ་ལྡན་ཕོ་བྲང་ [dga' ldan pho brang].

34 The Fourth Dalai Lama. Copper, gilded, with long inscription, Tibet, late 17th century, H 25.7 cm, W 20 cm, D 15 cm, Collection of Sandor P. Fuss, Denver. >>>

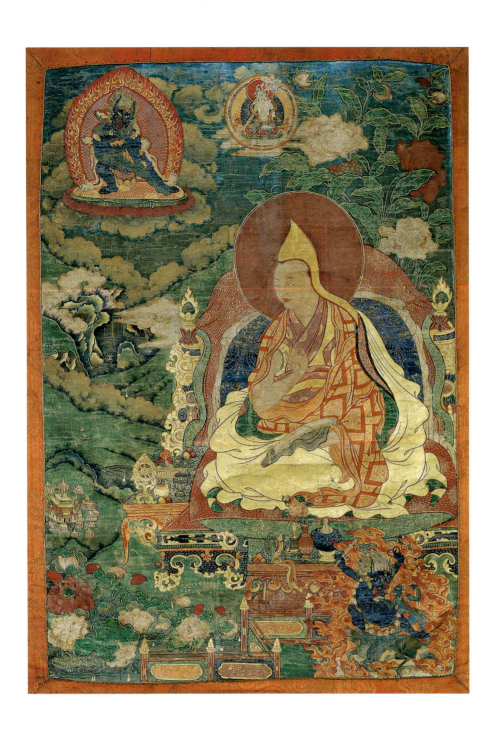

35 The Fourth Dalai Lama, surrounded by Two-Armed Mahākāla (upper left), Sitātapatrā (upper center), and Yamarāja Yapyum (Yab yum; lower right). Left possibly the Samye Monastery. Thangka, Tibet (restored 2004/05), 57 x 40 cm, Ethnographic Museum of the University of Zürich, Inv. No.: 14406.   **Detail of 35** Portrait of the Fourth Dalai Lama.

"His worship-worthy body, blazing with the brilliance created by turning the wheel of dharma day in and day out, is not sullied by even a speck of evil. He performs unceasing good works that open a hundred doors to welfare and happiness. His fame for having learned completely the five great knowledge systems...encompasses the three lands with a white umbrella of garlands. All *dharma*—the essence and extent of what can be known—have entered his mind. He has seen the end of the ocean of our philosophical systems and others."

(Mondrowa)

THE FIFTH DALAI LAMA NGAWANG LOPSANG GYATSO

ངག་དབང་བློ་བཟང་རྒྱ་མཚོ་

Kurtis R. Schaeffer

The 5th Dalai Lama, known to Tibetan history simply as the "Great Fifth," is renowned as the leader under whom Tibet was unified in 1642 in the wake of bitter civil war. The era of the 5th Dalai Lama—roughly the period from his enthronement as leader of Tibet in 1642 to the dawn of the 18th century, when his government began to lose control—was the formative moment in the creation of a Tibetan national identity, an identity centered in large part upon the Dalai Lama, the Potala Palace of the Dalai Lamas, and the holy temples of Lhasa. During this era the Dalai Lama was transformed from an ordinary incarnation among the many associated with particular Buddhist schools into the protector of the country. In 1646 one writer could say that, due to the good works of the 5th Dalai Lama, the whole of Tibet was now centered under a white parasol of benevolent protection. And in 1698 another writer could say that the Dalai Lama's government serves Tibet just as a bodhisattva—that saintly hero of Mahāyāna Buddhism—serves all of humanity.[1] In what follows we will survey the career of this important Tibetan leader by focusing on his youth and education, his assumption of power over Tibet, the role of Lhasa as a cultural center under his rule, the competition for authority in Lhasa, the Dalai Lama's literary corpus, the intriguing circumstances of his death, and finally his status as the Bodhisattva Avalokiteśvara and as a Buddha.

YOUTH, EDUCATION, AND EARLY TEACHING

The 5th Dalai Lama was born into a noble family in the Yarlung Valley, near the tombs of the Tibetan kings. According to the biography by Mondrowa Jamyang Wanggyal Dorje སྨོན་གྲོ་བ་འཇམ་དབྱངས་དབང་རྒྱལ་རྡོ་རྗེ་ [smon 'gro ba 'jam dbyangs dbang rgyal rdo rje],[2] the Dalai Lama's birth was portended by his mother's dreams. The account of the first years of his life, 1617 to 1619, is largely taken up with a description of his birth. The years 1620 to 1621 find the Dalai Lama engaged in "youthful play." Most importantly, it is during this period that this young resident of Chongye was recognized as the reincarnation of the 4th Dalai Lama. In 1622 the Dalai Lama was taken to the central Tibetan institution that was to be his home base for years to come, Drepung Monastery. His first years there were taken up with learning to read. At the beginning of 1623, the Dalai Lama undertook one of the first of the numerous public rituals he was to perform during his life, granting a large feast for New

Year. In the fourth month of that year, the Dalai Lama celebrated the Sagadawa Festival (Skt. Vaiśākha Pūrṇamā Pūjā). In that same month he embarked on a tour of central Tibet, travelling from Rigo to Chekar Dzong, on to Tsetang, and finally back to Drepung. Such annual tours of central Tibet were to form a constant obligation for the young Dalai Lama.

In 1622 the Dalai Lama began his studies at Drepung Monastery under Lingme Shapdrung Könchok Chöphel གླིང་སྨད་ཞབས་དྲུང་དཀོན་མཆོག་ཆོས་འཕེལ་ [gling smad zhabs drung dKon mchog chos 'phel] (1573-1646). The latter was a central figure in the young life of the Dalai Lama, and he would continue serving as tutor until 1646. In 1625, the Dalai Lama first met another figure who was to be prominent in his education, the First Panchen Lama, Lopsang Chökyi Gyaltsen བློ་བཟང་ཆོས་ཀྱི་རྒྱལ་མཚན་ [blo bzang chos kyi rgyal mtshan] (1570-1662). He received many teachings from the Panchen Lama, and, more importantly, he took novice vows under both the Panchen Lama and Lingme Shapdrung. It was under the Panchen Lama that he began studying Mahāyāna literature, and the next few years found him deeply enmeshed in the study of classical Buddhist literature. The years 1630 to 1632 were especially productive years, as during this time the teenaged Dalai Lama undertook studies in the *Prajñāpāramitā*, *Madhyamaka*, *Vinaya*, and *Abhidharma*, all under the tutelage of Lingme Shapdrung. In 1630 the Dalai Lama began his own career as a teacher by discoursing on the *Book of the Kadam* to a large crowd.

THE FIFTH DALAI LAMA ASSUMES POWER OVER TIBET

In 1637 the 5th Dalai Lama met with the Mongol leader who would become his greatest ally, Gushri Khan, who had come on pilgrimage to visit the great monasteries of central Tibet. At their first meeting, Gushri Khan offered 4,000 measures of silver and sat to hear teachings from the young incarnation (plate 42). This meeting made a great impression on the Mongol leader, for that night he dreamt that he beheld a gigantic Dalai Lama, wearing a golden scholar's hat, floating above the Ganden Kangsar. By the end of the year, encouraging signs appeared to both the Dalai Lama's retinue and to Gushri Khan, portending, from the perspective of Mondrowa's hindsight, the impending victory over the Geluk's enemies that would be brought about by the collaboration of Mongol leader and the Geluk incarnation. On one occasion, while Gushri Khan was

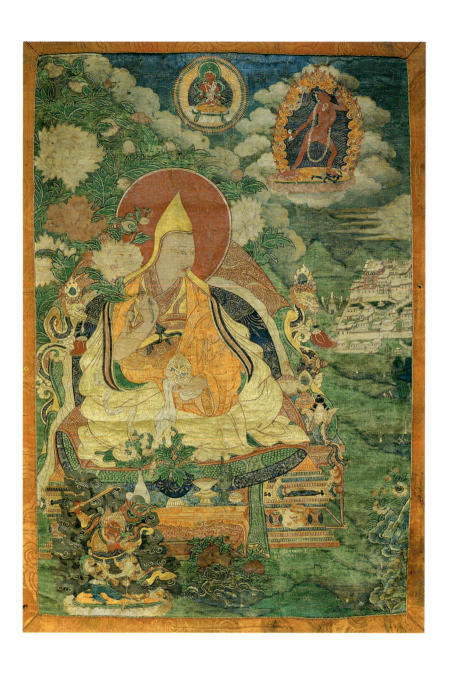

36 The Fifth Dalai Lama, surrounded by Buddha Amitāyus (upper center), Ḍākinī Narokhachöma (Na ro mkha spyod ma; upper right) and Bektse (lower left). The Potala on the right. Thangka, Tibet (restored 2004/05), 57 x 39 cm, Ethnographic Museum of the University of Zürich, Inv. No.: 14403. **Detail of 36** The Potala, the construction of which was begun during the regency of the Fifth Dalai Lama. On the left, the Great Chörten Gate (bar sgo bka gling), the western entry gate to old Lhasa, two obelisks below (rdo ring). See also plate 41.

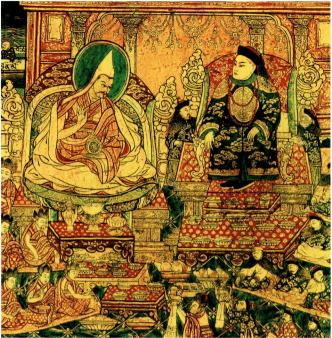

37 The Fifth Dalai Lama initiating the Mongolian ruler Thubeng (Bingtu ?) Wang in Avalokiteśvara. The lower section of the picture shows extensive gifts from the Chinese Emperor. Mural, late 17th century (1690–1694), Potala, Great Western Meeting Hall (tshoms chen nub), west wall.　**38** The Fifth Dalai Lama (left) meets the still youthful Emperor Shunzhi in 1653 in Beijing. Mural, late 17th century (1690–1694), Potala, Great Western Meeting Hall (tshoms chen nub), west wall.

travelling by night, a great white light came from the north, illuminating all the bushes and the pebbles along the path. When he asked about the significance of this omen, he was told that "this is very auspicious. The stainless teachings of Lord Tsongkhapa will spread in all regions and grow. This is a sign that you, the king, will perform all actions toward that end." Gushri Khan accepted this prophecy and went once more to Lhasa, where he received teachings and oral transmissions from the Dalai Lama. Now filled with faith in the teachings of Tsongkhapa, Gushri Khan dedicated himself to the protection of the Geluk School. In Mondrowa's estimation, "even though some had blocked the golden bridge between central Tibet and India, and had blocked the hundred rivers of offering to the monks of Ü and Tsang, this king repaired them." Together, Gushri Khan and the Dalai Lama, now referred to as *yönchö* ཡོན་མཆོད་ [yon mchod] "patron-spiritual teacher" or "donor-donee," went to the Rasa Trulnang Temple, "the Vajrāsana of Tibet," where the Dalai Lama blessed Gushri Khan and gave him the title "Upholder of the Teaching, King of the Dharma" or Tenzin Chökyi Gyalpo བསྟན་འཛིན་ཆོས་ཀྱི་རྒྱལ་པོ་ [bstan 'dzin chos kyi rgyal po], the title by which Mondrowa refers to Gushri Khan henceforth. Mondrowa describes the Dalai Lama's blessing with vivid imagery:

> The elephant trunk of the words and their connected blessing of our world-protecting master was raised high. Then with a golden vase completely filled with ten-million [types of] the nectar of merit, [the Dalai Lama] empowered the king in order to benefit

and soothe all the people and cover [them] with one all-encompassing white umbrella.

So blessed, Gushri Khan put his ten fingers together at his heart and said that he must return to Mongolia. Toward the end of the year 1638 Gushri Khan returned to Tibet with three hundred people to whom the Dalai Lama gave teachings. At this time the Dalai Lama also began to bestow full monastic vows upon others, exercising his new status as a full monk. Earlier, in the third month of the same year, he had taken full monastic vows from the Panchen Lama in the presence of ten monks of Sera and Drepung and in the presence of the Jobo (Śākyamuni). At this time he was given the name Ngawang Lopsang Gyatso ངག་དབང་བློ་བཟང་རྒྱ་མཚོ་ [ngag dbang blo bzang rgya mtsho]. In 1642 Gushri Khan—now styled by Mondrowa as "this King who grasped the three worlds [of gods, humans, and serpents]"—asked the Dalai Lama to come to Tsang, now firmly in the hands of the Mongol leader and his army. It was in Shigatse that the Mongol king offered the thirteen myriarchies of Tibet to the Dalai Lama, as if he were offering a maṇḍala. The relationship of these two as donor and donee was now firmly established, "just as it was earlier between Chogyal Phakpa and Sechen Gyalpo." Because of this momentous event, "the whole of the Snowland was covered by a single white umbrella of prosperity and happiness." Gushri Khan had "achieved dominion over all the earth with a golden wheel that is victorious over all regions. [He] bound the crown that is the seal of the kingdom to [his]

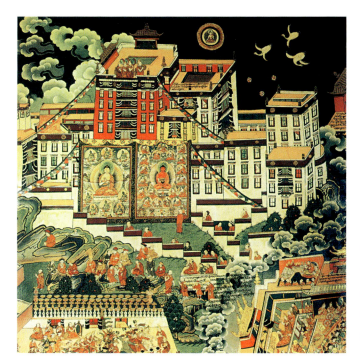
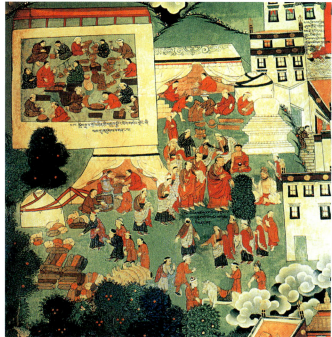

39 Potala with two large scrolls, on the occasion of the completion of construction. Mural, late 17th century (1690–1694), Potala, "Lhasa Fresco Gallery." **40** Construction of the stūpa tomb of the Fifth Dalai Lama. Mural, late 17th century (1690–1694), Potala.

head, opened the hundred doors of [such] auspicious acts and took hold [of Tibet]." In Mondrowa's account, the new arrangement between Gushri Khan and the Dalai Lama was met with widespread praise. Abbots from every Geluk, Kagyü, and Druk religious establishment came to meet the Dalai Lama, despite the fact that, as Mondrowa boasts, "in the presence of this our Omniscient Lama, other scholars were like fireflies in the presence of the sun, making it difficult to be impressed with their qualities." The Dalai Lama gave a teaching on the Book of the Kadam to a large assembly at Tashilhünpo: "not just thinking of the faithless, but also of all the lay and clerical people of Tsang, [he] planted the seeds of good karma, and wished to accomplish the desires of the people of Tsang."

In 1645 the Dalai Lama set his sights on the establishment of a permanent location from which to rule. In this endeavor he was influenced by prophecies "explained by those with the untarnished clear eyes of dharma," which stated that

> when great fortresses were established on Menpori, Chuwori, and Hepori in this glorious Snowland, the harvest of the Victor—in which the life root of the precious teaching naturally dwells—grew ever greater like the waxing moon, and perfect happiness gathered in the human realm, knowing no exhaustion, like rain during summer time...

Gushri Khan and the Dalai Lama agreed "to carry the burden of the precious teaching" by building a fortress in Lhasa. Thus the Dalai Lama granted that a new palace be constructed on Mount Marpori, a palace that would be known as the Potala. Here Mondrowa makes a clear equation between Avalokiteśvara and the Dalai Lama, averring that "our protector of the Snowland, this very Avalokiteśvara, came from Drepung to the Potala in order to subdue the land."

In the Spring of 1645 the Dalai Lama performed purification rituals along the outline of the future building's foundation, after which the foundation was laid for the construction of the new palace. Usually at that time of year great winds would blow through the valley. But now not even a little wind came up, and the sky was completely clear. A tent of rainbows wrapped the hill without interruption and a rain of flowers fell. Such wonders "were an object of perception for all, high and low." In addition, Gushri Khan beheld a divine mansion in the sky, with many immortal sons and daughters making offerings. The King and the Lama remained on the hill for some time, taking tea on the hill that was to be Avalokiteśvara's residence in Tibet. With the new palace well underway, the Dalai Lama's position of power in Lhasa was firm.

LHASA AS CULTURAL CENTER

Throughout the 1640s the influence of the Dalai Lama's new government grew, in great part due to the work of the Dalai Lama's senior advisors, the regents of the government, who were technically in charge of administrative affairs. It was Sönam Rapten བསོད་ནམས་རབ་བརྟན་ [bsod nams rab brtan] (1595-1658, assumed office in 1643), who was most instrumental in guiding the Dalai Lama's rise to power, though traditional biographies tend to downplay his influence so as to portray the Dalai Lama as de facto leader of Tibet. By 1651 the Dalai Lama had achieved considerable renown throughout Asia, so much so that Emperor Shunzhi 順治 (1638-1661) invited the Tibetan leader to pay a visit to Beijing. He began his journey in 1652 and arrived in Beijing the next year (plates 38, 46).

China was certainly not the only country with which the Dalai Lama's government had relations, nor the only culture with which it interacted during the latter half of the 17th century. It is well known that during this period Lhasa was host to a multitude of foreign travellers. Armenians maintained a fixed trading outpost, Mongols travelled to Lhasa on diplomatic missions, and Newā artisans were continuously employed as painters, sculptors, and builders. Indians were also present in Lhasa during this period. According to the Dalai Lama's autobiography, nearly forty Indian guests resided at his court at some time or other during the thirty-seven years between 1654 and 1681,[3] though it appears that the 1670s were the greatest period of Indian activity at the court. The majority of Indians mentioned were intellectuals heralded as experts either in the medical arts or the language arts. This South Asian presence at the Dalai Lama's court coincides in part with the emergence of new intellectual trends in certain regions of India itself at that time.

Some of the Indian scholars visiting Lhasa under the patronage of the Dalai Lama spent considerable periods of time there. Gokula, a Brahman scholar from Vārāṇasī, spent the entire decade from 1654 to 1664 either residing in Lhasa or travelling between India and Lhasa. Vārāṇasī appears to have been the most common point of origin for the trip to Tibet, as fully ten of the forty Indian scholars are said to have come from that city. However, this does not necessarily mean that all ten were natives of that city. For example, although Gokula is said to be a scholar of Vārāṇasī, a letter addressed to him from the Dalai Lama relates that he was born in the Indian region of what is now Kēraḷā.

A visit to the Dalai Lama could be economically rewarding for those Indian scholars who made the trip, for the Dalai Lama bequeathed a variety of items to his visitors, most usually gold, but also cotton, tea, clothing, silk, Chinese red satin,

and provisions for the road. Indeed, many of the dated entries in the 5th Dalai Lama's autobiography report no more than that the Dalai Lama met a certain Indian and gave him certain goods. In 1677, for instance, he gave to two mendicants from Mathurā, named Hemagiri and Nīlakaṇṭha, three measures of gold each, while to a Brahman of Vārāṇasī named Sītādāsa he gave two measures of gold. He also provided a travel document allowing the three travellers to move as they wished between India and Tibet. Such travel documents, what we might call passports, were routinely issued to Indian visitors by the Dalai Lama.

In addition to these records of material gifts, a few passages from the autobiography hint at conversations about culture. For example, an entry from 1677 records the Dalai Lama questioning two Brahmans from Vārāṇasī on their skills and religious background. The two Brahmans, Jīvanti and Gaṇera, respond that they are learned in the science of mathematics and are followers of Viṣṇu. Whenever the Dalai Lama offers descriptive remarks about his Indian guests, they are nothing but laudatory, praising both India and its scholars. In a letter to the grammarian Gokula dated 1663 the 5th Dalai Lama addresses him as a "son of the world's grandfather, Brahman, supreme in effort among those who speak of the Vedas." In a letter written in 1670 he praises Vārāṇasī as "the great city where gather many scholars of vast intellect, skilled in all linguistic and philosophical topics," and he bids the scholars farewell as they prepare to return south through the Himalayas, having illuminated the darkness of Tibet with the moonlight of Pāṇini's grammar. Though we cannot make too much of these passages, they do at least suggest that in the 17th century, the court of the Dalai Lama held Vārāṇasī in high regard because of its visiting scholars.

COMPETING FOR AUTHORITY IN LHASA

Though the 5th Dalai Lama and his government were largely in control of the political and cultural affairs of central Tibet, this does not mean that they were without competition, even from within the Geluk School. A short work composed by the 5th Dalai Lama, entitled *Guidelines for Seating Arrangements at the Mönlam Chenmo Festival of Lhasa* (1675), exemplifies such struggles for power in its prescription of cultural practices surrounding the ritual calendar of Lhasa.[4] The ostensible purpose of the

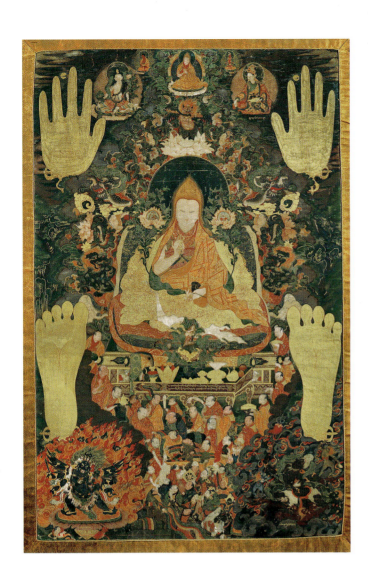

42 The Fifth Dalai Lama, with hand and footprints. Above him in the middle is one of his teachers, Dorje Peljor Lhündrup, and top left Amitābha (small) and Avalokiteśvara, top right Amitāyus (small), one of the kings of the mystical kingdom of Śambhāla, lower left Heruka, and lower right Brāhmaṇarūpa-Mahākāla. Tibet, late 17th century, 77.5 x 50 cm, Musée national des arts asiatiques Guimet, Paris, Inv. No.: MG 19107. **Detail of 42** The Mongolian ruler Gushri Khan (in clothes with fur collar) brings gifts, including precious jewels, rolls of cloth, etc., for the Fifth Dalai Lama during his visit in 1637 or 1642.

43 and 44 The Fifth Dalai Lama and Regent Sanggye Gyatso. Miniature paintings from the "Secret Visions" of the Fifth Dalai Lama. Tibet, between 1674 and 1681, Musée national des arts asiatiques Guimet, Paris, Inv. No.: MA 5244. **45** Two pages from the "Secret Visions" of the Fifth Dalai Lama; ritual objects used for consecration ceremonies. In the center stands Lokeśvara, another name for Avalokiteśvara. Gold and colors on paper, Tibet, after 1674, each page 29 x 6 cm, Musée national des arts asiatiques Guimet, Paris, Inv. No.: MA 5244. >>>

work was to establish a hierarchical seating arrangement for monks participating in the Mönlam Chenmo Festival, an annual event founded by Tsongkhapa in 1409. The more pressing concern, however, was to establish the monks of the Dalai Lama's own Drepung Monastery at the top of that hierarchy, while placing the monks of Sera Monastery, the other large Geluk institution near Lhasa, in a secondary position. To this end the Dalai Lama's *Guidelines* focuses on one crucial point—he argues that individuals and sectarian groups should not foment discord in the Buddhist monastic community, the *saṅgha*, for to do so vitiates the authority of the *saṅgha* as a unified moral body in the eyes of the lay public, thereby bringing negative karma upon those who perpetuate such discord.

The Dalai Lama then addresses the matter of hierarchy within the *saṅgha*, building his argument almost exclusively on canonical citations strung one after the other. It is a given, he argues, that when so many monks gather for a single event, there will be present both those who are models of virtue and some who know little virtue. The latter are often inappropriately motivated by the desire to gain a name for themselves or their particular faction, and thus are led to disrupt the proceedings. Not only do such people bring a bad reputation to the *saṅgha* as a whole, but they bring unthinkable suffering upon themselves. As the Dalai Lama describes the troubles that have plagued the Mönlam Chenmo Festival in past years, it becomes plainly obvious that his criticisms are directed not at the full set of participants but are targeted specifically on the monks of Sera Monastery. Because certain monks of Sera have sought gains for themselves, without thinking of the *saṅgha* as whole, the festival has been delayed, extra rules have become necessary, and the aisles needed for the proper performance

of ritual have been blocked. More seriously, fighting has broken out over seating arrangements, usually provoked by the inmates of Sera. A Mongolian monk of the Je College at Sera even hit a discipline officer from Drepung, and then received praise from his abbot.

By contrast, says the work, the monks and officials of Drepung have promoted a communal perspective and have "sought friendship with the troublemakers, whatever their impure previous actions." It is in this spirit of harmony that the Dalai Lama has decided to impose strict seating arrangements for the festival, all of which, as one might expect, favor the monks of Drepung. Earlier he has argued that, according to the *vinaya*, the eldest among the *saṅgha* are to be accorded the highest respect at all times. It now becomes clear that the monks of Drepung are in his estimation the "elders" of the *saṅgha*. Thus, under the guise of reforming the *saṅgha* and maintaining order at this massive festival, the Dalai Lama shifts both moral and administrative authority to his own monastery. He accomplishes this by arguing that his institution has continually fulfilled the intentions of Buddhist scripture, whereas the monks of Sera have failed to do so. It is his monastery who has lived up to classical ideals of the Buddhist *saṅgha*, and now it is his monastery that is in charge of the largest public ritual in central Tibet.

WRITINGS OF THE FIFTH DALAI LAMA

The 5th Dalai Lama was also a most prolific author. He composed over twenty-five volumes of writing, a corpus that covers nearly every aspect of Buddhist thought and practice. He is particularly well known for being one of the most prodigious authors of autobiographical literature in the history

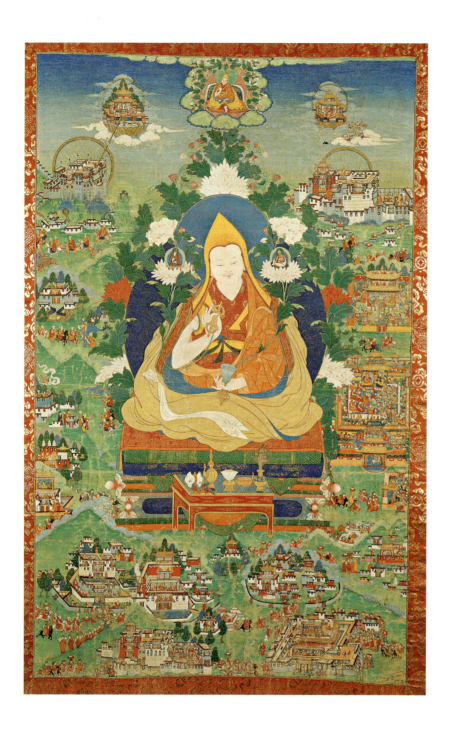

46　The Fifth Dalai Lama and important scenes from his life. Thangka, Tibet, 18. century, 180.3 x 101.6 cm, Rubin Museum of Art, NY, Inv. No.: HA 65275.　**Detail of 46**　The Fifth Dalai Lama meeting the Chinese Emperor Shunzhi in the Forbidden City in Beijing (mid-January, 1653), Tibetan dignitaries on the left side of the court, Chinese on the right.　**Detail of 46**　Birth of the Fifth Dalai Lama, arriving at his parents' home as Avalokiteśvara on a ray of rainbow-colored light, as if from the realms of the heavens.　**Detail of 46**　Death of the "Great Fifth," which had been kept secret for about twelve years, and the temporary return of the Dalai Lama to the heavenly realm. The crow flying over the Potala has a direct tie to Six-Armed Mahākāla: in 1663, as the Great Fifth was thinking about how to honor Mahākāla, a crow alit on his window ledge, which he interpreted as Mahākāla asking that a new ritual be written down, which he did. The inscription on the painting says, "While he was meditating, a crow came down as an emanation of Mahākāla through karma."

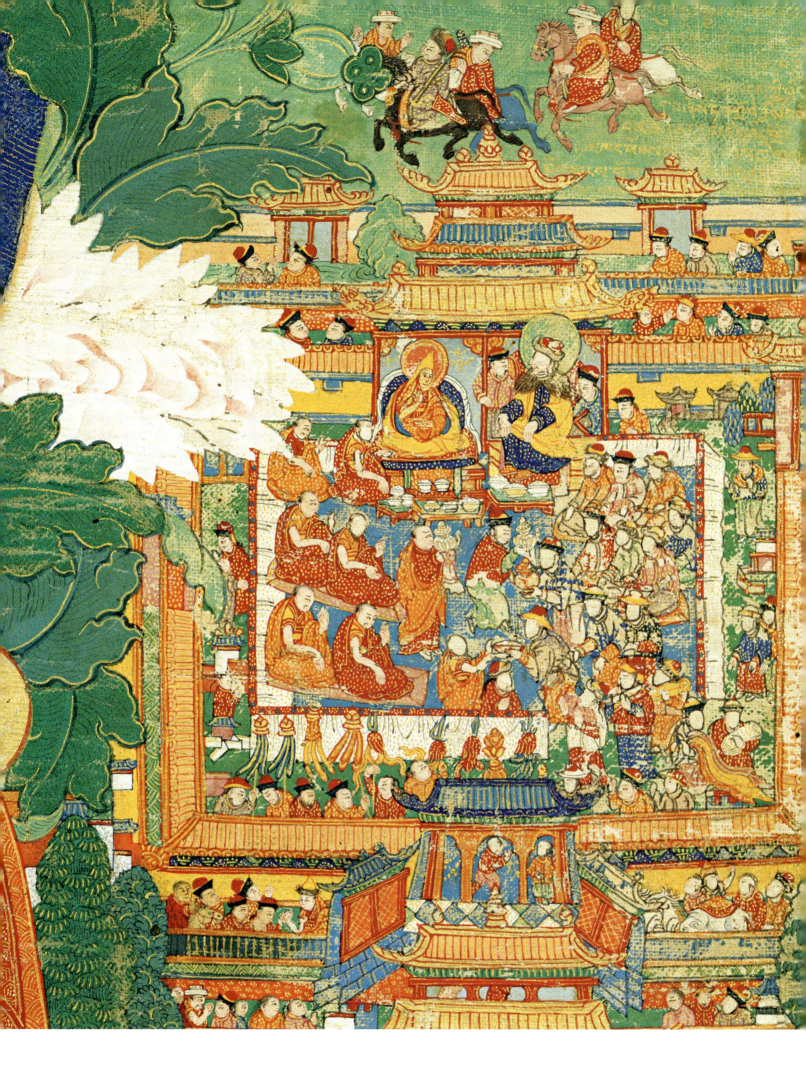

47 Demo Tülku, who accompanied the Fifth Dalai Lama on his journey to Beijing in 1653 and later was apparently one of his regents. Thangka, Tibet/China, dated to 1667, 251.5 x 157.5 cm, Rubin Museum of Art, NY, Inv. No.: F1997.45.2 (HA 578). >>>

of the Himalayan plateau. The Dalai Lama's autobiographical corpus consists of three principal works amounting to some 2,500 folios. The first of these works is a four-volume record of texts and teachings he had received. Suggestively entitled *River Gaṅga's Flow*, we might be tempted think of the work as a massive survey of Tibetan literary history rather than a single person's reading list. The second work, entitled *Fine Silken Dress*, is a three-volume account of the Dalai Lama's life from 1617 to 1681, covering all save his last year.[5] This work, a veritable mine of political, social and cultural detail, is the single most important portrait of courtly life at the Potala from the 1640s to the middle of 1681. The final work is an account of the many visions of gods, kings, queens, and demons that the Dalai Lama experienced between the ages of six and fifty-six. To-

gether these three works fit well into the traditional three-fold rubric for life writing, which distinguishes external, internal, and arcane aspects of the subject's life.

The 5th Dalai Lama is also renowned as a writer of history, though this reputation stems entirely from a single, early work. One year after he took the throne as leader of central Tibet, he composed a history of Tibetan political institutions entitled *Song of the Spring Queen: The Annals of Tibet*. This influential history begins with a short life of the Buddha and a brief discussion of the Kālacakra Tantra, then moves quickly to the history of imperial Tibetan rulers. The central chapters detail the political institutions of Ü and Tsang in central Tibet from the 12th to the beginning of the 17th century, including sections on the Sakya, Phakmodru, and Rinpung hegemonies. The concluding chapter lauds the 5th Dalai Lama's Mongolian patron, Gushri Khan, who had requested the work's compilation. In this work the 5th Dalai Lama is occasionally critical of other historians, and he states in the conclusion that his work is meant to correct "the foolish and baseless words of proud and haughty 'learned men.'" Throughout the book are interspersed examples of ornate poetry, giving the work a tone of both formal eloquence and rhetorical authority. In both style and content, *Song of the Spring Queen* is one of the most important historical works on central Tibet that we possess.

One cannot discuss the writings of the 5th Dalai Lama without also mentioning those of the fifth regent, Sanggye Gyatso སངས་རྒྱས་རྒྱ་མཚོ [sangs rgyas rgya mtsho]. The latter would be a prolific writer during his twenty-four years as ruler (1679-1703), and much of his work complements that of the Dalai Lama. Sanggye Gyatso was perhaps the most influential writer on secular arts and sciences that Tibet has ever produced. From his early 1681 work on governance to his 1703 history of medicine, he touched on subjects as varied as language arts, building techniques, the politics of ritual, funeral rites, astrological and calendrical theories, methods of healing, and rules for court servants. Sanggye Gyatso spent much of the 1690s molding a public vision of the 5th Dalai Lama. His literary activities between 1693 and 1701 were almost entirely concerned with the 5th Dalai Lama's life, death and legacy, marshalling the vast resources of canonical literature in what is surely one of the great biographical projects of Tibetan literature. In all the regent devoted more than 7,000 pages to extolling the 5th Dalai Lama from a variety of perspectives—a staggering amount of writing by any account, and likely the largest biographical project ever attempted in Tibet. Sanggye Gyatso's writing efforts during these few years were not random occasions, but were almost certainly connected with major events such as the 1695 installation of the 5th Dalai Lama's remains in the great *stūpa*, the completion of the Potala's Red Palace in which the *stūpa* was housed, and the 1697 enthronement of the 6th Dalai Lama.

Rather than to slavishly follow the standard canons of tradition, both the 5th Dalai Lama and Sanggye Gyatso argued with them, remade them, and—using the advantage of their position as rulers of Tibet for over six decades combined—implemented a new vision of Tibetan culture by means of wide-ranging reforms (plate 63). Over the course of their careers they sought to systematize Tibetan cultural life and practice in a number of specific areas through writing, systematizing bodily practices in the form of medical treatises, spatial practices in ritual manuals, time in the form of astrological writings and the institution of an officially sanctioned New Year, administrative practice in the form of rules for court servants, and religious discourse in the form of polemical, historical, and philosophical writings. Although their vision remains to be borne out in detail, it is probably no exaggeration to say that the corpus of writing left by the Dalai Lama and his regent represents the boldest attempt ever to create a broad cultural hegemony in Tibet.

48 The Fifth Dalai Lama, surrounded by Bodhisattva Avalokiteśvara (upper center), Songtsen Gampo (upper left), Domtön (upper right), the First Dalai Lama (left) and the Second Dalai Lama (right), the Third Dalai Lama (lower left), the Fourth Dalai Lama (lower right) and the deity Jambala (lower center). Gold painting on red ground, Tibet, 18th century, 66 x 42.5 cm, Rubin Museum of Art, NY, Inv. No.: HA 506.

THE DEATH OF THE FIFTH DALAI LAMA

In 1679, after thirty-three years of leadership, the Dalai Lama abdicated his rule over Tibet to Sanggye Gyatso. He died three years later, on 7 April 1682, though few were to know of his death until more than a decade later.[6] In April of 1695 the desiccated body of the 5th Dalai Lama was removed from the wooden casket in which it had been placed the day after his death thirteen years earlier. Wrapped in silk and cotton, packed with cinnamon, saffron, camphor, and salts, the body had mummified over the years, and it was now time to install it in the sixty-foot-tall golden reliquary housed in the recently completed Red Palace of the Potala. Known as the Single Ornament of the World, this *stūpa* was intended to form an essential part of ritual and political life not only within the massive Potala but also

in the nearby city of Lhasa and its environs and more widely throughout Tibet. At least, this is what Sanggye Gyatso hoped as he prepared to unveil the reliquary to the public and reveal the long-hidden fact of the Dalai Lama's death.

The lengthy mummification presented some practical problems. From 1682 to 1695 the corpse of the Great Fifth had been preserved in a sandalwood casket, wrapped in cotton and packed in two types of salt. Because of the effects of this preservation, Sanggye Gyatso admitted, the all-important relics gathered after cremation would not be forthcoming and thus will not be available for the people's benefit as had been the case with the previous Dalai Lamas. But this is no cause for dismay; one merely needed a substitute—in this case, embalming salt. This salt was efficacious because it had been in contact with the body

49 Three-dimensional maṇḍala that the Fifth Dalai Lama presented to the Emperor Shunzhi on the occasion of his visit to Beijing in 1652/1653. It was initially kept in the Western Yellow Temple and later, on the advice of Rölpe Dorje, Emperor Qianlong's Tibetan Buddhist teacher, in the innermost section of the Imperial Court. Tibet, ca. 1650, gold, turquoise and corals, Dm: 32 cm, National Palace Museum, Taipei.

of Dalai Lama, a fact which alone should be reason enough to accept the efficacy of its blessing power. In order to convince people of this, Sanggye Gyatso composed a reasoned defense of the Dalai Lama's salt relics in November of 1697, issuing it as a proclamation that very month. The timing of the proclamation was not coincidental. It fell between two events of crucial import for the continuing success of the Dalai Lama's government—the announcement of the 5th Dalai Lama's death and the enthronement of the young 6th Dalai Lama. The 5th Dalai Lama had now been dead for fifteen years, and his tomb had been complete for three, yet knowledge of these events did not extend beyond the few privileged insiders at the Potala court.

The regent had begun to reveal the secret in June of 1697. In that month he laid the groundwork for revealing the existence of a new Dalai Lama by providing select people with an account of the transference of consciousness from the 5th Dalai Lama to the 6th, an event that would have occurred fifteen years earlier. In November of 1697 he had the proclamation and the account read to large assemblies at the major monasteries around Lhasa—Drepung, Sera, and Ganden—as well as

at the Tashilhünpo Monastery in Tsang. According to Sanggye Gyatso's biography of the 6th Dalai Lama, during the proclamations the skies were clear and there were many wondrous signs, such as a rain of flowers at Tashilhünpo. In Lhasa, two laymen read the account of the transference of consciousness to citizens gathered in a public park. As the people heard the news of the Dalai Lama's death some years earlier, an old woman remarked that "from that year to now the regent has accepted the responsibility of *dharma* and worldly affairs. Not even knowing the dusk, we now see the dawn!"

The "dawn" in this case was of course the coming of the new Dalai Lama, and the timing of these proclamations was no doubt planned carefully to prepare the lay citizens of Lhasa and the thousands of resident of its monasteries for the upcoming enthronement of the 6th Dalai Lama, an event of great pomp that was to occur on 8 December of the same year. Most people reportedly met the news with a mixture of sorrow and joy, and they wept a great deal. As the proclaimation and the account were read at Sera Monastery, each monk present was given a portion of the embalming salt, and each commoner was given a small molded figurine of the Dalai Lama made of materials mixed with the salt, a memento of the previous Dalai Lama in expectation of the next.

THE DALAI LAMA AS AVALOKITEŚVARA AND AS BUDDHA

At the beginning of his autobiography, the 5th Dalai Lama goes to great lengths to de-emphasize his status as author, authority, and unique subject. In his autobiographical writing he presents as a very human figure simply recounting the mundane details of everyday life. Yet the 5th Dalai Lama is also considered by tradition to be the reincarnation of a previous Buddhist master, the 4th Dalai Lama, as well as the incarnation of that ever-benevolent celestial being, the Bodhisattva Avalokiteśvara. The contrast between his self-effacing presentation and his sublime public status can be seen by comparing the tone of his autobiographical production with the praise Mondrowa accords him. Even more striking is the contrast between the Dalai Lama's self-presentation and the writings dedicated to him by his regent and most zealous biographer, Desi Sanggye Gyatso. Let me thus conclude with a few remarks about this latter set of writings, which we might consider an elaboration on Mondrowa's early effort.

50 Eight-Armed Avalokiteśvara. Bronze, gilded, decorated with semi-precious stones, Tibet, H 91 cm, W 43 cm, D 20 cm, Ethnographic Museum of the University of Zürich, Inv. No.: 14497.   51 Four-Armed Avalokiteśvara. Bronze, gilded, Chahar, Inner Mongolia, ca. 1700, H 180 cm, W 115 cm, D ca. 70 cm, Folkens Museum Etnografiska, Stockholm (Collection of Sven Hedin), Inv. No.: 1935.50.1712. >>>

Not content with the Dalai Lama's self-presentation in his autobiographical writings, Sanggye Gyatso contributed a further 5,000 folios of biographical work, much of which is concerned with extolling the Dalai Lama as Avalokiteśvara. His most concentrated effort in this regard is no doubt the introduction to his 1,000-folio supplement to the Dalai Lama's *Fine Silken Dress*, where he assembles fifty-eight biographical narratives of the various incarnations of Avalokiteśvara. Expectedly, the last of these narratives deals with the 5th Dalai Lama himself, who, Sanggye Gyatso argues, is at once the incarnation of Avalokiteśvara and the rebirth of those numerous masters of the past, who also happen to have been incarnations of Avalokiteśvara. The tone of this hagiographic project contrasts starkly with the self-deprecation of its subject. For example, Sanggye Gyatso writes that it is by definition impossible to capture in words the fullness of the Dalai Lama's activities as Avalokiteśvara, for "what person," he asks, "can speak of the profound, vast, and ineffable interior life of this holy omniscient one and not exceed the bounds of propriety?" The Dalai Lama, by contrast, suggests in his introductory remarks to *Fine Silken Dress* that it is all but impos-

sible *not* to exaggerate. Nevertheless, the tension between the two writers may be more a matter of rhetorical technique than anything else. The Dalai Lama's modesty fits the norms of the autobiographical genre while also being expressive of the Bodhisattva Avalokiteśvara's character as a model of empathetic compassion. The regent's laudatory style was shaped by this same vision, and it was only because his persistent and lengthy efforts to promote the cult of this same *bodhisattva* in the person of the Dalai Lama that the Dalai Lama's government and its rule from the Potala Palace continued to be perceived as the center of Avalokiteśvara's benevolent reign in Tibet.

Sanggye Gyatso was not the first to associate the Dalai Lama with Avalokiteśvara. In 1646 Mondrowa was already placing this identity at the center of his hagiographic efforts. Indeed, the first chapter of this work consists in the main of a defense of this notion that the Dalai Lama was Avalokiteśvara. Mondrowa even goes so far as to equate the 5th Dalai Lama with the Buddha himself. In an apologetic tone, Mondrowa assures the reader that his subject's enlightened activities are beyond description. The Dalai Lama "is no different from the Victor of

52 The Fifth Dalai Lama, possibly his teacher, the First Panchen Lama, on a lotus. Silver, Tibet, ca. 1650, made especially for the visit to the Chinese Emperor Shunzhi (late January 1653), H 50.5 cm, National Museum of Chinese History, Beijing.

53 The Fifth Dalai Lama. Bronze, gilded, on wooden base (not original), Tibet, H 23 cm, W 24.5 cm, D 20.5 cm, Collection of Markus O. Speidel, Birmenstorf.   54 The Fifth Dalai Lama. Gold statue, with inscription: "The victorious king, the omniscient Ngawang Gyichuk Lopsang Gyatso, the virtuous, we honor [him]." Tibet, 17th century, H 4 cm, Nyingjei Lam Collection.   55 The Fifth Dalai Lama. Painted clay, Tibet, 17th /18th century, H 21 cm, W 23 cm, D 18 cm, Collection of Jean-Pierre and Helga Yvergnaux, Sint-Martens-Latem.   56 The Fifth Dalai Lama. Bronze, gilded, with engravings, Tibet, 18th century, H 10.5 cm, The State Hermitage Museum, St. Petersburg (Collection of Prince Ukhtomsky), Inv. No.: U-1028. >>>

57 The Fifth Dalai Lama. Painted wood statue, Tibet, 17th century, H 26 cm, Collection of Carl Sommer, John Dimond and Hans Zogg, Zürich.   58 The Fifth Dalai Lama. Bronze, gilded, with inscription on the reverse in Lentsa script and in Tibetan: "the most wise, powerful, noble Ngawang Lopsang Gyatso," Tibet, 18th century, H 12 cm, The State Hermitage Museum, St. Petersburg (Kozlov Collection), Inv. No.: U-1368.   59 The Fifth Dalai Lama. Bronze, with two long inscriptions composed by the Fifth Dalai Lama and the person who commissioned the statue (Ngawang Sherap), a very close confidant of the Fifth Dalai Lama, Tibet, ca. 1679, H 13 cm, Museum of Fine Arts, Boston, Inv. No.: 50-3606 (Gift of Lucy T. Aldrich). >>>   60 The Fifth Dalai Lama. Bronze, gilded, chased, Tibet, no later than 17th century, with inscription, H 20 cm, Rose Art Museum, Brandeis University, Waltham, MA; today at the Tibet House, New York, Inv. No.: 1971.267 (Gift of N.L. Horch to the Riverside Museum Collection). >>>

61 Decree of the Fifth Dalai Lama appointing Sanggye Gyatso as regent, ca. 1679, wall calligraphy at the Potala, entry hall (sgo khang) of the "White Palace," left wall. >>> **62** The Regent Sanggye Gyatso. Thangka, late 17th century (1690–1694), Potala.

the Three Kālas ["Times"] and his Sons" he writes. "Because he is indivisible from them, the total accumulation of facets of his life story are inconceivable and inexpressible. His manner is not a matter for *arhats*, *śrāvakas*, *bodhisattvas*, or *vajradharas*, so even if one were to make an effort eon upon eon, one could not tell even a fraction of his life story, because how could it be a matter for normal, foolish people?" Though the middle chapters of *Life of the Dalai Lama* are devoted largely to chronological narrative, in the conclusion Mondrowa returns to praise the Dalai Lama:

> His worship-worthy body, blazing with the brilliance created by turning the wheel of dharma day in and day out, is not sullied by even a speck of evil. He performs unceasing good works that open a hundred doors to welfare and happiness. His fame for having completely learned the five great knowledge systems— language, logic, plastic arts, medicine, and inner knowledge, as well as divination, poetics, synonymy, and prosody, together comprising the ten knowledge systems, encompasses the three lands with a white umbrella of garlands. All *dharma*—the essence and extent of what can be known—have entered his mind. He has seen the end of the ocean of our philosophical systems and others. He has become a lord of those who speak of scripture and reasoning. The melodies of his *dharma* explanations fill the ears of all intelligent people with nectar. His voice of debate confounds backward speakers with a thunderous downpour of diamonds. The sensitivity in his elegant compositions creates a charming delight that makes the hearts of scholars grow joyful.

Countless acts such as this delight like nectar the minds of all fortunate beings.

A measure of Mondrowa and Sanggye Gyatso's success at promoting the enlightened qualities of the 5th Dalai Lama can be gleaned from an anecdote from Lhasa related by Sir Charles Bell in the early part of the 20th century. In describing folk memories of the 5th Dalai Lama's death, more than two centuries after the event, Bell notes that "you will hear from some of the simpler folk that it is only since this calamity that the branches [of the weeping willows around Lhasa] drooped, whence they call it the 'tree of sorrow.' Even those who use the ordinary name, 'Chinese Willow,' aver that since those days all the trees and flowers have drooped a little."[7] Likely I make too much of this anecdote, yet I very much doubt whether the willows around Lhasa would still be drooping more than two centuries later without the help of Sanggye Gyatso in memorializing his master, the 5th Dalai Lama.

63 Chayik (bca' yig) "Edict" of the Fifth Dalai Lama, rules of conduct for monks in the Gaden Rapgyeling Monastery. Painted on silk, Potala, Lhasa, Tibet, 1664 (with the seal of the Fifth Dalai Lama), 451 x 85 cm, Collection of C. Lequindre, Paris. >>> **Details of 63** *Upper*: The reformer Tsongkhapa with his two main disciples Khedup Je and Gyaltsap Je and two protective deities. *Lower*: Several protective deities of the Geluk School, upper left: Vaiśravaṇa, and below Rematī (a form of Palden Lhamo), in the middle, the Six-Armed Mahākāla, upper right Yama, and below Dorje Lekpa and an assistant.

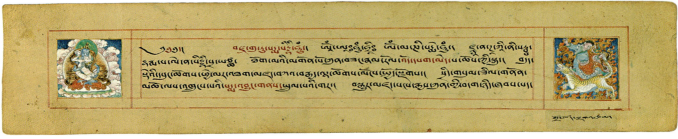

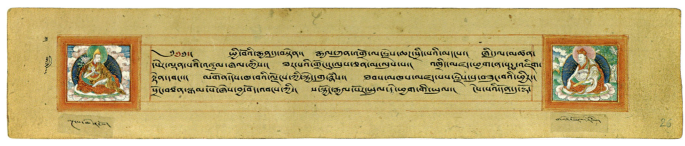

64 Three pages of the "Secret Autobiography" of the Fifth Dalai Lama with red thumb print of the "Great Fifth," which he used to authorize the text, and miniature paintings that show the Fifth Dalai Lama (lower left), among others. Cursive writing on paper, Lhasa, ca. 1680, each page: 6 x 32 cm, Bayerische Staatsbibliothek, Munich, Cod. Tibet. 500. >>> **65** Manuscript: description of the Tsokdag (Tsog dag) ritual, commissioned by the Fifth Dalai Lama, ten pages (of a total of almost two hundred pages). Inks and pigments on paper, Central Tibet, ca. 1665, dimensions of one sheet: ca. 44 x 8 cm, Collection of Thomas Isenberg, NY. >>>

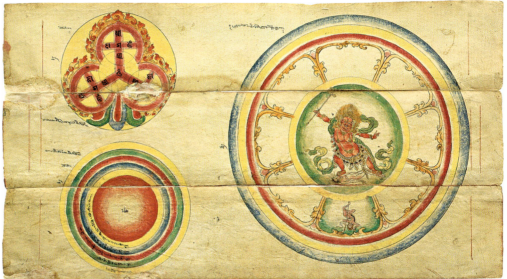

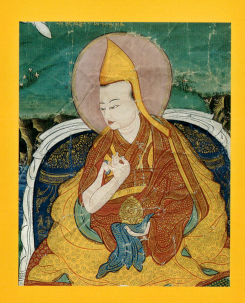

"Eastwards, from the mountains' peaks
White, the shining moon appeared:
The countenance of a fair maiden
Again and again took shape in my mind."

(Tsangyang Gyatso)

THE SIXTH DALAI LAMA **TSANGYANG GYATSO**

ཚངས་དབྱངས་རྒྱ་མཚོ

Erberto Lo Bue

HIS LIFE

The 6th Dalai Lama, Tsangyang Gyatso ཚངས་དབྱངས་རྒྱ་མཚོ [tshangs dbyangs rgya mtsho] (1683-1706), occupies a special place in the Tibetan historical and literary tradition which portrays him as having long hair adorned with rings and jewels, wearing an elegant blue brocade tunic, and holding a bow and a quiver. He was born in Mön, a Himalayan area now divided between the Tibetan Autonomous Region in the People's Republic of China and the Arunāchal Pradeś in India. Three years before his birth Mön had been incorporated into the vast theocratic state the 5th Dalai Lama created with the military support of his Mongol ally, Gushri Khan, at the expense of the lay kingdoms of Tsang, which corresponds to southwestern Tibet, and Beri, in eastern Tibet.

His paternal family belonged to the tradition of the Nyingma རྙིང་མ [rnying ma] "Ancient" teachings related to Padmasambhava, a Tantric *yogin* from Swāt who was active during the early spread of Buddhism in Tibet. His maternal family belonged to the milieu of the Geluk དགེ་ལུགས [dge lugs] "Virtuous Order," founded in the early 15th century by the followers of the great religious reformer Tsongkhapa ཙོང་ཁ་པ [tsong kha pa]. The child was born during a rather troublesome period in the history of Tibet following the deaths of Gushri Khan and the 5th Dalai Lama. In spite of being officially under the rule of Gushri Khan's successors, the country was largely controlled by the Geluk administration. In order to avoid a power vacuum, the regent Sanggye Gyatso སངས་རྒྱས་རྒྱ་མཚོ [sangs rgyas rgya mtsho] had concealed the Great Fifth's demise and announced that the latter had entered a long period of retreat. To make his announcement credible, he forced a monk bearing some resemblance to the Great Fifth to dress and behave like him. The sound of ritual bells and prayers could be occasionally heard coming from the room where the 5th Dalai Lama was supposed to be meditating and meals were regularly served to the impersonator, who—wearing a tantric hat covering half his face—even received Mongol dignitaries in the darkness of his room. In the meantime the regent addressed special prayers to the embalmed body of the Great Fifth entreating him to be reborn quickly. He also asked his closest collaborators who knew of the 5th Dalai Lama's death to pay attention to any dreams they had which might provide clues about the reincarnation.

Relying on such clues and others provided by three oracles, and on the fact that one or two years had elapsed between the death of the previous Dalai Lama and the discovery of his reincarnation, in the summer of 1685 the regent instructed two monks to travel to southern Tibet to start searching for the child in secret, under the ruse that they were looking for the reincarnations of two other religious masters who had recently died. The monks travelled to Urgyenling in central Mön based on the indications with which they had been provided. There they found a child who seemed a likely candidate in spite of the fact that his parents doubted that he might be the reincarnation of a great lama and even tried to prevent the envoys from seeing him.

That first meeting was a failure—the child appeared confused and did not recognize the 5th Dalai Lama's rosary. Thinking he was not the right candidate, the two monks left. But one of them fell ill during the return journey and dreamt that the rosary had not been shown to the child correctly. Later divinatory signs obtained at the monastery of Samye indicated that the child had indeed been the right one. The regent ordered them to return to Mön and to examine the child with greater care. After doing so, they were convinced that this boy was the real reincarnation of the Great Fifth and returned to Lhasa to report their new findings. Despite all the precautions, some people had come to suspect that the Great Fifth had died and it was soon rumored that not only had his reincarnation been found, but that the Bhutanese (who had suffered two Tibetan invasions during the time of the 5th Dalai Lama) were preparing to kidnap the child. The regent decided to hasten the child's recognition, so in 1685 he had him and his parents secretly transferred to Tsona, north of the Himalayan watershed. Along with a servant, the three spent twelve years isolated in the fortress of Tsona under the guard of soldiers and watchdogs. They were at the mercy of two hostile governors who did not know that the child being held was a candidate to succeed the Great Fifth. Like his parents, they believed him to be a reincarnation of the abbot of the monastery of Shalu in southwestern Tibet.

In 1686 two monks took over the child's education from the parents. They first taught him reading and arithmetic, then religion and astrology—he was eight when he wrote his first letter to the regent. In 1694 he was made to listen to a list of

66 The Sixth Dalai Lama, surrounded by Eight-Armed Avalokiteśvara (upper left), the Second Panchen Lama Lopsang Yeshe (upper right) and Bhairava. Thangka, Tibet (restored 2004/05), 56 x 39.5 cm, Ethnographic Museum of the University of Zürich, Inv. No.: 14407.   **Detail of 66** The Eight-Armed and Eleven-Headed Avalokiteśvara.

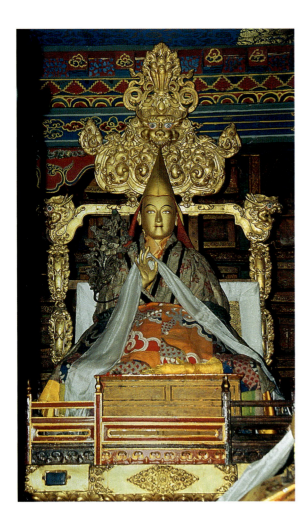

67 The Sixth Dalai Lama. Bronze, gilded, Tibet, first half of 18th century, Lama Lhakhang, Potala. Photographer: Guido Vogliotti, Turin.

the death of the 5th Dalai Lama as well as the discovery of his successor. The Panchen Lama ordained the boy as a novice, who received the monk's name under which he is known. Before taking the tonsure, he burst into tears—years of hardship at Tsona and recent changes in his life, including the sudden loss his father, no doubt contributed to his reaction. Tsangyang Gyatso ascended the golden throne on 8 December 1697 in the palace rising on Potala hill near Lhasa, in the presence of a number of Tibetan and foreign dignitaries including the Mongol ruler Lhazang Khan. From that time onwards Tsangyang Gyatso had to cope with private and public audiences, protocol, religious duties, rituals, and ceremonies in addition to study. He received many courtesy and political visits, including from the sons of the kings of the Kāṭhmāṇḍū Valley, Ladākh, Zangskar, and Sikkim, as well as envoys from Mongol princes and from the Manchu emperor. Sanggye Gyatso personally took on the task of Tsangyang Gyatso's education while the Panchen Lama was in charge of his religious instruction.

Sport was also part of Tsangyang Gyatso's education, and he turned out to be a clever archer. He devoted more and more time to archery, shooting with friends in the park behind the Potala and going on excursions into the valleys near Lhasa. With his restlessness, he started to disappoint and worry the regent, who informed the Panchen Lama and suggested that the youth should receive his final ordination. In the exchange of letters with the Panchen Lama that followed, the young Tsangyang Gyatso tried to justify his behavior explaining that he had no desire to sit on the throne during monastic meetings. Eventually he agreed to meet his religious tutor, but it is significant that, after a first encounter, they followed different routes to Tashilhünpo, the Panchen Lama's seat at Shigatse. Tsangyang Gyatso arrived five days after his teacher and established himself in a mansion rather than in the monastery itself.

During the ensuing meetings, Tsangyang Gyatso admitted having violated the Panchen Lama's precepts yet repeatedly refused to undergo his final ordination or even sit on the abbot's throne in spite of his teacher's entreaties. On the contrary, having prostrated in front of the Panchen Lama's apartment three times, he informed his tutor in a very loud voice that he was renouncing his vows and went as far as threatening suicide if his choice were not respected. He resisted the pressures

the teachings his predecessor had received and the following year he started reading his predecessor's secret autobiography, which the regent hoped would remind the child of the religious experiences undergone in his previous life. Only in 1696 did Sanggye Gyatso inform the parents that their son had been identified as the reincarnation of the 5th Dalai Lama.

By that time the rumor that the Great Fifth had died had already reached the ears of Kangxi 康熙, the Manchu emperor of China. The regent thus moved the boy to Nangkartse, on the shore of Lake Palti (also called Yamdrok), and then announced exerted by Lhazang Khan, the religious leaders of the three great Geluk monasteries in the Lhasa area, and members of a delegation the regent specially sent to solve the crisis. If not resolved, the situation might have negative repercussions not only on the image of the Geluk order, but also on the political situation of Tibet. After seventeen days, Tsangyang Gyatso returned to Lhasa. From then on he refused both to take the tonsure and wear the monk's robe, but instead wore aristocratic garments and ornaments, and felt entitled to lead the lifestyle he preferred —bowshooting, going riding with friends around Lhasa during the day and spending nights in taverns or private houses, courting young ladies (including the regent's daughter), and expressing his love for women in songs he composed. Official religious iconography generally portrays him wearing the yellow hat of the Geluk order, his right hand in the teaching *mudrā*, his left in the attitude of meditation. He holds either the *dharmacakra* or a vase containing the elixir of immortality (plate 70). Yet popular tradition remembers the 6th Dalai Lama on the basis of of a contemporaneous description—with long black hair falling on a blue silk garment, his fingers with rings and holding a bow.

Tsangyang Gyatso's decisions dismayed and embarassed the Geluk religious and political establishment, and strained the already difficult relationship between the regent and Lhazang Khan, who wanted to exert more effective control over Tibet than his predecessors had. In order to ease tensions, Sanggye Gyatso transferred the regency to one of his sons, Ngawang Rinchen, yet he retained political power behind the scene. He further conspired to murder the Dalai Lama's most faithful companion who often accompanied him on his amorous adventures and affairs even in the Potala area. On the evening of the ambush, however, Tsangyang Gyatso, his friend, and his servant arrived at the Potala after having exchanged garments following a custom among pleasure-seeking aristocrats. In the ensuing scuffle, the servant was mistaken for his companion and stabbed to death. Tsangyang Gyatso reacted firmly by having the conspirators arrested and tried. Some were even publicly executed, which forever spoiled his relationship with the former regent.

Sanggye Gyatso found himself isolated. He had irritated Emperor Kangxi by hiding the death of the Great Fifth for a number of years, infuriated Lhazang Khan by attempting to

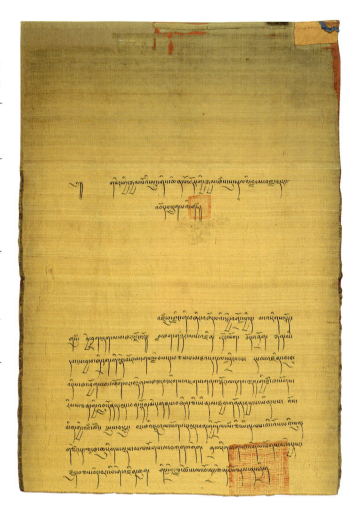

68 Document of confirmation of the Sixth Dalai Lama from the Year of the Wood Monkey (1704/1705), silk, 84 x 59 cm, Museum für Völkerkunde, Vienna, Inv. No.: MVK 176.992. >>>

have him poisoned, and finally upset the Dalai Lama himself. The Geluk order used diplomacy to avoid the worst and negotiated that the former regent would retire to an estate far from Lhasa and that the Mongol ruler would return to the pastures where his tribe resided. But neither man intended to give up the struggle for the political control over Tibet. Sanggye Gyatso continued to plot in secret. Lhazang Khan set up an army which marched on Lhasa. Sanggye Gyatso fell into the hands of one of the Mongol ruler's wives, who repaid a grudge by having him beheaded on 8 September 1705. His son was deposed, and although Lhazang Khan was able to force his rule upon Tibet, he had yet to solve the thorny issue of a Dalai Lama who had given up his religious vows, led a life morally and politically incompatible with his rank, and whom both he and Emperor Kangxi regarded as illegitimate and spurious.

The conclave summoned to take a decision on the issue did not deny that Tsangyang Gyatso was the reincarnation of the 5th Dalai Lama, but it merely acknowledged that the spirit of Buddhist enlightenment had abandoned him. The Mongol ruler, however, thought the verdict justified him in carrying out the order of arrest and deportation which he had received from the Manchu emperor, who was obviously concerned with the events taking place in Lhasa. This did not prove easy— when the soldiers escorting Tsangyang Gyatso to China passed the monastery of Drepung, the monks came out to rescue the Dalai Lama. Lhazang Khan's troops started to shell the monastery and so Tsangyang Gyatso decided to surrender. On 29 June 1706, after announcing that he would meet the monks of Drepung again during his next lifetime, he left the monastery with a few companions who fell fighting with the Mongols, and then gave himself up. Before leaving Tibet, the Dalai Lama arranged to receive teachings from the abbot of Phabongkha.

Tsangyang Gyatso fell ill during the journey. Arriving at a small lake south of Lake Kökönor, he refused to proceed any further and, feeling his end approaching, left instructions that his personal belongings—including his ritual implements— should be given to his successor. He addressed his attendants and personal physician, stating that there was not much to say at the point of death—they should remember what he had told them repeatedly earlier on and all would go well. It was the night between the fourteenth and fifteenth of November 1706. Tibetan historical sources agree that the 6th Dalai Lama died from illness. According to information Orazio della Penna later gathered in Tibet, Tsangyang Gyatso died from dropsy, but it is not inconceivable that he had been poisoned. His body was cremated at Xining 西寧 in Qinghai 青海 province. Many people came to pay homage to his body in the days before cremation. The Manchu emperor sent orders to dishonor the body by scattering the remains, but they arrived too late.

The grief was universal when the news of the Dalai Lama's death reached Lhasa. All manner of tales in line with Tsangyang Gyatso's life of romance began to circulate. In addition to the promise made to the monks of Drepung, he had also written a song in which he announced his rebirth at Lithang. Together these created such expectations that leaflets announcing the rebirth began circulating in Lhasa despite the fact that Lhazang Khan had already placed his illegitimate son on the throne in the Potala, declaring him the real reincarnation of the Great Fifth. According to Orazio della Penna, a riot followed whereby Lhazang Khan returned to Lhasa, had fourteen leaders beheaded, and forfeited their relatives' property. Tsangyang Gyatso's mother was apparently blinded and her property confiscated while the authors of the leaflets had their hands cut off before being executed.

The life and death of the 6th Dalai Lama were given a further romantic twist half a century after his demise. A Mongolian monk edited a secret hagiography based on "confessions" made to him by his own teacher, who maintained that he was Tsangyang Gyatso in person, having survived and led an adventurous life after escaping from his guards. The practice of passing oneself off as a famous person who actually died has been documented at least since the 12th century in Tibet.

The secret hagiography is interesting from a literary, social, and anthropological viewpoint inasmuch as it has contributed to the growth of a myth that has struck not only Tibetan, but also the Western imagination. Professional historians, such as Luciano Petech, Michael Aris, and Per Sørensen, have given it no credit.

HIS POEMS

Tsangyang Gyatso was eleven when he wrote his first religious composition, a piece devoted to the Buddhist deity Hayagrīva, a wrathful protector of the Buddhist doctrines. The 6th Dalai Lama is however more famous for his secular songs, of which at least two collections are attributed to him. The first and most famous collection of about sixty songs has been transmitted through various editions. The second collection, discovered only recently, consists of as many as 459 poems including most of the songs of the previous one, although it is incomplete.[1] Both are made up of uninterrupted verses and might be thought of as lyrical autobiographies. The shorter collection appears to have been exclusively compiled by Tsangyang Gyatso, while the longer one likely betrays the hand of its editor.

70 The Sixth Dalai Lama, interestingly shown with a *phurbu* "ritual dagger" in his belt, which would usually indicate the Fifth Dalai Lama, if the inscription did not clearly identify the statute as the image of the Sixth Dalai Lama. Bronze, gilded. Provenance unknown.

In both collections love appears in all its facets, more often physical, whether irresistible or unreachable, and is expressed through a variety of feelings: hope, complicity, nostalgia, doubt, mistrust, disappointment, pain, resignation, and even carelessness. The author occasionally complains about gossip and a few times he is even at odds with a particular religious figure. Religion generally appears difficult to follow or else merely provides a background to the poem and becomes a pretext. Only once does the author view it as a refuge, and that is because of the impossibility of keeping his lover with him. Such songs reflect the situation in which the 6th Dalai Lama found himself. Some, like those referring to the protagonist's escapades from his palace or to the Snake Temple on the islet in the pond behind the Potala, have a particularly autobiographical tinge. Others refer to Mön, the region where Tsangyang Gyatso was born.

References to the 6th Dalai Lama's interest in secular poetry are extremely rare in Tibetan historical sources and are altogether absent from the official biography Sanggye Gyatso started writing on his rebellious pupil, a job he gave up when matters got out of hand. A religious aristocrat reports in his diary that he had seen Tsangyang Gyatso in a house composing verses and singing poems, not in the least altered by alcohol, while some of his companions were drunk to the point of hardly being able to stand up. No mention of the poetry collections is found in contemporaneous Tibetan historical records, except for a bit of information which may indeed refer to them: on his death bed the 6th Dalai Lama asked his servant not to lose his unfinished writings and explained that they should be returned to him later on. This suggests that he might have wanted his love songs to be given to his next incarnation.

Tsangyang Gyatso's songs represent a historical and literary document of exceptional value not only because of their authorship, but because of their intrinsic stylistic qualities, both factors accounting for the popularity they still enjoy among Tibetans of all social classes. They belong to a traditional genre of secular poetry, of which several collections are known to exist, and represent a literary adaptation of Tibetan popular love songs in which colloquial expressions are inserted into a formal and elegant context drawn from a vast repertory of images and metaphors. The charm of this poetry lies in the simplicity of its images and its plain structure. The first half of the poem evokes an image generally related to nature (the moon, sun, water, birds, insects, flowers, fruits, trees) that anticipates the latter part, which describes a particular moment in the poet's sentimental life, typically the presence or absence of the beloved, who is described with a wide range of epithets and adjectives. The rhythm, conciseness, and imagery of the 6th Dalai Lama's verses may be illustrated by the first poem in the collection (with phonetic transcription and translation below):

ཤར་ཕྱོགས་རི་བོའི་རྩེ་ནས།
དཀར་གསལ་ཟླ་བ་ཤར་བྱུང་།
མ་སྐྱེས་ཨ་མའི་ཞལ་རས།
ཡིད་ལ་འཁོར་འཁོར་བྱས་བྱུང་།།

Shar-chòk ri-wò tse-nè
Kar-sèl da-wà shar-chùng.
Ma-kyé a-mè she-rè
Yi-là khor-khòr che-chùng.

Eastwards, from the mountains' peaks
White, the shining moon appeared:
The countenance of a fair maiden
Again and again took shape in my mind.

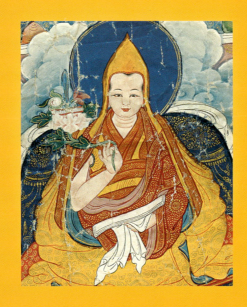

"The sun of the Sage's Teaching has been dragged off
To set in the west in a carriage of folly;
And now, when an evil fog gathers,
True friends are the rarest of flowers.

When flocks of self-seeking owls,
Birds spurned by the noble and wise,
Fill all Tibet with their mournful cries,
Who's so bold as to think himself joyful?"

(Kalsang Gyatso to Janggya Rölpe Dorje)

THE SEVENTH DALAI LAMA **KALSANG GYATSO**

སྐལ་བཟང་རྒྱ་མཚོ་

Matthew T. Kapstein

The life of the 7th Dalai Lama, Kalsang Gyatso སྐལ་བཟང་རྒྱ་མཚོ་ [skal bzang rgya mtsho] (1708-1757), spanned a troubled period in Tibetan history, during which the Land of Snows was transformed from the battleground of competing Mongol factions into a protectorate of the Manchu Qing 清 dynasty. This transition provided a precedent for the modern Chinese assumption that maintaining control over Tibet plays a key role in ensuring the stability of China's western frontiers overall. The varied fortunes of the 7th Dalai Lama reflected not only the vulnerability of his office, but also its remarkable symbolic power among the peoples of Inner Asia. It may be said that the institution of the Dalai Lama, given its religio-political foundations under the leadership of the Great Fifth, assumed its mature form under the Seventh, whose relations with the Manchus set the pattern for Sino-Tibetan affairs throughout the remainder of the Qing dynasty.

RECOGNITION AND YOUTH

Kalsang Gyatso was born in the region of Lithang the eastern province of Kham during the Year of the Earth Rat of the 12th Tibetan calendrical cycle (1708). His father was named Sönam Dargye བསོད་ནམས་དར་རྒྱས་ [bsod nams dar rgyas] and his mother Sönam Chötso བསོད་ནམས་ཆོས་མཚོ་ [bsod nams chos mtsho]. The child's birth was said to have been accompanied by wonders including his uttering marvelous words. A maternal uncle gave him the auspicious name *Kalsang Gyatso,* "Ocean of Good Fortune." Sometime later, a local monk was possessed by the protective divinity White Lustre, Öden Karpo འོད་ལྡན་དཀར་པོ་ ['Od ldan dkar po], who declared that the boy was the rebirth of the teacher "fulfilling to see," a phrase that was taken to refer to the late Dalai Lama. The oracle further stated that the boy should be taken immediately to a monastery.

The report that the Dalai Lama had been reborn in Kham gradually spread throughout far eastern Tibet, whose Tibetan and Mongol leaders welcomed the news. Soon rumors started circulating in central Tibet, where Lhazang Khan, who had inherited the title of "King of Tibet" from his ancestor, the 5th Dalai Lama's patron Gushri Khan, was displeased by this turn of events. Following the deposition and death of Tsangyang Gyatso, Lhazang had named his own son Yeshe Gyatso as Dalai Lama, an act for which the Tibetans generally despised him. Once apprised that a competitor had been discovered in Kham,

Lhazang sent two of his military commanders, a Tibetan and a Mongol, to investigate. On learning that the child was a rebirth of Tsangyang Gyatso, the Tibetan officer, Norbu Ngödrup ནོར་བུ་དངོས་གྲུབ་ [nor bu dngos grub], sought to defuse the situation by maintaining that because Tsangyang Gyatso had been judged—by the Mongols and Manchus at least—not to be the true Dalai Lama, Kalsang Gyatso posed no threat because he was therefore not the emanation of the Dalai Lama at all, but only a false pretender. At the same time, however, Norbu Ngödrup recognized that this ruse would protect the boy for only a short time and so he counselled Sönam Dargye to find refuge. The family fled into the wilderness that very evening, returning home only after Lhazang's emissaries had returned to central Tibet.

In 1714, upon hearing once more that some of Lhazang's men would again be in the vicinity, Sönam Dargye decided that it would be best to seek haven for his son in Derge. Though well-received by the prince of Derge, Tenpa Tsering བསྟན་པ་ཚེ་རིང་ [bstan pa tshe ring], it was by no means sure that should Lhazang decide to send troops there, Derge would be as safe as was hoped. The Mongol chieftain of Kökönor, Qingwang Ba-thur-tha'i-ji, and others therefore arranged for the boy's passage to Amdo. There it was at last possible for representatives from the great central Tibetan monasteries to examine him. As a result, Kalsang Gyatso was finally recognized officially but in secret as the new Dalai Lama. The Namgyal Tratsang རྣམ་རྒྱལ་གྲྭ་ཚང་ [rnam rgyal grwa tshang], the personal monastic institution of the Dalai Lamas that had been founded by the Great Fifth, was now reestablished. Its continuous history until the present is said to date from this time.

When Kalsang Gyatso reached the age of eight, the Qing emperor Kangxi 康熙, following the precedent his father had established in his relations with the 5th Dalai Lama, sent representatives of the court so that a combined Chinese-Tibetan-Mongol cavalry could escort the rebirth to Kumbum, the famous monastery near Xining 西宁, marking the place of Tsongkhapa's birth. It was here that Kalsang Gyatso was enthroned and an imperial proclamation publicly read affirming that "this emanation is the veritable rebirth of the former Dalai Lama...As the Omniscient One comes into the world like the sun, which cannot be blocked out with the hand, the lightrays of his compassion and enlightened deeds embrace the whole world, so that the Buddha's teachings expand and increase."

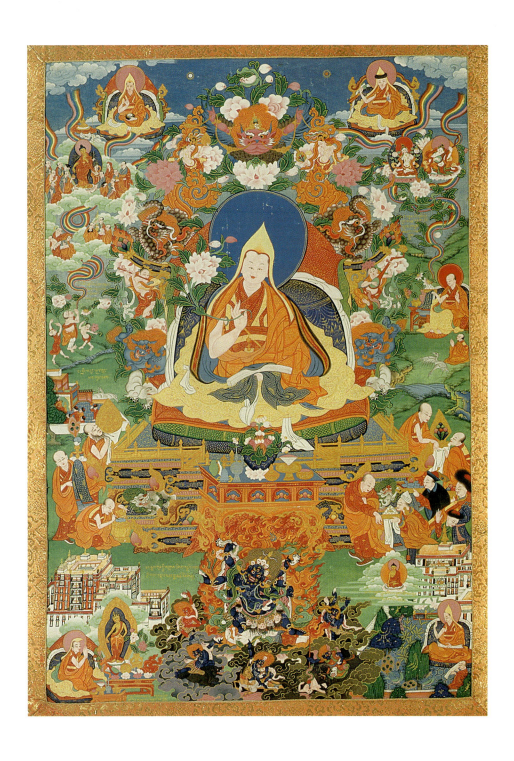

71 The Seventh Dalai Lama. Thangka, presented to King George V of Britian in 1913 on behalf of the Thirteenth Dalai Lama, Tibet, early 20th century, 183 x 61 cm, Victoria and Albert Museum, The Royal Collection © 2005 Her Majesty Queen Elizabeth II, London, Inv. No.: RL 485.   **Detail of 71**   Inscription: "As [he] had a vision of the very noble Buddha—arising from 100,000 rays of light—he became the keeper of the Buddha's teachings." Scene above that: On the occasion of assuming temporal power, the Seventh Dalai Lama receives guests (probably from China and Mongolia), who present him with gifts.   **Detail of 71**   Inscription: "At the tender age of four, [he had] a miraculous vision of Buddha and the Arhats."   **Detail of 71**   As he withdrew to meditate, he had a vision of White Mañjuśrī and Sarasvatī.

72 The Seventh Dalai Lama, with dharmacakra, book, and a sword on a lotus blossom. To the left and right of the throne, the faithful can be seen paying homage to him and presenting gifts, with Mongolians below, as their head coverings indicate. The scenes in the lower section are difficult to interpret since the inscription cannot be deciphered, but are apparently at the court, as the clothing and architecture indicate. Thangka, Tibet, mid-18th century, 86 x 54 cm, Schleiper Collection, Brussels.

At the same time, the emperor continued to affirm the legitimacy of Lhazang Khan's rule, so for the time being central Tibet remained under Lhazang's control. The young Dalai Lama's protectors had no choice but to raise him at Kumbum where he pursued his studies under a succession of noteworthy tutors. In 1717 the Dzungars invaded central Tibet and Kham, where they came to be hated for their religious persecutions, particularly of the Nyingma School. Nevertheless, by defeating Lhazang Khan they also deposed his son, the false Dalai Lama Yeshe Gyatso. When the Dzungars began to crumble under the assault of combined Manchu and Tibetan forces in 1720, the time had arrived for Kalsang Gyatso, then thirteen years, to claim his throne in Lhasa. The Kangxi emperor favored this move and sent his own fourteenth son, Prince Yinti 胤禵, to

accompany the Dalai Lama together with leading representatives of Tibetan Buddhism at the Qing court, and Manchu, Chinese, and Mongol military leaders. Clearly, the emperor wished to demonstrate to the Tibetans that the Dalai Lama was an object of his reverence yet at the same time a dependent of the court. Manchu devotion thus always contained an element of menace—both were equally real, and it required probity and skill on the part of the Tibetans to find the appropriate balance between these apparently opposite tendencies. The career of Kalsang Gyatso—the 7th Dalai Lama for the Tibetans but for the Manchus the 6th—would in effect be played out in the crosscurrents between imperial faith and power.

Kalsang Gyatso arrived at the Potala during the autumn of 1720. That same winter he was ordained by the foremost Geluk master of the day, the Panchen Lama Lopsang Yeshe པཎ་ཆེན་བློ་བཟང་ཡེ་ཤེས་ [paṇ chen blo bzang ye shes] (1663–1737), who gave him the monastic name Lopsang Kalsang Gyatso བློ་བཟང་སྐལ་བཟང་རྒྱ་མཚོ་ [blo bzang skal bzang rgya mtsho]. Even on this joyful occasion, however, political complications could not be altogether avoided. The Tibetan government, in making seating arrangements for the honored guests invited to witness the event, gave preference to the Tibetan nobles and the emissaries of the Qing court and left only inferior seats for the Mongol lords. This perceived insult would later be cited as one of several causes of the rebelliousness of the Mongols and their Tibetan supporters during the years that followed.

In fact, it was in Amdo that opposition to the Manchus first erupted into open conflict. In 1723, soon after the death of the emperor Kangxi, just as the new ruler Yongzheng 雍正 was establishing his authority, Mongol tribesmen rose up against the Qing in the region of Kökönor. These Mongols, claiming the succession of Gushri Khan, together with their Amdo Tibetan allies were supported by some factions within the monasteries. The new emperor insisted on violent reprisals and the Manchu army unleashed a scorched earth campaign in Amdo, destroying villages and monasteries believed to have sided with the rebels and killing their inhabitants indiscriminately. Even Chupsang Nominhan ཆུ་བཟང་ནོ་མིན་ཧན་ [chu bzang no min han], who had been the Dalai Lama's chief tutor during his childhood at Kumbum, was numbered among the victims. On hearing of these events the Tibetan Buddhist leadership of Beijing, as well as Kalsang Gyatso himself, petitioned the court and pleaded for clemency.

Eventually the emperor relented and ordered that the damaged monasteries be rebuilt with funds from the imperial coffers. By extending direct patronage to the Tibetan Buddhists of Amdo, the Qing intended to ensure their loyalty henceforth. In this they proved to be at least partially successful.

One of the principal sites to feel the wrath of the Manchus was Gönlung Jampaling Monastery དགོན་ལུང་བྱམས་པ་གླིང་ [dgon lung byams pa gling] in the Monguor territory to the east of Xining. The monastery was thoroughly devastated and its six-year-old incarnation, Janggya Rölpe Dorje ལྕང་སྐྱ་རོལ་པའི་རྡོ་རྗེ་ [lcang skya rol pa'i rdo rje] (1717–1786), was taken into hiding in the surrounding wilderness. His predecessor, Janggya Ngawang Chöden ལྕང་སྐྱ་ངག་དབང་ཆོས་ལྡན་ [lcang skya ngag dbang chos ldan] (1642–1714), had been a close disciple of the 5th Dalai Lama and in later life a tutor of the Kangxi emperor. Accordingly, an order was issued that the boy should be found and brought to Beijing unharmed. Rölpe Dorje would be raised and educated under the direct protection of the court, groomed from childhood to serve as an intermediary between the seat of Manchu power and the Buddhists of Tibet and Mongolia.

EXILE AND RETURN

Although by now the young Dalai Lama had been installed in the Potala for some years, he was still in his minority and Tibet remained politically unstable. There was therefore no question that he should be made to rule. For the time being, he continued to be occupied solely with his religious education. In the aftermath of the war with the Dzungars in 1720, the Manchus had punished harshly those in the Tibetan government who had collaborated with the enemy while at the same time they sought to impose strict discipline upon the general population, measures that did nothing to endear them to the Tibetan people overall. They established an oligarchy of five leading Tibetan nobles to rule Tibet, led by Khangchenne ཁང་ཆེན་ནས་ [khang chen nas], who exercised authority in collaboration with two Manchu governors, the Ambans 安班. Adding to the complexity of these arrangements was the new status of the Dalai Lama's father, Sönam Dargye, who had been ennobled following his son's installation and soon became entangled in the affairs of the ruling oligarchy.

Throughout the 1720s relations among the Tibetan oligarchs grew increasingly fractious. Kangchenne, though in

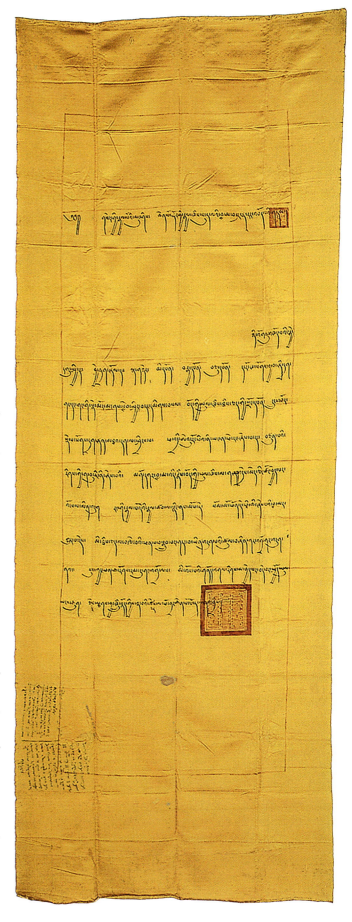

73 Decree of the Seventh Dalai Lama, dated 7 October 1741, to the Capuchin missionaries stationed in Lhasa. Handwritten on yellow silk, Lhasa, 1741, 200 cm x 69 cm, Bayerische Staatsbibliothek, Munich, Cod. Tibet. 507. >>>

74 Edict of Emperor Yongzheng from 1723, in which he confirms Kalsang Gyatso as the "Sixth" Dalai Lama and the legitimate successor to the "Great Fifth." 166 x 100 cm, Archives of the Tibet Autonomous Region.

many respects a capable leader, was arrogant and ill-suited to cooperate with others. Three of his peers, Ngaphö ངག་ཕོད་ [nga phod] and Lumpawa ལུམ་པ་བ་ [lum pa ba], whose daughters had married Sönam Dargye, and also Jarawa སྦྱར་ར་བ་ [sbyar ra ba], plotted rebellion. The fourth, Pholhane Sönam Topgyal ཕོ་ལྷ་ནས་ བསོད་ནམས་སྟོབས་རྒྱལ་ [pho lha nas bsod nams stobs rgyal], regarded Khangchenne as the rightful leader despite his character, and so for a time sought to distance himself from the conflict. In 1727, Khangchenne, his retainers, and family were assassinated in a coup d'état, whereupon Pholhane reacted by rallying armies in western Tibet and Tsang to overthrow the killers and their supporters. Though badly outnumbered, Pholhane was the superior strategist and by carefully concentrating his forces he secured control of important fortresses in the west, notably Shigatse, while waiting for Manchu reinforcements. Once these arrived, the rebellion was firmly suppressed, although it was now clear to the Qing that local governmental arrangements in Tibet needed to be thoroughly overhauled. The oligarchy was henceforth abandoned in favor of Pholhane's unified rule. Though in principle he exercised authority in concert with the Ambans, foreign observers during this period, such as the renowned Capuchin missionary Cassiano Beligatti de Maccrata, came to regard Pholhane as the real "king" of Tibet. Part of the price Pholhane exacted for accepting his newly elevated position, however, was the exile of the Dalai Lama's family. Because in Pholhane's view Sönam Dargye was a troublemaker who would continue to find supporters in central Tibet as long as his son remained there, Kalsang Gyatso would also have to go.

These developments placed the Manchus in an awkward position. On the one hand, Pholhane had in effect saved Manchu authority in Tibet and so had a justified claim for their support, while on the other, the emperors Kangxi and Yongzheng had themselves approved of Kalsang Gyatso's recognition so that the court was duty-bound to remain loyal to the Dalai Lama they had helped to install. The pragmatic—though perhaps not ideal—solution that was adopted did permit Pholhane to consolidate a stable regime in Tibet for the first time

75 Lama Janggya *Khutughtu* Rölpe Dorje, without the lotus blossoms on the left and the book on his right or sword on them. Bronze, gilded, fine traces of pigments, Tibet/China, 18th century, H 17 cm, W 12.5 cm, D 8.5 cm, Jacques Marchais Museum of Tibetan Art, NY, Inv. No.: 85.04.0162. **76** The Seventh Dalai Lama, without the lotus blossom on his right and the book on his left. Bronze, gilded and painted, Tibet/China, 18th century, H 19 cm, W 12 cm, D 10 cm, Jacques Marchais Museum of Tibetan Art, NY, Inv. No.: 85.04.0772.

in over a quarter century while giving the Dalai Lama every provision for the advancement of his religious vocation: a new monastery was built as Kalsang Gyatso's court-sponsored residence in Garthar མགར་ཐར་ [mgar thar], to the far east of Kham in Sichuan 四川, a place far removed from central Tibetan affairs. For the next eight years, Kalsang Gyatso devoted himself entirely to study and meditation while teaching and writing for those who gathered to receive his blessings. It was during this period that he came to be reputed as one of the great Tantric masters of the Geluk order and for this reason he is sometimes represented in Tibetan artwork as a *yogin* (plate 77). His great commentary on the *maṇḍala* and initiation rites of the Guhyasamāja Tantra is the most extensive of his works and is regarded among the leading masterpieces of Geluk Tantric exegesis.

The Qing decision simultaneously to support the Dalai Lama and to support his exile involved a contradiction that could not continue indefinitely. In 1735 it was decided that the time had come to authorize Kalsang Gyatso's return to central Tibet.

Pholhane was now secure in his own authority and though he clearly did not relish the idea of the hierarch's renewed presence in Lhasa, he recognized that it made no sense to oppose it. He therefore acquiesced to the imperial decision under the condition that Kalsang Gyatso only be permitted to assume religious and ceremonial functions. Under the order of the Yongzheng emperor, a royal entourage of five hundred religious, civil, and military representatives was sent to accompany the Dalai Lama from Garthar to Lhasa. The religious leader of the delegation was none other than Janggya Rölpe Dorje, then eighteen.

For the latter, this was the opportunity he had been waiting for and he eagerly grasped the occasion to continue his studies under the guidance of the Dalai Lama and his tutors. During the two years that followed, he became Kalsang Gyatso's confidant and close disciple, and many years later became his official biographer, too. In 1737, Janggya travelled to Tashilhünpo in Shigatse to receive his complete ordination from Panchen Lopsang Yeshe as the Dalai Lama himself had done. His sojourn

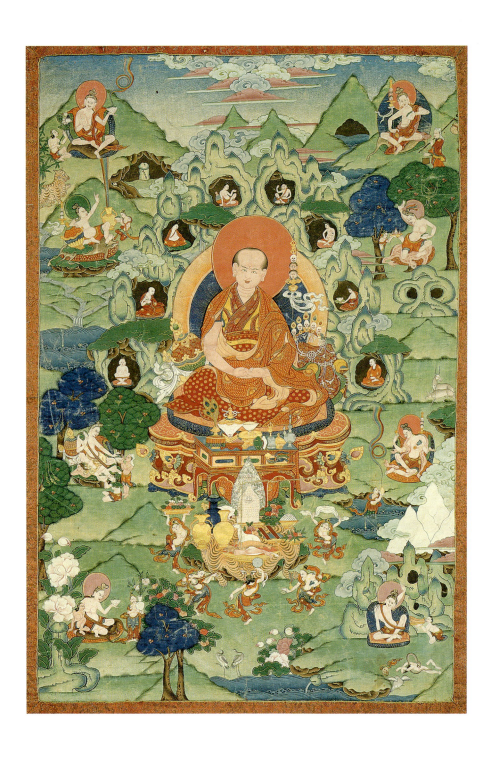

77 The Seventh Dalai Lama as scholar and Tantric master, showing the Seventh Dalai Lama's vision on the occasion of a Heruka (Cakrasaṃvara) initiation awarded by Lopsang Yeshe, the Second Panchen Lama. Left of the Dalai Lama are the objects used in that initiation. Eight of twenty-four holy sites of Cakrasaṃvara are also seen. Thangka, Tibet, 64 x 42 cm, Ethnographic Museum of the University of Zürich, Inv. No.: 13200. >>> **Detail of 77** Five ḍākinīs dance before the throne and altar tables—one with normal ritual items and the other with Tantric ones; objects symbolize the five senses (fruit, lute, mirror, *dāmaru*, and cloth).

78 Emperor Qianlong shown as a Tibetan lama. Detail of a larger painting on silk, China, ca. 1766, Total dimensions of the scroll: 113.5 x 64 cm, Freer Gallery of Art (Arthur M. Sackler Gallery), Washington D.C. >>>

with this master, however, was cut short by news of the emperor Yongzheng's death and Janggya was obliged to return to Beijing in haste. The new monarch turned out to have been his closest friend among the princes, who was elevated to the throne under the imperial title *Qianlong* 乾隆. Given Janggya's now established connections both with the Manchu ruler and Kalsang Gyatso, he came to play a uniquely important role in Sino-Tibetan affairs throughout the decades that followed.

MATURE ACHIEVEMENTS AND LEGACY

The death of Pholhane in 1747 ushered in a new period of instability. His second son, Gyurme Namgyal འགྱུར་མེད་རྣམ་རྒྱལ་ ['gyur med rnam rgyal], succeeded him and sought to renew ties with the Dzungars, forever the opponents of Manchu hegemony in Inner Asia. He is also said to have shunned the Dalai Lama. Tensions brewed and came to a head in 1750, when Gyurme Namgyal was assassinated at the hands of the Ambans. In retaliation, the office of the Amban was attacked by Gyurme Namgyal's supporters, the Ambans were killed, and a general massacre of the Chinese in Lhasa ensued. A delegation the emperor sent did

not hesitate to take severe punitive measures so that members of Gyurme Namgyal's faction who were captured were either executed or imprisoned. Their rebellion against both the Dalai Lama and Manchu rule made it impossible for Kalsang Gyatso to intercede on their behalf.

In the wake of these events, Emperor Qianlong decided that the Tibetans could no longer be trusted to rule themselves and that henceforth the two court-appointed Ambans would act as the sole governors of the region, therefore effectively transforming Tibet from a protectorate into a colony. Janggya Rölpe Dorje's value as the recognized intermediary between the Tibetan clergy and the emperor now became clear: he argued before the monarch that the attempt to place the Tibetans under direct Manchu rule would have untoward consequences, of which the outcome would surely be armed rebellion. He recommended that his teacher and friend, the Dalai Lama, now be allowed to assume his rightful role. For his part, the emperor came to recognize the merits of Janggya's position, and in a long proclamation addressed to the Tibetan authorities he justified the complete suppression of Gyurme Namgyal's faction while establishing a system of shared rule. In this arrangement the Ambans and the Dalai Lama, with the aid of respected officials such as Doring Paṇḍita རྡོ་རིང་པཎྜི་ཏ་ [rdo ring paṇḍita], would together take charge of Tibetan affairs. For the first time in his life, the Dalai Lama Kalsang Gyatso now occupied the political center-stage.

The 7th Dalai Lama's success as a political leader was unforeseen. Trained as a scholar-monk, the turmoil surrounding his youth and early adulthood had effectively excluded him from an active political role until the events of 1747-1750 propelled him to head the Tibetan government at the age of forty-three. His personal reputation for learning and spiritual integrity, together with the widespread devotion of the Tibetan people to the figure of the Dalai Lama, earned him the cooperation of the general population as well important factions of the clergy and aristocracy, not to mention the Manchu court. It was therefore possible for him to act with a degree of consensus that partisan elements in the Tibetan leadership had lacked.

Among the principle political institutions created under the 7th Dalai Lama, one must take special note of the *kashak* བཀའ་ཤག [bka' shag], the "leadership council" or "cabinet" serving as the apex of secular administration in Tibet until 1959 and continuing today under the Tibetan government-in-exile. Because prominent members of the first *kashak*—notably Doring Paṇḍita and Dokhar Shapdrung མདོ་མཁར་ཞབས་དྲུང་ [mdo mkhar zhabs drung]—had been important allies of Pholhane, an appropriate measure of continuity in government was also maintained. In 1754, the Dalai Lama moved to enhance the education of lay officials by founding a new school specializing in calligraphy, the literary arts, and astrology—the principle subjects required for Tibetan government service—as well as the famous Döpal འདོད་དཔལ་ ['dod dpal] artistic workshop in the Zhol quarter beneath the Potala. An archival office, *yiktshang lekhung* ཡིག་ཚང་ལས་ཁུངས་ [yig tshang las khungs], was later added to these new facilities, which together regulated the material aspects of Tibetan secular and monastic administration. During the following years, the Dalai Lama personally supervised a considerable production of religious art and publications. His health began to weaken, however, in 1756 and he passed away during the following year at the age of just fifty. A regent, the 6th Demo *Khutughtu* Jampel Delek Gyatso དེ་མོ་ཧོ་ཐོག་ཐུ་འཇམ་དཔལ་ བདེ་ལེགས་རྒྱ་མཚོ་ [de mo ho thog thu 'Jam dpal bde legs rgya mtsho] (1723–1777) assumed the reins of government.

In his political life Kalsang Gyatso no doubt wished above all to bring some benefit, in the form of peace and prosperity, to the Tibetan people who had suffered greatly from foreign invasion and civil war. His rise to power in 1751 ensured that a characteristically Tibetan form of government combining the religious and *chösi nyiden* ཆོས་སྲིད་གཉིས་ལྡན་ [chos srid gnyis ldan] "secular" would be the established norm in Tibet henceforth. For himself, however, one has the impression that he was most content in his meditations and scholarship and in his roles as Buddhist author and teacher. He is credited in the course of his life with the ordination of some 9,774 *śrāmaṇera* and 16,993 *bhikṣu,* as well as countless Buddhist laymen and laywomen. The seven volumes of his *Collected Works* make him the most prolific writer among the Dalai Lamas after the Great Fifth. His works include commentaries, liturgical texts, and a wide variety of official and consecratory documents. His most admired literary achievements, however, are his religious poems, which combine homely advice for the Buddhist religious life with profound instructions for contemplation. It is fitting, therefore, to conclude the present, brief account of his life with a short excerpt. In the original Tibetan the selections

79 Lama Janggya *Khutughtu* Rölpe Dorje, who bears the attributes of Bodhisattva Mañjuśrī on lotus blossoms to his left and right. Detail of thangka, Tibet/China, late 18th century, 72.5 x 43 cm (complete thangka), Musée national des arts asiatiques Guimet, Paris, Inv. No.: MA 4939. >>>

offered here were composed in the dance-song meter that his tragic predecessor, Tsangyang Gyatso, had favored for verses on worldly themes:

> When stirred by that demon, "Grasping-as-real,"
> Relative appearances arise.
> But cut through this, your own error,
> While investigating what reason can know;
> Turn back errant illusion,
> Just look at reality's show!

> In the face of an empty-clear sky,
> There is no independent true thing,
> But manifold causal conditions
> Together make rainbow designs.
> Just look at this! It's amazing
> How it all aimlessly seems to arise!

> Though you can't catch hold of anything
> By analysis that seeks out a "this,"
> It's in the nexus of conditions,
> The attribution of names alone,
> That all doings and deeds are established.
> Open your eyes to this illusion!

THE EIGHTH DALAI LAMA JAMPEL GYATSO[1]

འཇམ་དཔལ་རྒྱ་མཚོ

Derek F. Maher

The tenure of the 8th Dalai Lama was a tumultuous time filled with battles and intrigues. The rise in Nepāl of the Gurkha King Pṛthvī Nārāyaṇ Śāh in the 1760s brought the destruction of the Newā coalition in 1769, conflict with Sikkim in 1774–1775 and again in 1788, and the invasion of western Tibet in 1787 and 1791. In addition, Bhūṭān occupied Sikkim for a number of years until its strongman, Deb Judhar, prompted a British reprisal in 1772–1773. Meanwhile, the Manchurian representatives of the Qing 清 Empire enhanced its position in Tibet.

During the 18th century the Qing court had been increasingly concerned with Tibet, and its representatives often attempted to rule directly. Their efforts were partly a response to problems with the Mongols on China's northwest frontier. Since many of the most nettlesome Mongol tribes had strong links with Tibet, especially with the Dalai Lamas' Geluk School, the Qing often found that political influence in Tibet produced a more pacified environment among the Mongol nomads. Moreover, the Qing court wished to counterbalance the influence of the Mongols, the Gurkhas, and, beginning in the late 18th century, the British.

Prior to 1751, Tibet had been dominated for several decades by a series of Tibetan and Mongolian strongmen. In this period the Qing made their impact known by building alliances and playing factions off against each other. The primary instrument of these intrigues was the Qing representative known as the Amban 安班. Although the Amban's actual power was frequently quite limited, it is evident that these officials from China often influenced events in central Tibet. The degree of that influence is a matter of fierce polemical debate among historians. The Tibetan historian Tsepön Shakabpa རྩིས་དཔོན་ཞྭ་སྒབ་པ་ [rtsis dpon zhwa sgab pa] (1908–1989) claims that, aside from responding to invitations to ceremonies, dramatic performances, and festivals, the Manchu Ambans played no role in politics.[2] The opposite extreme is represented by the Chinese author Ya Hanzhang 牙含章, who portrays the Ambans as exercising strict control over minute details of Tibetan life, saying, "The eighth Dalai Lama was the leader of Tibet only nominally, for everything he did was dictated by the Amban."[3]

Upon the death of the 7th Dalai Lama, Kalsang Gyatso སྐལ་བཟང་རྒྱ་མཚོ [skal bzang rgya mtsho] (1708–1757), many of the ecclesiastical and political luminaries of the time gathered to discuss the institution's future. The assembly initially debated whether even to search for the new incarnation, apparently being influenced by prophecies indicating there would only be seven incarnations in the lineage.[4] Once they had decided in favor of conducting a search, they decided that, for the first time, an incarnate lama should be appointed as regent until the new Dalai Lama attained his majority. The 7th Demo incarnation Ngawang Jampel Delek Gyatso དེ་མོ་ངག་དབང་འཇམ་དཔལ་བདེ་ལེགས་རྒྱ་མཚོ [de mo ngag dbang 'jam dpal bde legs rgya mtsho] (d. 1777) was their unanimous choice.

In 1760 the 3rd Panchen Lama, Lopsang Palden Yeshe བློ་བཟང་དཔལ་ལྡན་ཡེ་ཤེས [blo bzang dpal ldan ye shes] (1738–1780), travelled from Tashilhünpo Monastery in Shigatse to Lhasa in order to consult with the regent on the process of selecting the new incarnation of the Dalai Lama. All of the major oracles were consulted, and reports of special children began to reach Lhasa. Consensus opinion settled on a boy born on the twenty-fifth day of the sixth month of 1758 in Tobgyel Hlari Gang in Tsang. Objects that had been owned by the 7th Dalai Lama were then mixed in with similar objects, and the child unerringly selected the correct items.

In early 1761 the young incarnation was taken from his parents' home to meet the Panchen Lama, and the latter ceremonially cut a lock of his hair and bestowed upon him the name Lopsang Tenpe Wangchuk Jampel Gyatso བློ་བཟང་བསྟན་པའི་དབང་ཕྱུག་འཇམ་དཔལ་རྒྱ་མཚོ [blo bzang bstan pa'i dbang phyug 'jam dpal rgya mtsho] (1758–1804). That same year, at the tender age of three, he began his education under the guidance of eminent scholars. In 1762 a large procession conveyed the youth to the Potala Palace in Lhasa, where the Panchen Lama presided over his enthronement on the Dalai Lama's Snow Lion throne. In 1765 the Panchen Lama bestowed novice vows. The occasion was marked by the appearance of rainbows around the sun, divine forms in the clouds, songs of praise resounding in the sky, an earthquake, a distant sound like that of a dharma drum, and the pervasive smell of sweet aromas.[5]

The young Dalai Lama's most influential teacher was his primary tutor, Yeshe Gyaltsen ཡེ་ཤེས་རྒྱལ་མཚན [ye shes rgyal mtshan] (1713–1793). A key disciple of the 2nd Panchen Lama, Lopsang Yeshe བློ་བཟང་ཡེ་ཤེས [blo bzang ye shes] (1663–1737), Yeshe Gyaltsen was recommended for the position of tutor by the 3rd Panchen Lama. Yeshe Gyaltsen was both an exceptional scholar and an accomplished adept. At the time he was appointed as the Dalai

80 The Eighth Dalai Lama at his enthronement as Dalai Lama, attended by high dignitaries, guests and even deities. Various scenes and figures surrounding the central figure, including his birth in Thopgyal (right) accompanied by many miracles, his teacher Yeshe Gyaltsen (upper right) and the Third Panchen Lama Lopsang Palden Yeshe (upper left). Thangka, Tibet, ca. 1780, 90 x 61.5 cm, Collection of R.R.E.   **Detail of 80** Portion of the throne decoration and behind it, the house where the Eighth Dalai Lama was born, with his parents visible in the window.   **Detail of 80** Reverence and presentation of gifts by the deities (including the Four-Faced Brahma)...   **Detail of 80** ...and people of this world, including foreigners, one of whom presents a dish full of jewels to the Dalai Lama seated on the Snow Lion throne.

Lama's tutor, Yeshe Gyaltsen was an obscure monk who had received his training at Tashilhünpo Monastery. Subsequently, he had withdrawn to remote regions in the Himalayas in order to undertake extensive retreats over a period of twelve years, during which he attained profound realizations. He exercised significant influence over the young Dalai Lama. The latter's contemplative nature and his emphasis on practice-oriented literature echo Yeshe Gyaltsen's own predispositions. Moreover, the tutor's disinclination to mix Nyingma practices with the strict Geluk regime persuaded the 8th Dalai Lama not to follow the eclectic nature of earlier Dalai Lamas.

At the beginning of 1771 the teenaged Dalai Lama's education entered a more advanced phase. He received transmissions and explanations on many of the primary root texts and commentaries of the Geluk school, along with a large number of tantric works.

In 1774, while the Dalai Lama remained in Lhasa, the Panchen Lama was occupied back in Shigatse with the visit of the British envoy George Bogle. Ostensibly, the latter had been sent by the Governor-General of Bengal, Warren Hastings, to thank the Panchen Lama for his efforts to facilitate peace in Bhūṭān. Clearly, however, the British also saw this visit as an opportunity to advance relations with Tibet on a broad range of issues. Bogle and the Panchen Lama developed a close personal relationship. However, conservative authorities in Lhasa ordered that the British delegation depart Tibet after only five months. By 1781, both men were dead and the opportunity to promote relations between their countries was lost.

The regent Demo Trülku died in 1777 after having served for two decades. As the Dalai Lama had reached the age of twenty by this point, the *kashak* བཀའ་ཤག [bka' shag] "cabinet," his personal attendants, the abbots of the great monasteries, and the monastic and lay government officials urged him to assume full political responsibility. However, he declined so that he could complete his studies unhindered, and Ngawang Tsultrim ངག་དབང་ ཚུལ་ཁྲིམས [ngag dbang tshul khrims] (1721–1791) was appointed as the new regent.

For some time, Emperor Qianlong 乾隆 (1711–1799) had wanted the Panchen Lama to visit China. The latter had been declining the invitations, in part out of fear of the smallpox then rampant, which had already forced him to retreat to a remote monastery for a while in 1774 when an outbreak occurred in Tsang. In 1779 he was no longer able to continue resisting the

Qing emperor's requests, and he consented to visit China, wintering at Kumbum Monastery before arriving in Shayho in 1780. As he had feared, smallpox was afoot when he arrived. Rituals were performed in order to abate the epidemic, and the Panchen Lama offered prayers to take upon himself the entirety of the illness. He went on to meet with the emperor, who was so enthused about the esteemed lama's visit that he had learned some colloquial Tibetan. Together they proceeded to Beijing, accompanied by a large party. Upon their arrival the Panchen Lama presided over the emperor's seventieth birthday. The two spent many hours discussing Buddhism. However, in the end the lama was overcome by smallpox and died.

As relations between the Qing court and Tibet became closer throughout the 17th and 18th centuries, it became rather routine for Tibetan incarnate lamas to spend some time in China. The 2nd Janggya Rölpe Dorje ལྕང་སྐྱ་རོལ་པའི་རྡོ་རྗེ [lcang skya rol pa'i rdo rje] (1717–1786), for example, was raised in the household of the emperor and served as a royal envoy on various occasions. These close connections between the Qing court and the Tibetan lamas, which would expand greatly during the life of the 8th Dalai Lama, reflected the mutual benefits each side received from the exchange. As had been the case since the very origins of the Preceptor-Patron relationship in the 13th century, the lamas in the equation received significant support of various sorts for their various projects, including patronage for the construction of temples, monasteries, *stūpas*, and the like; protection from indigenous and foreign enemies; and a certain species of legitimacy that derives only from a close relationship with a great power.

The patrons willingly participated because the relationship allowed them to construe themselves as Buddhist kings, following the paradigm laid down by the Buddha's own royal patrons. By taking on the role of patronizing a great religious figure, they thereby assimilated to themselves the authority and legitimacy inherent in that mythology. Tibetan lamas therefore served to uphold and authenticate Qing emperors by representing them within legitimizing religious narratives. Not only could these royal figures justifiably take pride in their contributions to Buddhist causes, but Tibetan lamas also found reason to portray them as *bodhisattvas*. As David M. Farquhar observes, "Mongols and Tibetans of the eighteenth and nineteenth centuries would not have been at all surprised to see [Emperor]

Qianlong presented as a reincarnation of Mañjuśrī," the representation of Buddha's perfect wisdom.[6] This mutual authentication between Tibetan Buddhist lamas and either emperors in China or Mongolian khans, an arrangement symbolizing the essence of the Preceptor-Patron relationship, had been going on since the 13th century and many Tibetans were anxious to see it continue. By the time of the 8th Dalai Lama, however, the Ambans had begun to go further, insinuating themselves directly into the administration of Tibetan affairs. The Manchu efforts to increase their control would become increasingly evident as the Dalai Lama's tenure continued.

In 1781, the religious and political elite of Tibet once again requested that the Dalai Lama assume full responsibility for the government. Being devoted to his education and his spiritual practice, he continued to resist, but in the end he reluctantly agreed to assume the throne, provided that the regent Ngawang Tsultrim remain in service at his side. This arrangement was maintained until the regent retired from his post in 1786. That same year, Janggya Rinpoche died in Beijing, and the emperor requested that Ngawang Tsultrim take his place, likely as a way of removing a strong figure from Lhasa so that the Amban would have a freer hand.

In 1783, at twenty-five years of age, the Dalai Lama travelled to Tashilhünpo Monastery, the original seat of the 1st Dalai Lama. While there, at the request of many of the senior lamas, he performed the flower consecration at the silver *stūpa* of the previous Panchen Lama. He then presided over the identification of the 4th Panchen Lama, ceremonially cutting a lock of the child's hair, and bestowing upon him the name Lopsang Palden Tenpe Nyima རློ་བཟང་བསྟན་པའི་ཉི་མ་ [blo bzang bstan pa'i nyi ma] (1782–1853). On this occasion, the Governor-General of Bengal, Warren Hastings, sent a congratulatory mission to mark the identification of the 4th Panchen Lama, delegating his own relative, Samuel Turner, for the purpose. This mission was meant to reactivate the relationship that had been dormant since the deaths of the 3rd Panchen Lama and the British emissary George Bogle. However, the renewed diplomatic efforts did not result in much enduring benefit, as Hastings was soon recalled to England.[7]

In 1784 the 8th Dalai Lama began construction of the Kelsang Palace at Norbulingka, a park a few miles west of the Potala where previous Dalai Lamas had traditionally bathed in the medicinal waters. From that point on, it became the custom of the Dalai Lamas to spend part of the summer at the Norbulingka. Grand processions would accompany the Dalai Lama's transit from Norbulingka to the Potala Palace and back.

From 1786 until 1790 the Dalai Lama ruled Tibet on his own. These years were trying and perilous for the country and distressing for the Dalai Lama. From early adulthood, he had evinced a powerful disinclination towards politics, and his attitude did not change when the Gurkhas in Nepāl began attacks along Tibet's southern border in 1787. As the situation worsened, he sought once again to transfer primary political power to others.

The tensions with Nepāl had been building for some time. The Gurkha King Pṛthvī Nārāyaṇ Śāh had consolidated control over the entirety of Nepāl in 1769, and he and his successors soon began working to extend their reach to the further stretches of the chaotic Himalayan region. Tensions between Nepāl and Tibet first emerged when the Gurkhas and the Tibetans sided with different parties in the 1775 Bhūtān-Sikkim conflict, and they were heightened by conflicts over trade and exchange rates. Additional opportunity for conflict arose when the Panchen Lama's two brothers disagreed over who should inherit the patronage the Lama had received in China. This latter dispute came to a head when one of them, the 10th Shamar Chödrup Gyatso ཞྭ་དམར་ཆོས་གྲུབ་རྒྱ་མཚོ་ [zhwa dmar chos grub rgya mtsho] (1741/1742–1792), also known as the Lama Shamarpa, went on a pilgrimage to Nepāl during which he encouraged the Gurkhas to seize the riches at Tashilhünpo Monastery in Shigatse.

In 1787, the first of two Gurkha–Tibet wars erupted as the Nepalese forces invaded Tsang, attacking several border towns in the middle of the year. In response, the Tibetan government called up troops and the Amban appealed to the emperor for reinforcements. The Tibetans were ambivalent about the Qing assistance, as the large army sent by Beijing threatened to strain available resources. Furthermore, the emperor's representatives seemed overly intent on settling, even on unfavorable terms. The resulting treaty required the Tibetans to pay an indemnity to Nepāl, an unhappy result that entailed further hardship for the Tibetans. In light of the many losses experienced by Tibet during this period, it was determined that the management skills of the regent Ngawang Tsultrim were required once again, and he was recalled from China in 1790,

81 The Eighth Dalai Lama, surrounded by his predecessors, the First through the Seventh Dalai Lamas, the Ninth and the Tenth Dalai Lamas, and other previous incarnations, including, the three kings, Domtön above the aura, and Sachen Künga Nyingpo (with bald head) left; with inscription on the obverse naming individual figures and a longer inscription on the reverse. Thangka, Tibet, mid-19th century, 152 x 103 cm, Ethnographic Museum of the University of Zürich, Inv. No.: 18593. >>> **Detail of 81** Portion of throne decoration of the Eighth Dalai Lama: Garuda and Nāga.

82 Golden Urn and five ivory plates, commissioned by Emperor Qianlong, for the selection of the Dalai Lamas and Panchen Lamas. Decorated with plant- and cloud-like swirling patterns, jewels and the Namchu Wangden (the Kālacakra symbol made up of ten mystical letters) intertwined on the front surface. China, late 18th century, H 35.5 cm, Dm: 21 cm (foot 14.4 cm), Palace of Harmony, Beijing.

ending an absence of four years. He soon passed away, however. His replacement in China, the 8th Tatsak Tenpe Gönpo རྟ་ཚག་བསྟན་པའི་མགོན་པོ་ [rta tshag bstan pa'i mgon po] (1760–1810), was then recalled to Tibet and appointed as regent.

The new regent took office just as tensions with the Gurkhas were on the verge of erupting into the war of 1791. The new war posed a serious threat to Tibet. When negotiations had resumed between Tibet and the Gurkhas, the Tibetan delegation was captured and sent to Nepāl. Meanwhile, the Gurkha armies once again attacked Tsang, forcing Tibet to recruit troops from throughout the country. Religious services were also performed at many of the large monasteries. When reports indicated that Gurkha troops had sacked Tashilhünpo Monastery, panic ran through Lhasa and the Amban Bao Tai 保泰 sent an appeal to the emperor. The Amban and many others urged the Dalai Lama to withdraw to Chamdo along with the Panchen Lama. However, he refused to leave, instead holding a large ceremony at Lhasa's Jokhang Temple. The Dalai Lama used the occasion to rally the public and steel its resolve. As he spoke, perspiration is said to have broken out on the face of the Palden Lhamo statue. The government and the monasteries were taking measures to conceal their valuable treasures.

Tibetans felt that the Gurkhas had been emboldened enough to attack a second time by the treaty the Qing negotiators had urged on them. Tibetan troops moved into Tsang, severing the Gurkhas' supply routes. Meanwhile, the Qianlong emperor had sent 20,000 troops under his brother Fu Kang'an 福康安, and a separate contingent of 10,000 imperial troops arrived during the first day of 1792. By that time, according to Tibetan sources, the main Gurkha army had already been repulsed.[8] Together, the Qing and Tibetan troops now drove the remnants of the Gurkha forces back across the border into Nepāl. The Gurkhas initially hoped to continue the war with British assistance, but Lord Cornwallis, the British Viceroy in India, rebuffed their appeals. In the end, the Gurkhas blamed the entire adventure on Lama Shamarpa, who died under mysterious circumstances soon thereafter.

In the aftermath of this unsettled period, all parties strove to avoid further conflict. Since conflicts over the debased coins issued in pre-Gurkha Nepāl had provided one of the initial causes of the war, Tibet began minting its own high quality coins in 1792. Meanwhile, the Dalai Lama withdrew entirely from political affairs. The Tibetan government, under the guidance of the regent Tatsak, punished several government officials for their part in recent events, and efforts were also made to reform the operation of the government. The Gurkhas, for their part, were confronted with a new political reality in that they were compelled to exhibit a subservient attitude towards the Qing emperor, and the official language of the settlement even implied that the Gurkhas were now assimilated into the Qing empire. Though China never exercised any tangible control over Nepāl, the latter continued to pay nominal tribute to the Qing until the empire collapsed in 1911.

Having had to dispatch two separate armies to the distant Himalayan region within just a few years, the emperor now resolved to play a more active role in Tibetan affairs. Accordingly, the *Twenty-Nine Article Imperial Ordinance* 二十九條章程 was issued, redefining the character of Sino-Tibetan relations (plate 83). As with the Gurkha-Qing settlement, some of the provisions and rhetoric were merely fanciful posturing, a continuation of the already ancient narrative of China as the Middle Kingdom around which all others compliantly orbited. On occasion, even Britain's mighty king was construed as a subservient vassal. Nonetheless, the ordinance was a watershed in

83 The Twenty-Nine Article Imperial Ordinance with instructions for better governance of Tibet, written at the commission of Emperor Qianlong. China, 1793, L: 359 cm, W 53 cm, Archive of the Tibetan Autonomous Region. >>>

Tibet-Qing relations, as from then onward the Qing court was able to enact a much tighter control over Tibetan affairs.

The provisions of the ordinance represented the Qing Amban as running the entire government in detail, as he now possessed authority to issue commands affecting the organization of the military, the ranks of government officials and nobility, appointments to positions of power within monasteries, visits to Tibet by non-Tibetans, and so forth. The authority and functions of the Dalai Lama and the Panchen Lama were also strictly defined. The most symbolically potent assertion of Qing imperial power related to the process of selecting the Dalai Lamas and the Panchen Lamas, as the ordinance declared that the new incarnations were to be selected by placing the names of candidates on pieces of ivory, metal, or paper and drawing one at random from a Golden Urn 金瓶 (plate 82) supplied by the emperor.[9] Although this last provision was justified as a depoliticization of the selection process, Tibetans disliked the interference intensely.

The 8th Dalai Lama was not as prolific an author as some of his more scholastically oriented predecessors. Primarily he wrote prayers, ritual texts, and other practice-oriented literature, specializing to a degree in rites relating to the lesser-known cycle of Mahāmāya Tantra. Aside from such texts, he composed two major works. The first of these was a catalog describing the reliquary of one of his principal teachers, the 3rd Panchen Lama. His most extensive text is a lengthy biography of Yeshe Gyaltsen, his primary tutor and his regent for twenty-one years. Furthermore, throughout his life the Dalai Lama worked in understated fashion to improve the status of Buddhist institutions in Tibet.

In 1804, the Dalai Lama's health began to deteriorate. Services were performed on his behalf, but ultimately he came down with a case of pneumonia. The court physician Tsarong wanted to administer a treatment of cold-water therapy, and the Dalai Lama was taken to Norbulingka for that purpose. He seemed to have improved over the next few days, but then his suffering increased. Tatsak Rinpoche presided over the performance of rituals intended to reverse his illness, but these were not effective. As his vitality declined, the Dalai Lama asked to meet with members of the *sangha*. Many monks visited him before he succumbed to death at the age of forty-seven years.

THE NINTH TO THE TWELFTH DALAI LAMAS

Derek F. Maher

Between the end of 1805 and the beginning of 1875, four incarnations of the Dalai Lama were born, identified, enthroned, and then mourned. These ill-fated youths lived as few as nine and as many as twenty-one years. Since none of them ever became strong and accomplished leaders, they were unable to serve as a rallying point for the Tibetan people during this time of territorial infringement from all sides. This era also witnessed a series of particularly ineffectual regents and comparatively inconspicuous Panchen Lamas. Consequently, outside parties were able to dominate Tibet, particularly the Qing 清 representatives, or Ambans 安班, who furthered the emperor's ambitions in Lhasa. The influence on and control over Tibetan affairs that the Qing had realized during the tenure of the 7th and 8th Dalai Lamas solidified in this atmosphere. Indeed, some observers suspect that some or all four of the youths were murdered by Qing agents in order to perpetuate the power vacuum in which official Manchurian influence could flourish. But others have theorized that Tibetan aristocratic officials may have killed the four Dalai Lamas so as to prevent a strong leader from undermining the interests of the noble class. Still others have supposed that regents or monastic officials may have been guilty of treachery. Surviving reports from Manchurian officials, Tibetan nobles, and monastic authorities are uniformly self-serving, either failing to raise suspicions or else pointing fingers at other factions. It is difficult to imagine what additional evidence might come to light on these cases. In any event, Qing institutional control certainly became far more elaborate during this era.

1805–1815
THE NINTH DALAI LAMA, LUNGTOK GYATSO
ལུང་རྟོགས་རྒྱ་མཚོ

As we saw in the previous chapter, Emperor Qianlong 乾隆 (1711–1799) announced a series of reforms in the wake of the Second Gurkha War of 1792–1793. The reforms were meant to solidify Qing control over Tibet and preclude the necessity of dispatching costly expeditions in its defense. Among these reforms, the *Twenty-Nine Article Imperial Ordinance* 二十九條章程 declared that the reincarnations of the Panchen Lamas and the Dalai Lamas should be selected by drawing lots from an ornate Golden Urn 金瓶 supplied by the emperor, but the Tibetans resented the Golden Urn as an encroachment. Consequently, when searching

for the 9th Dalai Lama, the regent Tatsak Tenpe Gönpo རྟ་ཚག་བསྟན་པའི་ མགོན་པོ [rta tshag bstan pa'i mgon po] (1760–1810) hoped to avoid ratifying the concept of the Golden Urn Lottery. Therefore he and the others involved in the selection process declared swiftly that the identification was absolutely unquestionable, thereby making the lottery unnecessary. Hence, on the first occasion that the Golden Urn might have been used, the regent, the previous Dalai Lama's attendants, and the others involved collectively demonstrated the Qing court's inability to control the identification process. In this they were aided by developments in Beijing. The Qianlong emperor had retired in 1795. His successor, Emperor Jiaqing 嘉慶 (1760–1820), exhibited less interest in Tibet, and most affairs there had been turned over to the discretion of the Ambans in Lhasa. Hence, the effectiveness of Qing policy at any given time depended to a great extent on the capability of the Ambans.

When initial inquiries had been made in the search for the 9th Dalai Lama, two children emerged as likely candidates. Consensus opinion soon settled on a fatherless boy born in Kham in 1805, and his candidacy strengthened when the previous Dalai Lama's attendants met the child and found that he remembered aspects of his previous life. By the end of 1807 he had been taken to Gungtang Monastery near Lhasa, where he was examined by the 4th Panchen Lama Tenpe Nyima བསྟན་པའི་ཉི་ མ [bstan pa'i nyi ma] (1782–1853) and also by the regent, the Qing Amban Wu, and members of the *kashak* བཀའ་ཤག [bka' shag] "cabinet." His identification was quickly confirmed by means of the traditional Tibetan methods, and in early 1808 the 4th Panchen Lama performed the tonsure ceremony and granted the boy the name Lopsang Tenpe Wangchuk Lungtok Gyatso བློ་བཟང་བསྟན་པའི་དབང་ཕྱུག་ལུང་རྟོགས་རྒྱ་མཚོ [blo bzang bstan pa'i dbang phug lung rtogs rgya mtsho] (1805–1815) (plates 84–87).

The entire process was surrounded by rhetorical maneuvering. The Tibetan ecclesiastical authorities wished to act in a way that fostered an image of autonomy, while the Qing wished to represent the emperor as fully in control. The Tibetans enacted their part by short-circuiting the Qing-imposed procedure and identifying the boy quickly and decisively. As the emperor could not afford to risk a confrontation, the Qing court countered this Tibetan strategy by trying to take control of the rhetoric, claiming that the selection had been made with the emperor's permission.

84 – 87 Scenes from the life and enthronement of the Ninth Dalai Lama. Details from a narrative scroll, Mongolia, 1809, total scroll: 637 x 44.5 cm, Bibliothèque de l'Institut des hautes études chinoises du Collège de France.   **84** Birth of the future Ninth Dalai Lama. The rainbow heralds an unusual event.   **85** The future Dalai Lama and his entourage travelling to Lhasa. The biography narrates that Tsongkhapa, the reformer and founder of the Geluk School, appeared to the Ninth Dalai Lama in a vision during this journey.

Thus, the first imperial envoy he sent to Tibet publicly declared his assent to the identification while emphasizing privately that this was a unique circumstance and that in the future the Golden Urn would have to be employed. Meanwhile, the Qing court enthusiastically declared, for public consumption, that the Golden Urn had not been required since the identification was so obvious, and it claimed that the omission was done with Beijing's consent. The Chinese apologist historian Ya Hanzhang 牙含章 remarked that since the child was "the genuine re-embodiment of the fifth Dalai Lama," the Panchen Lama, the regent, and the abbots of the great Geluk monasteries sought "the permission of His Majesty to dispense with the drawing of lots from the golden urn."[2] This humble supplication, if it occurred, seems to have passed unrecorded in Tibetan sources.

An exemplary contemporary instance of the Qing rhetoric appears in a travelogue recounting the journey to Tibet of the Mongolian Prince Manjubazar of Qaracin, the emperor's special envoy sent to supervise the enthronement of the 9th Dalai Lama.[3] For Tibetans, it is inconceivable that a military official in the Manchurian army could actually have played any real role in the identification process. Yet the Mongolian travelogue represents Tibetan officialdom in a subservient posture, describing the "*kashak* in Lhasa" as submitting "a request expressing the wish to identify a child born on the twenty-second day of the ninth month of this same year as the reincarnation of the Dalai Lama."

For their part, the Tibetan sources tend to emphasize the relative impotence of the Qing's representatives. The 9th Dalai Lama's biographer, the regent Demo Jigme Gyatso, remarks that aside from the traditional Preceptor-Patron relations, the Amban "had absolutely no influence in the Tibetan government's political affairs." According to the same source, when the Amban was preparing to return to China, he had an audience with the Dalai Lama in which he was given religious advice. Shakabpa says the Amban had such profound faith that he performed a full-length prostration with tears in his eyes.[4] Such an image is entirely inconceivable in a Qing narrative.

The regent Tatsak Tenpe Gönpo died at Kundeling Monastery on the last day of 1810. By acclamation, he was replaced by Demo Ngawang Lopsang Tupten Jigme Gyatso དེ་མོ་ངག་དབང་བློ་བཟང་ཐུབ་

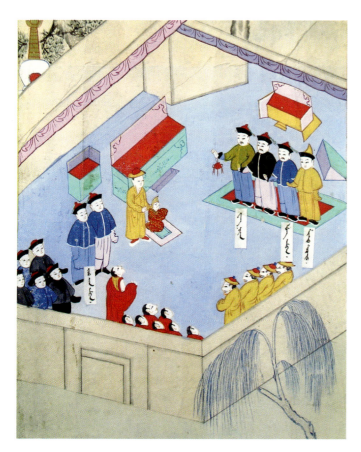

86 Enthronement of the Ninth Dalai Lama at the Potala on 10 November 1808 in the presence of the two Manchu Ambans and a four-person Qing delegation, led by Mongolian Prince Manjubazar, who commissioned this scroll (the man on the left, holding an object in his right hand).   87 The Potala with a rainbow hovering above as a sign of a special event, the return of the Dalai Lama (Lit. Charleux among others. 2004 a and b).

བསྟན་འཛིན་མེད་རྒྱ་མཚོ [de mo ngag dbang blo bzang thub bstan 'jigs med rgya mtsho] (1778–1819). Unfortunately, Demo suffered from episodes of mental illness, a fact that must have undermined his effectiveness. Few important public policies could be undertaken with such unsteady leadership.

In 1811 Thomas Manning, a British trade representative, reached Lhasa. Despite the opposition of the Amban and conservative Tibetans, he was permitted to remain and open a medical clinic in the city. During his stay he had several meetings with the young Dalai Lama, the first such meeting between a Dalai Lama and a British citizen. According to Manning's account, the boy was beautiful, elegant, refined, intelligent, and entirely self-possessed even at the age of six.[5] Some Chinese sources represent Manning and other British people who were in the Himalayan region during this time as spies collecting information in preparation for an invasion of Tibet.[6] There is little evidence for this, though it is clear the British were hoping to expand their trade relations and diplomatic contacts into the Tibetan plateau. Qing fears intensified, however, when open conflict erupted between the Gurkhas and the British in 1814.

The Tibetans were anxious not to be drawn into the war, but the Gurkhas appealed to the regent for assistance. The most the Tibetan authorities could do was to have monks at the great monasteries recite prayers on behalf of Nepāl.

In 1812, on the Dalai Lama's seventh birthday, the Panchen Lama gave him monastic vows. The boy continued his studies under the tutelage of Jangchub Chöpel བྱང་ཆུབ་ཆོས་འཕེལ [byang chub chos 'phel (1756–1838), who would go on to be the 69th Throne Holder of Ganden. However, before long the young incarnation came down with a cold while officiating at the Mönlam Chenmo Festival. Despite the performance of extensive rituals and the efforts of the best doctors, he died in early 1815, soon after his ninth birthday.

1816–1837
THE TENTH DALAI LAMA, TSULTRIM GYATSO
ཚུལ་ཁྲིམས་རྒྱ་མཚོ

The public was thoroughly shaken by the premature death of the beloved 9th Dalai Lama. Mourning was still underway when preliminary indications suggested that the new incarnation

88 The Ninth Dalai Lama. Detail of plate 81.

should be sought in eastern Tibet. Six candidates were discovered between Lhasa and Dartsedo, and consensus ultimately settled on a boy born in early 1816 near Litang 理塘. The boy's father was granted a title and the Yutok estate, thereby inaugurating an important noble family that would supply a steady stream of distinguished monastic and lay officials well into the 20th century.

The key oracles agreed with the selection, and the regent, the *kashak*, the main teachers at the big Geluk monasteries, and the ecclesiastical and lay government officials issued an edict bestowing recognition on the child. However, before the child could be officially enthroned, the regent contracted smallpox and died. He was replaced as regent by Ngawang Jampel Tsultrim Gyatso ངག་དབང་འཇམ་དཔལ་ཚུལ་ཁྲིམས་རྒྱ་མཚོ་ [ngag dbang 'jam dpal tshul khrims rgya mtsho] (1792–1862/1864) of Tsemönling Monastery. The new regent had very limited experience in government, and the power of the regency declined during his tenure, allowing the Ambans to expand their influence.

Eager to avoid being preempted from the selection process, the Qing managed to delay the formal enthronement of the Dalai Lama and had rival candidates brought to Lhasa. When the traditional tests were performed, the Litang candidate successfully identified the possessions of the previous Dalai Lama. However, Tibetan sources indicate that the machinations of the Qing authorities emboldened the families of the other candidates, who now insisted on the drawing of lots from the

Golden Urn. These delays meant that the Litang candidate was not enthroned until 1822, but the additional proceedings did not change the outcome. Shakabpa even goes so far as to say that the Golden Urn was not actually employed, claiming that the regent had merely pretended to use it in order to satisfy the Ambans.[7]

Within a week of the 10th Dalai Lama's ratification, the 4th Panchen Lama performed the tonsure ceremony and gave the youth the religious name Ngawang Lopsang Jampel Tsultrim Gyatso [ngag dbang 'jam dpal tshul khrims rgya mtsho] ངག་དབང་ བློ་བཟང་འཇམ་དཔལ་ཚུལ་ཁྲིམས་རྒྱ་མཚོ་ (1816–1837). He received his monastic vows from the Panchen Lama the following month. Lopsang Trinle Namgyel བློ་བཟང་འཕྲིན་ལས་རྣམ་རྒྱལ་ [blo bzang 'phrin las rnam gyal] (b. 19th century), a well-regarded scholar-monk from Sera Me Monastery, was appointed as one of his principal tutors, a post he would also hold for the 11th Dalai Lama. Other significant tutors included Ngawang Chöpel ངག་དབང་ཆོས་འཕེལ་ [ngag dbang chos 'phel] (1760–1839), the 70th Throne Holder of Ganden, as well as the regent Ngawang Jampel Tsultrim Gyatso, who would later become the 73rd Throne Holder of Ganden.

Throughout the remainder of the 1820s the *kashak* oversaw a variety of governmental reforms concerning taxation, regional population censuses, and the like. The Lhasa government also had to intervene in several local disputes in Tibet and in neighboring Bhūtān. In that same decade the Dalai Lama commenced his basic religious and scholastic training. He also undertook a tour of various monasteries, spending a particularly prolonged period of time at Sera Monastery. Early in the 1830s he commenced his studies of the great Indian treatises.

During 1834 and 1835 an epidemic raged around Lhasa, and as a consequence the Dalai Lama was confined to the Potala Palace. When the Panchen Lama was invited to Lhasa for the Dalai Lama's ordination ceremony, he stayed at Norbulingka Palace until the actual event. In order to limit the Dalai Lama's potential exposure, the ritual itself was conducted at the nearby Trungrab Temple. Despite these stringent health precautions the 10th Dalai Lama, never vital and healthy, became acutely ill in 1837. He did not suffer a great deal of pain, but he entirely lost his appetite and became short of breath. Although medicines were administered, he did not improve. Religious ceremonies were conducted in the hopes of averting his death and doctors examined him. When his attendants supplicated him to remain alive, he replied:

> As you perform extensive prayers, good results will come because of the great merit. However, as the saying goes, you can only build a statue to the extent that you have material.[8]

As he spoke, the regent, the ministers, and the Dalai Lama's personal attendants prayed for his well-being. Nonetheless, at the age of twenty-two, he died. Extensive services were offered on his behalf and he was implored to return swiftly in his next incarnation. Emissaries from Bhūtān, China, and Nepāl arrived later to make funerary offerings.

1838–1855
THE ELEVENTH DALAI LAMA, KEDRUP GYATSO
མཁས་གྲུབ་རྒྱ་མཚོ་

The regent Ngawang Jampel Tsultrim Gyatso began searching for the new incarnation of the Dalai Lama in 1840. Investigative parties were dispatched to Kham in eastern Tibet, among other places. The dignitaries received news of a remarkable child that had been born in late 1838 near Gartar Monastery. When the party reached central Tibet in 1841, the boy passed the customary tests before the Panchen Lama, the regent, the *kashak*, and the lamas and incarnations of the Drepung, Sera, and Ganden monasteries. The identification of the child was confirmed by use of the Golden Urn, though it is unclear if any rival candidates were in the running. The 11th Dalai Lama was received at the Potala Palace by a large array of Qing and Tibetan officials and lamas, including the 4th Janggya Yeshe Tenpe Gyaltsen ལྕང་སྐྱ་ཡེ་ཤེས་བསྟན་པའི་རྒྱལ་མཚན་ [lcang skya ye shes bstan pa'i rgyal mtshan] (b. 18th century), who brought the congratulations of the Daoguang 道光 emperor (1782–1850). In 1842 the 4th Panchen Lama performed the tonsure ceremony and bestowed on the child the monastic name Kedrup Gyatso མཁས་གྲུབ་རྒྱ་མཚོ་ [mkhas grub rgya mtsho] (1838–1855).

In addition to the Panchen Lama and Lopsang Trinle Namgyel, the 11th Dalai Lama's teachers included the 72nd Throne Holder of Ganden, Jampel Tsultrim འཇམ་དཔལ་ཚུལ་ཁྲིམས་ ['jam dpal tshul khrims] (b. 18th century); Ngawang Lopsang Tenpe Gyaltsen ངག་དབང་བློ་བཟང་བསྟན་པའི་རྒྱལ་མཚན་ [ngag dbang blo bzang bstan pa'i rgyal mtshan] (1811–1848), who was the reincarnation of

89 The Tenth Dalai Lama. Detail of plate 81.

Tatsak Tenpe Gönpo, the 8th Dalai Lama's regent; and Yeshe Gyatso ཡེ་ཤེས་རྒྱ་མཚོ་ [ye shes rgya mtsho] (1789–1856). Many of the people who were most influential in the 11th Dalai Lama's life had strong connections to Sera Me Monastery.

The new Dalai Lama was enthroned at a tumultuous time, for by 1841 tensions between Ladakh and Kashmir had spilled over the Himalayas. The Sikh King Gulab Singh and his general Zorowar Singh had conquered Ladakh, and eventually Sikh and Ladakhi troops marched into western Tibet. The Tibetans found themselves caught in the middle of a struggle beyond their control, as the invasion became part of a larger contest not only between British and Qing commercial, military, and territorial interests but also between those interests and the British efforts to pacify relations with north Indian kings and the Gurkha kingdom in Nepāl. Tibet could only hope to avoid becoming more deeply involved in these evolving power relationships.

As the situation deteriorated, the regent Ngawang Jampel Tsultrim Gyatso, who had been serving in that capacity since 1819, gradually lost the confidence of the Tibetan elite. Finally, in mid-1844, he was deposed for malfeasance. He had acquired a large number of powerful opponents, including the Panchen Lama and the Amban. Shakabpa asserts that the regent had alienated the common people by having pretended to use the Golden Urn in the selection of the 10th Dalai Lama, thereby establishing a precedent that resulted in its use in the selection

90 The Eleventh Dalai Lama. Statue at the Potala (Trungrab Lhakhang).

of the 11th Dalai Lama. There is also a suggestion that there may have been some financial improprieties. For all of these reasons, the regent's monastic estate was seized and he was detained elsewhere, though monks from Sera Me Monastery eventually rescued him and sheltered him in their monastery. While the transition was in process, the Panchen Lama took over as regent for about eight months. Then, in mid-1845, Reting Ngawang Yeshe Tsultrim Gyaltsen རྭ་སྒྲེང་ངག་དབང་ཡེ་ཤེས་ཚུལ་ ཁྲིམས་རྒྱལ་མཚན་ [rwa sgreng ngag dbang ye shes tshul khrims rgyal mtshan] (1816–1863) was appointed regent at the behest of the *kashak* and the Tibetan National Assembly.

In 1846 the Panchen Lama presided over the Dalai Lama's ordination at the Jokhang Temple in Lhasa. In 1848 the youth took up residence in Norbulingka Palace, which had recently been expanded and refurbished, and by 1852 the Dalai Lama had commenced his formal education at the great Geluk monasteries. The 4th Panchen Lama died the following year at the advanced age of seventy.

Between 1852 and 1854 the young Dalai Lama toured many of the most important monasteries in central and western Tibet, including Tibet's first monastery, Samye, which was then being restored. In the beginning of 1855 the 11th Dalai Lama assumed religious and political authority. This was the first time a Dalai Lama had ruled without a regent since the 8th Dalai Lama's brief tenure from 1786 until 1790. Before the year was over, however, the Dalai Lama became ill. Oracles were consulted, medicines administered, and prayers performed, but these measures were not sufficient to prevent his death. He was just seventeen years old.

1856–1875
THE TWELFTH DALAI LAMA, TRINLE GYATSO
འཕྲིན་ལས་རྒྱ་མཚོ

Soon after the death of the 11th Dalai Lama, Reting Ngawang Yeshe Tsultrim was asked to come out of retirement and reassume the duties of the regency, a position he would hold until his death in 1863. The Reting incarnation's first order of business was to reach a settlement with the Gurkhas. The old tensions with Nepāl had been re-ignited, partly because the Nepalese were attempting to transfer opium through Tibet and partly because they had been emboldened by the closer ties they had developed with the British in India. When the Gurkhas had invaded western Tibet, the Tibetans were unable to eject them. Neither Tibetan nor Qing negotiators were able to reach a favorable agreement with the aggressors. Ultimately, the Tibetans consented to rather one-sided terms that required the payment of an annual indemnity of 10,000 rupees. Both the Gurkhas and the Tibetans used the treaty to register their claims not to be under the jurisdiction of the Qing emperor.[9]

Meanwhile, the regent focused on identifying the 12th incarnation of the Dalai Lama. Three children came to his notice. In 1857 the three were brought to Lhasa, where senior ecclesiastical and governmental authorities examined them at Norbulingka Palace according to traditional methods. A ten-month-old boy from Olga correctly identified objects belonging to the previous Dalai Lama, thereby gaining decisive favor among the examiners. People had great confidence that he was indeed the reincarnation, but the Golden Urn Lottery was performed nevertheless, and the public was extremely relieved when the boy's name was drawn. The regent ceremonially cut a lock of the child's hair and bestowed upon him the name Lopsang Tenpe Gyaltsen Trinle Gyatso བློ་བཟང་བསྟན་པའི་རྒྱལ་མཚན་འཕྲིན་ལས་རྒྱ་མཚོ་ [blo bzang bstan pa'i rgyal mtshan 'phrin las rgya mtsho] (1856–1875). The child was formally enthroned in 1860. His earliest education began under his tutor, Lopsang Khenrap Wangchuk བློ་བཟང་མཁྱེན་རབ་དབང་ཕྱུག [blo bzang mkhyen rab dbang phyug] (d. 1872), the 76th Throne Holder of Ganden.

While this was happening, the regent became embroiled in a serious power struggle with the *kashak*, who felt his orders encroached on their authority. The *kashak* asked the regent to deposit his official seals with the Keeper of the Seals, noting that this practice was followed even by the Dalai Lama. An ally aroused the regent's fears by suggesting the *kashak* meant to depose him. *Kashak* Minister Shedra Wangchuk Gyalpo འཤད་ སྒྲ་དབང་ཕྱུག་རྒྱལ་པོ [bshad sgra dbang phyug rgyal po] (1795–1864) was blamed and sent into internal exile at Gyelje Tsel Monastery. Monks from the Ganden and Drepung monasteries rose to the minister's defense, while monks from the regent's Sera Monastery were deployed to guard the regent's estate. Because of the widespread tension among the monks, the Mönlam Chenmo Festival had to be suspended in 1862. Meanwhile, Shedra was publicly criticizing the regent. As the two sides became more polarized, some younger monks from Ganden and Drepung attacked the regent's home. He was eventually compelled to flee to China, and in his stead the *kashak* minister was appointed regent, in which role he was known as Desi Shedra.[10] The exiled former regent Reting was eventually permitted to return to retirement in Tibet, but he died on his way back from China.

In 1864 the Dalai Lama received the monastic vows from his tutor at the Jokhang Temple. Later that year the regent Desi Shedra died in Norbulingka Palace. The *kashak*, the Dalai Lama, and the Tibetan National Assembly appointed the tutor Lopsang Khenrap Wangchuk as the new regent. However, the Dalai Lama's personal attendant Pelden Döndrup དཔལ་ལྡན་དོན་གྲུབ [dpal ldan don grub] (d. 1871), a particularly strong personality, challenged the regent for power. With the support of the anti-Reting factions at Ganden and Drepung monasteries, Pelden aspired to supplant not only the regent but also the Dalai Lama and the Panchen Lama. He was opposed by the *kashak* ministers. When they tried to warn the regent of Pelden's scheming, at least one of them was murdered. The regent and the remaining ministers secretly attempted to arrest Pelden, but he got wind of the plan and fled to Drepung. As he was attempting to flee onward to Kham, he was killed.

After serving for nearly a decade, the regent-tutor died in 1872. In early 1873, at the age of seventeen, the Dalai Lama assumed nominal power over the government, but he was still assisted by Purbujok Lopsang Jampa Gyatso ཕུར་བུ་ལྕོག་བློ་བཟང་བྱམས་པ་རྒྱ་ མཚོ [phur bu lcog blo bzang byams pa rgya mtsho] (1825–1901), the future tutor of the 13th Dalai Lama. In 1875, five days after a total solar eclipse, the Dalai Lama became ill. Just two weeks later, he passed away at the age of nineteen.

As we saw in the previous chapter, the Qing *Twenty-Nine Article Imperial Ordinance* envisioned having Dalai Lamas and Panchen Lamas selected by the Golden Urn method. This was a key element in the assertion of Qing control over that distinctive Tibetan religio-political institution. The institution of the lottery method of selecting high incarnations was ostensibly meant to depoliticize the process. However, it also stood as a potent symbol of Qing control. A popular saying describes the Golden Urn as being like honey on a razor's edge. We have seen that the Tibetans were acutely aware of the symbolic importance of maintaining control over the process of selecting incarnations, and they resisted Qing interference as feverishly as the Ambans encouraged it. In the end, the Golden Urn was used at most in the selection of the 10th, 11th, and 12th Dalai Lamas. It was also employed in the identification of some of the Panchen Lamas. However, it seems never to have overturned the traditional Tibetan selection methods.

The Qing had hoped Golden Urn procedure would legitimize their control over events in Tibet by capturing the potency imbedded in the highly charged symbolic person of the Dalai Lama. In this institution the Qing emperor was represented as authenticating the identification of the Dalai Lama, just as the Qing Empire itself was represented as guaranteeing Tibet as a whole. Accordingly, Qing pronouncements, decrees, and histories from this period presume that Tibet had been unambiguously assimilated into the Empire, though the precise moments and means of this incorporation were never entirely clear. From then onward, the Qing government and later the Communist Party has sought to manipulate the symbols of reincarnation to their advantage, even as recently as the identification of the 8th Panchen Lama in the 1990s

The early deaths of the four Dalai Lamas discussed in this chapter denied the Tibetan people their most lively and potent symbol of Tibetan identity at a time when external pressures were threatening to tear Tibet apart. While the Qing, the Gurkhas, the British, and, more remotely, the Russians, jockeyed for position in the great game of diplomacy, the Tibetan public continually had to suspend and then transfer their allegiance—and thereby their national aspirations—as their beloved boy leaders died one after another. Nevertheless, the continued symbolic vitality of the institution was evidenced as, time and again, the Tibetans repeatedly invested their hopes in the new incarnations. Their hopes were ultimately fulfilled in the person of the Great 13th Dalai Lama.

"The Dalai Lama was about five feet six inches in height. His complexion was the darker hue of one who is lowly born. The nose was lightly aquiline. The large well-set ears were a sign that he was an incarnation of Chenrezik. Eyebrows curved high and a full moustache with the ends well waxed, accentuated the alertness of the administrator, rather than the priest meditating apart. His dark-brown eyes were large and very prominent. They lit up as he spoke or listened, and his whole countenance shone with a quiet eagerness. He had small, neat hands and the closely shaven head of the priest." (Charles Bell)[1]

THE THIRTEENTH DALAI LAMA **THUPTEN GYATSO**

ཐུབ་བསྟན་རྒྱ་མཚོ

Tsering Shakya ཚེ་རིང་དབང་འདུས

The British political officer Sir Charles Bell wrote the description to the left of the 13th Dalai Lama when he met him in 1910. At the time the Dalai Lama was thirty-four and had come to Dārjīliṅ in India after the Chinese invasion of Tibet. The Thirteenth is one of the few Dalai Lamas about whom we know a great deal, in part due to the fact that he lived to maturity. The early 20th century was a time when Tibet came into contact with the outside world whose events began to have an effect on Tibetan affairs. The reign of the 13th Dalai Lama was a turbulent period in the modern history of Tibet. According to the *namthar* རྣམ་ཐར [rnam thar] "biography" of the 13th Dalai Lama, when the 12th Dalai Lama Trinle Gyatso འཕྲིན་ལས་རྒྱ་མཚོ ['phrin las rgya mtsho] died at the young age of nineteen in 1875, his face turned toward the southeast. This *namthar* also tells us that after attendants placed the late Dalai Lama's body in a wooden box in preparation for mummification, when they returned and opened the box a few days later, his head had also turned in the direction of the southeast. This indicated that the next incarnation would be born in that direction.[2]

DISCOVERY AND ENTHRONEMENT

The Nechung གནས་ཆུང [gnas chung] Oracle confirmed the southeast as the direction in which lay the new Dalai Lama's birthplace, which another divination, the 5th Panchen Tenpa Wangchuk པཎ་ཆེན་བསྟན་པའི་དབང་ཕྱུག [paṇ chen bstan pa'i dbang phyug], did confirm. When the Nechung Oracle was consulted a third time, the oracle gave more precise details and foretold the names of the parents—the father's name would be Künga and the mother's name Dolma. The Regent Kündeling Chökyi Gyaltsen ཀུན་བདེ་གླིང་ཆོས་ཀྱི་རྒྱལ་མཚན [kun bde gling chos kyi rgyal mtshan] and the *kashak* བཀའ་ཤག [bka' shag] "cabinet" appointed the aged abbot of Gyutok Monastery, Khensur Lopsang Dargye མཁན་ཟུར་བློ་བཟང་དར་རྒྱས [mkhan zur blo bzang dar rgyas], to head a search party to find the new Dalai Lama. Following custom, Khensur Lopsang Dargye went to the holy lake of Lhamo Lhatso to seek a vision of the location and any other revelations on the Dalai Lama. On the surface of the lake, Lopsang Dargye saw a vision of a hamlet where a couple were bringing a child out from a house and saying that he was the Dalai Lama. The boy blessed the Khensur by touching his forehead. Later, when Khensur Lopsang Dargye arrived at the village he was able to recognize it from the vision he had seen on the surface of the lake.[3]

The 13th Dalai Lama was born on 27 May 1876. Many auspicious signs accompanied his birth. A year earlier, an earthquake had struck the Dakpo area and all the houses in the village where the Dalai Lama was born were destroyed or badly damaged. The house of the future Dalai Lama, however, remained intact. At first this was seen as inauspicious, but a lama told the family that this was an auspicious sign. Before the child was born, his mother had many dreams foretelling the birth of the Dalai Lama: in one dream, a woman dressed in the finery of an aristocratic Lhasa lady visited the house and offered them a *khatak* "white scarf"; in another, the mother discovered a white conch shell in a pond near the house. The Dalai Lama's *namthar* tells us the lady in the dream was Jetsün Dolma, and the conch shell represents the spread of the Buddha's teachings far and wide. In another dream, his mother had a vision of a prayer flag stretching from the top of their house to the Potala in Lhasa. Just before the child was born, a tree in front of the house began to flower even though it was not the season. On the twenty-fifth day of the third month of the Year of the Fire Mouse (1876), a rainbow appeared and a mysterious bright light shone over the house. A week later on the fifth day of the fourth month, the child was born at sunrise. That day there was a light rain, which was seen as auspicious. According to tradition, *drangchar* སྦྲང་ཆར [sbrang char] "light rain" always foretells good fortune because this drizzling rain is beneficial to all beings by nourishing the soil while not harming insects.

The *namthar* describes the infant boy as having a fair complexion, a parasol-like head, and shining black hair with a single strand of white hair in the center.[4] When the child was two, the search party Khensur Lopsang Dhargye led arrived in the village of Langdün གླང་མདུན [glang mdun] "Elephant Front" in the Dakpo area situated near a mountain in the shape of an elephant—hence the name. According to the *namthar*, the village was blessed with the ten perfections. Dakpo has also been associated with many religious figures, notably Gampo Pala Özhönnu སྒམ་པོ་པ་ཟླ་འོད་གཞོན་ནུ [sgam po pa zla 'od gzhon nu] (1079–1153), chief disciple of Jetsün Milarepa རྗེ་བཙུན་མི་ལ་རས་པ [rje btsun mi la ras pa] who was also known as Dakpo Lhaje དགས་པོ་ལྷ་རྗེ [dags po lha rje]. Tradition holds that the Dalai Lama's mother was a descendant of Gampo Pala's family.[5] Khensur Lopsang Dargye recalled the Nechung Oracle's pronouncement and recognized the landscape from the vision he had had at Lhamo Lhatso.

Lopsang Dargye examined the boy and saw his resemblance to the five-month-old boy he had seen on the surface of the holy lake. Lopsang Dargye thought this boy was slightly fatter than the boy he had seen in the vision. Later, other members of the search party visited the boy's house. When the young boy saw Jangchup Namdrol བྱང་ཆུབ་ཕྱུག་རྣམ་གྲོལ་ [byang chub rnam grol], the secretary of the *kashak*, he smiled and instinctively touched the forehead of each member of the search party. Each time the search party visited the boy's house, a rainbow appeared over it, indicating it as the birthplace of the Dalai Lama. The boy could recite many mantras by the age of two without having been taught. The search party was certain that they had found the right boy and reported to the regent in Lhasa who informed the Nechung Oracle with the search party's initial findings. On hearing the names of the parents, the Nechung Oracle immediately pronounced the boy from Dakpo as the Dalai Lama.

Since there were no other candidates, the regent submitted the boy's name and the details of his discovery to the Manchu emperor, who endorsed the boy as the 13th Dalai Lama. The young boy and his parents were brought to Lhasa in the company of an escort of a hundred Tibetan soldiers and monks. The party rested at Tshe Gungtang, a monastery fifteen miles outside of Lhasa, for three months while the city prepared to welcome the new Dalai Lama. The regent, the members of the *kashak*, the abbots of the three great monasteries, the Manchu Amban 安班, and Gorkha Vikal all came to pay their respects to the Dalai Lama while he was at Tshe Gungtang.

The new Dalai Lama's impending arrival caused great excitement in Lhasa. Every building in the city was painted with fresh coats of whitewash and rooftops were strung with new prayer flags. On the fourth day of the first month of the Year of the Tiger (1878), the Panchen Lama arrived to perform the naming ceremony. A few days later the new Dalai Lama also arrived with great pomp and ceremony and was taken to the Potala Palace. On the eleventh day of the first month of the Year of the Tiger (1878), the Panchen Lama performed the *tsüphü* གཙུག་ཕུད་ [gtsug phud] "tonsure" ceremony and bestowed on him the name Jetsün Ngawang Lopsang Thupten Gyatso Jikdral Wangchuk Chokle Namgyal Pelzangpo རྗེ་བཙུན་ངག་དབང་བློ་བཟང་ཐུབ་བསྟན་རྒྱ་མཚོ་འཇིགས་བྲལ་དབང་ཕྱུག་ཕྱོགས་ལས་རྣམ་རྒྱལ་དཔལ་བཟང་པོ་ [rje btsun ngag dbang blo bzang thub bstan rgya mtsho 'jigs bral dbang phyug phyogs las rnam rgyal dpal bzang po], although the 13th Dalai Lama generally came to be known by the abbreviated name, Thupten Gyatso ཐུབ་བསྟན་རྒྱ་མཚོ་ [thub bstan rgya mtsho].

The young Dalai Lama's family was ennobled and took the name Yapzhi Langdün ཡབ་གཞིས་གླང་མདུན་ [yab gzhis glang mdun]. As customary, the Manchu emperor gave the father of the Dalai Lama the title of *Gong* 公. The young Dalai Lama spent his early childhood in the Potala Palace during the winters and in Norbulingka Palace during summers, while the monk officials who had served the 12th Dalai Lama surrounded him. His formal enthronement took place on the first of August 1879. When he reached the age of six, his formal religious training began with the taking of the *getsul* "novice monk" vows, also known as the thirty-six precepts of a novice monk. Regent Kündeling was appointed as his senior tutor and the learned lama Phurcok Jampa Gyatso ཕུར་ལྕོག་བྱམས་པ་རྒྱ་མཚོ་ [phur lcog byams pa rgya mtsho] (1824–1894) of Sera Monastery, who had served as tutor to the 12th Dalai Lama, was appointed as junior tutor to guide and educate the young Dalai Lama, who became close to and held in great affection this junior tutor. Later the Dalai Lama was to write, "the kindness of my teacher cannot be repaid even at the cost of heaps of jewelry filling the three worlds."[6] The Dalai Lama wrote a moving biography of his teacher after his death.

Formality and a strict regime of learning governed the Dalai Lama's early years. Elderly monks attended him, teaching him to read and write. As he became proficient, Phurcok began formal instruction in the Buddhist scriptures. Before he attained his majority, Regent Kündeling undertook the day-to-day functioning of government until his death in 1886. Kündeling was succeeded by Regent Demo Ngawang Lopsang Trinle Rapgye དེ་མོ་ངག་དབང་བློ་བཟང་འཕྲིན་ལས་རབ་རྒྱས་ [de mo ngag dbang blo bzang 'phrin las rab rgyas]. During his childhood, the Dalai Lama suffered from various illnesses, the most serious in 1882 when there was a smallpox epidemic in Lhasa. According to his biography, he also suffered during the epidemic but recovered.

POLITICAL AFFAIRS

A major problem Tibet faced during the early years of the 13th Dalai Lama's reign was the menace of the British in India. The Tibetans became increasingly aware of British interest in their country and the strengthening of their rule in the Himalayan foothills. The British established a protectorate

over Sikkim and in 1885 sought permission from the Chinese government to send a mission to Lhasa. Colman Macaulay led a British mission, which arrived with a military escort at the frontier of Sikkim and Tibet, although the Tibetans refused to allow them to enter the country. There was nothing the British or the Chinese could do in the face of the Tibetan refusal. The Tibetans saw Macaulay and his military escort as proof of British readiness to invade Tibet. The *namthar* of the Dalai Lama details the anxiety felt in Lhasa which led the Tibetan government to mobilize a new army. The government brought in a thousand soldiers from Dagyap བྲག་གཡབ་ [brag g.yab] in Kham.

In 1880, nine hundred Tibetan soldiers went to the border with Sikkim. The army moved into Lungthar རླུང་ཐར་ [rlung thar], a high pass between Sikkim and Tibet, which the Tibetans regarded as part of their country. Yet the British demanded that the Tibetans withdraw, claiming the area was part of Sikkim. After the Tibetans refused, in March 1888, the British attacked the Tibetan camp and drove the Tibetans out of the area. This was the first armed clash between the Tibetans and the highly mechanized British army. In 1890 in Dārjīliṅg, the British and the Chinese signed a treaty, the "Anglo-Chinese Convention Relating to Sikkim and Tibet," which granted the British the right to trade, send missions to Tibet, and fixed the frontier between Tibet and Sikkim. Yet the Tibetans ignored any agreement signed between China and Britain regarding Tibet.

When the Dalai Lama was thirteen, he recorded that a black man visited him in a dream and told him that he would face many difficulties and that he would be forced to travel to Mongolia, China, and India.[7] This man further prophesied that the Thirteenth would live longer than any other Dalai Lama. This was indeed an uncanny prophecy: as we know, the Dalai Lama was later exiled to the countries foretold in the dream.

Until age twenty, the 13th Dalai Lama devoted himself to religious studies and refused to assume political power despite repeated requests. Generally, a Dalai Lama assumes political power at eighteen but the 13th Dalai Lama told the *kashak* that he wanted to wait until he had completed his religious studies. Traditionally the Panchen Lama administers these vows. However, at the time, the 6th Panchen Lama was too young to initiate the Dalai Lama into the *saṅgha*. On the first day of the eighth month of the Year of the Wood Sheep (1895), the abbots and monks of the three great monasteries gathered in the Jokhang. Phurcok Rinpoche presided and the Dalai Lama took the *gelong* དགེ་སློང་ [dge slong] vow, which requires observing two hundred and fifty-three precepts.

This marked the completion of the Dalai Lama's formal religious training. Now he could no longer avoid his responsibility to take political power. The public was also concerned that he had not assumed power two years earlier and began to voice their concerns. The general assembly was convened, which all the nobility and abbots of the three great monasteries attended. In their meeting, they called unanimously for the Dalai Lama to assume political power. The Dalai Lama himself responded by saying that the British threat had not yet passed, and as the country still faced danger, that more experienced leaders should administer it. He also told the assembly and the *kashak* to consult the Nechung Oracle first, but that he would follow the oracle's guidance.

The government did consult the Nechung Oracle, who while in trance held out a *khatak* and told the members of the *kashak* who had come to consult him to take it to the Dalai Lama, which indicated that the time had come for the him to reign the country. The Nechung Oracle's pronouncement was final. On the eighth day of the eighth month of the Year of the Wood Sheep (1895), a ceremony was held in the Potala Palace marking the Dalai Lama's assumption of spiritual and temporal power over Tibet.

The first two years of the new Dalai Lama's reign passed peacefully—his biography mainly records visits to monasteries and the recognition he conferred on other lamas. In 1896 the Governor of Sichuan, Lu Chuanlin 鹿傳霖, launched an attack on eastern Tibet and attempted to gain control of the Nyarong ཉག་རོང་ [nyag rong] region, which Lhasa governed. Zhou Wanshun 周萬順 led an army to attack a detachment of the Tibetan army in Nyarong and established Chinese control of the region. The Dalai Lama viewed this as the unilateral action of the governor of Sichuan and so dispatched to Beijing by sea via Kalkattā a secret mission which Sherap Chönphel ཤེས་རབ་ཆོས་འཕེལ་ [shes rab chos 'phel] led. This was a shrewd decision which circumvented the Chinese officials. The Manchu emperor readily agreed to the Dalai Lama's demand for the withdrawal of the Chinese soldiers from Nyarong and returned the territory to the direct rule of Lhasa.

92 The Thirteenth Dalai Lama on a throne with various ritual implements and sacrificial offerings on small tables to the left and right. In the left foreground is the protective goddess Palden Lhamo, to the right a form of the god of riches Vaiśravaṇa, in between a golden dharmacakra. An early example of the combined use of photography and painting: the head of the Thirteenth Dalai Lama is a (very faded) photo, while the rest has been painted in. Such images using a hybrid of photos and painting were also made later of the Thirteenth and Fourteenth Dalai Lama (see plate 126, 127 112, 128, 130). Miniature painting and photography (face), 10 x 7.7 cm, Collection of Lambert Verhoeven, Gouda.

93 Dharmacakra. Silver, partially gilded, decorated with rock crystals, Tibet/Mongolia?, 19th century, gift of the Thirteenth Dalai Lama to Tsar Nicholas II of Russia, H 51 cm, The State Hermitage Museum, St. Petersburg, Inv. No.: KO-884. >>> **94** Statue of the historic Buddha Śākyamuni sewn in cloth, with the seal of the Thirteenth Dalai Lama and inscription stating that this statue is a gift to Mr. Khodzolop (Koslov). The Thirteenth Dalai Lama probably gave the statue to Koslov, a Russian explorer, when he met the Dalai Lama in 1905 in Urga (Ulaan Baatar). Bronze, gilded, Tibet, 15th/16th century(?), H 11.5 cm, The State Hermitage Museum, St. Petersburg, Inv. No.: KO-12.

The *namthar* of the 13th Dalai Lama records that when he reached age twenty-four, he began to have recurring and disturbing dreams, which he wrote down. He consulted the Nyingma lama, Terton Sönam Gyalpo གཏེར་སྟོན་བསོད་ནམས་རྒྱལ་པོ་ [gter ston bsod nams rgyal po], who had discovered many hidden treasures and texts from these dreams. Terton Sönam Gyalpo saw these dreams as a irrefutable sign that the Dalai Lama's life was in danger.[8] The Nechung Oracle further confirmed this through his pronouncements. The Dalai Lama was advised to perform various rituals and good deeds to avert the danger to his life. In 1899, the Dalai Lama's tutor, Phurcok Rinpoche, advised him to take the *geshe lharampa* དགེ་བཤེས་ལྷ་རམས་པ་ [dge bshes lha rams pa] degree, the highest academic degree. On the seventh day of first month of the Year of Earth Pig (1899), the 13th Dalai Lama became the first Dalai Lama to obtain the degree of *geshe lharampa*.

THE CURSED BOOTS AND FLIGHT TO MONGOLIA

In 1894, the Dalai Lama's tutor, Phurcok Rinpoche, fell ill at age seventy-six. The Dalai Lama himself conducted the funeral rites and later wrote a moving biography of his teacher. According to Tibetan astrology, every thirteenth year is *kyek* སྐྱེག་ [skyeg] "obstructed." The year 1900 was seen as a particularly

dangerous year for the Dalai Lama, when he was twenty-five.

The Nechung Oracle repeated his prophecy that the Dalai Lama's life was in danger. That year the Dalai Lama was disposed to getting sick and began losing his appetite and started getting weak. He noticed his condition worsened whenever he wore the boots Terton Sönam Gyalpo had given him. When his retinue took apart the boots and examined them carefully, to their shock, they found a harmful mantra hidden in the sole of one of them. The government questioned Terton Sönam Gyalpo, who declared his innocence and said that when he put on the boots, he had a nosebleed. He told the officials the boots had been a gift from another lama from Nyarong who was renowned for his powers in black magic.

When that lama was interrogated, he confessed that the former regent, Demo Ngawang Lopsang Thrinle Rapgye, had recruited him. He confessed that he had hidden the mantra in the boot and that he had also buried mantras in the four corners of the Potala Palace and in Samye to harm the Dalai Lama. The government arrested Demo and members of his family. Under questioning, Demo admitted to attempting to eliminate the Dalai Lama through black magic in order to restore his own power.[9] The Demo's estates were confiscated and he was imprisoned in Lhasa. After the incident, the Dalai Lama went on a pilgrimage to the holy places of Tibet, most notably to Tsari in the south. In 1902 he ordained the 6th Panchen Lama, Chökyi Nyima ཆོས་ཀྱི་ཉི་མ་ [chos kyi nyi ma], in the Jokhang.

By 1900, the British government had started receiving reports from missionaries based in Tibet and on the Sikkim border that there were hundreds of Russian military advisors in Lhasa and that the Dalai Lama and the Tsar had formed a secret alliance. These reports alarmed Lord Curzon, Viceroy of India. In 1901, the Russian press reported the visit of the Buriyad Lama Dorjiev to St. Petersburg, which further fueled British suspicions. Dorjiev was a monk from Buryatia in the region of Lake Baikal who had first come to Lhasa in 1880 to study at Drepung, where it was customary for Mongolian monks to enroll at the Gomang College.[10] There he excelled in his studies and was appointed as a *tsenzhap* བཙན་ཞབས་ [btsan zhabs] "debating partner" to the Dalai Lama. As such, Dorjiev had ample opportunity to spend time with the Dalai Lama and it seems they soon established a close friendship. It was through Dorjiev that the Dalai Lama learned of Russia and its increasing influence in Central Asia. Tsar Nicholas and Empress Alexandra granted Dorjiev an audience.

For the Dalai Lama and the Tibetan government, this seemed a good time to establish closer relations with Russia. The Tibetans realized from their earlier clashes with the British at the Sikkimese frontier that China was in no position to come to their aid. Therefore, if they were to deter the British interest in Tibet, they had to establish contacts with other powers. In the summer of 1901, Dorjiev arrived in St. Petersburg with a letter from the Dalai Lama and one from the *kashak*. The Dalai Lama's letter was formal and expressed his appreciation of the treatment of the Tsar's Buddhist subjects. The *kashak*'s letter was explicit in soliciting Russian support against the British.[11] When the British learned of the purpose of Dorjiev's visit, they saw it as a serious threat to the security of British India.

Despite the fact that the Russians informed the British they would not intervene in Tibet, the British remained suspicious. At first the British demanded that the Chinese open up Tibet to them, but China was powerless to enforce any promise they made to the British. It finally dawned on the British that China lacked any real authority in Tibet. Lord Curzon decided to take a more direct approach by setting up a permanent British mission in Tibet to maintain British interests. Under the leadership of Colonial Francis Younghusband, the British mobilized over eight thousand soldiers in January 1904 and launched an invasion of Tibet from the Sikkimese frontier. The ill-equipped Tibetan army was no match for the well-trained British army. The Tibetans lost over a thousand men during the various battles. When it reached Lhasa, the news of the impending arrival of the invading army caused panic.

At that time the Dalai Lama was in the middle of three-year-long solitary mediation which prevented him from intervening in day-to-day state affairs. On the twelfth day of the sixth month, he came out of mediation. Several days earlier, the *Tsongdu* "National Assembly" had convened to discuss the situation. The majority members agreed that Tibet should fight the British to the last man. At the time, the senior-most *kalön* བཀའ་བློན་ [bka' blon] "minister" was Shatra, who argued that the Tibetans needed to reach a settlement with the British. He was one of the few Tibetan officials who had travelled outside Tibet and knew the strength of the British army. Some obstinate members of the *Tsongdu* accused Shatra of appeasement and accused him of being pro-British. The assembly decided unanimously to impeach four *kalöns* and imprison them. When the Dalai Lama came out of meditation and learned of their arrest, he immediately ordered their release.

The news reached Norbulingka that the British had arrived at Chakzham, a day's ride from Lhasa. On the night of the fifteenth day of the sixth month (30 July 1904), the Dalai Lama hurriedly appointed Gaden Thripa Lopsang Gyaltsen དགའ་ལྡན་ ཁྲི་པ་བློ་བཟང་རྒྱལ་མཚན་ [dga' ldan khri pa blo bzang rgyal mtshan] as regent. That night at midnight, the Dalai Lama fled Lhasa in the company of a few trusted servants. When the party arrived at Reting Monastery, the Dalai Lama changed into the costume of a wealthy Mongolian merchant and continued towards Ngachu in north Tibet. The journey proved arduous: on the plain of Jangthang, they encountered howling winds and were unable to pitch their tents, so that the Dalai Lama had to sleep in the open. After travelling for three months, the Dalai Lama and his party arrived in Urga, capital of Mongolia.

Apart from the close religious and cultural affinities between Mongolia and Tibet, serious political considerations influenced the Dalai Lama to decide to go to Mongolia. The first was that the Dalai Lama realized going to China would mean placing Tibet under further Chinese control. The second

95 Fear of Russia, shown here as an octopus attempting to seize parts of Europe and Asia, including Tibet, shown here as the yellow monk. Collection of Roger Denis, Bagnéres de Bigorre.

consideration was that following the advice of Dorjiev, who had accompanied the party, the Tibetans would be able to seek help from the Tsar from Urga. Thus soon after arriving in Urga, the Dalai Lama sent Dorjiev off to St Petersburg. When the Dalai Lama met Shishmaryov, the Russian Consul to Urga, he asked him directly whether Russia would protect Tibet from China and Britain.[12]

But Russia was facing more pressing problems at home and abroad and the Tsar was in no position to provide and help. The Russians had suffered a crushing defeat from the modernized Japanese navy in the Pacific in 1905, which precipitated the Russian Revolution of 1905. The Tsar could not afford to antagonize the British and the Chinese and so instructed his ambassador to Beijing to travel to Urga and meet with the Dalai Lama.

According to his *namthar*, the 13th Dalai Lama's stay in Urga caused a serious rift between him and Jetsün Dampa རྗེ་བཙུན་དམ་ པ་ [rje btsun dam pa], ruler of Mongolia. Every day hundreds of Mongolians sought blessings from the Dalai Lama and it appears his popularity exceeded that of Jetsün Dampa, who had personally refused to welcome him.[13] The increasing tension between the two high lamas along with the failure to receive any tangible support from the Tsar meant that the Dalai Lama could no longer stay in Urga.

For nearly two years thereafter, the Dalai Lama travelled through Amdo in northeastern Tibet giving teachings. There he visited Kumbum སྐུ་འབུམ་ [sku 'bum] Monastery, founded by the 3rd Dalai Lama Sönam Gyatso བསོད་ནམས་རྒྱ་མཚོ་ [bsod nams rgya mtsho] (1543–1588). While in Kumbum, the Dalai Lama

received a delegation from Lhasa urging him to return. He decided instead to go to Beijing to meet with the Empress Dowager Cixi 慈禧, who was the de facto ruler of China (plate 97). William Rockhill, scholar and American ambassador to China, witnessed the Dalai Lama's arrival in Beijing and later wrote "[the Dalai Lama] had been treated with all the ceremony which could have been accorded to any independent sovereign, and nothing can be found in Chinese works to indicate that he was looked upon in any other light."[14] This was the first formal contact between Tibet and the United States. The Dalai Lama presented Rockhill with a thangka of Tsongkhapa and a letter to President Roosevelt. After the meeting, Rockhill immediately wrote to President Roosevelt describing the meeting as "the most unique experience of [his] life."[15]

While in Beijing, the Chinese authorities tried to prevent the Dalai Lama from meeting foreign diplomats but the Tibetans were keen to establish contacts with Japan, whose standing as a major emerging power had risen since defeating the Russians. The Dalai Lama met the Japanese ambassador and a military advisor, who later sent military advisors to train and modernize the Tibetan army.

The Dalai Lama refused to meet with Chinese officials and insisted on discussing Tibetan affairs directly with the Empress Dowager, whom he met on 14 October 1908. Later that same day, the Dalai Lama met the young Emperor Xuantong 宣統 (Aisin-Gioro Puyi 愛新覺羅溥儀; 1906–1967). According to Rockhill, the Dalai Lama refused to *kowtow* before the young emperor.[16] The *namthar* of the 13th Dalai Lama does not mention this but states that when the Dalai Lama entered the imperial chamber,

96 The Thirteenth Dalai Lama is welcomed by Chinese military upon his arrival in Beijing in 1908. Mural, Potala, 1934–35(?). 97 The Thirteenth Dalai Lama visits the Empress Dowager Cixi in Beijing on 14 October 1908. Mural, Potala. Photographer: Michael Henss, Zürich.

the emperor rose from this throne to meet him but that the emperor's throne was raised slightly higher than his throne.[17] The Dalai Lama met with the Empress Dowager and the emperor several times. His *namthar* describes a close relationship between him and the Empress Dowager. When the Empress Dowager died in November 1908, the Dalai Lama performed funeral rituals and composed a long eulogy.

FLIGHT TO INDIA

On the ninth day of the eleventh month of the Year of the Earth Bird (1908), the Dalai Lama returned to Lhasa after nearly five years in exile. A few days after his arrival, a ceremony was held in the Potala Palace marking the formal handing over of power to the Dalai Lama. According to Tsepön Shakabpa རྩིས་དཔོན་ཞྭ་སྒབ་པ [rtsis dpon zhwa sgab pa], this signified the reassertion of native authority at a time when China was trying to claim control over Tibet.[18]

While in China, the Dalai Lama had received numerous reports about, and had seen for himself, Chinese attempts to gain control over Kham. The British invasion of Tibet and the contacts the 13th Dalai Lama established with foreign governments while he was in China alarmed the Chinese. In 1908, the Chinese government appointed the ruthless army officer Zhao Erfeng 趙爾豐 as Imperial Resident of Tibet. He was also given the task of bringing the Kham area under direct Chinese rule—he was brutal in his suppression of the Tibetan revolt in Kham, and put hundreds of Tibetans to death. According to his *namthar*, the Dalai Lama received a letter from the Amban in Tibet informing him of the appointment of Zhao Erfeng, and

which stated the Chinese would protect the religious authority of the Dalai Lama but made no mention of his political authority. Fearing that the Chinese planned to overthrow him as political ruler of Tibet, the Dalai Lama and the *kashak* sent a direct appeal to the Xuantong emperor from Kalkattā.

After facing fierce Tibetan resistance in Kham, Zhao and his army marched into Lhasa. After the British had annihilated the Tibetan army in 1904, the remnants of the Tibetan army were in no position to resist the invading Chinese army. The Chinese crushed the Tibetan resistance in Lhasa and took Yapzhi Phukhang ཡབ་བཞིས་ཕུན་ཁང [yab bzhis phun khang], head of the newly created Tibetan foreign office, as prisoner and killed two of his officials. The Dalai Lama decided to leave Lhasa because he feared there would be bloodshed with the public trying to protect him from the Chinese soldiers. On the night of the third day of the first Tibetan month, the Dalai Lama summoned Thri Rinpoche Ngawang Lopsang Tsemönling ཁྲི་རིན་པོ་ཆེ་ངག་དབང་བློ་བཟང་ཚེ་སྨོན་གླིང [khri rin po che ngag dbang blo bzang tshe smon gling] and appointed him regent, and then that night fled Lhasa in the company of members of the *kashak*. The next day when the Chinese learned of his flight, they sent an army to stop the party but the Dalai Lama managed to escape to India. According to his *namthar*, the Dalai Lama had planned to go to Beijing to negotiate with the emperor personally. Soon after arriving in India, however, he received a letter in which the emperor stated that he was powerless and had been deposed. By October 1910, Qing 清 rule in China had virtually collapsed and its authority severely restricted by the new government. For the new government under Yuan Shikai 袁世凱, Tibet was a lesser

98 Letter from the Thirteenth Dalai Lama to the ruling family of Nepāl in which the Dalai Lama expresses his hope that the friendship between Nepāl and Tibet may be eternal. Lhasa, no date, 120 x 93 cm, Collection of Wolfgang Hellrigl, Bozen. >>>

Monastery. The Chinese had arrested the ministers the Dalai Lama had appointed, and were threatening to execute some Tibetan officials.

With the Dalai Lama in India, the Chinese government realized they had miscalculated their policy. Far from strengthening their position, it had driven the Tibetans further into the British camp. Furthermore, Zhao Erfeng's army had antagonized the Tibetan populace, so the Chinese government rescinded Zhao's appointment as commissioner for Tibet. The Dalai Lama and his Tibetan party realized that the British were unwilling to assist the Tibetans actively against the Chinese. They decided that the Tibetans should organize a nationwide revolt. They secretly sent Dasang Damdül ཟླ་བཟང་དགྲ་འདུལ་ [zla bzang dgra 'dul], who had accompanied the Dalai Lama to Mongolia, to Lhasa to organize the revolt.

In 1911, the revolution in China caused chaos among the Chinese soldiers in Tibet—they mutinied and the Tibetans took advantage of the situation to gain control of the country. On the tenth day of the fifth month of the Year of the Water Mouse (1912), the Dalai Lama left for Tibet and a week later he arrived in Samding Monastery, where he remained for a month watching the situation in Lhasa. While at Samding he finally received a letter of surrender from the Chinese Amban.

The Panchen Lama came to meet the Dalai Lama at Ralung and on the sixteenth day of the eighth Tibetan month, the Dalai Lama entered Lhasa, where thousands lining the city streets welcomed him. Upon his return, he issued a proclamation that severed all ties with China and declared Tibet an independent country, saying that with the formation of a new government in China, the traditional relationship between two countries based on the *yönchö* ཡོན་མཆོད་ [yon mchod] "patron-spiritual teacher" model had "faded like a rainbow in the sky."[21] The Dalai Lama convened a special meeting of the *Tsongdu*. There he announced his decision to institute major reforms, and that the Amban and the Chinese army stationed in Tibet would be expelled. The *Tsongdu* also demanded that the Chinese that had settled in Tibet must leave within the next three years.

REFORMS AND MODERNIZATION

During his travels in Mongolia, China, and India the 13th Dalai Lama had witnessed changes in the world and realized how far Tibet lagged behind. He was therefore determined to bring

problem compared with the civil war he was facing at home.

In India, the British treated the Dalai Lama with great respect. Charles Bell, political officer in Sikkim, was appointed to look after him. Bell had been involved in Tibetan affairs since 1904 and was a fluent speaker of Tibetan. The British reception was a surprise to the Dalai Lama and his Tibetan party when they found that the British officers who dealt with Tibetan affairs were all fluent in Tibetan. This was in contrast to Chinese officials who were contemptuous of Tibetan culture and people.

The British found themselves in a predicament. The Tibetans were requesting direct military assistance, yet the Anglo-Russian agreement of 1907 forbade Britain from intervening in Tibet. Charles Bell writes, "The order came through from London that our attitude towards [the Dalai Lama] was to be one of neutrality."[19] He continues to say that when he delivered the message from the British government, the Dalai Lama "was so surprised and distressed that for a minute or two he lost the power of speech."[20] Without the tacit support of the British, the Dalai Lama had to rethink his strategies. While in India, the Dalai Lama received disastrous news that Chinese soldiers were looting Lhasa and were bent on attacking Sera

about political and social reforms—he established a new medical school, Mentsikhang སྨན་རྩིས་ཁང་ [sman rtsis khang], in Lhasa to improve the training of *amchi* "traditional medical doctors" and stated that every locality should have access to medical practitioners.

He sent four boys to study in England who returned to Tibet in the 1920s. Ringang, who had studied electrical engineering, installed the first power station in Tibet, and by 1924 the streets of Lhasa had electric lights. Gongkar, who had been trained as a military officer, began to train the Tibetan army. Kyibu, who had studied telegraphy, established a telegraph line from Lhasa to Gyantse, thus enabling Tibet to communicate with the outside world. In 1924, the Dalai Lama invited foreign advisors to Tibet to build schools and train the army. He appointed Frank Ludlow, inspector of schools in India, to set up a school in Gyantse modelled on English grammar schools. A Japanese military expert was appointed to train the Tibetan army and new military equipment was purchased from the British. The government established a communication system between parts of Tibet and introduced a government postal system for the first time. New paper currency was introduced to raise revenue for these modernizations.

After his return from India, the Dalai Lama was concerned not only with political matters: in the winter of 1913 he gave a major public teaching of the *lamrim chenmo* "Stages of the Path to Enlightenment," which hundreds of lamas and lay people attended. He also renovated the Jokhang and other temples in central Tibet, and sponsored the reprinting of important religious texts and established the Shol Printing Press in Lhasa, which later became the center of government printing not only for religious texts but for training manuals translated from Japanese, Russian, and English. In 1913, the Dalai Lama sent Lochen Shatra བློན་ཆེན་བཤད་སྒྲ་ [blon chen bshad sgra] to Śimla in India to attend a conference of representatives from China, Britain, and Tibet, whose main agenda was to define the boundary between Tibet and China. The Tibetans demanded the return of all Tibetan territories the Chinese were occupying in the Kham and Amdo regions. The British proposed the creation of Inner and Outer Tibet, which seemed to imply that the Dalai Lama was willing to surrender claims over territories east of the Drichu River in return for the tacit Chinese acceptance of Tibetan independence. Although all the

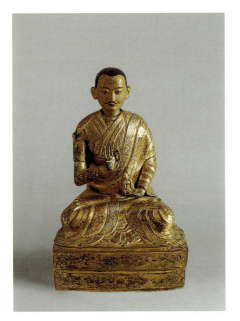  

100 The Thirteenth Dalai Lama. Bronze, gilded and pigmented, H 31 cm, W 20cm, D 18 cm, Collection of Claus-Peter Bach, Memmingen. **101** The Thirteenth Dalai Lama. Silver, partially gilded and pigmented, Tibet, 20th century, H 19.5 cm, Museum für Ostasiatische Kunst, Cologne, Inv. No.: Cd 77.1. **102** The Thirteenth Dalai Lama. Stucco and papier-mâché, Tibet, ca. 1900, H 23 cm, W 17 cm, D 13.5 cm, Collection of Enrico Bonfanti, Lucerne.

representatives initialled the final agreement, their respective governments never ratified it.

In 1917, fighting broke out between the Tibetan army and the Chinese troops in Chamdo. Under the command of *Kalön* Jampa Tender བཀའ་བློན་བྱམ་པ་བསྟན་དར་ [bka' blon byam pa bstan dar], the Tibetan army defeated the Chinese and reasserted Tibetan authority in most of Kham. Their success was largely due to the reforms and re-equipping the army that the Dalai Lama had carried out. The British, however, did not want to see Tibetan rule extended into Kham and refused to supply any more arms, thus halting Jampa Tender's progress.

The cost of the reforms and the war in Kham were enormous for the Tibetan government and the decision to increase government revenue was unpopular with the monasteries and wealthy estates. In order to pay for the larger Tibetan army, the government proposed that Tashilhünpo, the Panchen Lama's estate, should pay for one-quarter of its cost. In principle, Tashilhünpo agreed to continue to contribute as they had done in the past, but found it was a huge drain on their resources and never did. This lead to a serious strain in the relationship between Lhasa and Tashilhünpo, and so the Panchen Lama wrote the Dalai Lama asking for a personal meeting. The Dalai Lama responded by asking the Panchen Lama to come to Lhasa secretly with a small escort.[22] This alarmed Tashilhünpo officials, who feared that the Panchen Lama might be detained in Lhasa. In November 1923, in the company of few of Tashilhünpo officials, the Panchen Lama fled Shigatse and went into exile in China.

The *namthar* of the 13th Dalai Lama gives the impression that the personal relationship between the two was one of mutual admiration and respect, describing them as "sandalwood and its fragrance," one inseparable from the other. The Panchen Lama wrote to the Dalai Lama complaining that his religious training remained incomplete without receiving empowerment and initiations into various rites from the Dalai Lama. The relationship between the Dalai Lama and the Panchen Lama is complex: in religious terms, they are bound by the principle of "master and disciple." Yet their views on politics and secular affairs diverge seriously. The *namthar* says that they had differing opinions on the issue of taxation which led to the tensions between them. Whatever their personal relationship might have been, the flight of the Panchen Lama to China had disastrous consequences for Tibet. The Panchen Lama came under the influence of the Chinese government and never returned to Tibet.

The Dalai Lama was also facing opposition to his reforms. The school he established in Gyantse had to close because the monasteries saw it as an intrusion of foreign values that challenged their monopoly over the education of the young. They also feared the success of the schools would reduce the number of monks. Similarly, Mündro, who had been sent to England, returned after studying to become a mining engineer. He proposed developing goldmines in Tibet, but monk officials in the government argued that mining would disturb the spirit of the earth and the underworld.

103 a–c The Thirteenth Dalai Lama (possibly Rölpe Dorje?). Papier-mâché, polychrome, small wooden box, Mongolia, early 20th century, H 40 cm, W 28 cm, Collection of Joachim Baader, Munich. >>>

By the 1920s, Tibetan society started to change rapidly and new influences from outside the country were affecting people's lifestyles and habits. Fashionable people began to adopt western-style clothing and cigarettes became popular. In a policy that might be seen as far-sighted today, the Dalai Lama banned the importation of tobacco and ordered the customs office to seize cigarettes and tobacco. He also banned aristocrats from wearing western-style clothing, especially when attending government meetings and functions. He forbade ostentatious displays of wealth and aristocratic women from wearing expensive jewelry, saying that such displays created unnecessary envy and rivalry among the people. He then issued an order banning the slaughter of animals in Tibet; if this had been fully implemented, the Tibetans would have been forbidden to eat meat.

The Dalai Lama's religious practices were also a source of conflict with senior Geluk lamas. Like the 5th Dalai Lama, the Thirteenth was open-minded and accepted teachings from all schools of Tibetan Buddhism, undergoing initiations from Nyingma lamas as well as from other schools of Buddhism. This eventually led to conflict with one of the most influential Geluk lama, Pabongka Rinpoche པ་བོང་ཁ་རིན་པོ་ཆེ [pha bong kha rin po che], on the issue of the propitiation of Dorje Shukden རྡོ་རྗེ་ཤུགས་ལྡན [rdo rje shugs ldan].

In the end the Dalai Lama's reforms failed. His attempt to build a strong and well-trained army did not succeed, not only because of internal opposition but because the British refused to supply sufficient weapons. Further reforms could not be implemented because Tibet's feudal economy could not sustain the cost. This was illustrated when the Dalai Lama sent four boys in 1913 to be educated at Rugby, England's leading public school. The Tibetan government did not have the foreign currency to meet the school fees and had no means of raising hard revenue. The government's largest expenditure at the time was on religious services, any change to which the monastic community opposed.

As he neared the end of his life, the Dalai Lama became anxious about the fate of his country. During public sermons, he repeated the need for Tibet to change and be protected from foreign powers. A year before his death, he visited Reting Monastery, a few miles from Lhasa, where he departed from his usual religious teachings and told the gatherings mournfully, "I am talking as a father would advise his son." This introduction greatly perplexed the audience, which then became unusually attentive. His fatherly advice to his subjects became the famous last testament of the 13th Dalai Lama. He began by recounting his life and the troubles Tibet faced during his rule, then went on:

I am now in the fifty-eighth year of my life. Everyone must know that I may not be around for more than a few years to discharge my temporal and spiritual responsibilities. You must develop a good diplomatic relationship with our two powerful neighbours, India and China. Efficient and well-equipped troops must be

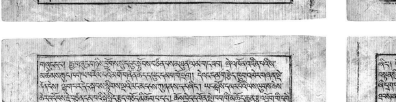

104 Four pages of the Thirteenth Dalai Lama's political testament. (pages 6 and 7, front and back of each). **105** Proclamation of the Thirteenth Dalai Lama "to all monks and laymen of the lower, middle, and higher classes living in Tibet," 1901, Library of Tibetan Works and Archives, Dharamśālā. >>>

stationed even on the minor frontiers bordering hostile forces. Such an army must be well trained in warfare as a sure deterrent against all adversaries.

Furthermore, this present era is rampant with the Five Degenerations, in particular the Red ideology. In Outer Mongolia, the search for the reincarnation of Jetsün Dampa was banned; the monastic properties and endowments were confiscated; the lamas and monks forced into the army; and the Buddhist religion destroyed, leaving no trace of identity. Such a system, according to the reports still being received, has been established in Ulaan Baatar.

In the future, this system will certainly be driven out, either from within or from without the land that cherishes the joint spiritual and temporal system. If in such an event we fail to defend our land, the holy lamas, including "the triumphant father and son [the Dalai and Panchen Lamas]" will be eliminated without a trace of their names remaining; the properties of the reincarnate lamas and of the monasteries along with their endowments for religious services will be seized. Moreover, our political system originating from the three ancient kings will be reduced to an empty name; my officials, deprived of their patrimony and property, will be subjugated as slaves for the enemies;

and my people subjected to fear and misery, will be unable to endure either day or night. Such an era will certainly come.[23]

The Dalai Lama had watched events in Mongolia after the Communist Revolution and refugees arriving in Lhasa told him of Stalin's repressive measures against Buriyads and Kalmyk Mongols. The Dalai Lama also saw the revolution in China as a threat to the well-being of Buddhism, and therefore saw these events as a danger to Tibet. He also realized that once the Chinese had gotten stronger, they would attempt to reclaim authority over Tibet. His prediction came true: under Communist rule, China enslaved Tibet and destroyed much of Tibet's cultural heritage with their barbaric policies.

On the thirteenth day of the tenth month of the Year of the Water Fowl (1933), the Dalai Lama became ill and began to suffer a coughing fit. A day later, he lost his appetite and became short of breath. Despite his illness, for several days he continued with his duties, meeting officials and monks. The Tibetans began to notice ominous signs that the Dalai Lama might not live much longer. There was an earthquake in Kongpo, and a fire destroyed Tsari Monastery, which the Dalai Lama had visited. In the western and eastern halls of the Potala was heard

the sound of a woman weeping, as had been reported at the time of the death of the 7th Dalai Lama. An owl perched on the roof of Nechung Monastery and hooted *ha ha ha* continually for two nights. The Dalai Lama's devoted servants began to worry and asked him the meaning of these phenomena. He replied that the portentous sound of the owl indicated that the time had come for him to depart his earthly existence. On the thirtieth day of the tenth Tibetan month the Dalai Lama lay down on his bed, feeling weak at midday. At seven-thirty in the evening, the Dalai Lama sat up and placed himself in a posture of meditation, closed his eyes, and departed from his earthly existence.

As noted in the introduction, the Thirteenth was one of two Dalai Lamas who lived to maturity and reigned over his subjects with full authority. His rule saw invasions from British India and China. It was also a time when Tibet was beginning to shape an international personality. He saw the need for Tibet to reform and establish a strong army. Looking back, we can see that he had foresight and his vision of an independent country was feasible. Those who met him saw him as an intelligent and politically aware figure, while the Tibetans who worked under him knew of his hot temper. Those who served him feared his constant scolding. He was generous to those he favored and who served him faithfully but ruthless towards his enemies. For example, after his return from India, Tsarong Shape was accused of collaborating with the occupying Chinese forces and was brutally beheaded along with his son at the foot of Potala. Another five government officials were executed in the same manner. Since the Dalai Lama did not intervene to save the lives of his officials, it must be assumed that he approved of these executions. Tsarong's estate was given to Dasang Damdül, who had served the Dalai Lama throughout his life and led the revolt against the Chinese in Lhasa in 1911.

The Dalai Lama also weakened his own reforms with some of his policies. Until the time of the 13th Dalai Lama, a monk could not serve in the *kashak*, thus barring them from interfering in the highest decision-making body of the government, but the Thirteenth allowed monks to become *kashak* members. Later, these monk officials in the *kashak* obstructed his reforms. Before the 13th Dalai Lama, there had been an unwritten consensus among the Tibetan ruling elite that no member of the current Dalai Lama's family could occupy a senior post in the government during the lifetime of that Dalai Lama. Yet in 1926,

the Dalai Lama appointed his nephew Langdün Künga Wangchuk ཀུན་དགའ་དབང་ཕྱུག [kun dga' dbang phyug] as one of the *silön* སྲིད་བློན་ [srid blon] "Prime Ministers" when he was only nineteen and lacked any experience in political affairs. This appointment left Tibet without an experienced and able leader.

The Thirteenth was also the first Dalai Lama to be photographed and he distributed hundreds of his photographs to the public. This brought a new sense of familiarity with him among the people. Only the Fifth rivals the Thirteenth in public estimation. When the golden tomb was built for his body, after much discussion it was agreed that the 13th Dalai Lama's tomb should be the largest and a fraction higher than the 5th Dalai Lama. This symbolized that no other Dalai Lama had matched the greatness of the Thirteenth.

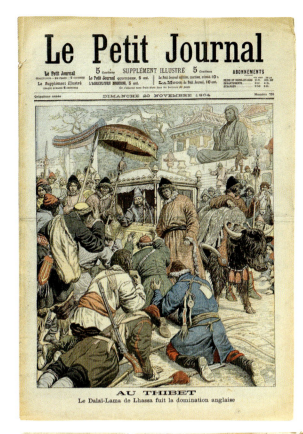

Le Petit Journal

AU THIBET
Le Dalaï-Lama de Lhassa fuit la domination anglaise

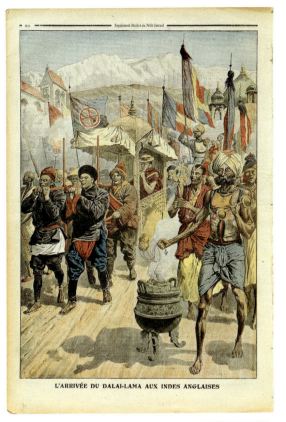

L'ARRIVÉE DU DALAI-LAMA AUX INDES ANGLAISES

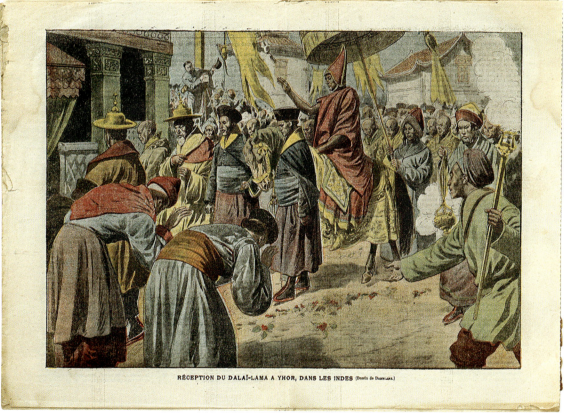

RÉCEPTION DU DALAÏ-LAMA A YHOR, DANS LES INDES (Dessin de Damblans.)

106 a–c Western depictions of the Thirteenth Dalai Lama. **a)** Le Petit Journal, Supplément illustré, 20 Nov. 1904, No. 731: "Au Thibet, Le Dalaï-Lama de Lhassa fuit la domination anglaise." **b)** Le Petit Journal, Supplément illustré, 20 March 1910, No. 1 009 : "L'arrivée du Dalaï-Lama aux Indes Anglaises." **c)** Le Pèlerin 21 March 1926 : "Réception du Dalaï-Lama à Yhor, dans les Indes." Ethnographic Museum of the University of Zürich (courtesy of Jean Lassale, Paris, and Roger Denis, Bagnéres de Bigorre).

107 The Thirteenth Dalai Lama by Ralung during his return to Tibet, July 1912. Photographer: Sonam W. Laden-La, © Collection of R.J. and E. Gould.   108 Khünphela and Tashi Döndrup, who were very close to the Thirteenth Dalai Lama, with one of his Baby Austin autos. In Dekyi-Lingka, on 20 Sept. 1933. Photographer: Sir Frederick Williamson, Cambridge University Museum of Archaeology and Anthropology (P.97071. WIL).   109 Portrait of the Thirteenth Dalai Lama during his exile in India. Kalkattā, ca. 1910. © The British Museum.

110 Portrait of the Thirteenth Dalai Lama. Photograph colored by a Tibetan artist. Kalkattā, 1910, Photographer: Sir Charles Alfred Bell Dirk: From: Bell, *Tibet – Einst and Jetzt*, Leipzig 1925, frontispiece.

111 Print of engraving. The Thirteenth Dalai Lama, in the Calcutta Museum surrounded by Tibetan officials, receives a gift of a stūpa with relics. During his exile in India. Kalkattā, March 1910, Collection of Roger Denis, Bagnéres de Bigorre.　　112 The Thirteenth Dalai Lama seated on his throne in a painting from the 1980s. Painter: Amdo Jampa.　　113 The Thirteenth Dalai Lama surrounded by high officials during his exile in India, ca. 1910. Photographer: anonymous, Sarah Central Archive.　　114 Portrait photograph of the Thirteenth Dalai Lama that served as the model for the painting above (plate 113). Lhasa, ca. 1932, Photographer: Leslie Weir. Collection of Maybe Jehu, London.

115 The Thirteenth Dalai Lama seated on a throne. In Norbulingka, ca. 1932, Photographer: Leslie Weir. Collection of Maybe Jehu, London.

116 The Thirteenth Dalai Lama at age fifty-six. 12 Sept. 1933, Photographer: Sir Frederick Williamson, Sir Charles Alfred Bell Collection. **117** Regent Reting Rinpoche and his servant in the garden of his summer palace. Lhasa, ca. 1936/37. Reting Rinpoche was the Fourteenth Dalai Lama's first main teacher. Photographer: Frederick Spencer Chapman, © Pitt Rivers Museum, University of Oxford, 2005. (1998.131.522). **118** Regent Reting Rinpoche, with two dogs in his garden, ca. 1940. Photographer: Hugh Richardson, © Pitt Rivers Museum, University of Oxford, 2005.(2001.59.18.14). **119** The Palace of Reting Rinpoche near Sera, Lhasa. Photographer: Frederick Spencer Chapman, © Pitt Rivers Museum, University of Oxford, 2005. (1998.131.512). **120** Regent Tadrak Rinpoche on his throne, ca. 1942/43. Before he became regent, he was the Fourteenth Dalai Lama's second main teacher. Photographer: Ilya Tolstoy, Collection of R.J. and E. Gould.

"I always pray: as long as space remains and as long as sentient beings' suffering remains, may I remain to dispel their suffering. So I pray that I am born somewhere where I will be useful." (Tenzin Gyatso)[1]

b. 1935

THE FOURTEENTH DALAI LAMA TENZIN GYATSO
བསྟན་འཛིན་རྒྱ་མཚོ་

Alexander Norman

The present Dalai Lama was born on or about 6 July 1935. As traditional Tibetan culture was far less time-conscious than is common today, the date may not be exact. It is certain, however, that on 23 August 1939, just over four years later, he was formally recognized as the longed-for reincarnation of the Precious Protector. His identification is reported to have been preceded by a multitude of portents indicating where he would be found. First, the seated corpse of the 13th Dalai Lama turned from south to east not once but twice as it awaited entombment. On several occasions, the state oracles of Nechung, Gadong, and Samye threw *khataks* "white scarves" toward the east. Most compelling of all, the regent, Reting Rinpoche རྭ་སྒྲེང་རིན་པོ་ཆེ་ [rwa sgreng rin po che], experienced a powerful vision at Lake Lhamo Lhatso, which is associated with Palden Lhamo, one of the Dalai Lamas' personal protective deities. In his vision Reting saw three letters of the alphabet, then a monastery with a three-tiered roof surmounted by a golden pagoda, and finally a single-story house with a flat, blue-colored roof. On the basis of these indications, the government dispatched three parties eastward to search for the new incarnation, one going southeast to the Kongpo region, one going due east to Kham, and one going northeast to Amdo. En route, the seekers travelling to Amdo received from the 9th Panchen Lama a highly favorable report of an infant he had met while staying at Kumbum monastery. This boy would eventually pass the identification tests conducted by Keutsang Rinpoche, and when he was ordained as a novice monk he would receive the name Jampel Ngawang Lopsang Tenzin Gyatso འཇམ་དཔལ་ངག་དབང་ བློ་བཟང་བསྟན་འཛིན་རྒྱ་མཚོ་ ['jam dpal ngag dbang blo bzang bstan 'dzin rgya mtsho].

From the moment he was identified, the 14th Dalai Lama's biography shifts decisively from the supernatural world to the natural. No sooner had the regent confirmed, via secret telegram, that this was indeed the boy being sought, then the child became caught up in political maneuverings. At the local level, for almost two years Ma Bufang 馬步芳, the Muslim warlord who had gained control of the Sino-Tibetan borderlands, kept the boy from travelling to Lhasa. At the national level, the nationalist Guomindang 國民党 government agreed to help the Tibetans persuade Ma to permit the boy to travel, but sought to impose conditions of its own, including the right to have a Chinese escort accompany the Dalai Lama on the journey to Lhasa. Rejecting these conditions, Lhasa finally obtained a travel permit for the child in exchange for two substantial bribes, one paid in cash and the other promised in due time.

The situation in the capital was no less complicated. Reting Rinpoche had been just twenty-two years old when he was appointed regent after the death of the 13th Dalai Lama in 1933. He was highly regarded for his spiritual attainments but a disastrous political leader. The high standards of probity and selfless devotion to duty set by the 13th Dalai Lama had, in the space of just six years, fallen away just as surely as the government's treasury had emptied and its grain reserves had been squandered. In the end, Reting resigned in 1942, apparently to avoid compromising the *getsul* "novice monk" vows he was about to confer on the young 14th Dalai Lama. It was an open secret that he had broken his own vow of celibacy, and he dared not stand accused of performing what would thus have been an invalid ceremony.

Reting's successor, the elderly Taktra Rinpoche སྟག་བྲག་རིན་པོ་ཆེ་ [stag brag rin po che], dedicated himself to restoring discipline, but he proved no more capable than Reting at providing the imaginative and decisive leadership that was required. The pressures were many and conflicting. On the one hand, there was an urgent need for modernization, owing not only to external events but also to the venality of several key figures within the administration. On the other hand, the monastic establishment resisted change of any sort. Faced with these complexities, Taktra could do nothing to forestall the eventual invasion by China, which began during the winter of 1949.

Meanwhile, the young Tenzin Gyatso turned out to be energetic, highly intelligent, playful, and deeply curious. Together with his immediate elder brother, Lopsang Samten བློ་བཟང་བསམ་ གཏན་ [blo bzang bsam gtan] (also destined for monkhood), he had begun his education under the supervision of two of the most highly regarded figures within the Geluk hierarchy, Ling Rinpoche གླིང་རིན་པོ་ཆེ་ [gling rin po che] and Trijang Rinpoche ཁྲི་བྱང་རིན་ པོ་ཆེ་ [khri byang rin po che]. The 14th Dalai Lama's studies followed the standard Geluk curriculum with its emphasis on formal logic, debate, and *Madhyamaka* (the middle-way philosophy of Nāgārjuna as expounded by Tsongkhapa). In only one respect did his education differ markedly from that of his predecessors. Thanks to the presence of a handful of Europeans in Lhasa at the time, Tenzin Gyatso was exposed to modern

121 Ritual implement presented to the Fourteenth Dalai Lama in 1942 by the Tibetan government. Inscription: "This 'Seven Jewels of Royal Reign'...of gilded cast bronze were presented by the Government in the Water-Horse Year [1942] to his Holiness, the Highest Lord Fourteenth Incarnation, in gratitude for his kindness in assuming the preparation for ordination." 17.5 x 10.2 cm, Collection of Lambert Verhoeven, Gouda.

cosmology at an early age. This came to him via a number of cinema films, some old copies of *Life* magazine, and, notably, several informal conversations with the Austrian mountaineer Heinrich Harrer. As a result, when he later came to study the traditional Indo-Tibetan cosmology of the *Abhidharmakośa* and related texts, he found them largely unsatisfactory. This history is no doubt what underlies the dialogue the 14th Dalai Lama has been pursuing with members of the western scientific establishment for much of the past two decades.

The Dalai Lama's education was severely disrupted when, on 17 November 1950, Taktra Rinpoche resigned the regency

in favor of the now barely fifteen-year-old Tenzin Gyatso. It was an almost impossible situation. The Chinese People's Liberation Army had already penetrated as far as Chamdo, and it was clear that little could be done to keep it from advancing to Lhasa. Accordingly, the Dalai Lama decided immediately to seek refuge at Tromo, in the south of Tibet close to the Indian border. There he would consider whether to seek exile or to remain in Tibet.

In early 1951, while the 14th Dalai Lama was staying at Tromo, the Chinese government imposed its so-called Seventeen Point Agreement on the Liberation of Tibet 西藏和平解放十七條協議. Because the Tibetan delegation that signed it did not have the authority of the Lhasa government, this was an entirely spurious document. Yet there was nothing the Dalai Lama could do to alter its terms. He decided, therefore, to return to the capital and try to work with the Chinese for the benefit of his people, a decision that was inspired in part by his sympathy for the aims of socialism. Thus began a period of some eight years in which the young leader acted, in some degree, as Beijing's man in Tibet.

In 1954 the Dalai Lama travelled to Beijing, where he was received by Chairman Mao 毛主席 (毛澤東; 1893–1976) (plates 156–158). While there, he became convinced—as to an extent he remains—that there could be a fruitful relationship between Communism and the way of the Buddha, the one attending to society's material needs and the other to its spiritual needs. However, on his final meeting with Mao, he learned that this vision was not shared by the Great Helmsman, who envisaged an entirely secular society.

From that moment on, while outwardly cooperating with Beijing, the Dalai Lama began to search earnestly for some way of engaging external support in hopes of checking the despoliation of Tibet. An invitation to visit the Republic of India during 1956 seemed to offer a promising opportunity. On this visit the Dalai Lama participated in the celebrations marking the 2,500th birthday of the Buddha. But although he was able to meet with Pandit Nehru (1889–1964) (plates 163, 165), the then Prime Minister of the largest democracy the world has ever known, he found no support in that quarter. Personally, Nehru was well disposed toward the plight of Tibet, but he was also committed to a policy of appeasement toward China and made it clear that there could be no prospect of Indian intervention

122 The Fourteenth Dalai Lama and important Tibetan and Indian saints, including Atiśa (upper left), Tsongkhapa (upper right), four (of six) "Jewels of India": Nāgārjuna (with snakes over his head), Asaṅga on the other side of the throne, Dharmakīrti below him (with beard), and Vasubandhu across from him. They are followed by the historical Buddha with both of his main disciples and all the protective deities: Dharmarāja Yama (left), the Six-Armed Mahākāla and Vaiśravaṇa (right). Between, the sacrifice of the six senses (left for the angry deities, right for the peaceful ones). Also shown are the "Eight Auspicious Symbols" and the "Eight Auspicious Objects" (left and right of Buddha's throne). Mural at Sera Monastery, Photographer: Ian Cumming, © Tibet Images.

123 The Fourteenth Dalai Lama. Bronze, gilded, painted face, made in 2005 by Rajesh Awale, Hangrib Handicrafts, Kāṭhmāṇḍū, Nepāl, H 41 cm, W 38 cm, D 27 cm, Ethnographic Museum of the University of Zürich (Gift of the Swiss-Tibetan Friendship Society), Inv. No.: 23856. >>>

on Tibet's behalf. Thus Tenzin Gyatso returned to Tibet with no alternative but to try to find some way of working with the Chinese.

From the middle of the decade the situation within Tibet deteriorated markedly. The Chinese government showed little intention of keeping to the terms of the so-called Seventeen Point Agreement, and all opposition to collectivization and other reforms was brutally crushed. In early 1956, for example, the monastery at Lithang was subjected to aerial bombardment because of its reluctance to embrace the new dispensation. Yet a burgeoning resistance movement, later to be funded, armed, and trained by the American CIA as part of its efforts to destabilize China, was beginning to achieve sometimes startling successes against the invaders. It was clear that matters were heading toward a climax. It was equally clear, to the Dalai Lama at least, that the outcome of direct confrontation would be disastrous for Tibet. Given that Tibet lacked

determined support from the international community, the People's Liberation Army, with its all but limitless manpower reserves, would inevitably smash whatever resistance the Tibetans could muster. Thus, to the intense disappointment of many of his countrymen, the Dalai Lama refused to endorse the resistance movement.

Even had he been inclined, the special nature of his position would have kept Tenzin Gyatso from devoting all his energies to managing the worsening political situation. There was also the question of his religious education, as throughout this intensely traumatic period the young leader had continued with his studies, at which he excelled. Having access to the best teachers and debating partners, he had an enormous advantage over other novices of his age. Nevertheless, there is no doubt that the standards required of the Dalai Lama were as high, if not higher, than those required of his contemporaries. In view of this, and in view of the desperate circumstances then prevailing, it is remarkable that in his final, public examinations he acquitted himself with distinction, though he was just age twenty-four (several years younger than the norm). Almost as remarkable is the fact that there survives some cine film of the event. This footage makes it plain that the Dalai Lama was not given preferential treatment in his quest to prove himself worthy of the title of *geshe lharampa* དགེ་བཤེས་ལྷ་རམས་ པ་ [dge bshes lha rams pa], or doctor of Buddhist philosophy.

This same year, 1959, was the moment of climax in the political sphere. Since the beginning of the year thousands of mainly Khampa warriors had been converging on Lhasa. The Chinese had meanwhile moved reinforcements into the vicinity of the capital. A final showdown had become inevitable. Following a series of mass demonstrations and protests, on the very eve of what promised to be a general uprising, Tenzin Gyatso fled the Norbulingka, the summer palace of the Dalai Lamas (plates 167–173). Just a fortnight later, having formally repudiated the Seventeen Point Agreement, he arrived at the border with India. Immediately granted refugee status by an abashed and regretful Nehru, he was among the first of an estimated 80,000 Tibetans who fled the ensuing bloodbath in and around Lhasa.

On arrival in India, the Dalai Lama briefly enjoyed the full attention of the world's media, profoundly impressing observers with his obvious sincerity and humility, though some detected a degree of shyness about him. However, once the story of his near-miraculous escape had been told, Tibet and the Dalai Lama largely disappeared from sight, not to reappear for a full twenty-five years. In the meantime, to the discomfort of many of his closest advisors—including such foreign friends as Hugh Richardson, the British and then Indian government's last political officer in Lhasa—the 14th Dalai Lama declared that new circumstances demanded new protocols. Effective immediately, he would abandon the formality that had surrounded and to some extent imprisoned the person of the Dalai Lama. From now on, for example, he would sit on chairs of height equal to those of visitors, retaining his accustomed mark of status only in religious settings. Other reforms followed soon after. The one which most distressed people was his order that a draft constitution for a free Tibet be drawn up. This constitution even included provisions for the Dalai Lama's impeachment and forced resignation as head of state. The Dalai Lama had grasped that it was precisely measures such as these that would give his newly formed government-in-exile credibility in the eyes of the international community.

Throughout his first decade as a refugee, the Dalai Lama was prevented from travelling abroad due to energetic opposition from the People's Republic of China. This period of containment was nonetheless fruitful both for his leadership of the exile community and for his spiritual development. He applied himself with great diligence to ensuring the settlement of the Tibetan diaspora in stable, well-run communities, mainly in the south of India. In this effort he enjoyed at last the full and unstinting support of Nehru and his government, whose supine approach to China was repaid by Mao's invasion of Arunāchal Pradeś in 1962. At the same time, the Dalai Lama pursued his monastic vocation with added determination and vigor. Inspired by the example of the 5th Dalai Lama, of whom he is a great admirer and with whom he feels a close spiritual connection, he began to devote himself to the study and in some cases the practice of traditions other than his own Geluk school. Controversially, these have included incorporation of a considerable number of Nyingma teachings. This has provoked dismay among some Tibetans, notably those devoted to the *dharmapāla* "protective deity" Dorje Shukden རྡོ་རྗེ་ཤུགས་ལྡན [rdo rje shugs ldan]. But Tenzin Gyatso's ecumenical approach has also won him a large and admiring audience among members of other faith traditions.

124 The Fourteenth Dalai Lama, surrounded by Uṣṇīṣavijaya (upper left) and the White Tārā (upper right), Palden Lhamo (lower right). The five monks at the foot of the throne present the Dalai Lama with offerings representing the five senses. Thangka, Tibet/Nepāl, 20th century, 88 x 63 cm, Museé d'Ethnographie, Geneva, Inv. No.: 53946.

When during the 1970s the Dalai Lama began to travel outside India, at first neither he nor the Tibetan cause aroused much interest. In 1987, however, he was given the opportunity to address the United States Congress. Responding to post-Mao China's apparent willingness to reach a negotiated settlement on Tibet's future (provided that the demand for independence from China be dropped), the Dalai Lama used the occasion to propose his Five Point Peace Plan. Unfortunately, the mode of his announcement greatly affronted the Chinese government, who perceived him to be internationalizing the issue. China had recently been allowing representatives of the Dalai Lama to visit their homeland, but it now abandoned its relatively liberal attitude. Equally regrettable was the reaction of Tibetans, some of whom viewed the Dalai Lama's acquiescence on independence as a betrayal. As the Chinese government continued to respond negatively to his proposals, the Dalai Lama issued a new statement during a 1989 speech to the European Parliament in which

125 The Fourteenth Dalai Lama selects the correct items from among several objects at his parents' home, which identifies him as the successor to the Thirteenth Dalai Lama. Mural at Norbulingka, South Meeting Hall (Tshomchen Lhoma Sizhi Dogukyil), Photo and © Thomas Laird, New Orleans.

he further softened his position on independence, articulating a vision of a "genuinely autonomous" Tibet working in "association" with the People's Republic of China.

At first, the renewed international interest in Tibet and the Dalai Lama was confined largely to the political issue. This focus was thanks in no small part to the western media's reporting on the independence demonstrations in Lhasa in the late 1980s. More recently, especially since his reception of the Nobel Peace Prize of 1989, Tenzin Gyatso has been focusing on more universal causes. He has been an eloquent spokesman for the concept of peace based on dialogue and mutual understanding, and he has put much effort into promoting what he calls secular ethics. Accepting that only a minority of people in the modern world are religious practitioners, he has, without referring to religion, spoken of the need for developing further such basic human qualities as compassion, patience, tolerance, forgiveness, and generosity. These, he suggests, can be grounded in the simple proposition that all desire happiness and that none desires to suffer.

Though the Dalai Lama is best known for his advocacy of peace, interreligious harmony, and secular ethics, he remains closely involved in the preservation and promotion of Tibetan culture. In particular, he has been committed to the establishment of a flourishing, and to some extent modernized, monasticism in exile. In the manner of the 13th Dalai Lama, he has done much to encourage high standards within the monasteries. For example, the natural sciences, which were traditionally taught only to a few monks, are now part of the Geluk curriculum required of all. In a major break with recent practice, he has also revived the ancient tradition of full monastic ordination for nuns. The resultant flourishing of the female *saṅgha* within the Tibetan tradition has been one of the most vital and promising developments of the last half-century.

At the same time, it is clear that Tenzin Gyatso is working gradually to decouple the monastic community from secular affairs. Should he succeed, he may finally be able to dedicate himself wholeheartedly to spiritual practice, something

126 Portrait of the young Fourteenth Dalai Lama. Hand-colored photograph, © Brian Beresford/Nomad Pictures.　**127** The Fourteenth Dalai Lama on the occasion of a Tantric initiation. Hand-colored photograph, © Brian Beresford/Nomad Pictures.

he has frequently stated to be his fondest wish. It will also mean that, for the 15th Dalai Lama, the institution will have been returned to something like the position it held before the tenure of the 5th Dalai Lama, when political and religious leadership became united. Even so, the chief legacy of the 14th Dalai Lama will undoubtedly be the internationalization of his role. Before him, the Dalai Lamas were merely holders of the foremost lineage within the Tibetan tradition. In the future, they will surely continue to play an increasingly important role in the spiritual leadership of the world.

128/129 Photographic model from the 1960s and painting by Amdo Jampa (Amdo Byams pa) from the 1980s. Photograph: Archives of the Norbulingka Institute, Sidhpur, India.   **130** The Fourteenth Dalai Lama on the occasion of his assuming power on 17 November 1950. Mural in the reception hall of the Fourteenth Dalai Lama in "Traktrak (Tagdu) Mingyur Phodrang," Norbulingka, 1955/56, painted by Amdo Jampa. >>>

FROM PROTECTIVE DEITIES
TO INTERNATIONAL STARDOM:
AN ANALYSIS OF THE FOURTEENTH DALAI LAMA'S STANCE TOWARD MODERNITY AND BUDDHISM

Georges Dreyfus

In recent years, the 14th Dalai Lama has acquired the stature of international star. His travels are media events, his lectures are sold out, and his books almost invariably land on the bestseller list. For many, he has acquired an iconic status, representing what is most authentic and valuable in the Buddhist tradition, a source of inspiration and moral guidance. This admiration is widely shared not just among Tibetans but also among the educated public of the industrial world. From France to Taiwan to the United States, many see him as an embodiment of Buddhist compassion.

Why are people so taken now by the Dalai Lama, who had previously been ignored or considered an oddity? This question is all the more intriguing when one considers that in the West the Dalai Lama rarely displays his enormous learning and considerable intellectual acumen, instead mostly offering plain exhortations about being compassionate and tolerant. Normally such exhortations would leave most people cold, but when spoken by the Dalai Lama, they win enthusiastic audience response. Why this enthusiasm? A first answer is that there is more to communication than mere words, and the experience of seeing a person who has devoted himself to the well-being of his people and hence whose life is to a large extent in agreement with his words is itself a great source of inspiration. When the Dalai Lama exhorts his hearers to be compassionate, they respond not only to the content of his words but also, indeed mostly, to their recognition of his very real compassion, intelligence, charisma, and communicative skills. However, this answer is not sufficient, as his fame also depends in part on peoples' perceptions of him and the ideals he has come to represent. What are these ideals? And are the views of his audiences appropriate, or are they groundless projections shaped by orientalist expectations?

This essay addresses these questions by examining some of the ideas with which the Dalai Lama is associated, particularly among Westerners who see him as embodying the fundamental principles of Buddhism. I will argue that these ideas are part of what many have called *Buddhist modernism*, a modern reconfiguration of the tradition rather than the expression of its timeless essence. I will also argue that this description of the Dalai Lama as a Buddhist modernist only partly corresponds to his own views and practices. My investigation will be focused on the recent controversy that has surrounded a previously obscure deity, Dorje Shukden རྡོ་རྗེ་ཤུགས་ལྡན་ [rdo rje shugs ldan]. I will argue that the Dalai Lama's actions in this controversy show that in many ways he is a traditionalist Buddhist master whose ideas and practices are quite different from the irenic version of Buddhism that many associate with him. I will conclude by reflecting on the complexities and tensions created by the coexistence of these two seemingly conflicting frameworks in a single person.

THE DALAI LAMA AS A BUDDHIST MODERNIST

Buddhist modernism refers to an understanding of Buddhism developed first in the Buddhist (mostly Theravada) world at the end of the 19th century as a reaction to Western domination.[1] Buddhist modernism sought to respond to the colonial negative portrayal of Buddhism by presenting the tradition in modern and positive terms. The modernist perspective came to depict Buddhism as a world religion on par with the other world religions, particularly Christianity, as far as having its own founder, sacred scriptures, philosophical tradition, and so on. Moreover, in this view Buddhism is in many ways superior to the other religions, because it is based on reason and experience and does not presuppose any blind acceptance of authority. Buddhist practice is held to be a highly rational endeavor that is fully compatible with modern science, whose authority it claims. Buddhism is even at times presented as an empirical inner science whose findings are waiting to be discovered by the modern West. As a religion, if it can be so called, Buddhism is said not to be interested in dogmas and institutions but merely to provide its followers a path leading to the overcoming of suffering. This perspective considers Buddhism to be strongly ethical, devoted to nonviolence, and providing valuable resources for social action. Its recommended practice is said to be meditation, while ritual is devalued as popular superstition or adaptations to the demands of the laity.[2]

This greatly simplified description characterizes quite well the belief system of many contemporary Buddhists, particularly in the West, where many have come to regard Buddhism as more a philosophy than a religion, a spirituality consonant with the scientific spirit of inquiry rather than a faith based on the acceptance of dogmas. The Dalai Lama expresses this view of Buddhism when he says:

Suppose that something is definitively proven through scientific investigation. That a certain hypothesis is verified and that a certain fact emerges as a result of scientific investigation. And suppose, furthermore, that that fact is incompatible with Buddhist theory. There is no doubt that we must accept the result of scientific research. You see, the general Buddhist position is that we must accept *fact*. Mere speculation devoid of an empirical basis, when such is possible, will not do. We must always accept the fact. So if an hypothesis has been tested and has been found to be one hundred percent sure, then it is a fact and that is what we must accept.[3]

In addition to viewing Buddhism as based on empirical investigation and in agreement with the contemporary scientific spirit, many in the modern world consider it expressive of the freedom of personal inquiry, considering its essence to be the tolerance, compassion, and wisdom gained through that inquiry. For modernists, these qualities are the true essence of the tradition. Everything else is the result of deformations created by historical contingencies and local cultures.

Many have argued, however, that this view of Buddhism is a rather selective reinterpretation of the tradition, which in fact contains much more than that. This is not to say that the modernist view lacks ample basis in the tradition. The canon is full of exhortations for monks and nuns to practice diligently and to rely on themselves rather than on external salvation. But it should be clear that this view of Buddhism leaves out more than it includes. In particular, in overlooking rituals, mythology, and metaphysics, it omits central aspects of the tradition that are grounded in well-established canonical material and have played foundational roles in all the historically known Buddhist traditions. Thus, far from corresponding to the essence of the tradition, the contemporary perspective is an innovation inspired by modern ideas about religion and philosophy, ideas that are often inspired by the Protestant view of religion as a matter of individual belief and commitment rather than communal practice.

Some scholars have argued that many of the Dalai Lama's ideas about Buddhism correspond to Buddhist modernism and that his success is in large measure a function of his ability to embody the virtues associated with that stance. One of them, Donald Lopez, has described the Dalai Lama as "the leading proponent of Buddhist modernism."[4] Those highlighting the Dalai Lama's modernist orientation have cited his Ghandhian advocacy of nonviolence, his participation in interfaith dialogues, and his strong interest in encounters with scientists. The Dalai Lama has also said that the essence of the tradition consists of virtues such as wisdom and compassion, which he contrasts with the more superficial trappings of culture. For example, he says:

When we speak of the essence [of a religious tradition], there is no question about suitability and no need to change the basic doctrines. However, on the superficial level change is possible. A Burmese monk in the Theravada tradition whom I met recently in Europe and for whom I developed great respect makes the distinction between cultural heritage and the religion itself. I call this a distinction between the essence of a religion and the superficial ceremonial and ritual level.[5]

In making this fundamental distinction between the essence of Buddhism and its cultural expressions, the Dalai Lama seems to agree with Buddhist modernism, as the distinction allows for adapting the tradition to the new circumstances of modernity while claiming to preserve its integrity.

This flexibility has enabled him to connect with great success to modern audiences, especially in the international arena, for his ideas correspond to his audiences' needs and fit their worldviews. This may seem surprising, since most people who come to hear the Dalai Lama expect to meet an extraordinary personality expressing the views of a different and even exotic tradition. But what they hear is often surprisingly familiar to them, and this odd mixture of the familiar and the foreign has a profound influence on the outcome of the encounter.

This is especially the case with the Dalai Lama's distinction between superficial ritual and the essence of Buddhism. As noted above, this idea appeals to the modern audience because it corresponds to the individualized conception of religion that has come to be widely accepted in the modern West. When expressed by a personality with such obvious authority and respectibility as the Dalai Lama, this idea acquires for his listeners a new legitimacy, being seen as a deep and eternal truth rather than an expression of the views of the time.

Few in the Dalai Lama's audience realize that what they are hearing is a reflection of modern developments in Buddhism rather than the traditional Buddhist conceptions.

For most of its history, however, Buddhism has encouraged a very different attitude, for example, reserving the actual practice of meditation mostly for monastic elites and arguing that in an age of degeneration such as ours it is very meritorious just to practice ritual or to hold Buddhist views. Hence, when the Dalai Lama distinguishes the essence of the tradition from rituals, and when he exhorts his followers to engage in personal religious meditative practice and not to worry too much about traditional orthodoxy, he is not so much following an age-old tradition as innovating, adapting Buddhist ideas to a modern context by advocating lay adoption of prescriptions traditionally reserved for elite practitioners.

THE DALAI LAMA AS TRADITIONALIST

Yet the description of the Dalai Lama as a Buddhist modernist does not fully capture the Dalai Lama's thought. Though he certainly believes in some of the tenets of Buddhist modernism, and though he also uses the modernist idiom as a way to help his audience understand Buddhism, in accordance with the classical doctrine of skillful means, there is much more to the Dalai Lama's ideas and practices than Buddhist modernism. Overattention to the "modernist" label would obscure the complexity of his positions and the way his ideas have evolved. Some of this complexity is revealed by his stance on the controversy surrounding the Dorje Shukden deity.

The Dorje Shukden dispute concerns the propitiation of a protective deity, Shukden, a practice that the Dalai Lama has come to condemn in an increasingly vocal manner.[6] Shukden's followers claim that the practice dates back to a rather obscure and bloody episode of Tibetan history, the violent death of Drakpa Gyaltsen གྲགས་པ་རྒྱལ་མཚན་ [grags pa rgyal mtshan] (1618–1655), an important Geluk lama and a rival of the 5th Dalai Lama (1617–1682). Because of his premature death, Drakpa Gyaltsen is said to have been transformed into a wrathful spirit bent on the protection of the doctrinal purity of the Geluk tradition. He is also said to be particularly irked at those Geluk lamas, such the 5th Dalai Lama, who study and practice the teachings of other traditions, and he is said to have contributed to the deaths of several of them.

However, it is only during the early part of the 20th century that this systematic connection between Shukden and Drakpa Gyaltsen was clearly established. Prior to this date Shukden seems to have been a worldly god with a relatively limited following. The linkage between Shukden and the Geluk tradition was mostly the work of Pabongka (1878–1941), a charismatic teacher who spearheaded a revival movement within the Geluk tradition, partly in reaction to the success of the nonsectarian revival among the other schools. Connecting Shukden to Drakpa Gyaltsen seems to have been a way for Pabongka to justify his adoption of this originally non-Geluk deity as the main protector of his movement. The elevation of Shukden's status was one of three key elements in Pabongka's new understanding of the Geluk tradition: Vajrayoginī was upheld as the main meditational deity, Shukden as the protector, and Pabongka or his successors as the guru. Pabongka's vision was strongly exclusivist: not only was the Geluk tradition considered supreme, but its followers were warned of dire consequences if they showed interest in other traditions. Shukden would deal harshly with them, it was said, just as he had with several earlier eclectic Geluk lamas who had died prematurely at his hands.

In recent decades the Dalai Lama has opposed this understanding of the deity in increasingly vigorous ways, going so far as to ban its followers from some of his teachings. The reasons for his opposition are complex. In part he is concerned about the sectarian orientation that accompanies the Shukden tradition. He is also personally committed to a rival protective deity named Nechung གནས་ཆུང་ [gnas chung] and to the accompaying ritual system underlying the institution of the Dalai Lamas. The latter institution rests on an elaborate and eclectic ritual system that has close ties with various schools of Tibetan Buddhism. It has particularly close ties with the Nyingma School, the one most closely associated with the early empire and its mythological figures and gods. This link with the Nyingma School is particularly visible in the roles given to Padmasambhava, one of the foundational figures of Tibetan Buddhism, and Nechung, an early Tibetan god who is said to be in charge of protecting the Dalai Lama and his government. The propitiation of Shukden undermines this eclectic system and its close links with the Nyingma School. In particular, by presenting Shukden as an exclusivist deity in charge of visiting

131 The Fourteenth Dalai Lama at a meeting with Nelson Mandela. South Africa, August 1997. Photographer: Francisco Little, Archives of the Norbulingka Institute, Sidhpur, India. **132** The Dalai Lama at a visit with Pope John Paul II. Rome, 1982. Archives of the Norbulingka Institute, Sidhpur, India. **133** The Dalai Lama with actor Richard Gere. Palermo, 1996. From a photo album given as a gift to the Dalai Lama. Sarah Central Archive. **134** The Fourteenth Dalai Lama is made an honorary member of John Moores University. Liverpool, 2004. Archives of the Norbulingka Institute, Sidhpur, India.

retribution upon those in the Geluk order who have adopted practices from other traditions, the cult of Shukden threatens the Dalai Lama's reliance on Padmasambhava and Nechung and hence the integrity of the entire ritual system underlying the institution of the Dalai Lamas, at least as conceived by its present incumbent. This threat is captured by the opposition between Shukden and Nechung. Shukden is said to undermine Nechung, who resents Shukden's role and actions. Nechung is therefore seen to be prodding the Dalai Lama to act against Shukden by urging people to abandon the propitiation of this deity and even acting directly to ban the practice. The Dalai Lama himself has described on numerous occasions the strength of his relation to Nechung and the role of this deity in his decisions concerning Shukden.[7]

An interesting facet of the Shukden affair has been its illustration of the Dalai Lama's reliance on divination and other traditional means to decide important issues. This appears in the Dalai Lama's description of the way he decided to abandon Shukden, whose practice he himself had taken on at an early

age.[8] The Dalai Lama says that, after long considerations, he decided to submit the question to his other important protector, the Great Goddess Palden Lhamo འཕགས་སྒྲུན་ལྷ་མོ ['pal ldan lha mo], the Tibetan equivalent of *Mahādevī*. Should he continue publicly the practice of Shukden, he asked, should he do it only secretly, or should he stop altogether? Each of these alternatives was written on a piece of paper, each of which was put in a separate small ball of dough. All three balls were then put in a cup on the altar of the Great Goddess. After propitiating the deity for a long time in the company of several ritual specialists, the Dalai Lama took the cup and rolled the balls around in it until one of them came out. The answer it contained decided the issue: the Dalai Lama would abandon Shukden completely. This decision has had enormous consequences. It has changed his personal practice and the ritual system of the Dalai Lama institution, and has also prompted him to become increasingly vocal in his opposition to Shukden.

The Dalai Lama's use of divination may surprise those who think of Buddhism as a rational philosophy shunning rituals.

135/136 The Dalai Lama speaking about peace and inner happiness at an event with 60,000 participants. Central Park, New York, on 21 Sept.2003. Photographer: Manuel Bauer, © Manuel Bauer, AGENTUR FOCUS, Hamburg, 2005.   **137** Public address by the Fourteenth Dalai Lama at the Fleet Center, Boston, on 14 Sept. 2003. Photographer: Manuel Bauer, © Manuel Bauer, AGENTUR FOCUS, Hamburg, 2005.   **138** The Dalai Lama and his translator, Matthieu Ricard, in La Villette, Paris, at an event with Mrs. Mitterand for France-Libertés. 11 Oct.2003. Photographer: Manuel Bauer, © Manuel Bauer, AGENTUR FOCUS, Hamburg, 2005.

But for most Asian Buddhists, ritual is an essential element of the tradition and adherents make no excuse for its importance. The Dalai Lama is no exception. He has been open about his reliance on this form of divination and his general commitment to the rituals of protectors. In an unpublished interview, the Dalai Lama expressed to me his complete confidence in the value of this practice, one he has used at several key junctures of his life, justifying it with the phrase: "I am a Buddhist after all, am I not?"[9] This statement speaks volumes for the Dalai Lama's own understanding of his tradition, an understanding in which protective deities, rituals of propitiation, and modes of divination are self-evidently valid. For him, it is obvious that being a Buddhist implies that one believes in protective deities, follows their rituals, and relies on them for important decisions in life.

WHO IS THE "REAL" DALAI LAMA?

The traditionalist Tibetan Buddhism of the Dalai Lama's personal practice seems quite different from the modernism underlying his distinction between "the essence of a religion and the superficial ceremonial and ritual level."[10] One could

be forgiven for asking: Who is the real Dalai Lama? Is he the traditionalist who believes in protective deities or the modernist who engages in dialogue with scientists?

The answer is that the Dalai Lama is both. In his personal practice, he is a traditionalist. Every day he does a brief ritual for his main protective deity, the Great Goddess, without whose protection he would not undertake any important task. Even travel must be placed under her auspices, and in all his journeys the Dalai Lama carries with him a painted scroll of this deity. In addition, the Dalai Lama has monks from his monastery Namgyal Dratsang རྣམ་རྒྱལ་གྲྭ་ཚང་ [rnam rgyal gwra tshang] come to his residence to perform the appropriate daily and monthly rituals for all the relevant protective deities. The Dalai Lama considers all these rituals foundational to the Dalai Lama institution and essential to his personal practice. At the same time, in his public work he is a modernist who extols the practice of meditation, urges his Western audiences to go to the essence of the tradition (instead of being caught in the cultural trappings of Tibetan Buddhism), and engages in ongoing dialogues with scientists that include discussion of empirical findings. On the international scene he is, in addition, an inspired speaker who argues for the rationality of compassionate actions and the irrationality of armed conflicts.

The coexistence of such disparate belief systems in a single person may seem surprising, but recognition of this complexity is important for understanding who the Dalai Lama truly is. Clearly, depictions of the Dalai Lama as a Buddhist modernist fail to capture a large part of his actual practice and thinking. In contrast to figures like Dharmapāla and Buddhadāsa, the Dalai Lama is not, for the most part, a reformist of his own tradition, which he tends to uphold firmly but without rigidity. It is primarily in his dealings with the West that the Dalai Lama acts as a Buddhist modernist, using that idiom to express to this audience some of the Buddhist ideas that he strongly believes. He has also acted as a modernist in some of his advocacy within the Tibetan community, for example promoting democratic ideas and practices as being in accordance with Buddhist ideals.

The Dalai Lama's modernism is not just an act for Western audiences. For him, wisdom and compassion truly are the essence of the tradition. It is also true, however, that for him the protectors, divinations, and traditional rituals are also important. He sees no contradiction between the traditional and the modern, for the two orientations operate at different levels and are relevant to different contexts. The orientation that deals with the ultimate goals of Buddhism is traditionally considered a higher level of practice reserved for elite practitioners, but it also resonates with modern expectations about religion. The other orientation is equally important, but is reserved for traditional contexts and relates to more immediate concerns. Thus it is that the Dalai Lama's addresses to Western audiences can reflect his perceptions of their needs, while his personal practice can be guided by other considerations. There is no inherent contradiction in this.

But the lack of a logical contradiction does not mean a lack of tension, and the scope of what the Dalai Lama thinks he can share with his Western audiences has shifted over the years. Again, this can be illustrated by reference to the *Shukden* affair, where in the early years of the quarrel the Dalai Lama restricted his remarks to Tibetan audiences. In the late 1970s, when I first learned about this quarrel, the Tibetan monks I spoke with were surprised by my ignorance of it. Yet at the time very few Westerners were even aware that the split existed. Only gradually, as devotion to Shukden was slowly spreading among Westerners, did the Dalai Lama begin speaking of it to Western audiences, and even then he did not immediately express the full extent of his opposition. Only after the Dalai Lama had banned Shukden followers from his teachings, and only after the 1997 murder of three monks in apparent response to this ban, did he begin expressing his views on Shukden more fully to Western audiences. His new openness was greeted with puzzlement. I was sitting in such an audience near New York a few years ago when the Dalai Lama started to explain his views and policies regarding this deity. I remember the reaction of malaise among the members of the audience, who were puzzled and made uneasy by this confrontation with an aspect of Tibetan Buddhism that they did not understand. "Why should we be concerned by this?" they seemed to be saying.

This reaction shows the degree to which the two aspects of the Dalai Lama's thinking had formerly been distinct, as the Dalai Lama had usually kept from his Western audience those ideas and practices that he felt would not be understood. But this separation has not been rigidly maintained. When the Dalai Lama estimates that the stakes are too high or that the time is right for putting things more clearly, the separation breaks down, regardless of the audience's discomfort. At this point the extent to which the Dalai Lama is not a Buddhist modernist becomes clear, and the audience often reacts with great discomfort.

The Dalai Lama's modernism also has deep roots, and clearly is important him. Thus, it is more than just a display for Western audiences. Though he understands his primary task to be one of winning not just converts to Buddhism but sympathizers to the Tibetan cause, and though he has shaped his presentation accordingly, he has also been influenced by his contacts with modern institutions. He was initially educated in a traditional Buddhist way, mostly following the curriculum of the great Geluk monastic universities. The Dalai Lama would later remark that this education was unbalanced and inappropriate for a person who was to assume a leadership role.[11] He was therefore completely unprepared when the modern world came crashing in on him in 1950, and he coped by trying to learn on the job how to deal with the modern world.

As he did so, he encountered several important sources of influence. One of them came from his dealings with the Chinese. Particularly important in this regard was his trip to China in 1954–55. His encounter with Chairman Mao on that occasion made a lasting impression, as did his visits to Chinese factories. More important, however, may have been his encounters in India, which he visited extensively in 1956 before settling more permanently in 1959 (see page 189). There the Dalai Lama encountered people he could identify with, including not only Prime Minister Nehru but also other lesser-known figures such as Jayaprakash Narayan, Acharya Tulsi, and President Rajendra Prasad. Through their own Hindu or Jain modernism, these people modeled how to be religious while also participating fully in the modern world. Their modernism influenced the Dalai Lama greatly as he developed the outlook and style that have marked his relations with the West.

The Dalai Lama's modernism has also led him to take fairly radical positions within the Tibetan community. On the political level, he has insisted that the community in exile adopt, despite the misgivings of most of its members, a constitution in which the Dalai Lama's role is limited and submitted to democratic oversight. The Dalai Lama has also consistently supported the spread of modern education among both lay and monastic Tibetan communities, often against the vigorous opposition of more conservative elements. On the religious level, he has voiced, often sarcastically, his distrust of the institution of reincarnated lamas. I remember hearing him say in the early 1970s that many reincarnated lamas seem great when they are young but disappoint when they grow older: "It is like the teeth of children. They are so cute and yet they rot when they age." On the other hand, the Dalai Lama has never embraced the modernist distrust of ritual, and in many respects he remains deeply imbued with traditional Tibetan attitudes.

The Dalai Lama's orientations have changed in subtle but important ways over the years, though their evolution has not been noticed by most observers. Living in Dharamśālā in the 1970s and 1980s, I was able to observe some of these changes firsthand. At the beginning of the 1970s I was struck by the Dalai Lama's refreshingly unconventional ideas, particularly his willingness to relativize and even put to the side certain aspects of his tradition. For example, once when I asked about the practice of the *lamrim* ལམ་རིམ་ [lam rim] "Stages of the Path,"

he replied, in essence, "Leave it out. It is just what is in the book, not what you actually need to do." However, sometime in the 1970s he seems to have become more traditional. The turning point appears to have been the winter of 1975–76, when the Dalai Lama was undergoing an important retreat. The Dalai Lama has never fully explained what happened at that retreat, yet from that date onward he began expressing publicly his opposition to Shukden and evidenced a more traditional approach to Buddhist practice. Also, he almost completely dropped his unwillingness to recognize reincarnated lamas, and his formerly biting remarks were replaced by more conventional admonitions.

This return to a more traditionalist attitude, which perhaps could have been expected, did not entail a repudiation of Buddhist modernism. Indeed, modernism remained his favored way of interacting with the West, which he started to visit seriously only at the end of the 1970s, when he was already well over forty. Nevertheless, his traditionalist turn made him more committed to practices such as the propitiation of protectors, particularly those protecting the Dalai Lama institution. This in turn led to the confrontation with the followers of Shukden, which has threatened to split the Geluk tradition. His change in attitude has also had consequences for the Tibetan community in exile, particularly for its Buddhist institutions, where some of the promises of Buddhist modernism have yet to materialize.

In sum, to describe the Dalai Lama simply as a Buddhist modernist is to ignore the important role that traditionalist practices and ideas play in his life. It is also to simplify greatly the views of this complex figure. Very real tensions exist between his traditionalist and modernist stances, and the balance among those stances has changed over time. To international audiences he continues, in modernist fashion, to emphasize the core notions at the heart of Buddhism, and he does not expect his Western disciples to take on the full array of Tibetan customary practice. At the same time, he personally practices the full array of Tibetan Buddhist ritual, and continues to uphold the concepts underlying the institution of the Dalai Lama. Inhabiting these two very different aspects allows him to fulfill his main mission, that of promoting the Tibetan cause and leading the Tibetan people. His modernism allows him to function as an internationally recognized spiritual leader at ease

139 The Tsangpa Oracle, a government oracle, strides by the throne of the Fourteenth Dalai Lama during the annual "Losar Tsechu Sabsöl" at the main palace. Dharamśālā, 1999. Photographer: Manuel Bauer, © Manuel Bauer, AGENTUR FOCUS, Hamburg, 2005.

within the various contexts of modernity, whereas his commitment to practices such as that of protectors puts him in touch with the more traditional aspects of the religious culture of his people. However useful this inhabitation may be, it is also not without its difficulties, as we have seen in this essay. Moreover, there is the nagging question of the future of such a stance. Will a future Dalai Lama be able to conciliate so brilliantly the conflicting demands of tradition and modernity? This question is inherent to the Dalai Lama institution and the mode of selection on which it is based. But this question acquires a particular urgency in the modern context where the very existence of Tibet seems to be at stake.

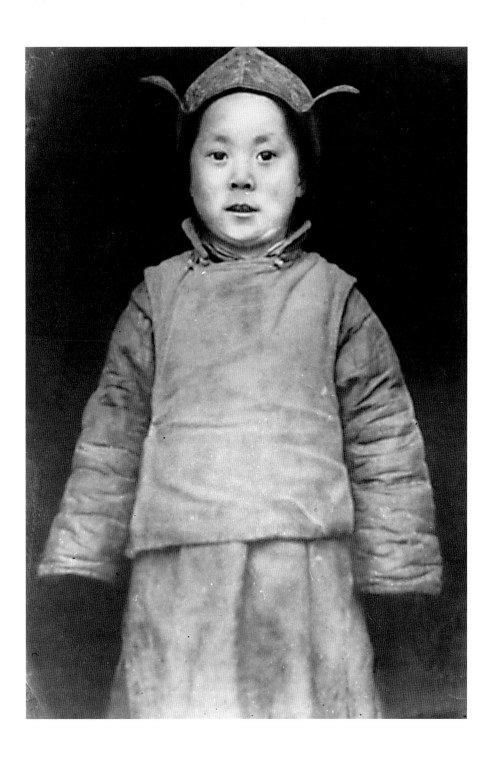

140 Portrait of the Fourteenth Dalai Lama, about four years old, in Amdo, ca. 1939. Photographer: anonymous, Archives of the Norbulingka Institute, Sidhpur, India.   **141 a–c** Portrait of the Fourteenth Dalai Lama, about four years old, in Amdo, ca. 1939. Photographer: probably Archibald Steele, a: © Pitt Rivers Museum, University of Oxford, 2005. (1998.131.630) b: © Pitt Rivers Museum, University of Oxford, 2005. (SC-T-2-631) c: © Pitt Rivers Museum, University of Oxford, 2005. (SC-T-2-629).   **142** The Fourteenth Dalai Lama before departing for Lhasa, surrounded by local dignitaries. Amdo, 1939. Translation of the Chinese text: "The Fourteenth incarnation of the (reborn) Dalai Lama is five years old" (according to Tibetan calculation of age). Photographer: anonymous, Archives of the Norbulingka Institute, Sidhpur, India.

転世達頼喇𡃤十四歲年方五歲

143 The Fourteenth Dalai Lama seated on his throne, about 10 years old. Ca. 1945. Archives of the Norbulingka Institute, Sidhpur, India.   144 Fifteen-year-old Dalai Lama, to the right the Regent Tadrak Rinpoche. Lhasa, 1950. Photographer: Lowell Thomas, James A. Cannavino Library, Archives and Special Collections, Marist College, Poughkeepsie, New York.   145 In the center, the fifteen-year-old Dalai Lama, far left Lowell Thomas, Sr. Lhasa, 1950. Photographer: Lowell Thomas, Jr., James A. Cannavino Library, Archives and Special Collections, Marist College, Poughkeepsie, New York.   146 The Fourteenth Dalai Lama at age seven seated in lotus position. 21 January 1943. Photographer: Brooke Dolan, The Academy of Natural Sciences of Philadelphia, Ewell Sale Stewart Library.   147 The Fourteenth Dalai Lama during tests that took the form of extended disputations with famous scholars. Here he faces the abbots of the Shar and Jang Colleges of the Ganden Monastery. Lhasa, 1958/59. Archives of the Norbulingka Institute, Sidhpur, India.   148 The Fourteenth Dalai Lama at about 10 years of age. Ca. 1945. Photographer: probably Archibald Steele, The Tibet Museum/DIIR, Dharamśālā.

149–155 The Fourteenth Dalai Lama and his entourage on the flight to Dromo, near the Sikkim border, 1950/51.   149/150 Residents of Phari greeting the caravan in flight as the Dalai Lama passes in his sedan chair. Photographer: Heinrich Harrer, Ethnographic Museum of the University of Zürich (VMZ 400.07.12.029/VMZ 400.07.GD.007).   151 "The monastery in Phari in which the Dalai Lama lived. On the left soldiers and monks form an honor guard. The first flag is the banner of the Dalai Lama, the second flag is the national flag." (quoting H. Harrer) Photographer: Heinrich Harrer, Ethnographic Museum of the University of Zürich (VMZ 400.07.13.017).   152 Departing after a rest break. The Dalai Lama is once more seated in the sedan chair, which is carried by monks during the flight. Photographer: Heinrich Harrer, Ethnographic Museum of the University of Zürich (VMZ 400.07.12.024).   153 Incense offering during a reception for the Dalai Lama in the courtyard of the Dungkhar Monastery, The Tibet Museum/DIIR, Dharamśālā.   154 The Dalai Lama with his closest entourage in the courtyard of the Dungkhar Monastery. Photographer: Heinrich Harrer, Ethnographic Museum of the University of Zürich (VMZ 400.07.XY.066).   155 Surrounded by his highest officials, the Dalai Lama receives a stūpa with an important relic. Dungkhar Monastery, early 1951. Photographer: Heinrich Harrer, Ethnographic Museum of the University of Zürich (VMZ 400.07.GD.008).

156 Meeting in Beijing, from left to right: the Panchen Lama, Mao Zedong, and the Fourteenth Dalai Lama. 1954. Ethnographic Museum of the University of Zürich.   **157** Mao Zedong, Zhou Enlai, Liu Shaoqi, and the Panchen Lama at a banquet given by the Dalai Lama on the occasion of the celebration of the Tibetan New Year. Beijing, 1955. Archives of the Norbulingka Institute, Sidhpur, India.   **158** Mural in Norbulingka, in the Southern Meeting Hall (Tshomchen Lhoma Sizhi Dogukyil), photo and ©: Thomas Laird, New Orleans.

159 The Fourteenth Dalai Lama greeting Mao Zedong with a *khatak*. 1954. Archives of the Norbulingka Institute, Sidhpur, India.   160 The Fourteenth Dalai Lama with the Prime Minister of China, Zhou Enlai, 1956, in India. Archives of the Norbulingka Institute, Sidhpur, India.   161 The Fourteenth Dalai Lama and the Panchen Lama are greeted at the railway station by the Prime Minister of China, Zhou Enlai and Marshal Zhu De. Beijing, 1954. Archives of the Norbulingka Institute, Sidhpur, India.   162 The Fourteenth Dalai Lama and the Panchen Lama at a meeting with Mao Zedong in Beijing, 1954/55. Archive of the Ethnographic Museum of the University of Zürich.

163–166 The Dalai Lama and the Panchen Lama in India on the occasion of the Buddha Jayanti celebrations, 1956.   **163** Reception by the Prime Minister of India Pandit Nehru (second from left) and the Vice President Sarvepalli Radhakrishnan (in white) at the airport in New Delhi. Archives of the Norbulingka Institute, Sidhpur, India.   **164** The Fourteenth Dalai Lama is received with military honors by Indian plenipotentiaries in Sikkim. Nathu-la, on the Indian border. Archives of the Norbulingka Institute, Sidhpur, India.   **165** Ride on an elephant with Prime Minister Nehru. Archives of the Norbulingka Institute, Sidhpur, India.   **166** The Fourteenth Dalai Lama and the Panchen Lama during a visit in India. Archives of the Norbulingka Institute, Sidhpur, India.

167–172 During the exhausting flight from Lhasa to India, 1959. Lower left (plate 171), the Dalai Lama with his younger brother, Tenzin Chögyal. Archives of the Norbulingka Institute, Sidhpur, India. **173** The Dalai Lama and his entourage arriving at the Indian border. Right in the picture is Thupten W. Phala, head valet of the Dalai Lama. 1959. The Tibet Museum / DIIR, Dharamśālā.

174 The extended family of the Fourteenth Dalai Lama. In the center, father and mother, on her lap Jetsün Pema, his youngest sister, and to their right his oldest sister, Tsering Dolma. Next to the father is Gyalo Thöndup, brother. Behind them, some servants. 1940. The Tibet Museum/DIIR, Dharamśālā.   **175** The parents of the Fourteenth Dalai Lama, his sister Jetsün Pema, his brother Lopsang Samten and his niece Khando Tersing posing for the camera in Dekyi-Lingka (British Mission). Ca. 1946. © Pitt Rivers Museum, University of Oxford, 2005 (1998.131.628).   **176** Together with his parents and two brothers. Archives of the Norbulingka Institute, Sidhpur, India.   **177** The Dalai Lama and his mother, who was an important emotional reference point for him. In Indian exile, around 1960. Archives of the Norbulingka Institute, Sidhpur, India.

178 The Dalai Lama's mother on the roof of her home. In the background is the Potala. Prior to 1950. Photographer: Heinrich Harrer, Ethnographic Museum of the University of Zürich (VMZ 400.07.61.001). 179 The Dalai Lama's mother (left) and his older sister Tsering Dolma. Photographer: Heinrich Harrer, Ethnographic Museum of the University of Zürich. 180 The Fourteenth Dalai Lama's mother. Lhasa, prior to 1950. Photographer: anonymous, Hopkinson Archive, © The British Museum.

181 The two main teachers of the Fourteenth Dalai Lama, left Ling Rinpoche and right Trijang Rinpoche. Archives of the Norbulingka Institute, Sidhpur, India.   **182** Group portrait with the Fourteenth Dalai Lama seated between his two teachers. To the left, members of the government and monks and to the right members of the family. Archives of the Norbulingka Institute, Sidhpur, India.   **183–188** The Fourteenth Dalai Lama performing various ceremonies and rituals. The two pictures at the bottom were taken while still in Tibet in the 1950s. Archives of the Norbulingka Institute, Sidhpur, India.   **189** The Fourteenth Dalai Lama at prayer in the temple next to his residence in Dharaṁśālā. 1972. Photographer: Martin Brauen, Bern.

190/191 The Fourteenth Dalai Lama at home keeping up with the news. Archives of the Norbulingka Institute, Sidhpur, India.   **192–197** Meeting with various people. Archives of the Norbulingka Institute, Sidhpur, India.

198 Child with amulet containing a miniature photograph of the Fourteenth Dalai Lama. Ladākh, Hanle, 1999. Photo and ©: Michael Marchant, Zürich.

THE PANCHEN LAMAS AND THE DALAI LAMAS:
A QUESTIONABLE MASTER–DISCIPLE RELATIONSHIP

Fabienne Jagou

Tibetans call the Panchen Lama and the Dalai Lama the "Moon and Sun," "Father and Son," "Master and Disciple." The Panchen Lamas are seen as embodiments of Öpakme འོད་དཔག་མེད་ ['od dpag med] (Skt. *Amitābha*), Bodhisattva of Wisdom, while the Dalai Lamas are the incarnations of Chenrezik སྤྱན་རས་གཟིགས་ [spyan ras gzigs] (Skt. *Avalokiteśvara*), Bodhisattva of Compassion. This tradition gives the Panchen Lama a spiritual preeminence that in principle keeps him outside worldly affairs while making the Dalai Lama the unique spiritual and temporal leader of Tibet—a force in the world. Another tradition holds that the Panchen Lama is the *chöku* ཆོས་སྐུ་ [chos sku] "religious body of the Buddha," while the Dalai Lama is the *lungku* ལུང་སྐུ་ [lung sku] "handle-like body" onto which a sufferer can hold and be drawn upwards.

The 4th Dalai Lama (1589–1617) transferred the Panchen title to his spiritual master Lopsang Chökyi Gyaltsen བློ་བཟང་ཆོས་ཀྱི་རྒྱལ་མཚན་ [blo bzang chos kyi rgyal mtshan] (1567/70–1662), abbot of Tashilhünpo བཀྲ་ཤིས་ལྷུན་པོ་ [bkra shis lhun po] "Mountain of Good Fortune." Since then the master–disciple relationship between the two hierarchs has been transmitted from one incarnation to the next until this day.[1] By giving the title Panchen to Lopsang Chökyi Gyaltsen, the 4th Dalai Lama could celebrate the connection between the Dalai Lamas and Tashilhünpo. All abbots since Gendün Drup (1391–1474), the 1st Dalai Lama and direct disciple of Tsongkhapa who founded the monastery in 1447, have borne the title Panchen in recognition of their great learning,[2] including the 2nd and 3rd Dalai Lamas. *Pan* is a contraction of the Sanskrit term *paṇḍita*, which means "scholar," while the meaning of *chen* is "great" in Tibetan. The title means "great scholar." However, the 4th Dalai Lama gave few indications about the duties and rights attached to it, and that opened all possible interpretations of the Panchen Lama's role.

ORIGINS OF THE MASTER–DISCIPLE RELATIONSHIP

After the death of the 4th Dalai Lama, for the first time ever the Panchen Lama participated in the search for the incarnation of the next Dalai Lama. He ordained the 5th Dalai Lama (1617–1682) as a novice in 1625 and then as a monk twelve years later. With this he reaffirmed the master–disciple relationship that he had established with the 4th Dalai Lama. The master–disciple relationship between Panchen and Dalai became instutionalized, with one Panchen Lama able to serve several Dalai Lamas: the 5th Dalai Lama ordained the 5th Panchen Lama (1663–1737), who in turn ordained the 6th Dalai Lama (1683–1706) and the 7th (1708–1757). This master–disciple relationship is also closely connected to the transmission of Buddhist teachings. Holders of the Kālacakra, the Panchen Lamas taught the Dalai Lamas this highest teaching, which is important both to this lineage of transmission and to the future of Buddhism. It is said a Panchen Lama will become the 25th king of Śambhāla.[3]

The master–disciple relationship between the Panchen Lama and the Dalai Lama took on real significance after the 5th Dalai Lama was enthroned at the fort of Shigatse and became the spiritual and temporal ruler of Tibet with the support of the Mongol Khoshod in 1642. After the death of the 4th Panchen Lama (1662), the 5th Dalai Lama composed a prayer urging his master to reincarnate. He ordered the prayer to be recited in a general assembly of monks at all the great monasteries. He also supervised the selection of a candidate and recognized the boy as the incarnation of the Panchen Lama.

The two most important Geluk reincarnation lineages—that of the Dalai Lama and of the Panchen Lama—were thus established. The generosity of the disciple to the master then started to become significant. The 5th Dalai Lama conferred on his teacher the ownership of the monastery of Tashilhünpo in perpetuity. In subsequent years the Dalai Lama made ever more generous endowments to this teacher, until Tashilhünpo's properties covered almost the entire province of Tsang and a sizeable portion of neighboring Ngari to the West. In making these generous donations, the 5th Dalai Lama was taking up a challenge: spiritually, he was affirming the reincarnation lineage of the Panchen Lama, while at the same time he was trying to wield strong secular influence over an important Geluk monastery and the province of Tsang.

While under the guidance of the regent, the Dalai Lama also tried to keep the Geluk School in check. For example, the 5th Dalai Lama took the opportunity of a trip to Tashilhünpo in 1654 to assess whether his wish that the Mönlam Chenmo Festival be again celebrated at Drepung Monastery near Lhasa instead of at Tashilhünpo as was the custom. The King of Tsang had indeed transferred the right to head the festival to the Panchen Lama as a reward for his having served as a mediator between the king's army and the the Geluk, whom the

199 The First (fourth) Panchen Lama, Lopsang Chökyi Gyaltsen, teacher of the Fifth Dalai Lama, surrounded by a rare form of the White Saṃvara, below him Vaiśravaṇa (left) and Bektse (right). At head height, a vision of the First Panchen Lama can be seen, during which he arrived in the Tuṣita heaven where he was blessed by Maitreya (seen in the picture). Thangka, Tibet, first third of the 18th century, 69 x 53 cm, Musée national des Arts asiatiques Guimet, Paris, MA 5241.

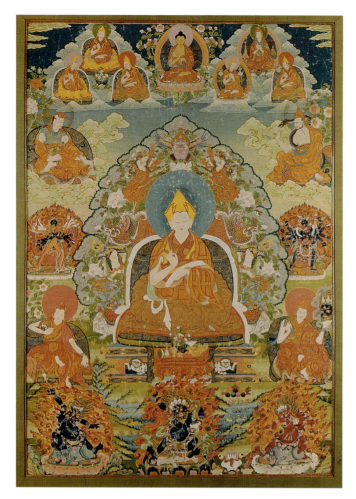

200 The First (fourth) Panchen Lama, surrounded by important monks from Ganden Monastery (upper left), Geluk dignitaries (upper right), other important holy men to the left and right, including among others Abhayākaragupta (with snake) and three aspects of the Geluk protective deity Dharmarāja Yama below. Thangka, Tibet, ca. 1835, 123 x 87 cm, Schleiper Collection, Brussels. >>>

Mongols had supported in 1621. The Mönlam Chenmo Festival had been celebrated in Lhasa since its institution.

From that point on, the Dalai Lama and the Panchen Lama became dependent on each other in many ways, for example becoming responsible for the search for the other's reincarnation and taking on the religious education of the other depending on their age. Because several Panchen Lamas were responsible for finding and educating important Dalai Lamas (see list at the end of essay), the Panchen Lamas held spiritual preeminence over the Dalai Lamas, at least until the mid-19th century. After that time, the Dalai Lamas could receive their ordinations from the Panchen Lamas because they were of the same generation. The matter of the age of Tibetan hierarchs and age difference has had a great impact on their master–disciple relationship. Today, we count fourteen Dalai Lamas and eight (or eleven by

the first reckoning; see end of essay) Panchen Lamas. On average, the Panchen Lamas, dying at fifty-nine, have lived longer the Dalai Lamas, dying at age forty. It therefore seems obvious that the Panchen Lamas would be spiritually preeminence over the Dalai Lamas, at least until the mid-19th century. If the Dalai Lamas had been able to ordain the Panchen Lamas after that time, the relationship would have been reversed with the Dalai Lamas becoming masters to the Panchen Lamas.

The spiritual preeminence of many Panchen Lamas, the uncertainty about their function, and the huge amount of land the 5th Dalai Lama had given the 1st Panchen Lama, in addition to such political factors as internal power struggles arising from the absence of adult and strong Dalai Lamas and the arrival of Manchus, British, and Chinese on the Tibetan political scene, all led outsiders to misinterpret the real power of the Panchen Lama and to force him to assume a political role for which most Tibetans did not consider him qualified.

OUTSIDERS' MANIPULATION OF THE MASTER-DISCIPLE RELATIONSHIP

The confusion surrounding the death of the 5th Dalai Lama, which the regent had hidden for fifteen years, the capricious personality of the 6th Dalai Lama, the appearance of a second 6th Dalai Lama (both of whom the 2nd Panchen Lama had recognized), the ascendancy of a Khoshod Mongol prince in Tibet who was soon considered untrustworthy, and finally a weak 7th Dalai Lama, all conspired to bring Tibet to its knees. Against this backdrop, each party courted the 2nd Panchen Lama, who was very careful in whom he supported in Tibet. He appears to have acted reluctantly, for example not answering all invitations. He continued to play his spiritual role in regard to the the Dalai Lamas, but could not keep a political career from developing. Both Tibetans and Mongols called on the 2nd Panchen Lama for help filling the vacuum left by the absence of an effective Dalai Lama. The Qing 清 emperors also understood that they needed the Panchen Lama to help them consolidate their growing power in Tibet.

Outside Tibet, the Great Powers had started moving. The Qing tried to bring the 2nd Panchen Lama under their sway (he was the first of the lineage to receive a Manchu title). They wanted him to recognize the 7th Dalai Lama whom they had finally put on the Tibetan throne in 1735 after having detained him in Kumbum Monastery. The 2nd Panchen Lama tried to act cautiously by being very late to recognize the 7th Dalai Lama and by not responding to the Qing emperor's requests to come to Beijing to meet him. But the arrival of the British at Tashilhünpo monastery in the middle of the 18th century only strengthened the Qing's position towards the Panchen Lama. When the 8th Dalai Lama was thirteen years old, the 3rd Panchen Lama (1738–1780) intervened as a mediator to re-solve a conflict between the Bhutanese and the British in 1771 and initiated contacts between his monastery and the British. From then until the beginning of the 20th century, whenever any British entered Tibet, they always stopped to see the Pan-chen Lama at Tashilhünpo, which was the seat of the Panchen Lama, on the road from India to Lhasa. Moreover since Lhasa was closed to foreigners, the British came to rely on the Pan-chen Lama instead of the Dalai Lama. This reinforcement of the relationship between the Panchen Lama and the British annoyed the Qing court and so they soon summoned the 3rd Panchen Lama to Beijing. There he died of smallpox in 1780. Tashilhünpo was also accessible to the Nepalese who made two raids there, in 1788 and 1791, that promped the Qing to initiate reforms of the Tibetan administration.

The Manchus tried to reshape the Panchen Lama and Da-lai Lama master–disciple relationship in two ways: First, they tried to put an end to the power each had to recognize the other's reincarnations by modifying the selection of high-ranking masters through the imposition of a new regulation governing the search process for incarnations, in particular the drawing of lots from the Golden Urn 金瓶. To the tradi-tional recognition process based on a series of tests and the visions of oracles, the Manchus added the drawing of lots done by inscribing on ivory plates the names and dates of birth of potential incarnations. The chosen ivory plate gave the name of the incarnation. Indeed, the Qing realized that the families of the Panchen Lama and Dalai Lama monopolized power in Tibet. For example, the 3rd Panchen Lama chose the 8th Da-lai Lama (1758–1804) from a family from Tsang (the province the Panchen Lama ruled de facto) after the death of the 7th Dalai Lama, and the same 8th Dalai Lama chose his cousin as the 4th Panchen Lama (1782–1853). Second, the Qing placed the Dalai Lama, the Panchen Lama, and the imperial Manchu agent in Tibet on the same level in the Tibetan government,

201 The First (fourth) Panchen Lama. Copper alloy, gilded, cast in two parts, Tibet 17th century, H: 27.5 cm, W: 22.5 cm, D: 20 cm, Oliver Hoare Collection, London, Inv. No.: 89.

even though the Panchen Lama was never supposed to hold any political office.

The 4th Panchen Lama even became both spiritual and tem-poral ruler of Tibet for nine months between 1844 and 1845 with Qing support after a series of intrigues leading to the premature deaths of the Dalai Lamas, from the 9th to the 12th, none of whom came to age. After returning to his estate in May 1845, the Panchen Lama remained de facto ruler of Tsang Province, a situation that would jeopardize the relationship between him and the Dalai Lama.

FISSURES IN THE RELATIONSHIP

The Dalai Lamas and the Panchen Lamas were about the same ages from the mid-19th century on. The 5th Panchen Lama (1845–1882) and the 6th (1883–1937) in addition to the 12th

Dalai Lama (1856–1875) and the 13th (1876–1933) were unable to participate in the recognition of each other's incarnations. Yet all maintained close relations as masters and disciples until an event damaged relations between Lhasa and Tashilhünpo, which lead to a split between the Dalai and Panchen Lamas. Ambiguity and conflict characterized the relationship between the 13th Dalai Lama and the 6th Panchen Lama.[4] If the Dalai Lama went one way, the Panchen Lama went in the other. When the Panchen Lama requested Buddhist teachings, the Dalai Lama refused to teach him. When the Panchen Lama asked permission to go on a pilgrimage, the Dalai Lama refused it. Although they were quick to reconcile, they would soon split again. This pattern ended with the departure of the 6th Panchen Lama for Outer Mongolia and China in December 1923.

The last argument between Lhasa government officials and Tashilhünpo concerned a new tax the Tibetan government imposed on the Panchen Lama's lands. The 13th Dalai Lama had declared Tibetan independence in 1913 after the Qing was overthrown and the Chinese Republic was created in 1912. Based on his political experience gained abroad, he embarked on a series of reforms to modernize Tibet and provide it with a well-equipped and well-trained army. Setting up an effective army, however, required considerable funding and consequently the 13th Dalai Lama and his government imposed a special levy. The government conducted new surveys of the properties the aristocracy and religious institutions held. This included Tashilhünpo, which they assessed a large sum based on its extensive holdings. The 6th Panchen Lama, who had previously not paid any taxes at all, declared the levy unfair and refused to pay the new taxes from the outset. Soon negotiations between Lhasa and Tashilhünpo became deadlocked and the Panchen Lama felt he had no choice but to leave Tibet, first for Outer Mongolia and then for China. Leaving Tashilhünpo on 22 December 1923, he left behind a letter explaining that he was setting out to find money to pay the taxes the Tibetan government demanded and to avoid creating more conflict with the 13th Dalai Lama and his *kashak* "cabinet." Soon the 13th Dalai Lama wrote the Panchen Lama to criticize his disciple's lack of confidence in his master and to reproach the Panchen Lama for his secret escape.

However, anecdote reveals that when the Panchen Lama left Tibet in fear of Lhasa government reprisals, he actually did so with the blessings of the 13th Dalai Lama. According to this legend, the Panchen Lama offered incense to the Dalai Lama in the fall of 1923. "Incense" is *pö* སྤོས་ [spos] in Tibetan, but is written the same as another word meaning "change of residence." In return the Dalai Lama sent him a white horse, still preserved at Kumbum Monastery in Amdo, which the Panchen Lama rode to leave Tibet. It is likely that the Panchen Lama would have informed the Dalai Lama of his departure and that the Dalai Lama would have given him his blessing by offering the Panchen a way to escape. Certainly this anecdote contradicts the disappointment the Dalai Lama expressed in his correspondence with the Panchen Lama later. Mystery still surrounds the Panchen Lama's trip.

In any case, the 13th Dalai Lama tried to compel the 6th Panchen Lama to return to Tibet, although by this time the influence the Dalai Lama held as head of the Tibetan government was very weak after the clergy forced him to abandon his reforms. He had also failed to convince his ministers of the Panchen Lama's loyalty to Tibet.[5] For his part, the Panchen Lama returned to Tibet only after the Dalai Lama died in 1933. It is still difficult to understand why he waited so long and why he insisted on being escorted by the Chinese army. Indeed, if he still feared reprisals from Lhasa, it would have been better to return to Tibet while the Dalai Lama was still alive.

Nevertheless, by remaining in northern China the 6th Panchen Lama was able to fulfill a different duty—he found the new incarnation of the 13th Dalai Lama in Amdo. The Republican Chinese, however, were not prepared to let the 14th Dalai Lama (b. 1935) go to Tibet so easily and they postponed his departure for Lhasa. In the meantime the 6th Panchen Lama died on the Sino-Tibetan border at the end of 1937, and like the Dalai Lama his incarnation was discovered also in Amdo. The Dalai Lama was too young to participate in the search for the Panchen Lama and many misunderstandings occurred over the recognition of the 7th Panchen Lama (1938–1989). From then on Chinese politics poisoned relations between the 14th Dalai Lama and the 7th Panchen Lama. The focus of the relationship between the two hierarchs shifted from religion to politics so that the 14th Dalai Lama tried to assert his spiritual authority against Chinese political pressures by recognizing the 8th Panchen Lama.

In response, officials of the new Chinese Republic tried to keep the 7th Panchen Lama in China, thinking that he could

202 The Sixth (ninth) Panchen Lama Lopsang Chökyi Nyima. Sarah Central Archive.   203 Portrait of Panchen Lama. Hand-colored and background painted by a Tibetan artist. His name and title are below, along with his seal, written in golden letters by Panchen Rinpoche himself. Library of Tibetan Works and Archives, Dharamśālā.   204/205 The Sixth (ninth) Panchen Lama Lopsang Chökyi Nyima. Sarah Central Archive.

206 The Seventh Panchen Lama, the Fourteenth Dalai Lama, and Prime Minister Nehru. New Delhi, 1956. Archives of the Norbulingka Institute, Sidhpur, India.

accomplish what his predecessor had not because of his death—he was supposed to help the Chinese by returning to Tibet and choosing a new incarnation for them. It was the Chinese Communists who eventually succeeded where the Republicans had failed. They brought back the 7th Panchen Lama, then fourteen, to Tibet under the escort of Chinese troops in 1952. The communists then adopted the Qing practice of putting the Dalai and Panchen Lama on equal footing.[6] The powers the Chinese granted the 7th Panchen Lama became even more important after the Dalai Lama fled to India and the the Tibetan government dissolved in 1959.

During this time the nature of the relationship between the Dalai Lama and Panchen Lama remained obscure. Did they share Buddhist teachings with each other? Did they exchange views on the future of Tibet? What we know for sure is that neither criticized the other's behavior. Indeed, after the Chinese began to destroy Tashilhünpo and its monks, the Panchen Lama rebelled against the Chinese and began to support the Dalai Lama and Tibetan independence. He was consequently imprisoned. After thirteen years there, he reemerged around 1980 to become the voice of Tibetans inside the Chinese government

and the Dalai Lama praised his courage. The 7th Panchen Lama died suddenly in 1989 under dubious circumstances. The Dalai Lama was then fifty-four years old, making him older than the Panchen Lama for the first time in Tibetan history. He was subsequently able to fulfill his duties as master to his disciple-to-be and thus reversed the traditional relationship between heads of the two most important Geluk incarnation lineages. A few years later he recognized a young Tibetan boy (plate 208) as the incarnation of the 7th Panchen Lama, although the Chinese denounced the choice, arguing that the search the Dalai Lama conducted did not conform to the rules the Qing had laid down. The 8th Panchen Lama has not been seen since then and the Chinese have placed another boy on the throne at Tashilhünpo whom they selected by drawing lots from the Golden Urn, although they omitted including the name of the boy the Dalai Lama had selected.

CONCLUSION

Although some masters of the Panchen lineage were spiritually learned, from the 18th century on they became not only a source of discord among the Geluk themselves, but also an object of political manipulation by foreign powers. These often created difficulties for the Panchen Lamas to maintain their earlier spiritual relationship with the Dalai Lamas. This master-disciple relationship could have been reversed, with the Dalai Lamas becoming masters to the Panchen Lamas if they had lived longer. This could only happen, however, in very recent history. The 14th Dalai Lama's long life allowed him to search for the 7th Panchen Lama and to recognize the 8th. Despite the Panchen Lama's disappearance, many still hope that the 14th Dalai Lama will one day be able to educate him in Buddhist teachings and that the relationship between both lineages will be a long-lasting one.

207 Portrait of the Seventh (tenth) Panchen Lama Lopsang Thrinle Lhündrup Chökyi Gyaltsen. Archives of the Norbulingka Institute, Sidhpur, India.

LIST OF PANCHEN LAMAS

In this list the lineage of the Panchen Lamas, with their names and dates, traces back to the time of the Buddha, as is the case for every great lineage in Tibet. It presents two ways of counting: 1) With Khedrup Gelek Namgyal Palzang (1385–1438) as the first Panchen Lama, although he was only declared as such posthu-mously; or 2) With Lopsang Chökyi Gyaltsen (1567/1570–1662) as the first because he was the first master to officially bear the title Panchen Lama. This is why the second row has been put in boldface. The first way counts from Lopsang Chökyi Gyaltsen as the fourth of the lineage.

Rapjor རབ་འབྱོར་ [rab 'byor], Subhūti, disciple of the Buddha

Jampel Drakpa འཇམ་དཔལ་གྲགས་པ་ ['jam dpal grags pa], Mañjuśrīkīrti, king of Śambhāla

Lekden Je ལེགས་ལྡན་འབྱེད་ [legs ldan 'byed], Bhavaviveka, a later follower of Nāgārjuna

Jikme Jungne Bepa འཇིགས་མེད་འབྱུང་གནས་སྦས་པ་ ['jigs med 'byung gnas sbas pa], Abhayākaragupta

Gökhukpa Lhaptse འགོས་ཁུག་པ་ལྷ་བཙས་ ['gos khug pa lha btsas], the Translator

Sakya Paṇḍita Künga Gyaltsen ས་སྐྱ་པཎྜི་ཏ་ཀུན་དགའ་རྒྱལ་མཚན་ [sa skya paṇḍi ta kun dga' rgyal mtshan]

Yungtön Throrgyal Dorje Pel གཡུང་སྟོན་ཁྲོ་རྒྱལ་རྡོ་རྗེ་དཔལ་ [g.yung ston khro rgyal rdo rje dpal], the Great Yogin

1		Khedrup Gelek Namgyal Pelzang མཁས་གྲུབ་དགེ་ལེགས་རྣམ་རྒྱལ་དཔལ་བཟང་ [mkhas grub dge legs rnam rgyal dpal bzang] (1385–1438), disciple of Tsongkhapa
2		Sönam Chokkyi Langpo བསོད་ནམས་ཕྱོགས་ཀྱི་གླང་པོ་ [bsod nams phyogs kyi glang po] (1439–1504)
3		Ensapa Lopsang Döndrup དབེན་ས་པ་བློ་བཟང་དོན་གྲུབ་ [dben sa pa blo bzang don grub] (1505–1566)
4	**1**	Lopsang Chökyi Gyaltsen བློ་བཟང་ཆོས་ཀྱི་རྒྱལ་མཚན་ [blo bzang chos kyi rgyal mtshan] (1567/1570–1662), the 1st Panchen Lama (plates 199–201)
5	**2**	Lopsang Yeshe བློ་བཟང་ཡེ་ཤེས་ [blo bzang ye shes] (1663–1737)
6	**3**	Lopsang Palden Yeshe བློ་བཟང་དཔལ་ལྡན་ཡེ་ཤེས་ [blo bzang dpal ldan ye shes] (1738–1780)
7	**4**	Lopsang Tenpe Nyima བློ་བཟང་བསྟན་པའི་ཉི་མ་ [blo bzang bstan pa'i nyi ma] (1782–1853)
8	**5**	Lopsang Palden Chökyi Drakpa Tenpe Wangchuk བློ་བཟང་དཔལ་ལྡན་ཆོས་ཀྱི་གྲགས་པ་བསྟན་པའི་དབང་ཕྱུག་ [blo bzang dpal ldan chos kyi grags pa bstan pa'i dbang phyug] (1855–1882)
9	**6**	Lopsang Chökyi Nyima Gelek Namgyal བློ་བཟང་ཆོས་ཀྱི་ཉི་མ་དགེ་ལེགས་རྣམ་རྒྱལ་ [blo bzang chos kyi nyi ma dge legs rnam rgyal] (1883–1937)[7] (plates 202–205)
10	**7**	Lopsang Thrinle Lhündrup Chökyi Gyaltsen བློ་བཟང་འཕྲིན་ལས་ལྷུན་གྲུབ་ཆོས་ཀྱི་རྒྱལ་མཚན་ [blo bzang 'phrin las lhun grub chos kyi rgyal mtshan] (1938–1989) (plates 206, 207)
11	**8**	Tenzin Gendün Yeshe Thrinle Phüntshok བསྟན་འཛིན་དགེ་འདུན་ཡེ་ཤེས་འཕྲིན་ལས་ཕུན་ཚོགས་ [bstan 'dzin dge 'dun ye shes 'phrin las phun tshogs] (1989–), also known as Gendün Chökyi Nyima དགེ་འདུན་ཆོས་ཀྱི་ཉི་མ་ [dge 'dun chos kyi nyi ma]

WHICH PANCHEN LAMAS FOUND, RECOGNIZED, AND TAUGHT WHICH DALAI LAMAS

1st Panchen Lama (4th by the first reckoning)	>	4th and 5th Dalai Lamas
2nd Panchen Lama (5th by the first reckoning)	>	6th and 7th Dalai Lamas
3rd Panchen Lama (6th by the first reckoning)	>	8th Dalai Lama
4th Panchen Lama (7th by the first reckoning)	>	9th, 10th , 11th Dalai Lamas

208 The Eighth (eleventh) Panchen Lama Gendün Chökyi Nyima. Modern painting based on an older photograph; the young Panchen Lama disappeared in May 1995 and his living conditions and location remain unknown.

THE PROTECTIVE DEITIES OF THE DALAI LAMAS

Amy Heller

In addition to believing that each person at birth has a protective deity associated with their body and birthplace, Tibetan Buddhists have great faith in the power of deities *sungma* སྲུང་མ [srung ma] "guardians" and *chökyong* ཆོས་སྐྱོང [chos skyong] (Skt. *dharmapāla*) "Protector of the Dharma." These deities are frequently invoked for physical protection against illness or accidents as well as from spiritual pollution or obstructions to meditation. Each person has the ability to influence them through worship in order to alleviate the suffering of existence. The political power of the Dalai Lama as an institution has derived its strength from deep belief in the powers of a clearly defined group of guardian deities that protect the lineage in addition to the Dalai Lama himself. These deities were therefore of the utmost importance and it is incumbent upon the Dalai Lama to worship them to get their benevolent influences for him both as an individual and as a religious hierarch. His worship of them has been all the more important in view of his eventual role as a political sovereign who wants to protect his people, government, and territory.[1]

For example, the sacred protective deities of the Great Fifth were entrusted with the heavy responsibility to safeguard the stability of the government, recently formed in 1642. In his capacity as an administrator, the 5th Dalai Lama progressively restructured government organization. Simultaneously in his capacity as a spiritual leader, he profoundly modified through his visions and literary compositions—both biographical and liturgical—the forms of worshipping certain protective deities to suit his political needs. He used the deities, or rather the power attributed to them, to legitimize his power, so that celebrations of their cults also became a celebration of the political regime. He glorified his own lineage by reinstating the religious preferences of earlier Dalai Lamas, as well as by celebrating rituals they had written, particularly those of the 2nd Dalai Lama and to a lesser extent of the 3rd Dalai Lama. With an eye toward creating an ideal central government, the 5th Dalai Lama also integrated the worship of the protective deities of other monastic orders into public celebrations in order to gain the support of their followers and to reinforce positive relations among the various schools. The geographic zone of influence of the Dalai Lama lineage's protective deities grew as political power extended far beyond the zone of the early Geluk monasteries in the Lhasa region, eventually under the 5th Dalai lama, encompassing areas in Mongolia as well as a territory stretching from Ladākh to the eastern regions of Sichuan 四川 and Yunnan 雲南.

According to the 14th Dalai Lama when he spoke in 2004,[2] there is a special relationship between Palden Lhamo; Nechung Dorje Drakden, then as a follower of Tsongkhapa; the Six-Armed Mahākāla; and Dharmarāja Yama. On other occasions, he has also mentioned Namthose. Among them Nechung, Palden Lhamo, Mahākāla, and Dharmarāja Yama are *dharmapāla*, while Namthose is a god of wealth and prosperity. Below we discuss differences in appearance and some of the mythology of the protective deities different Dalai Lamas have venerated. In reading the biographies about and autobiographies of preceding Dalai Lamas in addition to the essays of the Fourteenth himself, however, it is apparent that the significance individual Dalai Lamas have attributed to any given deity has greatly fluctuated over the years. This may be due in part to differences in each Dalai Lama's birth-gods, since these are linked with region of birth. For example, the 9th and the 11th Dalai Lamas were both born in Kham, so their protective birth-god was the Red Warrior deity Setap,[3] while since the 8th Dalai Lama was born in Tsang, he had Lijinhara as his birth-god.[4] A particular deity's popularity may also reflect their individual tutors, who emphasized the deities with whom they had personal affinities and initiated the Dalai Lamas for those deities. Another factor may be the dreams and visions a Dalai Lama has of a particular deity, which may result in more frequent worship. The State Oracle and the interpretations of his predictions may similarly influence the preference for certain deities.

HISTORICAL BACKGROUND

Let us now examine in chronological order some of the practices and preferences of earlier Dalai Lamas. According to his *namthar*, immediately after the birth of the 1st Dalai Lama (1391-1474), a crow suddenly appeared on the roof of his house and stayed there as a sign of the Four-Faced Mahākāla's protection.[5] Lhamo, especially in the form of Lhamo Makzorma, appeared in his visions and dreams first after he took his monastic vows in 1410 and later several times throughout his life. Once while teaching at Tanak, the ancestral monastery of the 2nd Dalai Lama, he had a vivid dream of Yama and the

209 Mahākāla. Copper (?) sheet metal, polychromy, Inner Mongolia, H: 41 cm, W: 35 cm, D: 14 cm, Folkens Museum Etnografiska, Stockholm, Inv. No.: 1935.50.2345.   210 Six-Armed Mahākāla of Wisdom with his four "ministers." Thangka, Tibet, 61 x 41.5 cm, Musée national des Arts asiatiques Guimet, Paris (Gift of Mrs. Toussaint), Inv. No.: MG23126. >>>

Four-Faced Mahākāla who told him that they were his friends.[6] These were the 1st Dalai Lama's main protective deities as described in his *namthar*.

Lhamo was particularly important for the 2nd Dalai Lama Gendün Gyatso in the late 15th century. Looking through his *sungbum* གསུང་འབུམ་ [gsung 'bum] "collected works," we find that he wrote a major history of her cult and several rituals for her. Gendün Gyatso focused great attention on Lhamo throughout his life. Both he and his father had several visions of Lhamo, particularly around the time that the *saṅgha* was hesitating to recognize Gendün Gyatso as the rebirth of Gendün Drup. As Gendün Gyatso grew older, Lhamo made an influential appearance when he started building the Chökhorgyal Monastery, and then another when he visited the lake nearby, an appearance which later generations in particular considered a major event.

With the expansion of the Geluk School under Gendün Gyatso, the cult of Lhamo and the guardians worshipped with her also grew. In 1509 he founded Chökhorgyal, which

he considered his personal monastery as did the succeeding Dalai Lamas. Just before construction began, Paldan Lhamo appeared to him in a vision to help him choose the exact place to build. Shortly thereafter, Gendün Gyatso went to a lake near the monastery in the company of a few of his disciples and again had more visions. Just as the 5th Dalai Lama did with his protective deities, in 1528 the 2nd Dalai Lama faithfully recorded his visions of Lhamo in his autobiography:

When I arrived at the edge of the lake, the surface was shining a brilliant white and I performed a ritual dedicated to Lhamo. At the moment of invocation a snowstorm suddenly arose from the east, but the snow falling on the lake did not change the color. Immediately after that, each of us saw rays of light forming the colors of the rainbow. Clearly above the five colors of the rays there were five turreted palaces. Then the lake took on the color of the sky. Next there was a frightening moment: the lake divided into two parts—a flat square area and an area rising like a mountain to the sky. I understood that this was the magic of Lhamo.

211 Vaiśravaṇa, represented as "Great Yellow Vaiśravaṇa," with the "Eight Masters of the Horse." Several Geluk priests in the upper section of the picture, such as the First Panchen Lama (far left) in the second row from the top, next to him is Je Sherap Sengge, an important disciple of Tsongkhapa, and at the same level on far right the Fourth Dalai Lama. Whether the figure to the left of him is the Third Dalai Lama is questionable, although the name of Je Sönam Gyatso is legible. The honorific title of Gyalwa, which accompanies the Fourth Dalai Lama, is missing, however. Thangka, Tibet, 67 x 49 cm, Ethnographic Museum of the University of Zürich, Inv. No.: 14415. >>> **Detail of 211** Mongoose spouting jewels.

We all witnessed these miraculous apparitions. It is certain that this place was protected by Lhamo because the infinite ways in which she acts cannot be expressed in words. What I write is only an approximation. Since I have become abbot of Tashilhünpo in 1512, I have been constantly performing rituals for Lhamo, three times a day with a *torma* offering and then in the evening, the performance of expiation rituals and more *torma* offerings. After making a *torma* offering for New Year's in 1514, I also had monks continuously perform rituals for several gods along with those for Lhamo, including for the Six-Armed Wisdom Mahākāla, Yama, and for the *dharmapālas* Four-Faced Mahākāla and Bektse. Continuing on to Kongpo, I also had performed uninterrupted ceremonies to the *maṇḍala* of Cakrasaṃvara.[7]

Reading this account, we can see how Gendün Gyatso was moved and became particularly devout towards Lhamo for the rest of his life. Since his lifetime, the lake where he had his visions has been known as *Lhamo Lhatso* "Soul Lake of Lhamo," a sacred place reputed to be particularly favorable for mystic visions. Today, the site is considered a sacred place for the Dalai Lama lineage because ever since Gendün Gyatso's visit, every Dalai Lama has made a pilgrimage there. The above excerpt from his autobiography shows us that already at the beginning of the 16th century, guardian deities were being venerated at the annual New Year's celebrations. All the Dalai Lamas ever since have continued these rituals to Lhamo and the other guardian deities.

Also in examining this passage, we may note a certain similarity between the protective deities that the 14th and the 2nd Dalai Lamas list: Palden Lhamo (plates 213–215), Six-Armed Mahākāla (plate 210), and Yama as *dharmapāla* (plate 226 left). In his autobiography, the 2nd Dalai Lama explains that Yeshe Gönpo Chakdruk ཡེ་ཤེས་མགོན་པོ་ཕྱག་དྲུག [ye shes mgon po phyag drug] "Wisdom Mahākāla" was the protective deity of his family's spiritual ancestors as well as being that of the Shangpa lineage teachings. Although he does not specifically discuss Namthose Vaiśravaṇa, the 2nd Dalai Lama did, however, write rituals in honor of aspects of Jambala, a deity often assimilated to Vaiśravaṇa. Gendün Gyatso's family performed rituals to *dharmapāla* Bektse (plates 217, 218), and Gendün Gyatso himself learned certain esoteric teachings on Bektse from his grandfather and from his father, who had studied them under the 1st Dalai Lama. He wrote three ritual offerings to Bektse describing him a red warrior—in his visions, Bektse always appeared to him as a red, wrathful warrior.[8]

For the life of the 3rd Dalai Lama, Sönam Gyatso, we must rely on the biography the 5th Dalai Lama wrote in 1646. It is noteworthy that before his birth, it was Lhamo who brought him to the home of his future mother and purified her womb. He had his first vision at eight months, of Lhamo with a sword and a skull cup full of jewels.[9] Lhamo is known as Padmasambhava's *kadö* བཀའ་སྡོད་ [bka' sdod] "special assistant,"[10] while also being known for her protection of Chökhorgyal.[11] Yet Lhamo was only one of many protective deities: in 1544 when he was one, Sönam Gyatso went to Drepung, where near the Nechung chapel, the great protective deity Dorje Öden Karpo རྡོ་རྗེ་འོད་ལྡན་དཀར་པོ [rdo rje 'od ldan dkar po] told him, "My friend, ...wherever you go, I will be with you."[12] In an essay, the 14th Dalai Lama uses the name Dorje Öden Karpo in tracing the history of Nechung and Pehar (a guardian deity who has lived at Samye since the 12th century) as two other protective deities.[13] The name Dorje Öden Karpo "Vajra of White Brilliance" itself signifies that the deity is a white manifestation and as such assimilated to Pehar himself.

When dignitaries came to investigate whether this young child was indeed a rebirth of the Dalai Lama, Sönam Gyatso clearly recognized the ritual flags of the Four-Faced Mahākāla and Bektse. Telling these gods' names to the assembled monks, he said, "Yes, those are their names, and sometimes my name is Mahākāla, but also they call me Gendün Gyatso. I have many other names."[14] When Sönam Gyatso was twelve, Bektse came into his dreams saying that he was Sönam Gyatso's personal *dharmapāla*.[15] Most significantly, in 1568 when the 3rd Dalai Lama was about twenty-five, he visited Tashilhünpo, where he had visions of Lhamo and then continued to Tanak, the family monastery of the 2nd Dalai Lama. There he had a vision of Bektse before returning to Tashilhünpo.[16]

During his childhood and again in 1558, the Nechung Oracle appears saying that he is a form of Pehar and works as Padmasambhava's *kadö*.[17] In 1570, the 3rd Dalai Lama visited Chökhorgyal to consecrate major images of Lhamo and Bektse,[18] which apparently reflected the 2nd Dalai Lama's ritual practices at Chökhorgyal. When the 3rd Dalai Lama left Lhasa to visit Altan

garlands of bones and either a tiger skin or an elephant hide, all evoking the frightening Hindu deities, especially Durgā, consort of Śiva, Lord of Destruction; or Kālī, the black goddess who receives blood offerings from goat sacrifices. The Tibetans also borrowed from the Indian goddess Revatī—"Rematī" in Tibetan—conceptually. She is as an ogress who in Indian mythology takes the lives of young children. Moreover, Lhamo has taken on the attributes and legends of several local pre-Buddhist Tibetan deities, which Tibetan Buddhism has traditionally associated with divination.

With so many distinct forms, a physical description of Lhamo will help explain her composite mythology and iconography of this. We find her described in a Geluk ritual of praise dedicated to her in her aspect of Palden Lhamo Makzorma དཔལ་ལྡན་ལྷ་མོ་དམག ཟོརམ [dpal ldan lha mo dmag zor ma], a fierce manifestation of Lhamo:

> Out of a vast, wild sea of blood and fat in the centre of a black storm, Palden Lhamo Makzorma Gyelmo Rematī comes forth from the syllable BHYO while mounted on a *kyang* "mule" with a white circle on its forehead, a belt of demon heads, a demon-skin cover, crupper, bridle, and reins made of poisonous snakes. Dark blue in color, she has one face and two hands. Her right hand wields a thunderbolt-adorned club which she raised above the heads of oath breakers; in front of her breast, her left hand holds the skull of a child born of incestuous union, full of magic substances and blood. Her mouth gapes open and she bares four sharp teeth; she chews on a corpse and laughs thunderously. Her three eyes, red and globular, move like lightning and her brow is furrowed with great anger. Her yellow-brown hair stands on end, her eyebrows and facial hair burning fiercely like the fire at the end of a *kalpa*. Her right ear is adorned with five human skulls. She wears a garland of fifty freshly-severed, blood-dripping heads. Her body is covered with splashes of blood and specks of fat, and is smeared with the ashes of cremated corpses. On the crown of her head shines the disc of the moon and on her navel that of the sun. She wears a black silk scarf and a human skin serves as covering; her upper garment is of rough black cloth, while her loincloth is a freshly-killed tigerskin of fastened with a belt of two entwined snakes. From the saddle-straps in front hangs a sack full of diseases; from the straps at the back, a magic ball of thread. A divination stick protrudes from her waist-belt. A

214 Palden Lhamo (Śrī Devi). Thangka, Tibet, 2nd half of the 17th century, 84 x 58.5 cm, Museum der Kulturen, Basel, Inv. No.: IId 13693. >>>

load of red tablets and a pair of white and black dice hang from the straps. On her head she wears an umbrella of peacock feathers.[24] (plate 226, far right)

Most of these attributes are linked with her mythology. For example, her mule has an eye on his flank resulting from an accident in one of Lhamo's previous lives in India when she was the spouse of a demon king living on the island Laṅkā. She decided to convert the inhabitants of the island to Buddhism forcibly and vowed that she would kill her own son if she did not succeed. Confronted with her failure, she had to sacrifice her son. She then attached his freshly-peeled skin to the saddle. The king chased her and injured her mule on the flank with an arrow. The eye is the trace of the wound, magically transformed through Lhamo's power.

We find Lhamo depicted alone or accompanying a form of Mahākāla as his consort or attendant. Although her attributes vary among her various forms, she is always depicted as a wrathful, dark-colored female. Sometimes we find a sword with a scorpion-shaped hilt substituted for her magic wand. She may sometimes have four arms—three holding weapons

215 Palden Lhamo and her two main attendants Siṃhavaktra "the Lion-headed one" and Makaravaktra "the Makara-headed one." Bronze, gilded, Tibet, H: 18 cm, W: 17.5 cm, D: 8 cm, Ethnographic Museum of the University of Zürich, Inv. No.: 14113.

and one holding a skull cup. The members of her entourage likewise vary considerably. There is often a lion-headed goddess and another with the head of a *makara*, a mythological creature resembling a combination of a crocodile and a feline (plate 215). As "Goddess of the Four Seasons," Lhamo has four attendant goddesses of different colors. She is also called "Mistress of the Twelve Tenma Goddesses" and is depicted standing in the center of a group of twelve female deities that have heads of various animals.

The cult of Lhamo has had a very long history in the world of Tibetan Buddhism. According to the 2nd Dalai Lama in his short history of the worship of Lhamo, teachers from Oḍḍiyāna, a land identified with either Bengal or the province of Swāt in Pakistān, introduced her cult to Tibet during the 11th century. *Ācārya* Marpo, "Red Master," an itinerant religious master also called Paṇḍita Sangwa Sherap པཎྜི་ཏ་གསང་བ་ཤེས་རབ [paṇ ḍi ta gsang ba shes rab] "Pandit of Secret Wisdom" was the first to transmit the

teachings in Tibet. Later, lamas of both the Nyingma and Kagyü Schools continued to spread the teachings. The most ancient depictions of Lhamo that we know of are those in the sanctuaries of Alchi in Ladākh, which probably date from the founding of this monastery in the late 11th century.

At about the same time, teachers of the Sakya School were initiated into the teachings devoted to Lhamo and chose her as Great *dharmapāla*, "Protector of the Dharma." Here Lhamo played the role of first consort to Mahākāla, principal protective deity of the Sakya School. A Sakya teacher transmitted her teachings to the 1st Dalai Lama (1391–1474), who was then abbot of Tashilhünpo, where he faithfully performed the rituals and taught them to his pupils, including the father of the 2nd Dalai Lama.

BEKTSE: GREAT FEROCIOUS MASTER OF VITALITY

When Gendün Gyatso would visit Lhamo's lake, he would first visit a smaller lake nearby, now known as Bektse's Lake. Even in 1933, the search party looking for the reincarnation of the 13th Dalai Lama sent a mission to these two lakes seeking clues to help them find the child. According to concepts of sacred geography, these two lakes symbolize the relationship between Bektse and Lhamo since these two deities had been made personal guardians of the Dalai Lama lineage.

Bektse is a ferocious warrior with three eyes. Red is the characteristic color of his skin and outfit. He is covered in copper armor from head to foot. This armor is called *bektse* in Tibetan and this has given him his principal name. His helmet with a diadem of five skulls is decorated with silk tassels at the sinciput. In his right hand, Bektse brandishes a sword with a scorpion handle, while his left hand clasps against his chest the heart and lungs of an enemy. In the crook of his arm, he carries the lance of victory and a bow. He tramples upon two bodies, horse and human.

This description of Bektse corresponds closely to that found in a ritual the 2nd Dalai Lama wrote, one of the earliest rituals now known for Bektse. The 2nd Dalai Lama writes that Bektse was worshipped in India before being introduced to Tibet during the 11th century. The Tibetan Buddhist master Nyen the Translator, who specialized in teachings on the Four-Faced Mahākāla introduced this form of worship to Tibet. This form of Mahākāla has two assistants: Bektse as a red warrior and

216 Oracle flag for Bektse. 94 x 79 cm, Ethnographic Museum of the University of Zürich, Inv. No.: 14910. >>>

Mahākāla himself in the form of a black *yogin.* Nyen the Translator taught these rituals to his disciples, principally students and teachers living at Sakya Monastery in southern Tsang. We will return shortly to discuss Bektse in the Sakya tradition. *Ācārya* Marpo or "Red *Ācārya,*" the teacher who introduced the cult of Lhamo to Tibet, also transmitted a series of rituals for worship of Bektse. In these we find Bektse represented completely differently, with three heads, six arms, and standing in embrace with a female deity. He transmitted these esoteric teachings to only a few restricted initiates.

Sakya monks were the first to elaborate the ritual traditions Gendün Gyatso had transmitted, although a *mahāsiddha*—a wandering holy man and miracle worker—also contributed to the elaboration. This *mahāsiddha* had visions of Padmasambhava in the company of protective deities with whom Bektse was associated. This master taught the rituals for Bektse to several Sakya lamas, one of whom was teacher to Gendün Gyatso's great grandfather. As discussed earlier in the chapter on the 2nd Dalai Lama, this ancestor of Gendün Gyatso's had been a follower of the mystic teachings of the Shang tradition of the Kagyü School. He founded Tanak "Black Horse" Mon-

astery in Tsang which specialized in the Shang tradition and also performed rituals dedicated to Bektse. These teachings descended from father to son, down to Gendün Gyatso, who had taken vows of monastic celibacy and so transmitted them to his monastic disciples. Hitherto, this tradition had been a family cult, but with Gendün Gyatso developed into an institutional cult within the Geluk School, which worshipped Bektse as one of their principal protectors, like Lhamo.[25]

DORJE DRAKDEN: STATE ORACLE

Today the deity Dorje Drakden, who bears the title of Nechung Chögyal, still holds a special position within the government of the Dalai Lama. This deity manifests itself through the medium of the Nechung Oracle—whose name is taken from Nechung Monastery—who acts as state oracle for the Tibetan government in exile. The tradition of such phenomena in Tibet seems to go back to ancient times. In 1436 Gendün Drup consulted the oracle Lama Donyö of Tanak for predictions, and later Gendün Gyatso also mentions in his autobiography that the same oracle was consulted to find Gendün Drup's rebirth.[26] However, the oldest accounts describing Nechung as possessing

217 Bektse. Copper (?) sheet metal, polychromy, Inner Mongolia, H: 43 cm, W: 34 cm, D: 13 cm, Folkens Museum Etnografiska, Stockholm, Inv. No.: 1935.50.2378. **218** Bektse, surrounded by respected Geluk masters, including the Second and Third Dalai Lama (top right beside Buddha Amitābha in the center), other wrathful gods (including his sister Rikpe Lhamo) and the group of the "Eight Knife Carriers"). Thangka, Tibet, 84.5 x 57.5 cm, Museum der Kulturen, Basel, Inv. No.: IId 13667. >>>

mediums date from the writings of the 5th Dalai Lama in the 17th century. Several other deities have also appeared through mediums over the centuries, including Dorje Öden Karpo discussed earlier. Yet at present, Nechung is the official oracle, and speaks primarily for Dorje Drakden.

As we see in plate 219, the Nechung Oracle is depicted as a warrior deity dressed in armor. In the center of his chest is a breastplate on which a letter is written; this is in fact a mirror used in séances. The letter is the "seed syllable" from which the deity emerges to enter the medium during trance. He also wears a helmet with a crown of five skulls and several triangular pennants at the sinciput. In his right hand, he wields a lance with silk pennants, while in the left he holds the loops of a lasso or slingshot used to coerce enemies of the Buddhist doctrine. Behind on his right, we see a quiver with a few arrows, with a bow on his left. A long sword is attached to the apron covering his armor. Beneath his feet, this stocky warrior crushes a human body. Iconographically, in certain respects there is a great similarity between Nechung and Bektse, which is perhaps related to a tradition which considers Nechung an emanation of Bektse.

Today it is generally accepted that Nechung Chögyal is an emanation of Pehar (plates 222, 223, 225). Several legends relate to the arrival of Pehar in Lhasa: during the reign of the 5th Dalai Lama, Pehar sent Nechung towards Lhasa in order for him to be near the capital. Nechung took up residence in a monastery but his presence was not appreciated and the lamas performed coercive rituals to oblige him to leave. He then chose a tree near Drepung in which to reside. Around this tree rose up a monastery which itself became a sanctuary for Pehar's emanation. Eventually Pehar himself went there. The name Nechung, literally "Small Place" or "Small Presence," came to be the name of the deity and of the medium through which he manifests himself.[27]

At present, the tradition of Nechung as emanation of Bektse is not widely known. This may derive in part from a vision the 5th Dalai Lama had in 1672: one day while performing rituals devoted to Padmasambhava, the latter appeared in a vision and again designated Bektse as assistant protector of the Dalai Lama. The vision continuing, Nechung appeared as Bektse's acolyte. From a purely iconographic perspective, it is clear that while Nechung and Bektse share many of the same attributes and both trample bodies, Pehar and his other emanations all ride on horseback. Yet Bektse and Nechung have differing official roles. When the 5th Dalai Lama was

219 Dorje Drakden, with probably the Fifth Dalai Lama (upper left), a very esoteric form of Hayagriva (upper center) and Pehar (lower center). Thangka, Tibet, 17th century, 63 x 41.5 cm, Nyingjei Lam Collection. >>>

220 Costume of Nechung Oracle. H: ca. 210 cm, Museum Rietberg, Zürich, Inv. No.: RTI. **221** Crown of an oracle. Metal, partially gilded, coral, turquoise, Dm: 30 cm, H: 15 cm, Ethnographic Museum of the University of Zürich, Inv. No.: 19826. Mirror of an oracle with the syllable hri. Dm: 20 cm, H: 18 cm, D: 8 cm, Ethnographic Museum of the University of Zürich, Inv. No.: 17007.

attending a special ritual for Bektse with many *torma* offerings, he watched as the tiered cakes suddenly collapsed. This sight provoked an unusual moment of prescience in the life of the 5th Dalai Lama. He immediately had the impression that he had seen before his eyes completely all the events of the coming years, and consequently established a series of political policies for the next two years. Yet according to all of the 5th Dalai Lama's accounts, Bektse never manifested himself through a medium to predict the future. Because the 5th Dalai Lama had greatly venerated Bektse throughout his entire lifetime, Bektse and Lhamo were appointed guardians of his funerary *stūpa*. The placing of special images of the two in the *stūpa*, along with the mummy of the Great Fifth, conferred divine protection to the monument and posthumous protection to the deceased. After the death of the Fifth, Nechung progressively superseded Bektse in his role as personal male protector of the contemporaneous Dalai Lama, a function that Nechung retains to this day. Lhamo has remained the principal female protector since the time of the 1st Dalai Lama.

While we have seen a certain fluctuation in the roles of various deities, the constant worship of and rituals devoted to the protective deities show how important they are. In a more abstract interpretation, we could say that the deities are all the same in essence, and may all give protection if worshipped appropriately. As far as which deities are major, it is above all the Dalai Lama's authority as religious hierach that determines to which deities homage must be given. Nevertheless, Palden Lhamo appears to be the most important deity to the Dalai Lama lineage, with her influence constant throughout the centuries. As the 5th Dalai Lama came to rely on the Nechung Oracle, Nechung Dorje Drakden came to great prominence. Today the 14th Dalai Lama has stated that these two deities are of paramount importance for his lineage.

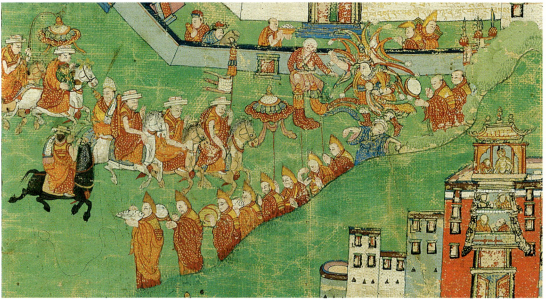

222 Pehar. Copper (?) sheet metal, polychromy, Inner Mongolia, H: 37 cm, W: 30 cm, D: 16 cm, Folkens Museum
Etnografiska, Stockholm, Inv. No.: 1935.50.2385.   223 Pehar. Thangka, Tibet, 44.5 x 32 cm, Ethnographic Museum
of the University of Zürich, Inv. No.: 14445. >>>   224 An Oracle wearing pennants receives the young Fifth Dalai
Lama who is riding a white horse beneath an umbrella of state, as he is brought to Lhasa. Detail from the scroll
of the Fifth Dalai Lama (see plate 46).   225 Pehar. Thangka, Tibet, 67 x 47 cm, Musées Royaux d'Art et d'Histoire,
Brussels, Inv. No.: Ver. 278. >>>   226 Details of a thangka (see plate 19 in this book): the most important protective deities of the Dalai Lamas, from left to right: Dharmarāja Yama, Bektse, Dorje Drakden and Palden Lhamo. >>>

WESTERN VIEWS OF THE DALAI LAMAS

Martin Brauen
Translated by JANICE BECKER

THE DALAI LAMA AS THE WORK OF THE DEVIL

The earliest report of the Dalai Lamas published in the West appears in *China Illustrata*, a compendium Athanasius Kircher published probably in 1667. His depictions were based on the reports of Father Albert d'Orville and Johannes Grueber, who spent a few weeks in Lhasa during 1661 but did not meet the 5th Dalai Lama. His description of Tibet begins with what is certainly a central symbol of both Tibet and the Dalai Lama, "Menipe." Kircher terms him the most important "Tibetan idol," referring to the Bodhisattva Avalokiteśvara, held to be reincarnated in the Dalai Lamas. According to Kircher, he was unusually tall and had nine heads arranged in the form of a cone (plate 229). "The dumb people pray to these gods, making unusual gestures as they do and repeating without pause the words, 'O Manipe mi hum, Om Manipe mi hum.'" Kircher was surely referring to the mantra of Avalokiteśvara, "oṃ maṇi padme hūṃ." A few lines later, Kircher writes:

> There are two kings in this country. The one is responsible for directing the actual affairs of the kingdom. He is called deva.[2] The other king is protected from all external influence and leads a life of leisure in the seclusion of his palace. He is revered as a god not only by the natives but by all the kings subject to him in the Land of the Tartars, who make the pilgrimage to him of their own accord. They pray to him like the true and living God. They even call him the Eternal and Heavenly Father and underscore their devotion with many gifts for him that they usually bring with them. He sits in the dark, closed chambers of his palace... (as seen in illustration XIX) (plate 230), bedecked in gold and silver and illuminated by many burning lamps. He sits raised on a pillow, under which are laid costly carpets. The visitors throw themselves humbly at his feet and touch the floor with their heads. They kiss his feet with unbelievable reverence, as if he were the Pope. This reveals in a most fantastic manner the entire cunning of the evil spirit, as such worship as is due only to Christ's representative on earth, the Pope in Rome, is directed to these pagan gods of primitive nations, as are all other mysteries of Christianity. The devil accomplishes this with the malevolence that only he possesses. As Christians refer to the Roman Pontiff as the Father of all Fathers, so these barbarians name their pitiful deity the Dalai Lama, which means the High Priest. They also call him the Lama of all Lamas, which means the Priest of all Priests...In order to prevent any

doubts arising as to his immortality, after his death the Lamas search the entire kingdom for a man similar in all respects to the deceased. When they have found him, they put him on the throne of the previous Dalai Lama. By these means, they convince the people in the entire kingdom, who know nothing of this swindle and deceit, of the eternal life of the Eternal Father lives, who is said to have arisen again from hell seven times in this century alone ...

Here Kircher anticipates later writings by comparing the institution of the Dalai Lama with that of the papacy. To some, the similarities were so striking that only one conclusion was possible for a devout Christian: the devil must have a hand in the matter.

Ippolito Desideri arrived in Lhasa in 1716, at a time when the young 7th Dalai Lama was still sojourning in eastern Tibet. His depictions of the Dalai Lama, which had remained undiscovered in library archives for almost 150 years, are still of interest. Desideri calls the Dalai Lama "the High Lama of Tibet," the head of all Lamas, Lord, Protector, and Pontiff of all the superstitious Tibetans, Nepalis, Tartars, and Chinese. He correctly describes the Dalai Lama as the incarnation of Chenrezik (Avalokiteśvara) and corrected misconceptions that Tibetans believed their High Lama was immortal, invisible, and never appeared to anyone. Quite the opposite, Desideri writes—he entertains not only his own countrymen but foreigners as well.

Desideri's conception of the system of reincarnation is also of interest. Strangely, he asserts the Tibetans were convinced that, upon finding a Dalai Lama, there was a fraudulent deal negotiated between the child's relatives and a group of Lamas and monks in order to deceive the credulous Tibetans. The child was said to be secretly instructed in exactly what he should say and do. Desideri himself does not accept this "conspiracy theory" apparently because the special qualities of the reincarnated monks impressed him. In his opinion, a young child would not be able to hatch all these "stories." Thus Desideri does not question the unusual abilities of the children held to be reincarnations; indeed he sees these abilities as self-evident. Rather, he seeks an explanation plausible from a Catholic perspective—that they were the work of the Devil.[3]

At various times between 1707 and 1745, Capuchin missionaries stayed in Lhasa[4] although there were only three longer and two brief meetings with the Dalai Lama living at that time, the

227–230 Images of Potala and the Dalai Lama published in Europe in the 17th century in compendia about foreign lands. These pictures were generally not made by travellers to Tibet but were instead based on their notes and sketches and were often copied. **227** "Bietala" (Potala), colored copperplate engraving, which was probably based on an engraving by Athanasius Kircher in *China Illustrata*. Collection of Jean Lassale, Paris. **228** This representation of the "Grand Lama," referring to the Dalai Lama, is also a copy of an earlier engraving from *China Illustrata* (see plate 230). Collection of Jean Lassale, Paris. **229** This engraving shows how the adoration of "Menipe" (Bodhisattva Avalokiteśvara) was imagined, who is curiously shown like a European bust without torso. Archive of the Ethnographic Museum of the University of Zürich. **230** Engraving from *China Illustrata*, which served as the model for the "Grand Lama" (see plate 228). Along with the Dalai Lama, the bust of the deceased King of "Tanguthen," Gushri Khan, is also visible. Archive of the Ethnographic Museum of the University of Zürich.

231 Depiction of the Dalai Lama, which was most likely based on one of the engravings seen on page 231. Archive of the Ethnographic Museum of the University of Zürich.

Seventh.[5] Father Gioacchino Da S. Anatolia describes the first audience with the Dalai Lama, which occurred in 1724. He discusses the types of blessing given, which the Capuchin monks did not have to undergo. He details the gifts the Capuchin missionaries and others presented to the Dalai Lama and goes on to describe seating arrangements and the drinks and dishes they were offered. This exact, even fastidious recording of the rituals and surroundings of the reception is striking in both this and in many later reports. The Father pays primary attention not to the content of the discussions with the Dalai Lama, but rather to the "set" and "action" of the event.[6]

Orazio della Penna and a few other Capuchin missionaries residing in Lhasa a third and final time after a twelve-year absence had another audience with the 7th Dalai Lama in 1741. Contrary to all expectations, the Dalai Lama received them informally, inviting them to sit and speaking directly to the Capuchin fathers, an honor which they describe as normally being bestowed on high-ranking personages. A casual conversation ensued during which the Dalai Lama asked about the health of the European monks and their travels to Tibet. At one of the final audiences in November 1742, there was no deep discussion even though there would have been occasion since the previous year Tibetan converts had been flogged. The Capuchin monks were only able to present the Dalai Lama with a book about the Christian faith written in Tibetan. They discussed trivialities and soon the missionaries received a few gifts and were shown the door.[7]

While deep discussions of religion did not characterize meetings with the Dalai Lama, there was correspondence and intimate discussion with his teacher. In 1741, the 7th Dalai Lama even signed an order permitting the Capuchin missionaries, the "white-headed Lamas," to preach their doctrine (plate 73).[8]

It would be sixty years before the next Westerner would again meet the Dalai Lama, this time the eccentric Thomas Manning, who arrived in Lhasa in 1811 during his private travels. On 17 December he went to the Potala to greet the "High Lama," the 9th Dalai Lama, then about six years old to present him with gifts, and to receive his blessing. The meeting apparently moved Manning greatly:

> The Lama's beautiful and interesting face and manner captured almost my entire attention. He was then about seven years of age and had the simple and unaffected manner of a well-brought up child of nobility. His face was, it seemed to me, poetic and touchingly beautiful. He had a cheerful and spirited disposition; his beautiful mouth incessantly tended to a charming smile that illuminated his entire face. Sometimes, especially when he looked at me, his smile would become almost a slight laugh. My ferocious beard and my glasses doubtless moved him to laughter …
>
> I was extremely moved by this meeting with the Lama, and I could have cried at the peculiarity of the feeling. I was completely lost in my thoughts as I arrived home. I wrote the following memorandum in my big book: "1 December, seventeenth day of the tenth month. Today I greeted the High Lama. Wonderfully beautiful youth. Face poetically touching; could have cried. Very happy to have seen him and his blest smile. Hope to see him again often.[9]

Almost a hundred years passed before any white people again saw the Dalai Lama. While Régis Évariste Huc and Joseph

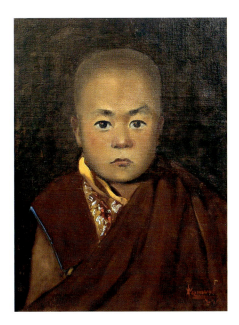 

232/233 The Fourteenth Dalai Lama at approximately age five on the occasion of his enthronement, at which apparently photographs were not allowed. The British delegation that attended the ceremonies included the Indian artist Kanwal Krishna, who painted several portraits of the five-year-old. Oil on canvas, Tibet, Lhasa 1940. 232 Collection of Lady Gould 233 Collection of R.J. and E. Gould Dm: 78 x 74 cm.

Gabet spent time in Lhasa in 1846, to their great regret they were not able to see the 11th Dalai Lama, then nine years old and living in the Potala, apparently because it was feared that they would infect the young monarch with smallpox.[10]

MATTERS OF CEREMONY

As mentioned above, many reports concentrated on ceremonial procedures that were often interpreted as evidence of the special deference bestowed on the particular visitor. What had fascinated all visitors since the first missionaries was the exchange of *khatak* scarves with the Dalai Lama.[11] A good example of these descriptions of ceremonial exchanges of scarves can be found in Macdonald's book, who was probably the first European after Thomas Manning to meet the Dalai Lama in Tibet. This occurred in 1910 in Yatung, when the 13th Dalai Lama was fleeing to India to escape the Chinese.[12]

Given the unique situation, court etiquette played no role during this meeting—Macdonald shared his room, his table, and his meal with the Dalai Lama. He leaves his reader largely in the dark, however, concerning the subjects of his discussions with the Dalai Lama.[13] Later when Macdonald met the Dalai Lama, this time in Lhasa, we learn nothing of the content of their discussions but only something about the ceremonies, namely the presentation of scarves and gifts. Macdonald notes with perceptible satisfaction that his reception included elements not afforded to every visitor—he received a scarf similar to the one he had presented to the Dalai Lama.[14] In general, all Western visitors observed and meticulously described the treatment they received from the Dalai Lama, no doubt because they thought they could read their own status through their treatment.

Especially interesting was an extremely rare ceremony which no Westerner had before observed, the installation of the 14th Dalai Lama in 1940. The most detailed description comes from Sir Basil Gould,[15] who characterizes the Dalai Lama:

> A solid solemn but very wide-awake boy, red-cheeked and closely shorn, wrapped warm in the maroon-red robes of a monk and in outer coverings, was seated high on his simple throne, cross-legged in the attitude of Buddha. (...) I noticed the steadiness of his gaze, the beauty of his hands, and the devotion and love of the Abbots who attend him. (...) It appears that His Holiness has a strong will and is already learning to exercise the privileges of his position.

AN AURA OF MYSTERY

Some depictions of the Dalai Lamas Western visitors provide are well-meaning, even rapturous. In a few, we can sense deep sympathy and real closeness; some of these authors seem to have believed that the Dalai Lamas were actually superhuman. We have already encountered one such example: Ippolito Desideri, who believed that the 7th Dalai Lama was so unusual that the devil must have had a hand in selecting him as the candidate. In later texts also there are suggestions of the extraordinary, if not superhuman, qualities of the Dalai Lama. While it remains unclear whether these are the opinions of the authors or of devout Tibetans, some passages clearly indicate the astonishment at the young Dalai Lama's abilities, such when Richardson writes:

> ...Today the Dalai Lama behaved with the same dignity as before but he seemed less solemn and occasionally smiled at his atten-

dants as if he were glad to have reached his old home again. (…) His behaviour during the exacting two days of his entry into Lhasa has been a source of wonder and delight to the people of Tibet and has confirmed their trust in the reincarnation. Indeed such calm assurance in so young a child seems to come from something more than mere schooling. He never smiled but maintained a placid, equable gaze. Much of his attention was directed to a calm inspection of members of the British Mission as though he were trying to recall where he had seen such people before.[16]

The following passage from a letter Richardson wrote to his parents also reflects something of his almost religious respect:

> When we saw him he was really extraordinary, and one almost believes in reincarnation. He seemed absolutely familiar with the ceremonies and what he should do and was not at all impressed by all the grandeur. There can be no doubt that he is exceptional and I continue to hear stories about him, in which there is a good deal of fact. Everyone says he behaves just like the late Dalai Lama.[17]

Sir Basil Gould was similarly impressed with the charisma of the young 14th Dalai Lama:

> Again a main impression produced was the extraordinary interest of the child in the proceedings, his presence, and his infalliable skill in doing the right thing to the right person and at the right time. He was perhaps the only person amongst many hundreds who never fidgeted and whose attention never wavered. It was evident that the Ser-Thri-Nga-Sol (the request to occupy the golden throne) was indeed the return, in response to prayer, of the Dalai Lama to a throne which by inherent authority was already his."[18]

Amaury Comte de Riencourt also wrote about his meeting with the young 14th Dalai Lama in 1947 in a mystical tone:

> I had to bite my lip to reassure myself that I wasn't dreaming, that I was really sitting in an audience with the Dalai Lama of Tibet, that I was sojourning in this strictly forbidden holy quarter…Scented mists of sandalwood incense surrounded the throne

of the Dalai Lama, as if they wanted to carry away the God King of Tibet on a magic cloud.[19]

Reading these quotations inevitably reminds us of Manning's description of the young 9th Dalai Lama.

CRITICAL DETACHMENT

While without exception almost all the male visitors[20] appear to have been overwhelmed by the sanctity of the Dalai Lama sitting across from them, the few European women who saw and spoke with him depict him in much less mystical tones. Writing with particular detachment bordering on sarcasm and disparagement, Alexandra David-Néel was disposed negatively towards the royal court clique. Her sympathies clearly lay with the Pancha Lama and the Chinese. She first met the 13th Dalai Lama on 14 April 1912:

> Tomorrow I will be introduced to the Dalai Lama; of course that is an event for me; to be received by the "Pope" of Asia is even less an everyday event for a European woman than to be received at the Vatican. It is an event for him, too, since I am the first woman from the Occident whom he has voluntarily received…I have prepared a series of questions that I want to ask him. What kind of a person will I meet?…I am delighted to be so lucky. To return with a study of Lamaism prepared with the Dalai Lama himself…that would really be a fantastic work of Orientalism! Unfortunately, his yellow Highness is greatly absorbed with political troubles and probably has little time for philosophical discussions. We will see… Suddenly I am standing before the Great Manitu…Laden La whispers nervously to me. "Don't you want to be blessed?" I sense that I would offend these people if I were to say it wasn't important to me. So I nodded, since the Lama was seated and was not tall. Quite powerfully—really!—he lays his hand on my hair. So now I have been blessed and his Narcissism is satisfied. Meanwhile we begin, or rather he begins, to talk. Of course, he asks me the unavoidable question of how long I have been a Buddhist and how I came to be one. But it would be difficult for his Tibetan brain to understand that one can become a Buddhist attending classes at a European university, as a student of Oriental philosophy. The fact that I had no guru, no teacher, exceeds his grasp…We chat about this and that. He seems to have quite a happy disposition. Of course he is not a moron, but by our standards no intellectual either.[21]

234 The Thirteenth Dalai Lama in a typical frontal photograph. However, in contrast to the norm, he is seated "Western" style—not on his throne. Photographer: David Macdonald, 1912, Sir Charles Alfred Bell Collection, © The British Library.

David-Néel met the Dalai Lama once again at the end of June 1912:

> The Dalai Lama wants to receive me at a private audience. A very special honor!...I speak with the Dalai Lama about the manuscript that he sent me, about a couple of points that are not clear in it...Despite that, this man does not appeal to me, he is a brother at most in the general sense of shared humanity. I do not hold the Popes in esteem and I don't care for the type of Buddhist Catholicism of which he is the chief. Everything about him is affected, he knows neither kindliness nor friendliness... well, the Dalai Lama doesn't seem to have the same disposition as the person he calls his teacher [referring to Buddha]. He is, however, much more educated and proficient in philosophical matters than is assumed in the Occident; in that regard, justice has not been done to him in the past.[22]

In an article for the *Mercure de France* (1912), David-Néel describes this same meeting, although curiously without the negative undertones. In the same article she mentions another, shorter meeting during which the Dalai Lama made a completely different impression on her. As she went to get her coat from the bungalow where the Dalai Lama lived, she unexpectedly encountered "the yellow Pope." He was standing in front of the doors of his room and looking out at the landscape. David-Néel regretted that, now in the moment she was completely alone with the Dalai Lama, she could not speak with him in the Tibetan language:

> ... without the chattering chamberlain who seemed to hold his Lord in leading strings. He had none of his official demeanor about him

as he looked at the rainfall, he seemed less and less like his photographs, and I liked him more, his look is resolute and open...At that moment he seemed like "someone" to me. I did not see that face in Kalimpong. A mystery of the royal court! Who knows how much freedom he has within his environment? ...The convocation of Lamas, the high dignitaries of the empire, cope well with a child-like Dalai Lama and had arranged things so that their almost divine pupil would not come of age. We had to make do with simply looking at each other, ... then the Dalai Lama went into his room, and I went my way. The regret was surely not just on one side.

Thyra Weir, the first Englishwoman to visit Lhasa, met the 13th Dalai Lama on 17 August 1930. She accompanied her husband, Col. Leslie Weir, who was attached to the official British mission in Tibet and who took several good portraits of the 13th Dalai Lama. Thyra Weir's description is particularly interesting because she did not write for publication but rather for her diary, which may explain the spontaneous, genuine tone:

> At 8AM we arrived at the Norbu Linga—a not very imposing building—the private residence of the Dalai Lama. Great was the excitement over my visit—the first European woman to be summoned in audience.
>
> We entered the throne room and there he was sitting on a marvellous throne (this was merely a minor throne room on the ground floor). We exchanged scarves, as is the custom, and seated ourselves on chairs— all our staff and everyone else standing throughout the interior. I was agreeably surprised over the appearance of the Dalai Lama. From photographs taken twenty years ago he appeared to be of the sickly "Gandhi" variety, but

here was a fattish man with a shaved bullet (Alpine?) head, bright though slightly watery eyes, teeth rather defective as they had mostly fallen out, one long one remaining in front —but withall a healthy looking man with a good colour. (His age is about 57.) He received us most genially and I managed to make him smile over the description of my reception by the crowds in the city. My apparent hilarity seemed to cause astonishment and concern in the room where people all assumed attitudes of the most subservient character, being nearly bent double—tongue slightly out and noise of intake of breath—very audible—tempered with saliva!

He was dressed in priceless yellow satin brocade and wore remarkable boots with turned-up toes and applice work on the uppers—very beautiful. By his side was the beautiful jade tea cup in its gold stand with gold lid. The gold is coloured a reddish shade here in Lhasa and in fact by all high officials everywhere. They do not value our pale gold at all.

We were given English tea flooded with milk and cream cracker biscuits. Our attendants—nothing. We talked of flowers, of his kind hospitality, of pictures. He wondered if my pictures could be as good as photographs—to which I replied in the negative. The visit was considered highly successful by the staff because it has been so cheerful and H.H. was in such good mood. I wonder what he thought of the queer English female! We shall see him again...[23]

WESTERN "HAGIOGRAPHY" OF THE DALAI LAMA

The Westerner with the best understanding of a Dalai Lama—in this case, the 13th—was Sir Charles Bell, a British political officer stationed for many years in Sikkim. After a twenty-three-year friendship with the Dalai Lama, ending only with the Tibetan ruler's death, Bell wrote his book, *A Portrait of the Dalai Lama*. In it he provides a very sophisticated, non-mystical depiction of the Dalai Lama, which is yet not as skeptical or detached as Alexandra David-Néel's. Furthermore, his work is of particular interest because it includes the first detailed depiction of the Dalai Lama by a non-Tibetan.

Bell describes the Dalai Lama as extremely open and honest, very interested in politics, brave, impulsive and humorous, cheerful and kindly, blessed with a hardy constitution and a love for work, authority, and a strong will. He loved to work—and he liked the power which work gave him. His was always the last word and he did not surrender any authority; he was an autocrat—in governmental as in religious matters, "perhaps

the most autocratic ruler in the modern world," "an absolute dictator," characteristics that apparently grew more pronounced toward the end of his life. Bell repeatedly refers to the Dalai Lama as impulsive and quick-tempered, traits which also became more pronounced with age. But Bell also describes the soft-hearted side of the ruler who loved to work in the garden and was interested in flowers and animals, especially dogs and birds. He also expected of others the same discipline that he demanded of himself. He raised the level and demands of religious training, especially for *geshes*, tested very carefully new abbots, intervened against certain monasteries' repression of the people, and improved hygiene in the monasteries—all measures that did not earn him sympathy from all quarters.

In his description of the 13th Dalai Lama, Bell alternately entitles him the "Precious Protector," the "Precious Sovereign," and the "Inmost One," while at the same time providing a description of power relationships in contemporaneous Tibet. The Dalai Lama had to contend with any number of enemies, critics, and oppositional forces, and it was only his skill and perseverance that averted rebellions, which could have easily grown into civil wars. Principal actors in these power plays included Loseling Dratsang of Drepung Monastery whose sympathies were with China; monks who opposed the improved position of the military and the lay bureaucracy; the Panchen Lama's entourage; fractions within the Dalai Lama's own retinue; and some of his closest associates, many of whom began to agitate against him when he moved to reorganize not only the monasteries but the criminal justice system and governmental administration as well.

Apart from Alexandra David-Néel's descriptions of the 13th Dalai Lama and a very few undifferentiated hatchet jobs aimed at the 14th Dalai Lama,[24] almost all Western depictions describe the Dalai Lamas as infallible, almost superhuman—in that respect they are not far behind Tibetan hagiographies. Charles Bell's book on the 13th Dalai Lama, and as a more recent and certainly more stimulating example, Georges Dreyfus's essay on the 14th Dalai Lama included in this volume represent revealing exceptions.

FROM RELIGIOUS ICON TO PHOTOGRAPHIC STAR

Although the depth of the friendship between the young 14th Dalai Lama and Heinrich Harrer remains controversial, there was without a doubt a close relationship of trust between them,

235 The Thirteenth Dalai Lama, taken in the traditional Tibetan "iconographic" style, i.e. seated on a throne and with a strictly symmetrical composition. Photographer: Leslie Weir, Collection of Maybe Jehu, London.   236 Western borrowing: Small product picture (Liebig-Libox-Oxo) based on the photography of Leslie Weir. Collection of Jean Lassale, Paris.   237 Deviation from conventional Tibetan rules of pictorial composition: The Thirteenth Dalai Lama is not seated in the center; neither he nor Sir Charles Bell are viewed from the front or the side but rather from a partial side view while still looking at the viewer. Another deviation from the norm is the person standing in the center, slightly to the rear, the Mahārāja of Sikkim. Photographers: Johnston and Hoffmann, 1910, Sir Charles Alfred Bell Collection, British Library London.

as the "secret" correspondence between the young Gyalwa Rinpoche and Heinrich Harrer evidence. The issue here is not to analyze how and what Heinrich Harrer wrote about the Dalai Lama,[25] but instead, to briefly discuss a different form of expression that had just begun to establish itself at the time Harrer was in Tibet—the photographic image.

We have seen how early missionaries tried to create images of the Dalai Lama and others attempted to do so after them. As photography became popular, so became possible the systematic documentation of reality through images. Heinrich Harrer and Peter Aufschnaiter were among the first to document Tibet, particularly central Tibet, intensively. It is striking that between the two of them, Aufschnaiter never photographed the Dalai Lama at all while Harrer did so only very rarely. There is not a single photographic portrait of the Dalai Lama among their unpublished photographs. Harrer took photos of the Dalai Lama only in 1950 when he was fleeing to southern Tibet, and those all taken only at a distance. The Dalai Lama is a relative central focus only of a series of photos from Dromo Monastery that were taken in the last days of Harrer's stay in Tibet (plate 155). One of the first photographs of the Dalai Lama, when he

was about four years old, was taken in northeastern Tibet by a Chinese man who claimed that he had to hide the camera in the wide sleeves of his clothing (plate 242).[26]

This inevitably poses the question of the reasons for the paucity of photographs. Harrer, for example, only got to know the Dalai Lama well toward the end of his stay in Tibet. But the lack of portraits among Harrer's collection must have another reason as well, since very few portraits of the 13th and 14th Dalai Lamas in Tibet are to be found elsewhere. Neither Gould nor any other Englishman attending the five-year-old Dalai Lama's coronation seems to have taken any pictures of him.

From that time on, there are only a few portraits of the Dalai Lama, those that Kanwal Krishna, who had accompanied the English to Lhasa, painted (plates 232, 233).[27] In subsequent years, the only known close-up photos of the young Dalai Lama taken while he was in Lhasa come from de Riencourt or Steele (1947); from Lowell Thomas, father and son (1949) (plates 144, 145, 241); and from Josef Vaniš (1954) (plate 244). Official Tibetan photographs of the young Dalai Lama are also rare.

We can trace the general lack of photographs of the Dalai Lama mainly to one primary reason: Tibetan opposition to this

238/239 Pencil drawing, rather than a photograph, which was not permitted at the time (1905). The two drawings were made by N. Kozhevnikov of the Thirteenth Dalai Lama in Urga (Ulaan Baatar). They were given to Tsar Nicholas II by P. Kozlov, Russian adventurer and explorer, at the request of the Thirteenth Dalai Lama (Lit.: Leonov 1991). 53 x 35 cm, The State Hermitage Museum, St. Petersburg, Inv. No.: ZK-V-740 / ZK-V-739.

modern, unknown form of pictorial representation over which they had no control, and which posed the danger that traditional iconographic and iconometric rules would be ignored. But who was the source of this skepticism? Certainly the clerical retinue, for one, and also the monks surrounding the Dalai Lama. Although the 13th Dalai Lama was perceived as tolerant and open to experiments, he too was first extremely skeptical about photography. At least two Western authors document his attitude. Finnish Field Marshal C. G. Mannerheim, meeting the 13th Dalai Lama at the end of June 1908 in a monastery in the Wutai Mountains near the Chinese city of Taiyuan, wrote:

> But he did not permit me to photograph him. He said that this request had been made of him many times but that he had always refused. The next time we met I would be allowed, he said, since by then he would view me as a good acquaintance, after I had met him again.[28]

Another was Koslov, a Russian researcher who reported that he was permitted to take photographs of the residence where the Dalai Lama and those who accompanied him to Urga were staying, but that he was not allowed to take any photos of the Dalai Lama himself.[29] Instead, the 13th Dalai Lama permitted Kozhevnikov, another Russian, to draw him not in colors, but in pencil and not in a frontal pose—thus breaking with tradition (plates 238, 239).[30]

A new phase of photographic iconography began in 1954 when the 14th Dalai Lama travelled to Beijing (plates 163–166) and gained momentum in 1956 when he participated in celebrations in honor of the Buddha in India. The number of photos of the Dalai Lama began to rise sharply, and the angle began to change from frontal portraits with their stiff composition reminiscent of traditional scroll pictures. Instead, we start seeing the more situational photos press photographers and visitors took. With his two trips abroad during the 1950s, a flood of images began whose extent is beyond measure and which has greatly influenced the Dalai Lama's image. In addition to the conventional short reports of the occasional visitor—the rule before 1958—there were now new types of representation, written as well as visual: biographies, including autobiographies written by ghostwriters; mural paintings, many in photorealist style; press photos; documentary and feature films; stamps; coins; and photographic portraits (with elements of photorealism, plates 122, 130).[31] Because of historic developments in Tibet, pictures of the Dalai Lama have also acquired a non-religious significance as symbols for Tibet as a whole, and thus of Tibetan aspirations for independence or genuine autonomy. Ironically, the Chinese occupation has been instrumental in this politicization of the his image—by substituting pictures of Mao[32] for images of saints during the Cultural Revolution (1966–1976) and later by banning the picture of the Dalai Lama altogether.

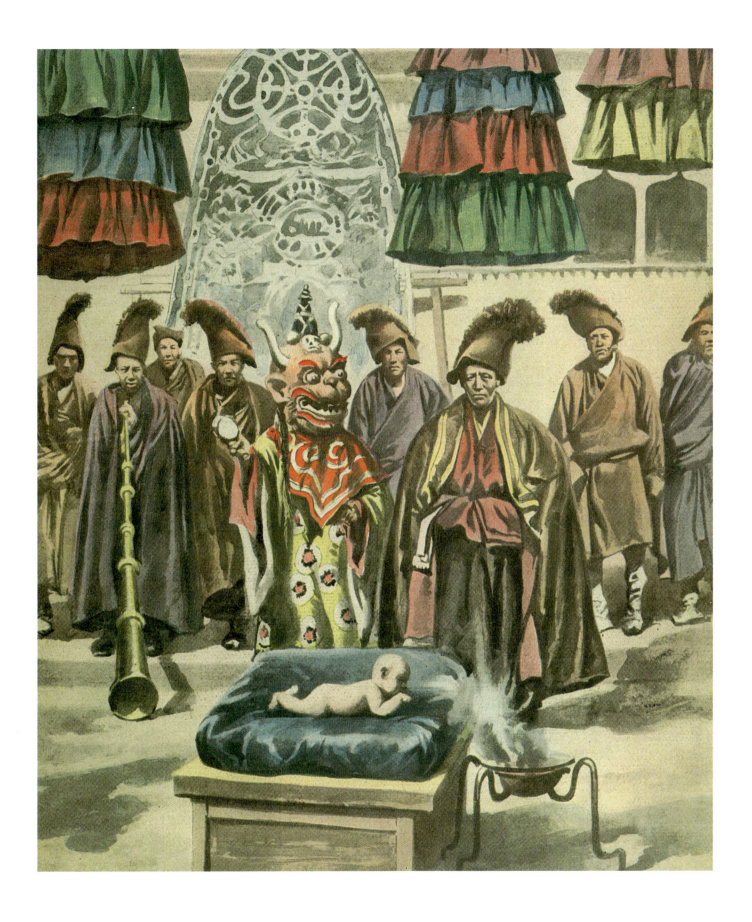

240 Western fantasy image: the birth and recognition of the Ninth Dalai Lama. Original text accompanying it: "In the Buddhist temple of Lhasa a strange ceremony was held according to ancient tradition in which a child was recognized as the new Dalai Lama, or Grand Priest, because the child was born at the same hour as the previous Dalai Lama died, which for the believers means that the spirit of the deceased passed to the body of the child." Collection of Roger Denis, Bagnéres de Bigorre, Illustrazione del Popolo, 28.1.1934. (The Fourteenth Dalai Lama was actually born on 6 July 1935. MB)

241 – 244 The photograph on the top left and both photographs below break the traditional rules of composition: The Dalai Lama is not photographed frontally nor does he stand or sit in the center; moreover, he is partially hidden by other people or cut off by the margin of the picture. The photograph on the upper right in a very traditional composition is certainly one of the earliest taken of the Fourteenth Dalai Lama (1939?). **241** Photographer: Lowell Thomas. **242** Photographer: Xing Suzhi. **243** Photographer: Dadul Namgyal Tsarong, Dehradun. **244** Photographer: Josef Vaniš, Prague.

245 Iconographic or thangka-like photograph of the Fourteenth Dalai Lama which only partially maintains traditional rules; while the composition is symmetrical, the picture is unusual in that it does not show the entire body of the Dalai Lama. Colored photograph. Ethnographic Museum of the University of Zürich.   246 – 248 All three pictures are distinguished by their unconventional composition.   246 The symmetry of the picture is broken and in which a Western scientific object, a globe, is included (the earth as a globe), © Brian Beresford / Nomad Pictures.   247 Picture of the Potala and the Thirteenth Dalai Lama in which traditional symmetry is maintained but which employs photography, a new technique, and which is in an unusual composition. Thus the picture is rectangle in format and the architecture dominates, which always played a secondary role in traditional thangkas. Postcard, probably around 1920, Collection of Harald Bechteler, Tutzing.   248 Picture similar to 247, but with the Fourteenth Dalai Lama as the protector of the Potala. Poster, late 20th century.

THE NINTH DALAI LAMA'S SET OF SEVEN LINEAGE THANGKAS

Per K. Sørensen

Celebrating the divine origin of the Dalai Lama, painting sets of his lineage usually grace the walls of the Dalai Lama's main residence in the Potala, where they serve as a source of inherent spiritual power and are treasured as prestigious heirlooms. They may have substantial artistic and historical value if nobles have commissioned or master artists executed them. A unique set of seven paintings illustrating several previous incarnations in the lineage of the Dalai Lama associated with the little-known 9th Dalai Lama, Lungtok Gyatso ལུང་རྟོགས་རྒྱ་མཚོ [lung rtogs rgya mtsho] (1805–1815), has recently appeared in the West, and is one of the few complete sets of this kind known to exist outside Tibet. Its extraordinary historical value, unique composition, and exquisite quality all warrant a comprehensive description.[1]

The motives behind the production of paintings of the Dalai Lama lineage needs some introduction. During the 16th century, a period of fundamental political changes in Tibet, the *yangsi* ཡང་སྲིད་ [yang srid] (Skt. *punarbhāva*) "conscious rebirths" system as a way to regulate access to religious positions and the succession of abbots gradually gained acceptance. These rebirths or incarnations formed unbroken lineages of *tülku* སྤྲུལ་སྐུ་ [sprul sku] "physical embodiments." This system absorbed and replaced the traditional family-based succession to monastic seats prevalent in the preceding centuries that had been transmitted from uncle to nephew or from father to son. Such lineages proved prone to rivalries among kin competing for primacy of ascent, often leading to endless disputes detrimental to the position itself. Ascent to a position through the Buddha or Bodhisattva reincarnation model therefore proved an ideal alternative. This reconfiguration of succession through recourse to the conscious rebirths of predecessors had been known in Tibet since the 13th century. Yet it was the Geluk School who diffused and strengthened the practice of regulating succession through lineages of rebirths, especially during their missionary quests for patronage among the powerful Mongols at the close of the 16th century. This new practice led to an inflated number of lineages claiming access to their religious positions through reincarnation not only among the Geluk, but other sects and schools as well.

Although Tibet had already seen paintings depicting the links in the transmission of individual religious and esoteric cycles, and lineages of abbots, from the mid–17th century onwards, there were concerted efforts to make prototypical sets of thangkas, and from the 18th century onwards, woodblock prints to illustrate the previous masters of the Kadam བཀའ་གདམས་ [bka' gdams] and Geluk དགེ་ལུགས་ [dge lugs] schools, in particular the lineage of the Dalai Lamas or their *thrung-rap* འཁྲུང་རབས་ ['khrung rabs] "rebirth succession." Later the lineages of other leading hierarchs also became increasingly popular subjects of depiction. The popularity and their ideological significance of the Dalai Lamas ensured a steady creation of such depictions, which came to be reproduced in a stereotyped format for dissemination throughout the Tibetan Buddhist world.

The production of sets of depictions of the Dalai Lama lineage began after the rise of the lineage as a central political institution, which came about through the state-based apotheosis of the Dalai Lama as a number of Geluk statesmen, including the 5th Dalai Lama himself and several regents, had masterminded. Part of the rationale behind these works of art was to symbolize an unbroken line within the institution of the Dalai Lama by alluding to former incarnates with a religious and historical background. The incarnations predating the Dalai Lamas played crucial roles in the past as mythic figures in the "Indian" lineage of Avalokiteśvara, while Tibetan incarnations part are recorded to have protected the Jokhang, or promoted the paramount cult of Avalokiteśvara. These selective—sometimes indiscriminately chosen—previous incarnations were essential to the new political order by bridging the past with the present. The emergent Geluk court, seeking symbols of legitimacy, adroitly ennobled a number of religious figures from the past to form an official coherent line of previous incarnations culminating in the Dalai Lamas.

We must see these endeavors of the court against the background of a Tibet that until that time had long lacked a unified central power. Their political consolidation of the country with the institution of the Dalai Lama at the center often required strategies between ideological reconciliation and coercion in order to justify their legitimacy. We should keep in mind that living manifestations of the Buddha or embodiments of Avalokiteśvara were far from being a Geluk invention. The 5th Dalai Lama likely took inspiration from the Druk and Karma schools, whose heads had long before established

249–252 Details of the first thangka.   249 The esoteric master and treasure-finder Nyangrel Nyima Wöser, a very important incarnation in the genealogy of the Dalai Lamas.   250 Ritual implements for performing esoteric and evil-dispelling rituals.   251 At Nyangrel Nyima Wöser's feet is one of his disciples, probably his son Namkhapel, whom Lhasa commended for performing rituals to ward off flooding.   252 Two tigers demonstrate the painting style of this series.

253–256 Details of the second thangka: scenes of nature and a monk presenting a maṇḍala offering to the First Dalai Lama, who is not seen here.

similar lineages of succession by making claims to be incarnations of these deities. The universal appeal and omnipresence of Avalokiteśvara help account for the great plurality of his forms in the Tibetan religious world. Understanding the ideological rivalries concerning incarnation helps us appreciate the politics behind Geluk hegemony in Tibet.

LIFE OF THE NINTH DALAI LAMA

Before giving a general description of the thangka set, let us briefly focus on the short life of the 9th Dalai Lama. We know deplorably little about him and what little we do is largely gleaned from his official biography dominated by trivial details of court life and of protocol with which the Ninth was to be manacled throughout his few years at the Potala. Lungtok Gyatso was born in Denma ལྡན་མ [ldan ma] district of lower Kham province in the twelfth lunar month of 1805. His father, belonging to a local *pöntshang* དཔོན་ཚང [dpon tshang] "ruling family," died prior to his birth and an uncle was to rear the infant. His biography records that he soon began exhibiting signs of his extraordinariness and claimed to be the reincarnation of the 5th Dalai Lama. He also often had visions and recollections of his previous lives as the 1st, 5th, and 7th Dalai Lamas and even of his bonds with Lama Zhang, a prominent 12th-century ascetic.

What is remarkable is not that the child could be a manifestation of Avalokiteśvara, but rather that he had strong bonds to the 5th Dalai Lama, which his biography addresses repeatedly. Remarkable also is that in the selection procedure, the non-Tibetan practice of drawing lots from the Goldern Urn 金瓶, which Beijing had introduced and insisted on using, was annulled in this case.[2] Lungtok Gyatso was formally enthroned in November 1808 at the Potala as the ninth *kuthreng gupa* སྐུ་འཕྲེང་དགུ་པ [sku 'phreng dgu pa] "manifestation." He proved to be bright and eagerly learned to read and write under the tutorship of his steward, Dechen Gyatso བདེ་ཆེན་རྒྱ་མཚོ [bde chen rgya mtsho].[3]

Thomas Manning presents a rare Western eyewitness account of the seven-year-old hierarch from Lhasa in 1811. He briefly portrays the young Dalai Lama, who was soon to engross all of his attention. Manning was impressed with his "simple and unaffected manners of a well-educated young princely child," and "his poetically and affectingly beautiful face and cheerful disposition."[4] The health of the young Dalai Lama appears to have not been very good, as he had a severe bout of pneumonia in the first month of 1815. Although an array of healing rituals and medicinal treatments were conducted, they offered him little relief. After an agonizing month he succumbed on the sixteenth day of the second lunar month of 1815, barely eleven.[5] Whatever the cause of his death, it remains a matter for speculation. A number of equally short-lived Dalai Lamas followed him until the Thirteenth, whose predecessors all died before reaching their majority, no doubt falling afoul of court intrigues. Today the remains of the Ninth rest in his Golden Tomb, also called the "Manifest Joy of the Three Worlds," which holds his golden *chörten* ossuary in the Potala.

GENEALOGY OF THE DALAI LAMAS

The 5th Dalai Lama, Ngawang Lopsang Gyatso ངག་དབང་བློ་བཟང་རྒྱ་མཚོ་ [ngag dbang blo bzang rgya mtsho] (1617–1682), was the key person who retroactively set the genealogy of the Dalai Lamas, although with the ingenious assistance of his regent, Sanggye Gyatso. The Fifth dealt with the issue on different occasions, at times even involving leading Nyingma ascetics like Terdak Lingpa in the discussions. These men have left us several sources that help us identify and assess the previous incarnations whom the court later codified and included in main and collateral lineages regarded as either "official" or "supplementary" to the succession. Yet because universality was the priciple underlying the concept of rebirth, there was basically no hierarchy and thus in theory no primacy among lineages or individual incarnates—each incarnation was unique and equally important. We therefore see the 5th Dalai Lama and his regent formulating and endorsing variant lists of rebirths, although to them these chronological inconsistencies never appeared contradictory. The selection and promotion of specific lineages clearly went through a number of stages, though space and the limitations of sources prevent us from going into greater detail here.

What is clear is that in their search for candidates from within their own schools to ennoble into their lineage, these men and their advisors took recourse to a selected number of sources containing references to mythic and historical figures from the early Kadam and later Geluk Schools. The popular collection of rebirth stories related to the Tibetan founder of the Kadam School, Domtön འབྲོམ་སྟོན་ ['brom ston] (1004–1064), proved a major source. Domtön in fact had paved the way for Kadam ascendancy by building its first monastery Reting རྭ་སྒྲེང་ [rwa sgreng] in 1057. Titled *Accounts of Rebirths,* these twenty-two stories of Domtön's previous lives found in the *Kadam Lekbam* བཀའ་གདམས་གླེགས་བམ་ [bka' gdams glegs bam] "Precious Book of the Kadam" were compiled in the Kadam monastery Narthang སྣར་ཐང་ [snar thang] in the early 14th century.

These *kyerap* སྐྱེས་རབས་ [skyes rabs] "stories of rebirths" were modelled on the Indian *jātakas,* and as such enjoyed considerable authority as a vehicle of moral values and ideal conduct. The tale "Dharmarāja Könchok Bang དཀོན་མཆོག་འབངས་ [dkon mchog 'bangs]"[6] in particular came to exert great scriptural influence. Like others in this Domtön rebirth collection, the tale narrates how an Indian prince came to be identified as a manifestation of Avalokiteśvara, who later transformed himself into a number of Tibetan kings and saints. This wholly Tibetan retelling of the life story of an ideal, pious Indian king links India to Tibet, and hence Avalokiteśvara to the Dalai Lama. The prophecies in the story foretell how King Könchok Bang would be reborn as Songtsen Gampo སྲོང་བཙན་སྒམ་པོ་ [srong btsan sgam po] (d. 650), Tibet's founding monarch, who in turn later remanifested himself as Domtön in order to disseminate Buddhism throughout Tibet. This narrative, with roots in 11th-century Kadam oral traditions, appealed strongly to members of the court in the 17th century when they reassembled an ideologically viable and scripturally authoritative lineage of succession.

257–260 Details of the third thangka.   **257** Nature scenes.   **258** Head of King Songtsen Gampo (Budda Amitābha is clearly visible on top of his head).   **259** Songtsen Gampo's Minister Thönmi, who invented the Tibetan script.   **260** Two men carrying the throne of the mythic king Nyathri Tsenpo "Neck-Throned One" on their shoulders.

Illustrative here are the analogies and parables this story contains. The Kadam and Geluk Schools both employ a popular narrative analogy in the *Shünpa Kokpa Rimpa Dünyö* ཤུན་པ་ལྐོག་པ་རིམ་ པ་བདུན་ཡོད་ [shun pa lkog pa rim pa bdun yod] "Seven Successive Bark Layers of the Juniper Tree" of Reting as an account of the emergence of the Dalai Lamas in Tibet. We may assume that this analogy was the first to serve as a model for reconstructing their lineage. While explaining the qualities of junipers growing in the lush groves at Reting Monastery, the narrative compares the seven successive layers of bark of juniper to the spread of Kadam teachings and the emergence of the seven *Jinas* or Buddhas in a degenerate era. The concept of the seven-layered bark came to be employed as a *tendrel* རྟེན་འབྲེལ [rten 'brel] "auspicious portent" of the emergence of Avalokiteśvara in Tibet to protect and safeguard the Tibetan people.[7]

This story of the juniper bark became a popular local cult associated with Domtön, who like his teacher Atiśa, was depicted as a manifestation of Avalokiteśvara. The importance of these *Accounts of Rebirths* for the Potala court for establishing the Dalai Lama lineage is reflected in their having all twenty-two stories painted in 1645–1648. Done in a mixture of *menthang* སྨན་ཐང་ [sman thang] and *khyentse* མཁྱེན་བྲྩེ་ [mkhyen brtse] styles, these murals decorate the Zimchung Kadam Khyilwa གཟིམས་ཆུང་ བཀའ་གདམས་འཁྱིལ་བ་ [gzims chung bka' gdams 'khyil ba] Chamber of the Potala.

Similarly in his construction of the lineage, the 5th Dalai Lama also used this and other tales in a small undated work he wrote on painting and displaying the *Succession of Avalokiteśvara's Rebirths in India and Tibet.* Here he refers to Avalokiteśvara's mythic origins and emphasizes the Narthang tradition with the legend of above-mentioned Indian prince Könchok Bang and his rebirth as Songtsen Gampo. He goes on to expand the succession by including a number of figures such as the remaining ancestral kings Thrisong Detsen ཁྲི་སྲོང་ལྡེ་ བཙན་ [khri srong lde btsan] (742–797) and Thri Ralpacen ཁྲི་རལ་པ་ ཅན་ [khri Ral pa can] (805–836). Later Domtön emerges in the list followed by a number of figures, some of whom had become famous for protecting the Jokhang, others of whom had been regarded as embodiments of Avalokiteśvara, including Khache Gönpapa ཁ་ཆེ་དགོན་པ་པ་ [kha che dgon pa pa]; Sachen ས་ཆེན་ [sa chen] (1092–1158); Zhang Yudrakpa ཞང་གཡུ་བྲག་པ་ [zhang g.Yu brag pa] (1123–1193); Nyangrel Nyima Wöser མྱང་རལ་ཉི་མ་འོད་ཟེར་

[myang ral Nyi ma 'od zer] (1136–1204); and Lhaje Gewabum ལྷ་རྗེ་དགེ་བ་འབུམ་ [lha rje dge ba 'bum] (ca. 1200–1250). After these follow the 1st to 4th Dalai Lamas.[9]

Significantly, the 5th Dalai Lama also explains the inclusion of each name on his list.[10] He counters the partial simultaneity of some incarnates by employing the *udakacandropamā* simile of illusion to say that these multiple appearances were "tantamount to the moon's ability to appear in myriad waters at one and the same time."[11] The reasons for the 5th Dalai Lama to include a number of non-Geluk masters in the lineage will become evident in the section on the set of seven thangkas below.

The regent Sanggye Gyatso also consulted such authoritative sources[12] to compile a list of members in the lineage of the Dalai Lamas. In the closing appendix of his lengthy biography of the 5th Dalai Lama, he introduces an extended list of reincarnations of Avalokiteśvara and the Dalai Lamas in India and Tibet.[13] Although drawn haphazardly from a number of sources and ideologically flavored, we may consider this list as official even though there are occasional discrepancies with other lists. This also indicates to us that still other slightly different lists may have been circulating during this period. Starting with Lokeśvara, Sanggye Gyatso lists thirty-six mostly royal Indian previous incarnations. This link with Indian roots—the hallmark of authenticity—is crucial for almost any Buddhist claim in Tibet, especially for such a prestigious line of succession. If there was no Indian connection with Avalokiteśvara, then one was fabricated as in the case of the Domtön, for whom a mythical link was projected into the distant past.

Sanggye Gyatso then continues with the *mewön namsum* "three ancestral kings" of Yarlung མེས་དབོན་རྣམ་གསུམ་ [mes dbon rnam gsum] (37–39); then Domtön (40), Nyangrel མྱང་རལ་ [myang ral] (1136-1204); Chökyi Wangchuk ཆོས་ཀྱི་དབང་ཕྱུག་ [chos kyi dbang phyug] (1212–1270); Ngari Panchen མངའ་རིས་པཎ་ཆེན་ [mnga' ris paṇ chen] (1487–1542); Trashi Topgye བཀྲ་ཤིས་སྟོབས་རྒྱས་ [bkra shis stobs rgyas] (1551–1602) (41–44). These latter were all Nyingma treasure-finders of the "Northern Treasury" School and so reflect the Fifth's prediliction for eclectic esoterica. He then lists Phakpa འཕགས་པ་ ['phags pa] (1235–1280) (45), no doubt because of his role as chaplain to the Yuan 元 court, which the Fifth's later administration considered a precursor to their

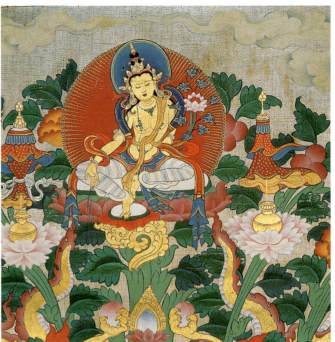

261–264 Details of the fourth thangka.   261 The Sixth and Seventh Dalai Lama floating in the clouds.   262 Detail of the mandorla surrounding the central figure of the "Great Fifth," including a White Tārā.

own master-disciple relationship first under Altan Khan in 1578 and later with the Khoshod Mongols in the 1640s. Then follows the Nepali Padmavajra.

The Fifth and Sanggye Gyatso included others in their list with whom the Fifth had close spiritual ties: Lama Zhang; Yamzangpa Chökyi Mönlam གཡའ་བཟང་པ་ཆོས་ཀྱི་སྨོན་ལམ [g.ya' bzang pa chos kyi smon lam] (1169–1233);[14] Sumtön Yeshe Zung སུམ་སྟོན་ཡེ་ཤེས་གཟུངས [sum ston ye shes gzungs], a medical master; Lodrö Gyaltsen བློ་གྲོས་རྒྱལ་མཚན [blo gros rgyal mtshan] (1366–1415); Rinchen Khyenrap རིན་ཆེན་མཁྱེན་རབ [rin chen mkhyen rab] (1436–97); and finally the historical 1st to 5th Dalai Lamas. Later the authoritative Geluk historian Longdol Lama ཀློང་རྡོལ་བླ་མ [klong rdol bla ma] (1719-1795) similarly discusses the former incarnations in his account of the cult and unbroken Avalokiteśvara line in Tibet. He too counts fifty-eight incarnations up to the 8th Dalai Lama.[15] Although we may consider his extended list the culmination of the efforts to create a genealogy, its fulcrum rests on the 5th Dalai Lama.

Many series of paintings of members of the Dalai Lama lineage consist of either five, seven, nine, ten, or thirteen paintings, all depicting former incarnations as individual *tsowo* གཙོ་བོ [gtso bo] "central figures."[16] Reasons for this variation in number may include the date of execution—if a set were executed more recently, the artist could include more Dalai Lamas—or the preferences of the donor or person commissioning the painting.

A standard format for such sets features the 5th Dalai Lama as the central figure of the lineage. Some—as in the set of seven thangkas that is the focus of this study—feature him as the central object of veneration not only because he founded the lineage, but because he was responsible for its propagation. With the possible exception of the Seventh, all subsequent Dalai Lamas could be considered extensions to the lineage and were therefore given a supplementary role to that of the Fifth in terms of artistic composition. Out of respect for his paramountcy in the genealogy, most sets reflect this format.

THE SET OF SEVEN LINEAGE THANGKAS: ARRANGEMENT, COMPOSITION, AND STYLE

With the 5th Dalai Lama as the *tsowo,* the remaining secondary paintings of his previous births are juxtaposed to the left and right parallel to the central thangka according to a system the painter and person commissioning the painting had arranged, as the texts added on the frames on the reverse side of each painting indicate. The center painting, identified by such inscription, is the *gyalwang ngawa* རྒྱལ་དབང་ལྔ་བ [rgyal dbang lnga ba] or central thangka of the 5th Dalai Lama. The remaining paintings are juxtaposed or aligned horizontally to the right and left,[17] an arrangement underscoring that this set was in essence of the Fifth. Each of the twenty-six hierarchs and saints depicted on the thangka, whether main or secondary figures, all belong to the extended Dalai Lama lineage. The figurative arrangement follows the traditional Tibetan layout in which the Indian incarnations are usually placed in the upper register of the painting.

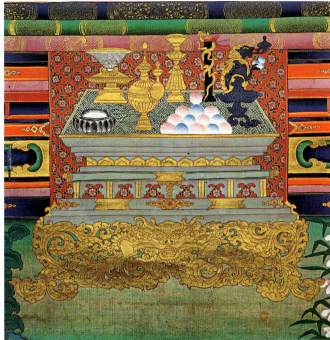

263 The "Great Fifth."   **264** Altar table with esoteric implements and jewels setting in front of the throne.

This set is a compelling work of art whether viewed from a distance or close-up. The style immediately suggests a late east Tibetan provenance, executed in a local or idiosyncratic *menri sar* སྨན་བྲིས་གསར་ [sman bris gsar] "New Menri" idiom, evident from its overall elaborate and naturalistic style. The artist himself was likely either from Lhasa or Kham. The artist likely painted at the Potala, where he was an unusual and innovative court painter. He has chosen a simple compositional layout which allows the hierarchs and saints to command our attention. Against an unobtrusive background of pale colors, the portraits become alive as if emerging from the painting. Some figures have idiosyncratic facial features while others follow standard, stylized iconographic conventions. Name labels are inscribed below each figure. The central figure and his elaborate surroundings immediately engross the attention of the viewer.

The painter was sensitive to details and delicate refinements, including a minute devotion to the multitude of outfits, brocades, multi-colored garments, and accoutrements as well as to the rich geometric floral motifs and multi-patterned patchwork details. The settings and repertoire display strong Chinese influences characterized by the elaborate figural and naturalistic flora and fauna motifs and by an opulent palette in varying tonalities. These mineral and polychrome colors are still unusually bright and fresh.

The set has likely been properly consecrated. On the reverse we find fairly large handprints—analysis may clarify whether they are from a nine- or ten-year-old Dalai Lama, though they appear to be from the hands of an adult. Based on similar sets of thangkas from the 17th century, it is likely they are the prints of the artist or a teacher. The reverse is stamped with a seal and covered with sacred inscriptions, often in three columns with "oṁ āḥ hūṁ" in huge letters in what appears to be a young, untrained hand. We know that Dechen Gyatso taught reading and writing to the 9th Dalai Lama from early, and so it therefore appears unlikely that these rather unsightly calligraphic exercises came from the Ninth's hand. Today when the set is put on full ceremonial display, it is usually adorned with a ten-meter red *khatak* scarf of woven silk decorated with a special border pattern and blessing signs.

The arrangement issuing from the central figure to the left and right is: No. I, third right: 3rd Dalai Lama; No. II, second right: 1st Dalai Lama; No. III, first right: Songtsen Gampo; No. IV, center: 5th Dalai Lama; No. V, first left: Domtön; No. VI, second left: 2nd Dalai Lama; No. VII, third left: 4th Dalai Lama. Reading the set chronologically and in terms of the prominence of the figures, we must depart from the central figure: the 5th Dalai Lama (No. IV), then proceed first right (No. III), then first left (No. V), then middle right (No. II), middle left (No. VI), then farthest right (No. I) and finally farthest left (No. VII). This perspective follows that of the central figure. For convenience, we will describe the individual thangkas left to right according to the perspective of the viewer.

No. I   No. II   No. III

265 First to Ninth Dalai Lamas; from left to right: Third Dalai Lama, First Dalai Lama, Songtsen Gampo, Fifth Dalai Lama, Domtön, Second Dalai Lama, Fourth Dalai Lama (see also a folding supplement accompanying this volume). Set of seven thangkas, 60 x 128 cm each, Collection of Veena and Peter Schnell, Zürich.

NO. I

The four figures illuminating this thangka are crowned with the central figure, the 3rd Dalai Lama, Sönam Gyatso བསོད་ནམས་ རྒྱ་མཚོ་ [bsod nams rgya mtsho] (1543–1588). In an opulent naturalistic setting, he sits on a fine throne robed in a richly and finely patterned religious garment like that of his predecessors and successors. With a bright red halo and his hands in the *vitarkamudrā* "bestowing teachings," he appears serene and absorbed.[18]

Above him in the upper right is seated another previous incarnation, the Indian royalty Gyalpo Gewapel རྒྱལ་པོ་དགེ་བ་དཔལ་ [rgyal po dge ba dpal] (Skt. Kuśalaśrī). Attired in royal robes with a red halo above his crowned head, he sits on a huge throne under a rocky landscape. Dharmarāja Gewapel is generally linked with the 3rd Dalai Lama.[19]

Below Sönam Gyatso in the lower left sits the Tibetan esoteric master and treasure-finder, *Ngadak* "Lord" Nyangrel Nyima Wözer མངའ་བདག་སྙང་རལ་ཉི་མ་འོད་ཟེར་ [mnga' bdag myang ral nyi ma 'od zer] (1136–1204). Richly dressed in both inner and outer garments, he is here depicted as an esoteric Nyingma lay ascetic, his head crowned with—typical of his portraiture—a hairknot in a blue halo. He holds a black rosary between his hands. On the right we see an array of ritual implements indicating his abilities in performing esoteric and evil-dispelling rituals (plates 249–251).

At his feet in a simpler ascetic's outfit we see what is probably one of his pupils, possibly his own son *Drogön* Namkhapel འགྲོ

འགྲོན་ནམ་མཁའ་དཔལ་ [*'gro mgon* nam mkha' dpal] (ca.1182–1244) who served Lhasa by performing water-abating rituals to protect the Jokhang from flooding, as did Lhaje Gewabum (No. VII and plate 275). Nyangrel was king of the treasury while also being the master mainly responsible for finding and distributing the *maṇi kabum* མ་ཎི་བཀའ་འབུམ་ [ma ṇi bka' 'bum] "testamentary literature" ascribed to Songtsen Gampo. Because of his close involvement, we may in fact consider him the most important figure of the entire Chenrezik cult in Tibet. He is therefore repeatedly listed as an important link in the chain of incarnations in the Dalai Lama genealogy.[20]

In the lower right we find the Sakya master Sachen Künga Nyingpo ས་ཆེན་ཀུན་དགའ་སྙིང་པོ་ [sa chen Kun dga' snying po] (1092–1158) in an elaborate garment seated cross-legged on a cushion with *vajra* and a bell in his hands. This is a traditional rendition of him as an elderly bald-headed man as found in most portraits of him. Numerous sources attest to his importance and hence his presence here, a foremost reason being that the Sakya tradition considers him a manifestation of Avalokiteśvara.[21]

NO. II

Three figures adorn this thangka. The *tsowo* is a depiction of the 1st Dalai Lama, Gendün Drup དགེ་འདུན་གྲུབ་ [dge 'dun grub] (1391–1474) in a monk's robe seated on an elaborate throne. With a blue aureole circling his head, he sits with his left hand holding a book while the right is in a *vitarkamudrā*.[22]

No. IV   No. V   No. VI   No. VII

The figure of nearly the same size to the right above him is a depiction of the Indian prince Gyalwu Depatenpo རྒྱལ་བུ་དད་པ་ བརྟན་པོ་ [rgyal bu dad pa brtan po] "Firm Belief." In Tibetan practice, the upper registers of a painting are usually reserved for Indian saints and ascetics, or as here royal dignitaries. Prince Gyalwu is also suitably seated in a royal gown. He too was a previous incarnation of Domtön, the tale of which is included in his *Accounts of Rebirths* and thus explains his presence here.[23]

In the lower center is a depiction of a Tibetan king, the second historical Dharmarāja Thrisong Detsen. His depiction here is quite conventional, with him majestically robed, and his hands in the *vitarkamudrā* and *varadamudrā* "boon-granting." An azure aureole circles his crowned head. During his reign Buddhism became the state religion. He invited Padmasambhava to Tibet and built Samye, the first convent in Tibet. He was thus incorporated into the Dalai Lama lineage.[24]

NO. III

Three figures adorn this thangka, possibly to add to the weightiness of the central figure, the oldest among the *tsowo*. This thangka depicts the first monarch of Tibet, Songtsen Gampo, founder of a Tibetan dynasty. In a rocky landscape, he is seated on a multitiered throne, its backrest decorated with dragonheads. He wears delicately designed royal garments and holds the usual accoutrements of a Buddhist Dharmarāja. A red aureole circles his crowned head, which in accordance with tra-

ditional portraits of him, is that of Amitābha (plate 258). He holds two lotus stalks in his hands which simultaneously form the *vitarkamudrā* and *varadamudrā*. At his feet we see his trusted minister Thönmi who would later invent the Tibetan alphabet and teach it to the king (plate 259).

The figure to the right above Songtsen Gampo is Gyalwu Jikten Wangchuk རྒྱལ་བུ་འཇིག་རྟེན་དབང་ཕྱུག [rgyal bu 'Jig rten dbang phyug], also known as Prince Lokeśvara "Lord of the World." Only slightly smaller in size, he is intimately associated with the *tsowo*.[25] *Lokeśvara* is a common epithet for Avalokiteśvara. Gyalwu Jikten is seated in the *ardhaparyaṅka* pose, resting on a curvilinear throne. He wears the richly designed garment of a monarch, his head crowned and surrounded with a halo. His right hand forms the *varadamudrā* while his left holds a bowl full of wish-granting jewels.

Below Songtsen Gampo we see the first mythic king of the Tibetan dynasty, Nyathri Tsenpo གཉའ་ཁྲི་བཙན་པོ་ [gnya' khri btsan po], the "Neck-Throned One." Indeed, we see his devotees carrying him using their necks as a throne (plate 260).[26] He is dressed as a king, here idealized with his left hand in the *abhayamudrā* "protection," while his right holds a rosary.

This painting in particular imparts a proper royal background to the institution and genealogy of the Dalai Lama. True to form, the figures are embedded in a refined and idyllic landscape of trees, rocks, birds, and fish, in all a remarkably non-Tibetan scenario reminiscent of Chinese landscape painting.

NO. IV

This painting is the key thangka of the entire set and depicts the 5th Dalai Lama, Ngawang Lopsang Gyatso, in full monastic name as given on the thangka: Ngawang Lopsang Gyatso Jikme Gocha Thupten Langtsöde དག་དབང་བློ་བཟང་རྒྱ་མཚོ་འཇིགས་མེད་གོ་ཆ་ ཐུབ་བསྟན་ལང་འཚོའི་སྡེ་ [ngag dbang blo bzang rgya mtsho 'Jigs med go cha thub bstan lang 'tsho'i sde] (1617–1682).[27] He is richly robed in the traditional garment of the Geluk hierarch in finely patterned red, yellow, and gold loose-folding swaths on his outer garment. He sits cross-legged on a multitiered throne-cushion behind a delicately painted ritual altar table (plate 263, 264). His face exudes serenity and dedication. A red aureole encircles his head. His right hand is in the *vitarkamudrā* while his left hand holds the vase of immortality, a common symbol of Amitāyus, the Buddha of Boundless Life. His seat is embedded in a mandorla-like array of flowers decorated with the *aṣṭamaṅgala* "eight auspicious signs." Above his head towers Tārā in the traditional *lalītaāsana* "pose of ease" with her right leg extended, the left folded (plate 262). She is arrayed with a blue nimbus within a larger mandorla and sits in her traditional apparel.

In the upper register of the painting are seated small figures embedded in an ocean of clouds, from left to right: the 6th Dalai Lama Tsangyang Gyatso ཚངས་དབྱངས་རྒྱ་མཚོ་ [tshangs dbyangs rgya mtsho] (1683–1706), the 7th Dalai Lama Kalzang Gyatso སྐལ་བཟང་ རྒྱ་མཚོ་ [bskal bzang rgya mtsho] (1708–1757) (plate 261), the 9th Dalai Lama Lungtok Gyatso ལུང་རྟོགས་རྒྱ་མཚོ་ [lung rtogs rgya mtsho] (1805–1815), and to the far right the 8th Dalai Lama Jampel Gyatso འཇམ་དཔལ་རྒྱ་མཚོ་ ['jam dpal rgya mtsho] (1758–1804). The two last figures were evidently misplaced as we would expect the Ninth to follow the Eighth. The figures are depicted smaller to indicate their hierarchical subordination to the *tsowo*.

NO. V

This first thangka to the left of the central image has a more strongly naturalistic ambience than the other paintings. Here only three figures are depicted: the *tsowo* is Domtön Gyalwe Jungne འབྲོམ་སྟོན་རྒྱལ་བའི་འབྱུང་གནས་ ['brom ston rgyal ba'i 'byung gnas] (1004–1064), the lay master and founder of the first Kadam monastery, Reting, and a cornerstone in the historical genealogy of the Dalai Lama.[28] Tradition holds that he started the Kadam School, from which later developed the Geluk School, by inviting the Indian master Atiśa to Tibet. Here Domtön is depicted conventionally with long, curly hair but here his rich earrings are framed in a red aura. He sits upon a multi-tiered throne with a huge backrest in a bed of flowers. Finely dressed in the opulent multicolored attire of a lay ruler, his left hand is in the *vitarkamudrā,* his right in the *varadamudrā.*[29]

The Indian Dharmarāja Lhe Gyalpo ལྷའི་རྒྱལ་པོ་ [lha'i rgyal po] is depicted in the upper register. Seated on a multi-tiered throne with a curvilinear backrest, the monarch displays the *vitarkamudrā.* He similarly wears opulent attire and a blue aureole encircles his crown (plate 266). He has been inserted into the hierarchy of incarnations by being made one of the thirty-six traditional Indian incarnations of Avalokiteśvara known from the Narthang narrative tradition, the *Accounts of Rebirths* associated with Domtön, in whose depiction he is also therefore included.[30]

The last figure in the lower right is the mythic twenty-seventh king in the prehistoric line of the Tibetan royal dynasty, Lha Thothori Nyenshel ལྷ་ཐོ་ཐོ་རི་སྙན་ཤེལ་ [lha tho tho ri snyan shel]. He too sits on a double-tiered throne with a curvilinear backrest, dressed opulently and holding a religious book in his left hand. To his right on a pedestal is a *stūpa*, both objects alluding to the sacred objects of the Avalokiteśvara cult. According to legend, these objects made their celestial arrival on the roof of the king's palace at the dawn of Tibetan history, an event heralding Tibet's first contact with Buddhism. Lha Thothori Nyenshel's role in this introduction ensured that he was listed as a former incarnation of Avalokiteśvara.[31]

NO. VI

The *tsowo* of this painting is the 2nd Dalai Lama Gendün Gyatso དགེ་འདུན་རྒྱ་མཚོ་ [dge 'dun rgya mtsho] (1475-1542).[32] Seated on a huge ornate, curvilinear throne and opulently dressed in a richly patterned yellow and red monk's robe, he holds a *vajra* in his right hand and a bell in his left, similar to the 4th Dalai Lama.

Above him in the upper left is the Indian prince Könchok Bang དཀོན་མཆོག་འབངས་ [dkon mchog 'bangs], whose life story was the basis upon which a major segment of the lineage rests. August in appearance, he sit on an elaborate throne dressed in ornate multilayered clothing of red, yellow, and blue, his hands

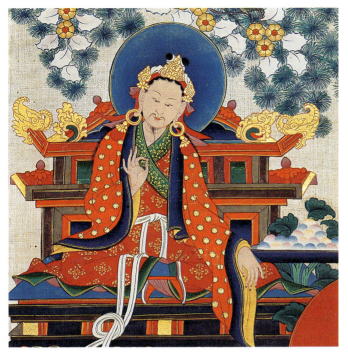

266 – 269 Details of the fifth thangka.   **266** The Indian Dharmarāja Lhe Gyalpo.   **267** Two birds.   **268** Two deer (?), a stūpa, and a disciple at the feet of Domtön.   **269** Man with vase.

270/271 Details of the sixth thangka. **270** A monk holding out a begging bowl to the Second Dalai Lama, not visible here, and carrying a book on his shoulders. To the right, the head of the Kāśmīrī yogin Khache Gönpapa. **271** A pair of birds.

forming the *vitarkamudrā.* The Narthang narrative attests to the link between him and the 2nd Dalai Lama.[33]

Below left is Ngawak Ralpacen མངའ་བདག་རལ་པ་ཅན་ [mnga' bdag ral pa can] "King Ralpacen" (805–836), one of the three ancestral Buddhist kings of the Yarlung dynasty. Elaborately attired in royal robes, he sits on a throne in the *ardhaparyaṅka* with a pink-red aura, his right hand in the *vitarkamudrā.* His inclusion is based on relevant sources.[34]

The last figure in the lower right is the great Kāśmīrī *yogin* Khache Gönpapa ཁ་ཆེ་དགོན་པ་པ་ [kha che dgon pa pa] (b. 1055) (also seen partially in plate 270) who sits on a broad cushion with a tiger skin underneath. Between his hands he holds a rosary. This nebulous figure is known to have brought esoteric cycles related to Vaiśravaṇa to Zangskar Lotsāwa of western Tibet. Khache Gönpapa is included in the lineage because he induced Lotsāwa to repair the ruined Jokhang in the 1080s, the first post-imperial renovation of the site.[35]

NO. VII

The *tsowo* of this painting is the 4th Dalai Lama, Yönten Gyatso ཡོན་ཏན་རྒྱ་མཚོ་ [yon tan rgya mtsho] (1589–1616), the Mongol-born prince whose epithet in the Narthang tradition is Dechen Chökyi Gyalpo བདེ་ཆེན་ཆོས་ཀྱི་རྒྱལ་པོ་ [bde chen chos kyi rgyal po]. Here he sits gracefully cross-legged upon a richly decorated throne wearing patterned yellow and red robes, the attire of a high Geluk hierarch. With a blue aura, the symbol of his attainment of enlightenment, he hold a *vajra* in his right hand and a bell

in his left. In front of him are attendants and Mongol nobles bearing costly gifts.

Supplementing to the *tsowo* is Zhang Yutrakpa Tsöndrakpa ཞང་གཡུ་བྲག་པ་བཙོན་འགྲུས་གྲགས་པ་ [zhang g.yu brag pa brtson 'grus grags pa] (1123–1193) in the upper left. His position in the upper register of the painting, normally reserved for Indian saints and figures, is unusual. Here he is sitting on a throne as a monk in a delicately patterned red and yellow garment. He wears a hat (plate 272) that according to tradition goes back to Dakgom Tshülthrim Nyingpo དྭགས་སྒོམ་ཚུལ་ཁྲིམས་སྙིང་པོ་ [dwags sgom tshul khrims snying po] (1116–1169), one of his main teachers. His mien reflects the characteristic violence of his personality as contemporaneous sources portray.[36] His stocky stature and corpulence are also conventional. His left hand forms the *dhyānamudrā* "contemplation," his right the *bhūmisparśa* "earth-witness," a standard posture of the true manifestation of the Buddha. He is the founder of the Tshelpa Kagyü sect, one of the first post-imperial polities established between 1175 and 1187 at Tshel Gungthang across from Lhasa.[37] He and his followers ruled the Lhasa valley in the 12th–13th centuries.

His younger contemporary Lhaje Gewabum ལྷ་རྗེ་དགེ་བ་འབུམ་ [lha rje dGe ba 'bum] (ca. 1200–1250) is at the lower left. Leaning against a green cushion seated on a throne, he is elaborately dressed in brocades and holds a black rosary in his left hand, a flower stalk in his right. A red aureole circumscribes his head. This ascetic and physician played a pioneering role in the

Lhasa area and actively built and maintained dikes to protect the Jokhang from flooding (plate 275).[38] In Jokhang a statue was erected in commemoration of his service. As did his mentor Nyangrel, he extensively repaired the Lhasa embankments. His flood-control measures and his promotion of the cult of Chenrezik ensure his inclusion in the list of previous incarnations.

The last secondary figure of this thangka is the little-known Nepalese ascetic Panchen Padmavajra (fl. 13th cent.). His positioning is somewhat asymmetrical, since Indian (or as here Nepalese) incarnates are usually found in the upper register of the painting. He sits in robes with the red hat of an Indian Buddhist *paṇḍita*. A prophecy from the *Accounts of Rebirths* assures his inclusion in the lineage. It is worth noting that these three secondary figures—otherwise historically unconnected to the main figure, the 4th Dalai Lama—are usually listed together, which probably indicates that they have initially been incorporated into a separate lineage.[39]

CONCLUSION

Apparently based on a similar set from the 17th century or some other model kept in the Potala, the artist has painted this set in a rather controlled and thematically simple manner and arranged so that the *tsowo* stands at the center of our attention. Unlike other Dalai Lama incarnation series, however, here he does not compose the individual paintings as a biographical sketch which highlights the idealized life of the hierarch. These portraits are far more forceful and bring out the distinct features of each individual as the artist saw. The portraits are unusual in a number of ways: the central figure of the set is the 5th Dalai Lama, the figure responsible for sanctifying the lineage. Clearly the artist was inspired by murals and thangka portraits of the Fifth from the Potala, such as his portrait executed in 1690. Yet this does not seem to be the case for the portraits of the other Dalai Lamas. Similarly, we can assume that the artist drew inspiration for the portraits of the Indian incarnations from the Menkhyen-style murals of 1645-1648 at the Potala.

The addition of successive authoritative individuals, including subsequent hierarchs, is therefore an artistic comment upon the set. Although these subordinate Dalai Lamas deserved positions of prominence in individual thangkas, since

this was intended to be a reproduction of an earlier 5th Dalai Lama set, their positions have been made secondary to that of the central figure. Thus their sizing is not due to economic reasons—to avoid executing three or four more paintings to the set. The ultimate motive for both artist and sponsor was that by glorifying the founder of the lineage, they forged a direct link between the 5th and the 9th Dalai Lamas in an unbroken line, as the arrangement of the figures indicates. During his short life, the 9th Dalai Lama repeatedly had visions of and claimed identity with the Fifth, which may have also influenced the compositional structure of the set. The motive for making the set was to establish legitimacy and documentation in addition to commemoration. The set is a faithful but innovative adaptation of the Dalai Lama lineage repertoire.

The artist has used conventional and idealized portraiture as found in individual portraits of the figures, or from another possibly identical lineage succession set evidently inspired by the prototypical murals in the Potala. Yet the predilection to experiment with the forms that portraiture allows seems to have captivated the artist. Some of the portraits appear to have been personally executed, with iconographical details and choice of color revealing the artist's hand. In representing the lineage, he may have taken some liberties or exhibited some ignorance: for example, we would expect Thrisong Detsen and Nyangrel Nyima Wöser to appear in the same painting because of their close bonds. Although artistic mimicry is paradigmatic to the Tibetan painting tradition, whatever model the artist may have used, he nevertheless has left his own idiosyncratic handprint. We can appreciate this through his slightly unorthodox deviations from the standard representations of the figures.

We do not yet fully know the precise date, explicit circumstances, artist or place of execution of this set. A reasonable guess would be that the artist was an unusual court painter from central or east Tibet active in Lhasa who used existing models found in the Potala. This would suggest a master of the New Menri painting school, someone from Denma in Kham, painting around 1815. The otherwise detailed biography of the 9th Dalai Lama does not mention the execution of the painting set, which suggests that it was not executed as part of an official commemoration. We may hazard that the set was commissioned around the time of the death of the 9th

Dalai Lama, either unofficially or by his family. His family was never ennobled as *yapzhi* ཡབ་གཞིས་ [yab gzhis] unlike the families of most other Dalai Lamas, who were granted sizable estates especially in central Tibet. This may have been because the head of the family, the Ninth's father, had already died and only his mother and sister(s) may have come with him to Lhasa. After his untimely demise, the reduced family and their descendants returned to Kham and therefore left no traces in central Tibet.

A minute art-historical comparison with other Dalai Lama *thrung-rap* sets including paintings of individual hierarchs should help contextualize this set in the development of this tradition and its many variations. There is little doubt with its personal style, this set is an exquisite example of Tibetan art. The fact that this rare set is directly associated with the little-known and ill-fated 9th Dalai Lama adds to its historical value and importance.

272–275   Details of the seventh thangka.   272   Head of Zhang Yutrakpa with a special hat dating back to one of his most important teachers. Zhang's expression seems to reflect his aggressive character.   273   Rock formations with plants.   274   Mongolian nobility and an attendant bringing gifts.   275   Lhaje Gewabum, who built dikes in Lhasa and thus protected the Jokhang from flooding.

TIBETAN EPISTOLARY STYLE

Hanna Schneider
Translated by JANICE BECKER

In Asia as in western Europe, epistolary and official styles of writing developed specific typologies as the state developed. These styles therefore came to reflect the administrative practices at each stage of the development of the state. Outside of Europe, particularly in the Middle East, as well as in Central and East Asia, conventions governing both form and content of letters gradually grew out of more ancient traditions. Long the object of great respect, letters of the literati and those educated in rhetoric served as models for official and private correspondence following set rules of style. In Tibet we find many parallels with Western traditions in the historical development of official and private epistolary styles and structures.

Over approximately the same period, between the 8th and 18th centuries, in Tibet as in western Europe there ensued a gradual development from loose collections of guidelines to formularies—books of forms—in which we find formulas organized by category for official use. "Formula" refers to those elements of the letter whose content is already set, such as the salutation, the opening and closing which were to be used exactly unchanged between sender and recipient. This has to be seen as standing in close connection to diplomatics, the language of official documents and the law which in Western traditions makes similar use of set phrases and formulaic portions. This development of guidelines culminated in the letter-writing guide, a kind of textbook which provided directions based on theory and examples of the correct and elegant composition of letters perfect in both form and content.

It is significant that letter writing and collecting came into vogue in Tibet precisely at a time of structural transformation, a time of the solidification of Tibetan Buddhism as state religion and a time of intensive contacts with Tibet's political neighbors. Independent anthologies of letters found their way into the collected works of many famous literati in Tibet. These were anthologies of the letters by individual masters representing all schools of Tibetan Buddhism composed during their lifetimes, collected like their spoken word, and bequeathed to posterity.

The 5th Dalai Lama, Ngawang Lopsang Gyatso དགའ་དབང་བློ་བཟང་རྒྱ་མཚོ་ [ngag dbang blo bzang rgya mtsho] (1617–1682), began to consolidate the Tibetan state during the second half of the

17th century, a process having a decisive influence over the development of the classical official style. By the second half of the 18th century, Tibet emerged as a centrally-ruled, well-organized state. The letter-writing guides that came into vogue just then paint a precise picture of the newly-modified social structures. The expansion of the administrative apparatus accompanying the development of a centrally-ruled state, the introduction of five ranks of nobility[1] in 1792, and the subsequent fine differentiations between administrative roles were all reflected in the need for new writing styles for letters and official use.

Individual elements appropriate to each rank of the administration were integrated under a new theoretical framework precisely regulated by protocol according to the situation. In the process, people fully exploited the capacity of the Tibetan language to make fine distinctions in speech levels. It is not surprising that the letter-writing guides of the Ganden Phodrang period placed particular attention on directions and samples of correct composition for letters and petitions to the Dalai Lama. These guides prescribed the correct level of respect to be maintained between author and addressee, beautiful handwriting, and careful folding and sealing of documents. For example, Norgye Nangpa's 1888 letter-writing guide[2] for official correspondence, found in offices and used as a reference work, tells us:

> For petitions to the Highest offices, to the protector, the Lord of the Jinas, the same guidelines apply to all senders from the rank of *kalön* བཀའ་བློན་ [bka' blon] "minister" and below: for the width of the letter paper, no more than three and a half handwidths and no less than three handwidths and eight fingerwidths should be used. The salutation should be placed one handwidth and eight fingerwidths below the upper edge of the page; a distance of seven fingerwidths should be maintained on both the left and right sides. The distance of respect between the salutation and the *güwang* གུས་འབངས་ [gus 'bangs] formula[2] is one handwidth and four fingerwidths. Inserts, abbreviations and corrections should be avoided. It must be ensured that the distance between lines does not exceed one fingertip.
>
> With a *khatak* and
> in respectful devotion,
> this petition is presented.

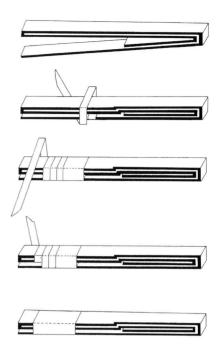

276 Manner in which a letter was folded and closed using a paper ribbon (drawing provided by Hanna Schneider, Bonn).

This sequence of three lines within the area of respect ends the closing.

The distance between the closing and the lower edge of the page depended upon the status of the sender. Even if a letter was supposed to be cut so closely that the final words were just legible, I have heard from oral tradition that this should not be done as it is inauspicious. According to this tradition, the distance to the bottom edge of the page should be one and one-half fingerwidths.

To ensure that the line of a fold is not lost or wasted on top, a letter should be folded as narrowly as possible. The form that the distance of respect should take on the presentation stamp on the outside is the same as described above. The external inscription must also be placed in a series of three steps, ending on the lower edge. The *takdam* རྟགས་དམ་ [rtags dam] seal to close the document must be affixed with half of its seal face, after the head of the seal has been aligned evenly. The paper ribbon required to seal the letter must be wrapped from below over the front and then down the back before inserting. After nine wraps made in this manner, the affixing seal is placed on the front aligned with the external inscription. The seal on the back face must be affixed evenly. The four ends of the sheet that will become the envelope are cleanly cut. The quantity of sealing wax should be just sufficient for the ground of the seal, so that the bulge is not too large. As for the presentation stamp, the forms of address should be repeated as in the petition.

The guidelines make no differentiation for the external framework whether the recipient was a Dalai Lama or Panchen Rinpoche, in contrast to all other recipients. Depending upon the rank of the sender relative to the recipient, the size of the letter paper may vary as may the distance of respect, being smaller for recipients other than the Dalai or Panchen Lama. Likewise, the number of wraps with the paper ribbon enfolding the letter would also vary. For the internal framework—the fixed elements of the opening and closing parts—the writer paid great attention to correct and elegant formulation. Naturally, they paid the greatest attention to these elements in a letter directed to the Dalai Lama.

We will briefly mention the individual elements here in the following order: the various formulas for the salutation, then the devotional formulas mentioned above, the opening section and the fixed transitional formulas leading to the narrative, and the petition which forms the main section or "heart" of the letter. Of course the sender must compose this section independently and cannot rely on any writer's guide. He or she here wants to engage both the eye and ear of the recipient for his personal report or request.

For the transition to the closing section with its closing protocol dealing with the date of composition, any accompanying gifts, and the devotional formula at the end of the letter, the writer could choose[4] from among a variety of formulas:

For letters addressed to the protector, the *Kyapgön Gyalwang Thamce Khyenzik Chenpo* སྐྱབས་མགོན་རྒྱལ་དབང་ཐམས་ཅད་མཁྱེན་གཟིགས་ཆེན་པོ་ [skyabs mgon rgyal dbang thams cad mkhyen gzigs chen po] "Great, Omniscient and All-Seeing Lord of the Jinas," the forms of address are the same for senders of the rank *kalön* and below:

Salutation: Before the Lord of the Jinas, jewel in the crown of all sentient beings in *saṃsāra* or those who have already entered *nirvāṇa*, fulfiller of all wishes for merit and well-being, including of the gods, the protector, the greatest, best, omniscient and all-seeing Lord of the Jinas.

or:

Before the throne carried by eight mighty lions, the footrest of the crown of all sentient beings in *saṃsāra* or those who have already entered *nirvāṇa*, majesty over the snowland, Lord of the Jinas, the Padmapāṇi,[5] the greatest, omniscient and all-seeing...

Devotional formula: ...With undivided religious devotion of body, speech, and mind, prostrating with my limbs stretched upon the earth, I present the heart of my request:

Captatio benevolentiae[6]: In these days of well-being and happiness extending their blinding glow in the splendor and virtue of a golden age...

or:

In these days when the splendor and virtue of well-being and benevolence have extended a hundred thousand-fold because of you who are the only refuge of those seeking shelter in this world, and who possesses the symmetrical arrangement of proportional features of the three secrets of the body, speech, and mind, revealing the demeanor of a youthful monk, clear, firmly formed and brightly radiant; you, who live and thrive by guiding the limitless number of sentient beings equal to the heavens along the path leading to superior rebirth and good and auspicious action: the accumulation of your immeasurable benevolence is as great as that of the lord of the mountains[7] stacked a billion fold upon each other—great, great! May even I, self-proclaimed subject living under the benevolence the Great Protector has granted so that I, who am barely touched by burdens, may live to fulfill my duties. I now prostrate myself and present as the heart of my request:

Here follow the narration and the petition, followed by the closing:

May you dwell securely under the Ten Powers and the Four Valors of the body armed with the Five Certainties. Through the brilliance of your teachings, meditation, activities in study, ethical conduct, and works of transcendence...may your solemn promise to all including me, for whom you have shown concern throughout my existences, that we may taste the nectar of your profound teachings as desired, may this deep vajra bond never in any way loosen. Acknowledge, acknowledge, acknowledge. Acknowledge, acknowledge. The great and devout dedication of my body, speech, and mind support my request submitted with this petition.[8]

Apart from corresponding on *samda* མསའ་ཁྲ་ [sam khra], white-washed wooden tablets, as a rule a Dalai Lama did not write personal or official letters in his own hand. Traditionally, specially trained secretaries instead did that. The Dalai Lama would dictate to his secretary, who then created a design, which after submission and approval, would be put on paper. After completion, the secretary sealed the letter in the presence of the Dalai Lama and then prepared an authorized copy of the original for safekeeping in the archives.

In addition to letters written on paper, notices could be sent either on chalk-covered wooden tablets[9] or with *dayik* མདའ་ཡིག་ [mda' yig] "arrow letters,"[10] generally used to transmit urgent official messages. For these, after the sender wrote the text on a piece of cloth with India ink and bamboo pen, he or she affixed the cloth to an arrow or wooden stick. The *samda* writing tablet was used primarily for personal correspondence over shorter distances. The sender applied lime powder to a small square wooden tablet and carved the text with a dry bamboo pen on the resulting writing surface. After reading the letter, the recipient could then easily wipe off the text like chalkboard, and send back an answer immediately. The Dalai Lamas also frequently wrote using *samda*. Rinchen Dolma Taring འཕྲེང་རིང་རིན་ཆེན་སྒྲོལ་མ་ ['phreng ring rin chen sgrol ma] describes a correspondence between the 13th Dalai Lama, Ngawang Lopsang Thupten Gyatso ངག་དབང་བློ་བཟང་ཐུབ་བསྟན་རྒྱ་མཚོ་ [ngag dbang blo bzang thub bstan rgya mtsho] (1876-1933) and her father, the famous Tsarong Shape Dasang Dadül ཚྭ་རོང་ཞབས་པད་ཟླ་དགྲ་འདུལ་ [tshva rong zhabs pad zla dgra 'dul].

The Great Thirteenth remains renowned for his unusual rhetorically nuanced style of writing. In their historical context, his letters reveal the complex politico-religious levels in which he communicated with secular and religious officeholders and men of state within Tibet and beyond. Written during turbulent times, his letters demonstrate the expressive power of a language rich in stylistic resources, revealing his character and

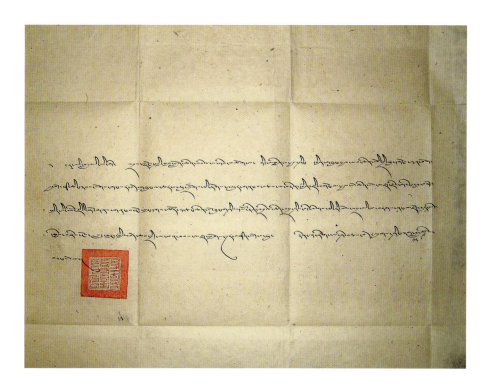

277 Letter from the Thirteenth Dalai Lama to Charles Bell, in which he congratulates Bell on receiving the title of C.M.G. (Commander of His Majesty's Government). Lhasa, 1915, British Library, London, Inv. No. Eur MSS F 80-19. >>>

the clear thinking of an experienced statesman, while standing firmly within the Tibetan *kāvya* literary tradition.

Sir Charles Bell (1870-1945) described the life of the 13th Dalai Lama from a Western viewpoint. He was in diplomatic service beginning in 1901 first in Kalimpong, then later as a political officer in Sikkim, Bhūṭān, and Tibet until 1919, then once again in the diplomatic mission to Lhasa in 1920. He enjoyed a close personal relationship with the Dalai Lama and became an outstanding authority on Tibetan culture and customs. He describes his correspondence with the 13th Dalai Lama below. It is interesting to compare the wording of his letter with that of the formal section translated from Tibetan above: [11]

The letters and reports were, of course, enclosed in a ceremonial scarf of thin white silk. And over all was the thick parchment cover, liberally sealed. Now and then, on the covers of letters from the Dalai Lama himself, there would be orders to the postal runners who carried them, "Do not stop even to take breath!" The Precious Sovereign did not lose time himself, and did not like others to do so.

It may be of interest to record the sort of phrases in which I began and ended letters to the Dalai Lama in accordance with Tibetan custom.

"To the golden throne of the excellent Dalai Lama, who is the protector and the unfailing refuge of all sentient beings, including

the gods. Thanks very much for your health being good, like the King of the Mountains, by virtue of the accumulated merits of countless ages and your good deeds increasing like stars in the sky. Here I am also in good health, and my affairs are going on as usual."

End of opening compliments. Now the business of the letter is written. The conclusion may be somewhat as follows:

"This letter is composed and written by myself, and so do not be displeased if there are mistakes in it. Kindly take what is good, and abandon what is bad, for your health, and send letters to me, whenever necessary, like a divine river. Know. Know. Know. Know. Know.

Sent with magnolia flowers by C.A. Bell, Administrator and Minister, on the eighth day of the ninth English month, a date of good omen."

THE ICONOGRAPHY OF THE DALAI LAMAS

Michael Henss
Translated by JANICE BECKER

This chapter represents a preliminary iconography and typology of the representations of all fourteen Dalai Lamas and provides an overview of the individual features of these Geluk hierarachs as passed down to us in scrolls, murals, and statues from the 16th through the 20th centuries. We will trace the origins and development of their portraiture, especially that of reincarnation lineages and how individual Dalai Lamas used them to buttress their sacred and historical legitimacy as the rebirth of Bodhisattva Avalokiteśvara, or their historical predecessors, including kings, lamas, and monks. We should point out that, aside from the prototypical images in which a largely fixed iconography became established starting in the late 17th century, there is no canon of obligatory motifs in the representations of the Dalai Lamas. Prior to that, the attributes and *mudrās* of the hierarchs were often interchangeable and only rarely do inscriptions provide reliable indications of the person represented in them, as in the case of small-sized metal figures.[1]

The earliest known portraits of a Dalai Lama are those of the 3rd Dalai Lama Sönam Gyatso who was also the first to bear the title Dalai Lama.[2] With the exception of a figure[3] allegedly executed during his lifetime in 1585, a thangka featuring a number of scenes from the life of Sönam Gyatso from Luk Monastery in western Tibet is of special importance. A local ruler likely commissioned a local artist to create the thangka shortly after the Dalai Lama visited Guge in 1572, though likely prior to his trip to Mongolia in 1578 (plate 29, 278).[4] Iconographically, this early likeness of the Dalai Lama follows the portraiture of monks that had been known in Tibet since the 12th century, with the lama as scholar and teacher, book in hand and gesturing in argument,[5] meditating,[6] or with the *tshebum* ཚེ་བུམ་ [tshe bum] (Skt. *jīvana-kalaśa*) "long-life vase" of Amitāyus.[7] Just as the essential features of monk portraiture had developed out of the image of the Buddha, the Dalai Lama began to appear as a deified lama.

This raises a more general question about the portrait in Tibetan art, which knows no profane images. There are only representations of saints and holy persons, with the lama as incarnation of Buddha or as manifestation of a *bodhisattva*,[8] such as a historical king or Dalai Lama. Ever since the time of the early kings, pictures of religious rulers have occupied the place of images of secular rulers. Content determines form, and

the "saint" or the divine do not allow for realist portraiture. Convention determines the likeness of the Dalai Lama and only occasionally, such as with the Fifth and much more rarely with other monks and masters (e.g. the first and second Karmapa, Marpa), do his representations take on portrait-like elements.[9] The objective is not the individual resemblance to the physical person but rather the ideal of the holy form and the visual representation of the institution of the Dalai Lama, "conveying the spirit through the form."[10] Certain attributes and *mudrās* later came to characterize individual Dalai Lamas, but they vary greatly or are interchangeable. In particular, metal sculptures of "regular" Geluk lamas are not sufficiently identifiable as a Dalai Lama and sometimes indistinguishable.

The fact that a particular image was created during the lifetime of a Dalai Lama does not mean greater portrait faithfulness. Thus the main figure in a thangka of the 5th Dalai Lama at the Rubin Museum follows completely conventional patterns, with only the walrus mustache characteristic of the Great Fifth indicating the figure's precise identity (plate 48). For historical reasons, the small metal statuette of the 5th Dalai Lama Ngawang Lopsang Gyatso from the Boston Museum of Fine Art (plate 59) was probably created around 1669, although its inscription does not exactly indicate the date of origin.[11] The Fifth's autobiography attests that other sculptures of him were produced during his lifetime: "I composed the inscription for a statue of me that the supervisor of sacrificial offerings had commissioned in gilded copper," referring to an event in 1679.[12]

We should also refer to the superb silver figure of himself that the 5th Dalai Lama presented to the Shunzhi 順治 emperor during his visit to Beijing on 14 January 1953 and which had been most certainly produced shortly before in Tibet (plate 52). A few other comparable figures have characteristics of a portrait: the massive round, hairless head with protruding ears give us an idea of the physical characteristics of the 5th Dalai Lama. In his autobiography, the Fifth uses the terms *drambak* འདྲ་འབག་ ['dra 'bag], *nge drambak* ངའི་འདྲ་འབག་ [nga'i 'dra 'bag] or *nga drama* ང་འདྲ་མ་ [nga 'dra ma] to describe how similar to himself were various images made of gold, silver, and other metals. The Tibetan means "according to the likeness [of the person]," a "a good likeness of me," or "just like me."[13] In each instance the 5th Dalai Lama himself approved such *nga drama* or "portraits" of himself done during his lifetime. That is, according to the

278 One of the earliest known representations of a Dalai Lama. Detail of a thangka of the Third Dalai Lama, Western Tibet/Guge, late 16th century, private collection (see plate 29). **279** The Sixth Dalai Lama. An example from the Stockholm thangka cycle, allegedly from the Imperial Summer Palace at Jehol (Chengde). Folkens Museum Etnografiska, Stockholm.

Tibetan, he "recognized [them] as the same as him." Thus the Great Fifth's writings verify what three-dimensional images like the Boston statuette demonstrate. What is remarkable is that there exist portrait-like figures only of the 5th Dalai Lama, with the exception of a few of the Thirteenth, as historical circumstance generally explains this situation. None of the other nine preceding or subsequent Dalai Lamas recognized as such during their lifetimes had a personality of comparable religious and political power or magnetism.

This depersonalization of the monk's image was both intentional and the objective: the point was not so much to reflect the individual physical appearance of a given title-holder, but rather to raise his image to a symbol of the Dalai Lama as an institution. This forms the intellectual backdrop to most representations of the Dalai Lama—not of individuals but as part of a series encompassing preceding and future incarnations.

TYPES OF IMAGES REPRESENTING THE DALAI LAMA: REINCARNATION SETS

The series of images of the previous existences of a particular Dalai Lama is of primary significance for describing the various types of images used in representing him. Although the biography of the 1st Dalai Lama written in 1494 refers to the concept of a line of reincarnations from Avalokiteśvara through King

Songtsen Gampo, and even before that reincarnation lines of the Sakya patriarchs were already known, monumental series of pictures became common only during the time of the 5th Dalai Lama. Indeed with him originates the first known text that sets forth these rebirth lineages starting with Avalokiteśvara,[14] on which he elaborates in his biographies of the 3rd and 4th Dalai Lamas (1646 and 1653). In 1644 he had the line of the 1st Dalai Lama painted in the assembly hall of Dzingpi Monastery ཛིང་ཕྱི་ [rdzing phyi] in Olkha District, about 8 km from the former Olkha Taktse Monastery འོལ་ཁ་སྟག་རྩེ་ ['ol kha stag rtse]. The Great Fifth describes similar paintings that included his previous existences—the first four Dalai Lamas—which have been preserved in the Great Eastern Hall[15] of the Potala Palace. In these paintings, he has used pictorial representation to reveal for the first time the lineage of both himself and his predecessors, and thus established a tradition of mural and statue series which his successors continued.

The Fifth's collected works include a short text written between 1673 and 1676 about "the foundation of the rebirth sequence, guidelines on how to paint it, including an explanation [called] 'clear mirror'," which contains "the rebirth sequence for the painting schools," as he states in a colophon.[16] Similarly, he had erected figures of the first four Dalai Lamas at the Potala around 1692 in the Thrungrap

Lhakhang འཁྲུངས་རབས་ལྷ་ཁང་ ['khrung rabs lha khang] "Shrine of the Holy Tradition." These figures were placed next to the central statue of the 5th Dalai Lama, whose lineage was traced there back to Jobo Śākyamuni—a copy of the Jokhang statue—seated that we see seated next to him (plate 292).[17] In another room, statues of Ngawang Lopsang Gyatso's seven successors down to the 12th Dalai Lama stand along both sides of the central figure of Tsongkhapa.[18]

The concept of the Dalai Lama reincarnation lineage, which the Great Fifth had so intensively propagated and expressed artistically, continued to appear in thangka painting unabated after his death in 1682. Likely only then or in the 1690s were the oldest of the extant scroll series made that illustrate the first five Dalai Lamas and the Fifth's previous fourteen incarnations reaching back to the legendary kings. Seven of the original nineteen images in this artistically outstanding series (plates 7, 21, 42)[19] have survived. The actual subject of this series is the 5th Dalai Lama and his previous incarnations. His own image, chronologically the last as well as the richest of the entire series, once occupied the central position with the remaining thangkas arranged symmetrically on either side.

Today the Stockholm Ethnographic Museum and the Palace Museum in Beijing are the repositories of two other series of thirteen pictures each depicting the 7th Dalai Lama Lopsang Kalsang Gyatso's previous incarnations. These two sets have survived intact and reveal very different painting styles. Here too the central thangka in the original arrangement is that of the chronologically last person—the 7th Dalai Lama—who is also the only one shown as a full frontal figure. Because complete, both sets are especially important for understanding the iconography of Dalai Lama reincarnation series. The Stockholm thangka series which Swedish researcher Sven Hedin acquired in 1930 in Beijing is said to have come from the imperial summer residence in Chengde, and it has been executed in a somewhat older painting style, possibly during the lifetime of the 7th Dalai Lama (plates 3, 282, 283). Twelve wooden blocks made at Narthang Monastery near Shigatse before 1737 served as models for prints to be painted over to make a series on the Panchen Lama's previous existences[20] in a very similar style, and thus the thirteen thangkas in Stockholm may also follow a no longer extant prototype of xylographs from the first half of the 18th century.[21]

This presumed Narthang set of the Dalai Lama lineage apparently became the model for several subsequent thangka sets in which individual images began to follow more or less fixed patterns of iconography and composition. Engraved wooden blocks made it possible to copy a set of images that the 7th Dalai Lama in particular propogated which traced the genealogy of the Dalai Lamas back to such Geluk ancestors as Domtön and especially Avalokiteśvara, of whom Dalai Lamas since the Great Fifth saw themselves as rebirths. Such wood engravings served as both prints that could be painted over and as iconographic and design models for painted "copies" in sample books. In many cases basic information about surviving reincarnation sets is lacking—especially whether the preliminary "drawing" was a wood engraving, as well as the format of the picture—so we can only begin to address the relationship between model and copy for these largely, but not entirely standardized sets. More precise investigation is encouraged.[22]

The Beijing series, only recently reproduced in full, is an example of the finest 18th century Tibetan painting. According to its catalogue entry, the Second Janggya *Khutughtu* Rölpe Dorje (1717-1786), the highest representative of Tibetan Buddhism in China since 1734, *guoshi* 國師 "teacher of the empire," and first art advisor to the Qianlong 乾隆 emperor,[23] gave the set a place among the imperial collection of Buddhist ritual art in 1761. We can take as certain the dating of these thangkas to around 1760, about two years after the death of the 7th Dalai Lama (plates 288, 289, 293-295). As with the Stockholm set, six thangkas of preceding rebirths—the eleven incarnations of Avalokiteśvara—balance the symmetry of the six previous Dalai Lamas on either sides of the central image, in addition to the 7th Dalai Lama. The five previous existences of the Dalai Lamas correspond to the original Narthang woodblock model also used for the Stockholm set: Avalokiteśvara, Songtsen Gampo, Künga Nyingpo, Domtön, and Sanggye Gömpa. Five partially-colored woodcut thangkas from this set of the Dalai Lamas and their previous existences have survived.[24]

PREVIOUS EXISTENCES OF THE DALAI LAMAS
The Tibetan concept of the reincarnation of a certain deity or person through succeeding personalities in a lineage of rebirths serves as a bridge between the past and the future. The writings of the 5th Dalai Lama include a detailed list of previous incarna-

280 King Songtsen Gampo. Bronze, gilded?, Tibet, ca.15th century, H 27 cm, Museum der Kulturen Basel, Collection of Essen, Inv. No. IId 14045. **281** The Eight-Armed, Eleven-Headed Avalokiteśvara. Bronze, gilded, H: 25 cm, W: 15 cm, Ethnographic Museum of the University of Zürich, Inv. No.: 9976

tions of the Dalai Lama exactly as we find them in the Stockholm and Beijing thangka series.[25] Such texts undoubtedly also served as the foundation for the sets of paintings .

At the beginning there was Chenrezik (Skt. Bodhisattva Avalokiteśvara) whose cult the 5th Dalai Lama particularly respected and propagated. "I myself have become an embodiment of Avalokiteśvara and exist in all his other manifestations," the Great Fifth said in a vision in front of the image of this bodisattva at the Potala in 1656.[26] According to Tibetan tradition, Avalokiteśvara took the form of *chögyal* ཆོས་རྒྱལ [chos rgyal] (Skt. *dharmarāja*) in the first historical king of Tibet Songtsen Gampo whose image is in the canon for all lineage sets of the Dalai Lama (Illus. xx).[27] Tibetan sources state that Songtsen Gampo was Avalokiteśvara's reincarnation, in other words, the sixth of the 5th Dalai Lama's eighteen previous incarnations.

As reflected in several of his visions, Lopsang Gyatso honored and revered Songtsen Gampo. A year after visiting the king's grave in the Yarlung Valley in 1651, when he was departing for the Chinese court, he had an apparition of the bodhisattva ruler. Later in 1656, during another vision, Songtsen Gampo initiated him into a *maṇḍala* in order to give instructions for restoring temples and paintings.[28]

Other Tibetan rulers also figure in image sets, like the third incarnation in the lineage, the mythic king Nyathri Tsenpo (found in the Paris-Brussels set), and Thrisong Detsen (in both the Paris-Brussels and Stockholm sets). Usually considered the incarnation of Mañjuśrī, other texts have classified Thrisong Detsen as Avalokiteśvara's seventh rebirth among the 5th Dalai Lama's previous existences, apparently because of his intensive efforts to spread Buddhism in Tibet.[29]

Numerous Tibetan texts state that Avalokiteśvara also came to Tibet for the ninth time as Domtön (1005–1064), founder of the Kadam School, to complete the reforms of his great teacher, Atiśa (982–1054) who while alive had declared his equally-learned disciple the incarnation of Avalokiteśvara and even described earlier Tibetan kings as his previous births.[30] Regent Sanggye Gyatso discusses Domtön in a prominent passage in the chapter "Avalokiteśvara Introduces Compassion to Tibet" from the volume he wrote around 1681 that was supplemental to the 5th Dalai Lama's. The idea of Domtön as an emanation of Avalokiteśvara made him a substantial prefiguration to the Dalai Lamas, because the 1st Dalai Lama—a rebirth of the founder of the Kadam School—had also been described as Avalokiteśvara's emanation. His image is present in every set (plate 282). His epithet *gyalwa* རྒྱལ་བ [rgyal ba] "vic-

282 Domtön, in the upper left his teacher Atiśa. Thangka, Tibet, 18th century, Folkens Museum Etnografiska, Stockholm, Inv. No.: 1935.50.966. **283** Sanggye Gömpa (not Phakpa as previously assumed). Thangka, Tibet, 18th century, Folkens Museum Etnografiska, Stockholm, Inv. No.: 1935.50.972.

torious," acknowledges his special connection with the Dalai Lamas, all of whom have also assumed the epithet.

The next of the Dalai Lama's previous existences from the Stockholm and Beijing series is Künga Nyingpo (1092–1158; plate 3), who is also viewed as an incarnation of Avalokiteśvara. He was the first of five great Sakya patriarchs and the son of the founder of the Sakya School, Khönchok Gyalpo. As Sanggye Gyatso's volume in the 5th Dalai Lama's autobiography explains, Künga Nyingpo reincarnated himself four times after entering *nirvāṇa*, the last time in the person of the 5th Dalai Lama as the 5th himself supposedly stated: "the omniscient Sönam Gyatso claimed that he was the re-embodiment of Sakya Chenpo [Künga Nyingpo]."[31] But we should not view Künga Nyingpo solely as the Avalokiteśvara's incarnation in the Dalai Lama lineage; he was also the founder of the Sakya clergy. His combining profane and religious power in the Sakya "state" served as a model for the subsequent Geluk theocracy in its political significance. Including earlier Sakya representatives thus solidified the Geluk School's position and legitimacy as well that of the Dalai Lamas.[32]

The last previous existence before the Dalai Lamas from this set has been associated with Phakpa Lodrö Gyaltsen འཕགས་པ་ གྲོས་རྒྱལ་མཚན་ ['phags pa blo gros rgyal mtshan] (1235–1280) who

was connected to the Sakya hierarchs and after 1268 served as *guoshi,* the "state religious teacher" who was head of the Chinese Buddhist clergy. Later tradition holds that he reincarnated himself as the 3rd Dalai Lama Sönam Gyatso (1543–1588) and also as his successor Yönten Gyatso *"Dharmarāja* Phakpa" (1589–1617) but Tibetan texts rarely mention the Dalai Lama's spiritual predecessors. An exception to this is the 5th Dalai Lama's autobiography, in which the Fifth says of himself, "I am Phakpa."[33] Phakpa's mission to Mongolia, which the Geluk revived with religious and political consequences in the 16th and 17th centuries, undoubtedly formed the basis for this statement. The Stockholm and Beijing sets illustrate these references in their portraits of the 5th Dalai Lama, where we see Phakpa seated next to Khubilai Khan in the lower right, probably Sakya Paṇḍita in the upper right, and Mahākāla Brāhmaṇarūpa (plate 293), connected with Hevajra Tantra, in the lower left.

The monk with the yellow pointed cap directly preceding the Dalai Lamas in the Stockholm[34] (plate 283) and Beijing[35] sets is likely, however the sixth abbot of Narthang and Phakmo Drupa disciple Sanggye Gömpa སངས་རྒྱས་སྒོམ་པ [sangs rgyas sgom pa] (1179–1250), whom texts repeatedly mention in connection with Domtön, and who was included in the lineage of Geluk hierarchs' previous existences as representative of the Kadam tradition. An inscription on a picture from the Stockholm set supports this identification: we find in the upper left Palden Gromochepa དཔལ་ལྡན་གྲོ་མོ་ཆེ་པ་ [dpal ldan gro mo che pa], also known as Gromoche Dürtsi Drak གྲོ་མོ་ཆེ་བདུད་རྩི་གྲགས [gro mo che bDud rtsi grags] or Grotön གྲོ་སྟོན་ [gro ston] (1153–1232), fourth abbot of Narthang Monastery, so significant for Kadam tradition, and teacher of Sanggye Gömpa, whom the inscription under the pillow upon which the main figure of the Beijing set is seated[36] specifically names. Another indication of the identity is the strikingly large enclosure charactistic of Narthang. We recognize Sanggye Gömpa in exactly the same iconographical form as the side figure in a thangka of the 8th Dalai Lama at the Ethnographic Museum of the University of Zürich, and then again in the upper right next to the Second and Fourth Dalai Lamas in a portrait of the 6th Dalai Lama at the Hahn Cultural Foundation.[37] Centuries later, Narthang itself may have referred to their own Kadam tradition as the 5th Dalai Lama and Sanggye Gyatso had done in order to legitimate the Geluk line of reincarnations. There, sometime around 1710 or 1720 a now-lost set of woodcut images of the Dalai Lamas and their previous incarnations was probably made.[38] Further investigation of the Kadam Lekbam བཀའ་གདམས་གླེགས་བམ་ [bka' gdams glegs bam] "book of Kadam teachings" may provide us with a deeper understanding of this.

Only individual thangkas have survived from other sets of reincarnation portraits, such as at the Ethnographic Museum of the University of Zürich, where we have the 2nd–6th Dalai Lamas (plates 26, 30, 35, 36, 66) who follow somewhat modified iconographic and compositional patterns and are somewhat modified compared to those of the Stockholm and Beijing series.[39] There are also series that include only the first eight Dalai Lamas as principle figures and have the previous existences as smaller ancillary figures. These include the five of an original eight thangkas at the American Museum of Natural History, and other truncated sets, such as the triptych of the 7th Dalai Lama with his predecessors the 5th and 6th Dalai Lamas at the Hahn Cultural Foundation in Seoul.[40] A set particularly interesting for its unusual iconographic and artistic style, strongly influenced by the Chinese (See essay by Per Sørensen in this volume) is that of seven thangkas from the time of the 9th Dalai Lama (1806–1815) that has portraits of the first four Dalai Lamas and two Tibetan kings arranged symmetrically around the central thangka of the Great Fifth, and four smaller figures of the 6th through the 9th Dalai Lamas painted in the upper margin.

A single picture, rather than a set, can also unite various previous existences of a single Dalai Lama and his predecessors such as in the thangka of the 5th Dalai Lama painted in gold on red at the Rubin Museum of Art in New York (plate 48). Here, the four previous Dalai Lamas along with Domtön, Songtsen Gampo, and the "primeval" bodhisattva illustrate the line.[41] For historic and biographical reasons, the large thangka at the Ethnographic Museum of the University of Zürich (plate 81) of the 8th Dalai Lama (1758–1804) and nine of his predecessors and successors painted in the late 1830s may well be the culmination of the tradition of incarnation lineage paintings. Here too the Tibetan religious kings Domtön, Künga Nyingpo, and Sanggye Gömpa stand in the rebirth lineage, although there have been a few changes in the pantheon: above the three personifications of Geluk Tantrism—Guhyasamāja, Yamantaka, and Cakrasaṃvara—there had been Śākyamuni opposite Avalokiteśvara, but now Amitābha, his spiritual father, replaces him. Two modern sets of all fourteen Dalai Lamas decorate the walls of the Kālacakra Temple at Namgyal Dratsang (the 14th Dalai Lama's personal monastery) in Dharamśālā and the temple at the Norbulingka Institute in Sidhpur, India (see p. 128).[42]

The reincarnation series and individual images in painting and sculpture described above have a central significance for the typology of Dalai Lama representations. We now turn to the other kinds of representations of the Dalai Lama.

BIOGRAPHICAL IMAGES OF THE DALAI LAMA

An individual Dalai Lama in a set of rebirth portraits is characterized by a generally canonical vocabulary of motifs: his own teacher; the founder of the Geluk School or the figure to first introduce a teaching of particular significance to that particular Dalai Lama; spiritual predecessors or previous Dalai Lamas; lamas who have initiated him; protective deities, and wrathful dharmapāla related to the school or teaching, all of which are grouped emblematically around the main figure. In biographical images of the Dalai Lamas including those in triptych form, however, numerous small scenes—

often explained in surround inscriptions—around the central figure illustrate his life story in the style of hagiographic texts, which also usually serve as models for these paintings. Thus the narrative in a thangka of the 2nd Dalai Lama at the Basel Museum of Cultures in which he is reciting from the Guhyasamāja Tantra in a double scenic "copy" is limited to a vision (as attested to in an inscription) that the hierarch had in front of a statue of Jobo Śākyamuni in the Jokhang during which his rebirth was prophesized (plate 27).

Other biographical thangkas have substantially more to say.[43] Just recently a scroll of the 5th Dalai Lama that came to light at the Rubin Museum of Art has interesting iconographic implications (plate 46) and probably dates to 1700 or shortly thereafter.[44] Like two other thangkas at the Musée Guimet and in the Tibet Museum, Lhasa[45] from around 1686, Padmasambhava appears on the lotus blossoms of the main figure. This and the presence of genial *yogin* saint Thangtong Gyalpo point to the influence of Nyingma teachings during his early years, as does the red-robed Nyingma teacher, Könchok Lhündrup (1561–1637), in the upper right. Beginning from the upper left, a number of scenes illustrate chronologically the Great Fifth's life and achievements, including a scene from a previous existence in which he descends as Avalokiteśvara from his paradise on the mythical Mount Potalaka and his birth in Chingwa Traktse Monastery in the Yarlung Valley; his visions of Atiśa and Tsongkhapa; his arrival at Ganden Phodrang དགའ་ལྡན་ཕོ་བྲང་ [dga' ldan pho brang], residence of the Geluk hierarchs from 1517 to 1650 (lower left); two other state monasteries, Sera and Ganden, which he expanded to their subsequent size; the beginning of the construction of the Potala and of instruction at the Jokhang (lower margin); the reverent reception he received from Mongolian princes during his trip to China in 1652; and his death in 1682 at the still-incomplete Potala, on whose white façade are written the Great Fifth's accomplishments including the training and ordaining of 14,000 novices and 20,000 monks.

Particularly interesting is the scene at the right margin of his audience with the fourteen-year-old Emperor Shunzhi in the Forbidden City in January 1653, in which the Dalai presents a silver statue of himself to his host. This statue can be dated to around 1651 and was thus crafted during his lifetime (plate 52).[46] This historically momentous meeting at the impe-rial palace is otherwise represented only in a mural from the early 1690s in the *Tshomchen Nup* ཚོམས་ཆེན་ནུབ་ [tshoms chen nub] "Great West Hall" of the Potala, and which probably also served as the model for the thangka at the Rubin Museum of Art. This state visit to Beijing does not appear in other biographical sets of the 5th Dalai Lama.[47]

Biographical images of the Dalai Lamas in the widest sense must also include those illustrating the "inner biography" of the main figure, such as the 5th Dalai Lama's various mystical experiences painted on a thangka at the Potala (plate 4).[48] The thirteen thangkas in a set on his life and visions are of a similar type and, according to his autobiography, the Great Fifth had them painted during his lifetime.[49] Other scrolls, usually forming a set, show the Dalai Lama in the "biography" of Tibet as the most recent representative in a historical tradition reaching back from Avalokiteśvara and the early Tibetan kings up through their presence at the Potala, although these individual scenes do not draw an explicit connection to the main figure (plate 1, 72).[50]

HAND AND FOOTPRINT THANGKAS

A small group of Dalai Lama "portraits" bearing their hand and footprints form another impressive emblem of the hierarchs' presence. We can trace this type of portrait which developed during the 16th century back to the much older *buddhapāda* "footprint of the Buddha" images which replicated the presence of the Buddha and formed part of early Tibetan painting.[51] Just as portraits of lamas developed in the 12th and 13th century to show teaching and meditating monks similar to the Buddha in attitude and *mudrā*, the *buddhapāda* also developed into the "lama-pāda" with the physical print coming to embody and serve as substitute for the master. Portraits for a lama's reliquary were similarly directly connected to the lama and as such attained extraordinary power to confer blessings.

But did the Dalai Lamas leave behind their actual hand and footprints? The size of the original format and certain obvious asymmetries, as well as other iconographic and stylistic features lend credence to their having been made during the subject's lifetimes and indicate that this indeed was the case at least sometimes.[52] Despite obvious standardizations, the first original handprints and footprints in the Paris-Brussels (plate 42) set could indeed have been made from the 5th Dalai Lama,

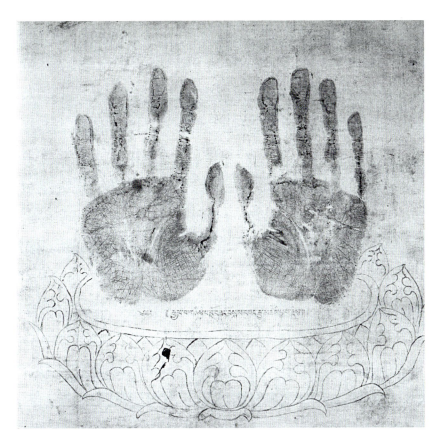

284 Handprint of the Seventh Dalai Lama and inscription on a thangka, on the obverse of which is a depiction of Tsongkhapa. Schoettle Catalog No. 32 (1976), No. 9265.   **285** Handprint of the Ninth Dalai Lama on one of the thangkas in the set of seven lineage thangkas (see p. 242). Collection of Veena and Peter Schnell, Zürich.

at least those in the last portrait.[53] Only rarely is it possible to show that a handprint made at the time of the consecration of the thangka happened during the lifetime of a Dalai Lama. At the Hanamaki City Museum 花巻市博物館 in Japan is a handprint of the 13th Dalai Lama "made from life" on paper and rolled like a Japanese scroll that the Thirteenth gave as a present to Tada Tokan 多田等観 (plate 99).[54] In another set of seven thangkas, it is presumably the 9th Dalai Lama who put both his handprints on their reverse (plate 285). [55]

The thangka from the Rubin Museum of Art mentioned above shows the 6th Dalai Lama Tsangyang Gyatso with his footprints and handprints (plate 69). Only an inscription on the throne pillow identifies the main figure as the 6th Dalai Lama and reads, "to honor the Sixth Royal Ruler, Tsangyang Gyatso." [56] The iconography and composition of this portrait are particularly interesting in that they have been quite obviously modelled on a similar thangka of the 5th Dalai Lama that survives in the Ford Collection. With the exception of the *phurba* ཕུར་པ [phur pa] "ritual dagger" peculiar to the Fifth as shown in any number of his representations, and apart from his rather youthful face, the 6th Dalai Lama conspicuously resembles his previous reincarnation. Even the walrus moustache points to the Great Fifth. We find a similarly conspicuous adaptation to

his famous predecessor only in a gold-plated Tibetan metal statuette holding a *phurba* from Beijing alluding to a Nyingma School orientation, but an inscription clearly identifies the figure as Tsangyang Gyatso (plate 70).[57]

OTHER REPRESENTATIONS OF THE DALAI LAMA

There are a very few images of the 7th Dalai Lama Kalsang Gyatso as a meditating monk and as a *yogin* practicing Tantric rituals in which he is not immediately recognizable as a Dalai Lama. Thus only with the aid of the textual source that served as the model for the portrait (plate 77)[58] has it been possible to identify the main figure in two very similar thangkas at the Ethnographic Museum of the University of Zürich and the Museum of Cultures in Basel as Kalsang Gyatso. In these he sits in a landscape dotted with rock caves and meditation sites, surrounded by various ritual objects and *ḍākinīs* who lend him the aura of secret knowledge and wisdom. We see him doing Tantric practices in several smaller scenes. According to the texts, the 7th Dalai Lama tried to achieve enlightenment during his lifetime with yoga in which a *ḍākinī* "she who traverses space" inspires and helps him towards this goal. Probably this "inner portrait" also contains biographical elements alluding to his experiences as a hermit.[59]

We have used examples overwhelmingly from painting as reference points to create the preceding typology of Dalai Lama representations which employ various iconographic "ingredients," including personal teachers and representatives of specific schools; protective deities; scenes from the life of the Dalai Lama concerned; and the Buddhist history of Tibet. All of these provide a rich and varied pictorial "repetoire": sets and individual portraits of reincarnation lineages; biographical and historical portraits from a larger narrative context; handprints and footprints which allude to the physical presence of the person portrayed; and reproductions of the Dalai Lama in other media.

INDIVIDUAL DALAI LAMA STATUETTES

Apart from a few monumental sets of statues of the Dalai Lama lineage found in the major Geluk monasteries—Potala, Drepung, Sera—of Lhasa, numerous small individual figures primarily constitute this essential type of representation. There are no reincarnation series among these generally small statuettes (between 10 and 30 cm high) since they are not designed for representational viewing and reverence by pilgrims in the way that large-scale temple sculptures were. The representational repetoire is here limited to such features as physical attributes and *mudrā*, which are sometimes interchangeable and do not allow exact identification of the specific Dalai Lama in each case. Often this is only possible with the aid of an inscription engraved on the figure, which is only present in a few cases.[60] A typology of these features forms the subject of the last part of this study, which encompasses a large number of these small individual figures.

PHOTOGRAPHY

The presence of Western visitors in Tibet starting around 1900 meant that a new type of representation, photography, emerged and with it came genuine individual images according to life. The earliest known photographic portrait of a Dalai Lama, that of the thirty-four year old Thirteenth, was taken during a meeting of a Tibetan governmental delegation with Sir Charles Bell, the British Political Officer for Sikkim, Bhūtān, and Tibet in 1910 in Kalkattā (plate 113).[61] Some of these "official" portrait photographs of the 13th Dalai Lama that Bell took into the 1920s came into the possession of religious and temporal figures or mon-

asteries and were later even reproduced as postcards or used as models for statuettes. The photograph often reproduced in Bell's books of the 13th Dalai Lama's enthronement in which he is wearing a yellow cap can be traced back to that meeting in Kalkattā, and according to the author, was the first shot with the hierarch sitting Tibetan style, "seated on a throne Buddha-wise ... as he would sit in his own palace at Lhasa for blessing pilgrims and others" (plate 110).[62]

A Tibetan painter subsequently colored in a few of these photographs, which were then provided with the 13th Dalai Lama's seal and a handwritten dedication. and were given back to the British diplomat. Photographs distributed of the Dalai Lama continue in a new form the earlier effect of figures and painting, as Bell had put it: "they all used the photographs in place of a statue with the same deference shown to images of buddhas and deities." As eyewitnesses, the photographic image no longer only showed the Dalai Lama in an official pose on his throne at the Potala or summer palace but also his private countenance, the "true likeness" of the youthful or aging human being Thupten Gyatso.

Forming both a bridge to photography and in this case a substitute for it, are the first Western-style hand-drawn portraits done of the 13th Dalai Lama who was residing in Urga (modern Ulaan Baatar) at the time. During a visit from Russian geographers in 1905, these drawings were done when the Dalai Lama refused to let them photograph him. Thus at the request of the Dalai Lama came into Tsar Nicholas the Second's possession two pencil drawings of the Dalai Lama on his throne by N. Kozhevnikov (plates 238, 239, 286).[63] These drawings generally correspond to the character of portraits and the iconography of metal statuettes and the photography of the 13th Dalai Lama. Russian sources also provide a remarkable comment that while in temporary exile in Mongolia, the Dalai Lama's entourage included several Tibetan painters who did a number of illustrations of different stages of the trip for a book about the life of the Thirteenth that was never published.[64] A Western-style painted likeness of the Dalai Lama did not appear again until around 1940, from the hand of Kanwal Krishna (1909–1993), an Indian artist who painted an oil portrait of the five-year-old 14th Dalai Lama based on a photograph taken during his enthronement at the Potala in February of that year (plates 232, 233).[65]

286 Pencil drawing of the Thirteeth Dalai Lama by N. Kozhevnikov (Urga, 1905; see also plates 238, 239) colored. Postcard "Dalai Lama, Buddhist High Priest," Collection of Jean Lassale, Paris.   287 The fifteen-year-old Dalai Lama on his throne. Lhasa, 1950, Photographer: Lowell Thomas, James A. Cannavino Library, Archives and Special Collections, Marist College, Poughkeepsie, New York.

With photography as a new medium of representation, the representation of the Dalai Lama had already been transformed during the lifetime of the Thirteenth, although other media generally fixed by canon and convention continued to have primacy. The exile of the 14th Dalai Lama after 1959 substantially changed Tibet's religious, political, and social foundations. Pictorial conventions that had been confined to traditional iconographic formulas marked by ritual gave way to a visual "pluralism" for representing the Dalai Lama. In the moving pictures of film and video, the boundaries between reality and artistic reproduction are transcended in a sequence of individual representations. The omnipresence of photographic images of the current Dalai Lama has created an iconography rich in variety, alongside traditional *mudrā*s and motifs in which the image of the real person has replaced the traditional image of the supra-personal institution.

ICONOGRAPHIC TYPOLOGY OF THE FOURTEEN DALAI LAMAS

Although over time certain individual features became obligatory and exemplary for pictoral representations including particular attributes and hand gestures (*mudrā*), but also teachers and founders associated with a specific Dalai Lama, or representa-

tives of specific traditions or protective deities. We can trace several iconographic schemata for each Dalai Lama, each with a vocabulary of motifs that is often interchangeable. Through selected examples, we will describe below detailed iconographic types based on the images of the Dalai Lamas surviving in Tibet and abroad. These images include mural and thangka painting, and both monumental and smaller sculptures. The individual sequences primarily reflect how frequently a particular pictorial vocabulary was employed. Unless stated otherwise, "right" and "left" will refer to the vantage point of the observer. The Sanskrit term for each *mudrā* comes first together with the main attributes of the central figure.

Abbreviations: AMNH: American Museum of Natural History (New York); MG: Musée Guimet (Paris); MKB: Museum of Cultures (Basel); NID: Norbulingka Institute Dharamśāla; RMA: Rubin Museum of Art (New York); SO: Schoettle Ostasiatica (formerly Stuttgart); TTC: Tamashige Tibet Collection (Tokyo) 玉重コレクションチベット仏教美術; VKM= Ethnographic Museum of the University of Zürich; Qing Gong 清宮: Qing Gong Zangchuan Fojiao Tangka 清宮藏傳佛教唐卡; TST=Thupten Samphel and Tender.

FIRST DALAI LAMA, GENDÜN DRUP

Type A   *vitarkamudrā* "bestowing teachings" and almsbowl.[66] (plate 288)

Type B   *vitarkamudrā* and *poti* སྤོ་ཏི [spo ti] book in the traditional oblong format, lotus blossom.[67]

Type C   *varadamudrā* "boon-granting" Tib. *chokjingyi chakgya* མཆོག་སྦྱིན་གྱི་ཕྱག་རྒྱ [mchog sbyin gyi phyag rgya] and *vitarkamudrā*, lotus blossom.[68]

Type D   *vitarkamudrā* and *dhyānamudrā* "meditation" Tib. *nyamzhak chakgya* མཉམ་བཞག་ཕྱག་རྒྱ [mnyam bzhag phyag rgya] *mudrā*, lotus blossom.[69]

Type E   *dharmacakramudrā*, lotus blossom. This *mudrā* of "turning the wheel of dharma," Tib. *chökyi khorlö chakgya* ཆོས་ཀྱི་འཁོར་ལོའི་ཕྱག་རྒྱ [chos kyi 'khor lo'i phyag rgya] is very rare in representations of Dalai Lamas. See also the 5th Dalai Lama.[70] (plate 22)

SECOND DALAI LAMA, GENDÜN GYATSO

Type A   *vitarkamudrā* and book (similar to type B, 1st Dalai Lama). By far the most common type of image for the 2nd Dalai Lama.[71] (plate 289)

Type B   *vitarkamudrā* and book (like A).[72] (plate 26)

Type C   *vitarkamudrā* and *jīvana-kalaśa* Tib. *tshebum* ཚེ་བུམ [tshe bum] "long-life vase."[73] (plate 25)

Type D   both hands in *semnyi ngalso* སེམས་ཉིད་ངལ་གསོ [sems nyid ngal gso] "gesture of serenity." *Panzha* པན་ཞ [pan zha] cap to protect against the sun, rather than the typical *paṇḍita* cap.[74]

THIRD DALAI LAMA, SÖNAM GYATSO

Type A   *Vajra* and bell.[75] (plate 290)
            1) sub-type: same emblems but different side figures.[76] (plate 30)
            2) sub-type with different side figures and narrative scenes.[77] (plate 1)

Type B   *Vajra* and bell.[78] The Dalai Lama in frontal view.

Type C   *bhūmisparśamudrā* "earth-witness" and book. *Panzha* cap, rather than the otherwise typical *paṇḍita* cap.[79]

Type D   *bhūmisparśamudrā* and long-life vase.[80] (plate 33)

Type E   *vitarkamudrā* and *dhyānamudrā*.[81]

Type F   both hands in *dhyānamudrā*.[82] (plate 32)

FOURTH DALAI LAMA, YÖNTEN GYATSO

Type A   *abhayamudrā* "protection" and *kapāla* "skull cap."[83] (plate 291)

Type B   *vitarkamudrā* and *kapāla*. The Dalai Lama in frontal view.[84]

Type C   *vitarkamudrā* and book.[85] (plate 35)

Type D   *vitarkamudrā* and almsbowl. The Dalai Lama in frontal view.[86]

Type E   with foot and handprints (of the 5th Dalai Lama). *Bhūmisparśamudrā* and *kapāla*. The Dalai Lama in frontal view.[87]

Type F   *vitarkamudrā* and lotus blossom, long-life vase with *sphaṭika*, Tib. *shel* "crystal."[88]

FIFTH DALAI LAMA, NGAWANG LOPSANG GYATSO

Type A   *vitarkamudrā*, lotus blossom (with figure on it), *cakra*.[89] (plate 292, 293)

Type B   *vitarkamudrā*, lotus, and *poti* book.[90]

Type C   *bhūmisparśamudrā* and book. Although not exclusively so, this type of representation is still overwhelmingly—at least in the case of sculpture—characterized by a draped girdle-type robe with only the *phurbu* and knob protruding which highlight the strong Nyingma religious influence since his early years. The absence of this Tantric dagger connected with Padmasmbhava from figures of the 5th Dalai Lama has been interpreted chronologically and explained as an indicator of anti-Nyingma sentiment after his death. This would mean that all representations with the *phurbu* originate prior to 1682 or after 1750, when the 7th Dalai Lama assumed temporal power.[91] (plate 59)

Type D   *Vajra* and bell. To left, small figures of Padmasambhava and a Nyingma *yogin* on the two lotus blossoms the Dalai Lama holds.[92]

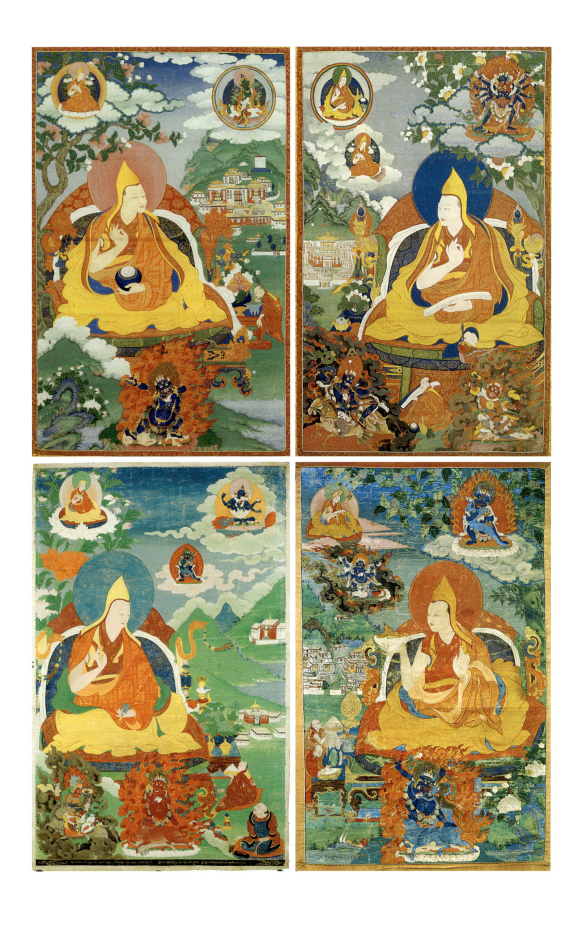

288 The First Dalai Lama. Thangka, 76 x 50.5 cm, ca. 1761, Palace Museum, Beijing. Above: his teacher Tsongkhapa, Green Tārā. Below: the Dharmarāja Antarasādhana, the Inner Dharmarāja, Yama, Tib. Chögyal Nangdrup (Chos rgyal nang sgrub). Right: Tashilhünpo Monastery, founded in 1447 by Gendün Drup. **289** The Second Dalai Lama. Thangka, 76 x 50.5 cm, ca. 1761, Palace Museum, Beijing. >>> **290** The Third Dalai Lama. Thangka, 70.5 x 47 cm, 18th/19th century, Collection of Karl-Dieter Fuchsberger, Kempten. >>> **291** The Fourth Dalai Lama. Thangka, 72 x 44.5 cm, 18th century, Collection of Mr. and Mrs. Solomon, Paris. >>>

292 The Fifth Dalai Lama and Jobo Śākyamuni. Larger-than-life statues of gilded copper, ca. 1692, Potala, Red Palace, Shrine of the Sacred Tradition.   **293** The Fifth Dalai Lama, Thangka, 76 x 50.5 cm, ca. 1761, Palace Museum, Beijing. >>>   **294** The Sixth Dalai Lama. Thangka 76 x 50.5 cm, ca. 1761, Palace Museum, Beijing. >>>   **295** The Seventh Dalai Lama. Thangka 76 x 50.5 cm, ca. 1761, Palace Museum, Beijing. >>>

Type E   *vitarkamudrā,* (usually) lotus blossom, and long-life vase.[93]

Type F   *vitarkamudrā* and *dhyānamudrā,* and (usually) lotus blossom.[94]

Type G   *bhūmisparśamudrā* and *dhyānamudrā.* These *mudrā* correspond exactly to the posture of the 5th Dalai Lama at his death, with the right hand in *bhūmisparśa* and the left in *dhyāna,* sitting in upright with legs crossed, right eye closed and the left motionless, looking straight ahead.[95]

Type H   *dharmacakramudrā.* This *mudrā,* rare in Dalai Lama portraits, appears only once for the 5th Dalai Lama, in the "Gold Manuscript" of the Lionel Fournier Collection that he himself composed.[96] (plate 43)

Type I   *abhayamudrā* and almsbowl.[97] The walrus moustache found in almost all representations of the Fifth is however absent on statues, as on the silver figure in Beijing dated to around 1651, and as on those statues whose original physical features were painted on in cold gilding that has not survived. As a rule, for the 5th Dalai Lama, the moustache is drawn bending downwards, while for paintings and sculpture of the 13th Dalai Lama, it bends upwards. In exceptional cases, the 6th and 7th Dalai Lamas are depicted with walrus moustache as a conscious reference to their predecessors.

SIXTH DALAI LAMA, TSANGYANG GYATSO

Type A   *vitarkamudrā* and *cakra.*[98] (plate 294)

Type B   *bhūmisparśa mudrā* and *cakra.*[99] (plate 66)

Type C   *vitarkamudrā,* lotus and *poti* book.[100] (plate 69)

Type D   *vitarkamudrā* and *dhyānamudrā.*[101]

Type E   *vitarkamudrā,* lotus and long-live vase. Represented as the "Fifth Dalai Lama" with walrus moustache and *phurba* in his robe.[102]

SEVENTH DALAI LAMA, KALSANG GYATSO

Type A   *vitarkamudrā,* lotus blossom with book and sword, book.[103] (plate 295);
          1) sub-type: variations in the surroundings.[104]

Type C   *vitarkamudrā,* lotus blossom with book and sword, *cakra.*[105] (plate 72)

Type D   *vitarkamudrā,* long-life vase.[106]

Type E   *vitarkamudrā,* lotus blossom, sometimes without book and sword, and *dhyānamudrā.*[107] (plate 76)

Type F   As meditating monk or *yogin.* To date, such representations of the Dalai Lama are known only for the Seventh.[108] (plate 77)

EIGHTH DALAI LAMA, JAMPEL GYATSO

Type A   *vitarkamudrā,* lotus blossom alone or with book, the book with or without sword, and *cakra.* For the 8th and subsequent Dalai Lamas, there are no known "pattern book designs" like the reincarnation set at Stockholm, VKM, Beijing or TTC.[109] (plate 276)

Type B   *vitarkamudrā,* lotus blossom with *cakra,* book.[110] (plate 81)

Type C   *varadamudrā* and *dhyānamudrā,* long-life vase and double lotus blossom with small figures of White Tārā and Uṣṇīṣavijaya.[111]

NINTH DALAI LAMA, LUNGTOK GYATSO

The only known historic representations of Dalai Lamas Nine through Twelve, each living only a few years, are almost exclusively the murals at the Potala. Only in exceptional cases have we taken into account the set of modern portraits in Dharamśālā and the illustrations in Lokesh Chandra's *Buddhist Iconography of Tibet,* also from the 20th century. Since the large sculptures of the Dalai Lamas at the Potala, Drepung, and Sera are usually at least partially covered by their robes, they were only occasionally useful for this study.[112]

Type A   *vitarkamudrā,* lotus blossom and *cakra.*[113] (plate 297)

Type B   *vitarkamudrā,* lotus blossom and book.[114] (plate 88)

TENTH DALAI LAMA, TSULTRIM GYATSO

Type A   *vitarkamudrā,* lotus blossom, with or without sword, and cakra.[115] (plate 89)

Type B   *vitarkamudrā,* almsbowl.[116]

ELEVENTH DALAI LAMA, KEDRUP GYATSO

Type A   *vitarkamudrā,* lotus blossom and cakra.[117]

Type B   *bhūmisparśamudrā,* almsbowl.[118]

296 The Eighth Dalai Lama, Detail of plate 80.

297 The Ninth Dalai Lama. Bronze, with inscription: "In reverence to the most revered [Ninth Dalai Lama] Lungtok Gyatso; Lord of the Word and Source of the Teachings of Lopsang [Drakpa, Je Tsongkhapa]." Tibet, ca. or after 1815, H 17. 5 cm, W 17 cm, D 11.5 cm, Collection of Markus O. Speidel, Birmenstorf.   **298** The Thirteenth Dalai Lama. Larger-than-life statue of gilded copper. Lhasa, ca. 1934/36, Potala Palace, Mausoleum of the 13th Dalai Lama.   **299** The Fourteenth Dalai Lama, here with "modern" mudrā, i.e. hands placed forward, an example of modern iconography no longer bound by tradition. Photographic realist painting by Amdo Jampa.

TWELFTH DALAI LAMA, TRINLE GYATSO

Type A   *vitarkamudrā*, lotus blossom and *cakra*.[119]

Type B   *vitarkamudrā*, lotus blossom and *poti* book.[120]

THIRTEENTH DALAI LAMA, THUPTEN GYATSO

Type A   *vitarkamudrā*, lotus blossom with book and sword, *cakra*. The moustache drawn in an upward curve distinguishes the 13th Dalai Lama from the Great Fifth, the ends of whose moustache were almost always downward turning. Most paintings and statues of the Thirteenth have the character of portraits.[121] (plate 298)

Type B   *vitarkamudrā*, book.

Type C   *vitarkamudrā*, long-life vase.

Type D   *bhūmisparśamudrā* and *dhyānamudrā*, lotus blossom with book and sword. With the *mālā* "rosary" on his left wrist characteristic of the 13th Dalai Lama's photographs.[122] (plate 101)

Type E   Both hands in front in a modern *mudrā*, an exemplary posture of this Dalai Lama in numerous photographs. An example of modern iconography no longer marked by tradition.[123] (plate 110)

FOURTEENTH DALAI LAMA, TENZIN GYATSO

The few painted representations of the 14th Dalai Lama that we can trace iconographically to the earliest mural dating to around 1955 in the Norbulingka Palace—which itself follows the 1930s murals of the 13th Dalai Lama from the Potala, Samye, and Gyantse (plate 130).[124]

Main Type *vitarkamudrā*, lotus blossom with book and sword, *cakra*, also the *khakkhara* "monk's staff" and the *khaṭvāṅga* "Tantric staff," along with the usual ritual implements on the throne table.

APPENDICES

NOTES

INTRODUCTION AND INTERVIEW WITH HIS HOLINESS THE FOURTEENTH DALAI LAMA
Martin Brauen

1 Per Sørensens' precise reasoning cannot be reproduced here for reasons of space.

2 Byang chub sems dpa': one who has developed the Bodhicitta (literally "enlightenment mind") and whose only goal is to be of use to others.

3 What the Dalai Lama seems to be saying here is that all Dalai Lamas from the first to the seventh were undoubtedly reincarnations of themselves, in other words, one and the same person. As for the eighth Dalai Lama and his successor, there is not the same certainty.

THE DALAI LAMAS AND THE ORIGINS OF REINCARNATE LAMAS
Leonard W. J. van der Kuijp

1 See Eric Hobsbawm and Terence Ranger, eds. *The Invention of Tradition*. New York: Cambridge University Press, 1992. [eds]

2 ghayiqamsigh vcira dara sayin coghtu buyantu dalai, Tib. [vajradhara dspal bzang po bsod nams rgya mtsho], in which "coghtu buyantu dalai" Tib. [dpal bzang po bsod nams rgya mtsho] inverts the order of Sönam Gyatso's full religious name which he received at age four from Sönam Drakpa [Bsod nams grags pa] (1478–1554) in 1547. "Ghayiqamsigh vcira dara" means "wondrous Vajradhara," where *vajradhara*, "Thunder-bolt-bearer" connotes not only his expertise in tantric theory and practice, but more importantly his buddha-hood.

3 Later, this monastery was to become the seat of the Panchen Lamas from the late 16th century onward.

4 That is, Palgyi Dechen [Dpal gyi sde chen] in Shingkun (Lintao in Gansu Province).

5 Son of Chögyel Phuntshok Trashi [Chos rgyal phun tshogs bkra shis] (1547–1602), the 22nd abbot of Drigung monastery.

6 "Cultural Tibet" are all those areas that share some form of Tibetan culture and language, including the modern Tibetan Autonomous Region, Amdo, Kham, Ladākh, Bhūtān, Sikkim, and other areas. The area this term covers is far greater than what has ever been unified in "Political Tibet." [eds.]

7 That is, Avalokiteśvara with Dromtön; Mañjuśrī with Ngok Lekpe Sherap [rNgog Legs pa'i shes rab]; and Vajrapāṇi with Kutön Töndrü Yungdrung [Khu ston brston 'grus g.yung drung] (1011–1075).

8 Here Avalokiteśvara with Zhönnu Gyaltsen [gZhon nu rgyal mtshan] (1031–1106); Mañjuśrī with Potowa Rinchen Sel [Po to ba Rin chen gsal] (1027–1105); and Vajrapāṇi with Tsülthrim Bar [Tshul khrims 'bar] (1033–1103).

9 *trülku* [sprul sku], Skt *nirmāṇakāya*, "emanation body,' the form in which the Buddha appears to ordinary beings or "form of magical apparition." The third of three *kāya*, besides the "truth body" or Skt *dharmak-*

āya, Tib [chos sku] and the *long ku* [longs sku], Skt. *sa bhogakāya* "enjoyment body."

10 This text from Buddhist India has been preserved in Tibetan translation. [eds.]

11 Suggested further reading: Kollmar-Paulenz (2001), Mullin (1988), Sorenson (1990), Shen (2002), Tenzin Gyatso (1991), Ya (1991).

THE FIRST DALAI LAMA
Shen Weirong

1 *Die Biographie des allwissenden Lamas, genannt 'Die Zwölf wunderbaren Taten,'* by Shen Weirong, 2002, p. 310. English translation by Mullin, 1985, p. 19.

2 *upāsaka* lay ordination

3 Bo dong Phyogs las rnam rgyal had already given him this title in 1431.

4 Such as gSang phu, Gro sa, 'Chad kha, and Thang po che.

5 Including Rong ston sMra ba'i seng ge (1367–1449), Bo dong Phyogs las rnam rgyal and others.

6 All the writings of Maitreyas, the Six Jewels of Jambudvīpa—Nāgārjuna, Āryadeva, Asaṅga, Vasubandhu, Dignāga and Dharmakīrti—and the Two Sublime Ones, Śakyaprabha and Guÿaprabha. He studied Tantric teachings primarily with Sherap Sengge, who instructed him in the complete cycle of the Guhyasamāja. He studied the Cakrasaṃvara dharma cycles under Tsongkhapa. Originally he had wanted to study the Kālacakra with mKhas grub rje dGe legs dpal bzang po (1385–1438), but in the end had to study it with 'Jam dbyangs rin chen rgyal mtshan at a Sakya monastery because mKhas grub died in 1438.

7 In 1416, one of Tsonkhapa's primary disciples, Vinayadhara Grags pa rgyal mtshan (1374–1434), initiated him in the *vinaya* at Ganden. Shortly after he continued systematically study it for two years at Drosa, the origin of the *vinaya* in Tibet, with dMar ston dPal ldan rin chen pa and rGya mtsho rin chen pa, two renowned vinaya teachers of central Tibet. Along with Zhonnu Gyalchok [gZhon nu rgyal mchog], these two Sakya teachers characterized him as one of the two best disciples of *vinaya* in Tsang and urged him to spread the vinaya teachings through Tsang.

8 Atiśa attempted to incorporate rgya chen spyod "vast action" and zab mo lta "profound view" as part of the *lam*. Another *lamrim* tradition is the theg chen blo sbyong gi gdams pa "instruction in Mahāyāna mind training," the essential concern of which is exercising an enlightened character through exchanges between oneself and others. Gendün Drup studied this tradition initially with lHa zung khang pa bSod nams lhun grub pa at the Kadampa Monastery 'Chad kha during his second period of study in Ü (1438–1440). Previously he had studied Tsongkhapa's sKyes bu gsum gyi lam gyi rim pa chen mo and Lam rim chung ngu, the *summa* of *lamrim* teachings, directly with Tsongkhapa himself as well as with rGyal tshab rje and mKhas grub rje.

9 Gling stod mthong smon

10 Shangs pa bKa' brgyud pa—Lama Don yod pa

11 Pramāṇavārttika, Prajñāpāramitā, Vinayasūtra, and Abhidharmakośa.

12 The first work, Legs par gsungs pa'i chos 'dul ba'i gleng gzhi dang rtogs pa brjod pa lung sde bzhi kun las btus pa rin po che'i mdzod, a commentary on the 'Dul ba'i gleng 'bum chen mo, is the best-known Tibetan commentary on that text, along with the 'Dul ba'i gleng 'bum blang dor gsal byed commentary by Vinayadhara Grags pa rgyal mtshan. The other is a commentary on the Vinayasūtra of Guÿaprabha, the Legs par gsungs pa'i dam pa'i chos 'dul ba mtha' dag gi snying po'i don legs par bshad pa rin po che'i phreng ba.

13 Theg pa chen po'i blo sbyong gi gdams pa and Theg chen blo sbyong chung zed bsdus pa. Both are commentaries on Blo sbyong don bdun ma of 'Chad kha pa.

14 Phu chung ba gZhon nu rgyal mtshan (1031–1106), sPyan snga ba Tshul khrims 'bar (1038–1103), Po to ba Rin chen gsal (1031?–1105).

15 (chu lho kha'i grva tshang chen po)

16 Including 'Phyong rgyas rtse pa, Dar rgyas pa bSod nams dpal bzang po and other local nobles such as Adlige rGya bar ba, rDo rings pa and Drang tshal pa.

17 The large treasury hall with six columns in the middle, the dukhang ('du khang) convocation hall with forty-eight columns, the temple of Maitreya with twelve columns on the left side, the temple of Tārā with six columns on the right side, the temple of the tutelary deities with two columns, the bla brang rGyal mtshan mthon po with twenty-four columns, and the single-storey monks residence and the temple of the Four Major Kings.

18 For example, sMan thang ba Don grub rgya mtsho and Sle'u chung pa

19 Shar rtse grva tshang, dKyil khang grva tshang, and Thos bsam gling gi grva tshang.

20 bla brang rGyal mtshan mthon po

Additional sources:

1. *pan chen* Ye shes rtse mo (geb. 1433), *rJe thams cad mkhyen pa dGe 'dun grub pa dpal bzang po'i rnam thar ngor mtshar rmad byung nor bu'i phreng ba bzhugs so, The Collected Works of the First Dalai Lama dGe 'dun grub pa*, vol. 5. Published by DoDrup Lama Sangy, Deorali Chorten, Gangtok (Sikkim). Printed at Jayyed Press, Ballimaran, Delhi 1981, pp. 385–509.

2. las chen Kun dga' rgyal mtshan, *Bla ma thams cad mkhyen pa'i rnam thar ngo mtshar mdzad pa bcu gnyis pa bzhugs so. The Collected Works of the First Dalai Lama pa dGe 'dun grub pa*, vol. 6. Published by DoDrup Lama Sangy, Deorali Chorten, Gangtok (Sikkim). Printed at Jayyed Press, Ballimaran, Delhi 1981, pp. 1–43.

3. las chen Kun dga' rgyal mtshan, *bKa' gdams chos 'byung khas pa'i yid 'phrong*. Indologisches Seminar der Universität Bonn, folio 380r–409r.

4. Shen Weirong, 2002 (See Works Consulted)

THE SECOND DALAI LAMA

Amy Heller

1 This essay on Gendün Gyatso was originally titled: *The Second Dalai Lama, 1476–1542: His perception of himself and of his birth*. It is based on previously unpublished research for my thesis presented in 1992. My primary sources were his autobiography and the biography of his father which he wrote in 1509. The reader may also wish to read Glenn Mullin's translatation of the biographical account of the Vaidurya Serpo, written in the late 17th century by the Desi Sanggye Gyatso (*Tibet Journal*. 1986: vol.11/3:3–16). Mullin, in *The Fourteen Dalai Lamas* (2001) refers to this biography and also the autobiography. I would like to thank the Venerable Tsenshap Rinpoche for reviewing my translations from the autobiography again in 2004. Prior to 1959, Rinpoche's family estate had been in Tanak where the 2nd Dalai Lama was born. This allowed him to understand the local colloquial expressions of the Tanak region which Gendün Gyatso used in his writings.

2 *Autobiography*, fol 22a describes the patronage of the leaders of Olka district leading to the foundation of Chökhorgyel monastery there.

3 See *Autobiography*, fol 35a for the offerings in 1523 from patrons in Ngari, Guge, and Mustang, and fol 36a for offerings from Kham.

4 The autobiography, fol 2a, and father's biography, fol 2a, are very clear about this family line and the role of the ancestor as chaplain at Samye during the reign of Trisong Detsen. Glenn Mullin refers to Trisong Detsen as an ancestor of Gendün Gyatso in the sense that Trisong Detsen is counted among the previous births of Dömton—this is not how Gendün Gyatso described himself because he is discussing his personal biological and spiritual lineage.

5 According to his biography, fol 17a, he took his full monastic vows at Tashilhünpo in a ceremony presided by Gendün Grup.

6 According to Luciano Petech, his precise date of birth was December 30, 1475 [See "The Dalai Lamas and Regents of Tibet," *T'oung Pao*, 1959: 368–394. [Reprinted in L. Petech, *Selected Papers on Asian History*. Rome: 1988, pp. 125–148.)

7 Sanggye Pel means literally "development of the Buddha," signifying that the boy who bears this name has an intrinsic link to Buddha.

8 Autobiography, fol 2–5; the story of Mahākāla of Wisdom is in fol 4b.

9 See *Biography of Künga Gyaltsen*, fol 25b for the passage describing this Mahākāla as the protector of the ancestors' teachings and fol 34b for his invocation at the funeral ceremonies to ensure a propitious rebirth.

10 *Autobiography*, fol 5–6, for the preparations prior to the visit to Tashilhünpo at age eight, fol 6b, then his return home fol 7a–b.

11 *Autobiography* fol 8b for the Guge ruler's visit. See, Lobsang Shastri, "Relations between Dalai Lamas and Rulers of mNga' ris skor gsum: From Late 14th–mid 19th century," in *Tibet Journal*, 2004.

12 Biography, fol 26b.

13 *Autobiography*, fol 9a for the date and description of his vows. Note that Vaidurya Serpo has this as age thirteen, which is historically inaccurate.

14 *Autobiography*, fol 11a for discussion of the Narthang Lama's dislike of Gendün Gyatso's father.

15 See chapter 14 on the protective deities of the Dalai Lama lineage for the discussion of the visions of Lhamo by Gendün Gyatso and other Dalai Lama.

THE THIRD AND THE FOURTH DALAI LAMAS

Karénina Kollmar-Paulenz

1 From the *Erdeni Tunumal Neretü Sudur* "Sütra called Jewel-like Translucence," a Mongolian chronicle written after 1607 by an unknown southeast Mongolian author. This quotation illustrates the importance that the 3rd Dalai Lama attached to missionary work among the Mongolians and the spiritual connection between Tibetans and Mongols that has prevailed ever since.

2 If not otherwise attributed, details throughout this section are based on the 5th Dalai Lama's 1646 biography (or *namthar*) of the 3rd Dalai Lama [rJe btsun thams cad mkhyen pa bsod nams rgya mtsho'i rnam thar dngos grub rgya mtsho'i shing rta] here abbreviated as *Ngödrup Gyatsö Shingta*, in [’Phags pa ’jig rten dbang phyug gi rnam sprul rim byon gyi 'khrungs rabs deb ther nor bu'i 'phreng ba] here abbreviated as *Norbü Threngba*, vol. 2, p. 1–171. For comparative purposes I also used the brief biography Tshechok Ling-yeshe Gyaltsen [tshe mchog gling ye shes rgyal mtshan] wrote in the 18th century; see G. Mullin, "Tse-Chok-Ling's Biography of the 3rd Dalai Lama," in *The Tibet Journal*, Vol. XI, No. 3, Autumn 1986, pp. 23–39. The transposition of the Tibetan annual cycles into modern dates is based on K.-H. Everding, "Die 60er-Zyklen. Eine Konkordanztafel," in *Zentralasiatische Studien* vol. 16, 1982, pp. 475–476.

3 See *Ngödrup Gyatsö Shingta* p. 18.

4 Panchen Sönam Drakpa was the fifteenth to occupy the throne of Galden, living from 1478–1554. See A.I. Vostrikov, *Tibetskaja istoričeskaja literatura*, Moscow 1962, note 510. Vostrikov bases this on the [re'u mig of sum pa mkhan po ye shes dpal 'byor], unavailable to me at the time of this writing.

5 The *namthar* of the 3rd Dalai Lama contains a detailed list of the instructions various lamas gave him. See *Ngödrup Gyatsö Shingta* p. 47–48.

6 See *Ngödrup Gyatsö Shingta*, p. 60.

7 See *Ngödrup Gyatsö Shingta*, p. 109. On ordination according to the rules of the *vinaya*, see G. Tucci, "Die Religionen Tibets", in: G. Tucci/ W. Heissig, *Die Religionen Tibets und der Mongolei*, Stuttgart 1970, pp. 31–32.

8 See M. Henss, *Tibet. Die Kulturdenkmäler*, Zürich 1981, p. 89.

9 With the exception of the Buriyads in the north, who would not be converted until the early 19th century.

10 The Tibetan term "Hor" refers to both supposedly Mongolian tribes assimilated to the Tibetans and more generally to nomadic groups and peoples who live in the nothern regions of Tibet and in northeastern Kökönor. See P. Kessler, *Laufende Arbeiten zu einem Ethnohistorischen Atlas Tibets (EAT), Lieferung 41.1.: Die historische Landschaft TEHOR (tre hor) unter besonderer Berücksichtigung der frühen Geschichte Südosttibets (Khams)*, Rikon 1984, p. 15 ff.

11 *Ngödrup Gyatsö Shingta*, p. 83.

12 *Erdeni Tunumal Neretü Sudur*, fol 21r10-11. This passage is translated in K. Kollmar-Paulenz, *Erdeni tunumal neretü sudur. Die Biographie des Altan qaghan der Tümed-Mongolen. Ein Beitrag zur Geschichte der religionspolitischen Beziehungen zwischen der Mongolei und Tibet im ausgehenden 16. Jahrhundert*, Wiesbaden 2001, p. 279.

13 Here Mongolian and Tibetan reports differ. Acoording to *Erdeni Tunumal*, fol 21r18-23, this temple had already been established in 1574. *Sanang Secen* also tells us in his 1662 chronicle, *Erdeni-yin Tobci*, fol 74v14-15, that the temple had been built prior to Sönam Gyatso's arrival. In contrast, his *namthar* states that the temple was built only after the meeting in 1578; see *Ngödrup Gyatsö Shingta* p. 149.

14 Abbreviation for *yöndak* [yon bdag] "patron," and *chöne* [mchod gnas] "place of sacrifice."

15 This is certainly the reinterpretation of later Tibetan historiographers on the Tibet–Mongolia bilateral relations of the 13th century.

16 In his *namthar*, abbreviated as Tale Lama Bara Dara [ta la'i bla ma badzra dha ra], "Dalai Lama Vajradhara," with Tibetan *ta la'i* coming from Mongolian *dalai*.

17 This is according to *Erdeni Tunumal*; his *namthar* gives 1585.

18 *Erdeni Tunumal*, fol. 45v13; again in the colophon of the Mongolian translation of the *Mahāmantrānudūri-sūtra*, which the 3rd Dalai Lama directed Ayusi Güsi to render into Mongolian sometime after 1587.

19 *Erdeni Tunumal*, fol. 45v15-18.

20 From Altan Tobci, *Goldene Chronik*, by an anonymous Mongol after 1655.

21 I base the following discussion of Yönten Gyatso's biographical information as found in the Mongolian chronicle, the *Erdeni Tunumal*, as well as his *namthar*. used the edition in *Norbü Threngba*, vol. 2, p. 173–238.

22 This place name probably corresponds to Chörten Karpo [mchod rten dkar po] in the *namthar*; see *Norbü Threngba*, p. 189.

23 See *Norbü Threngba*, p. 207.

24 See G. Tucci, *Tibetan Painted Scrolls*, Rome 1949, vol. 1, p. 51–56 for a detailed description based on dates from the 4th Dalai Lama's *namthar* and other Tibetan sources.

THE FIFTH DALAI LAMA

Kurtis R. Shaeffer

1 A number of sources and studies have informed this essay. Two accounts of the 5th Dalai Lama's political career have become standard reference works: Tucci (1949, 57–66) and Ahmad (1970, 108–145). A number of additional studies dedicated to the 5th Dalai Lama have appeared in the last several decades. Petech (1988) provides dates for all the Dalai Lamas and their regents, while Petech (1950) surveys the history of the closing years of the era of the 5th Dalai Lama. Karmay (1988) introduced the corpus of visionary autobiography. Karmay (2002) follows up on his earlier work. Uspensky (1996) describes a related collection of visionary autobiography. Macdonald (1977) details a statue of the Dalai Lama. Ishihama (1992) compiles evidence of the investitures granted by the Dalai Lama. Ishihama (1993) offers an insightful reading of the 5th Dalai Lama's autobiography and related works as they pertain to the cult of Avalokiteśvara. Richardson (1993) offers firsthand accounts of the annual rituals performed in and around Lhasa, many of which have their origins in the era of the 5th Dalai Lama. Tuttle, Schaeffer (2006) details the Dalai Lama's important diplomatic trip to China. In the same volume, Kurtis R. Schaeffer (2006) discusses Sanggye Gyatso's adaptation of Lhasa ritual life around the figure of the 5th Dalai Lama. The 5th Dalai Lama's history of Tibet has been translated into English in its entirety by Ahmad (1995). Ahmad (1999) translates the first half of the first volume of Sanggye Gyatso's three-volume continuation of the Dalai Lama's autobiography. All of the essays contained in Pommaret (2003) pertain to a greater or lesser degree to the 5th Dalai Lama. Bazin (2002) offers a glimpse of many ritual implements described in the visionary autobiographies of the Dalai Lama. Meyer (1987) introduces artistic features of the Potala. Richardson (1998) translates an important source for the history of Dalai Lama's regents. Cüppers (2001) introduces the form and content of the Dalai Lama's many diplomatic letters. Lange (1976) provides a preliminary bibliography of Sanggye Gyatso's writings. Aris (1989) describes the transfer of consciousness from the 5th to the 6th Dalai Lama.

2 Smon 'gro ba 'Jam dbyangs dbang rgyal rdo rje, *Rgyal dbang thams cad mkhyen pa ngag dbang blo bzang rgya mtsho'i mtshan thos pa'i yid la bdud rtsir byed pa'i rnam thar mthong ba don ldan mchog tu dga' ba'i*

sgra dbyangs sarga gsum pa, 128 folios (Cultural Palace of Nationalities, Beijing, catalog number 002555). The present narrative of the 5th Dalai Lama's life up to the year 1646 is taken from Mondrowa's important work. I gratefully acknowledge the assistance of Leonard W. J. van der Kuijp, who provided me with a photocopy of Mondrowa's *Life of the Dalai Lama*. I would also like to thank Christoph Cüppers of the Lumbini International Research Institute (LIRI), who generously made available to me an extremely useful digital text of Mondrowa's *Life*.

3 Ngag dbang blo bzang rgya mtsho, *Za hor gyi ban de ngag dbang blo bzang rgya mtsho'i 'di snang 'khrul ba'I rol rtsed rtogs brjod kyi tshul du bkod pa du ku'u la'i gos bzang* (Lhasa: Bod ljongs mi dmangs dpe skrun khang, 1989).

4 Ngag dbang blo bzang rgya mtsho (1617–1682). *Lha ldan smon lam chen mo'i gral 'dzin bca' yig*, in *Bod kyi snga rabs khrims srol yig cha bdams bsgrigs* (Lha sa: Bod ljongs tshogs tshan rig khang gi bod yig dpe rnying dpe skrun khang, 1989): pp. 324–345.

5 Ngag dbang blo bzang rgya mtsho, *Za hor gyi ban de ngag dbang blo bzang rgya mtsho'i 'di snang 'khrul ba'I rol rtsed rtogs brjod kyi tshul du bkod pa du ku'u la'i gos bzang* (Lhasa: Bod ljongs mi dmangs dpe skrun khang, 1989).

6 The following is largely taken from Sangs rgyas rgya mtsho, *Mchod sdong 'dzam gling rgyan gcig rten gtsug lag khang dang bcas pa'i dkar chag thar gling rgya mtshor bgrod ba'i gru rdzings byin rlabs kyi bang mdzod* (Bod ljongs mi rigs dpe skrung khang, Beijing. 1990); Sangs rgyas rgya mtsho, *Thams cad mkhyen pa drug ba blo bzang rin chen tshangs dbyangs rgya mtsho'i thun mong phyi'i rnam par thar pa du ku la'i 'phro 'thud rab gsal gser gyi snye ma* (Lha sa: Tshe ring phun tshogs, Ed. Bod ljongs mi dmangs dpe skrun khang, 1989); and Sangs rgyas rgya mtsho *Pur tshwa me 'dzin ma'i dkar chag dad pa'i sa bon gyis bskyed pa'i byin rlabs ro bda'*. Unpublished blockprint.

6 Bell, 1992 (1928): pp. 135–136.

THE SIXTH DALAI LAMA
Erberto Lo Bue

1 Per K. Sørensen (1990) *Divinity Secularized. An Inquiry into the Nature and Form of the Songs ascribed to the Sixth Dalai Lama*, Vienna.

THE SEVENTH DALAI LAMA
Matthew T. Kapstein

1 *Gangs ljongs mkhas dbang rim byon gyi rtsom yig gser gyi sbram bu*, vol. 2, p. 1125.

THE EIGHTH DALAI LAMA
Derek F. Maher

1 Except where noted, this paper is based on (1) Tsepön Shakabpa, *Political History of Tibet*, Volume 1, Chapter 10, titled "The Eighth Dalai Lama and the Gurkha Wars" (the full work is forthcoming in English as *One Hundred Thousand Moons: An Advanced Political History of Tibet*, translated by Derek F. Maher), hereafter, including Chapter 10, referred to as Shakabpa (1976)"; and (2) Demo Ngawang Losang Tubten Jikmay Gyatso (hereafter referred to as Demo), *An Ornament for the Entire World, Biography of the Powerful Conqueror, the Omniscient Losang Tenpe Wangchug Jampel Gyatso*.

2 Shakabpa (1976), volume 1, p. 609.

3 Ya Hanzhang, *The Biographies of the Dalai Lamas* (Beijing: Foreign Languages Press, 1991), p. 87. The work is hereafter, including Chapter 10, referred to as Ya (1991).

4 Glenn H. Mullin, *The Fourteen Dalai Lamas: A Sacred Legacy of Reincarnation* (Santa Fe, N.M.: Clear Light Productions, 2001), pp. 325–327.

5 Demo, p. 500.

6 David M. Farquhar, "Emperor as Bodhisattva in the Governance of the Ch'ing Empire," *Harvard Journal of Asiatic Studies* 38 (1978), no. 1, p. 8.

7 Alastair Lamb, *Britain and Chinese Central Asia: The Road to Lhasa 1767 to 1905* (London: Routledge and Kegan Paul, 1960), pp. 14–15.

8 Shakabpa (1976), volume 1, pp. 642–643.

9 Ya (1991), pp. 72–83.

THE NINTH TO THE TWELFTH DALAI LAMAS
Derek F. Maher

1 Except where noted, this paper is based on (1) Tsepön Shakabpa, *Political History of Tibet*, Volume 1, Chapter 11, called "The Ninth and Tenth Dalai Lamas" and Volume 2, Chapter 12, titled "The Eleventh and Twelfth Dalai Lamas" Shakabpa (1976) and (2) the series of extended biographies of each of the Dalai Lamas published in five volumes as *Garland of Jewels, the Birth Stories of the Series of Incarnations of (Avalokiteshvara), the Superior Lord of the World*. (Dharamśālā: Sku sger yig tshang, 1977). Volumes 3 and 4 of the latter contain the biographies of the 9th through 12th Dalai Lamas.

2 Ya (1991), p. 87.

3 For an extended analysis of this document, see the forthcoming article by Isabelle Charleux titled "Un document mongol sur l'intronisation du IXe Dalai lama." The latter's French translation of the document is contained in her "Annexe 2: Traduction du texts mongol," also unpublished. I am grateful to Amy Heller and Ms. Charleux for making these materials available to me.

4 Shakabpa (1976), pp. 672–673.

5 For Manning's description of this encounter see the essay *Western Views of the Dalai Lamas* by Martin Brauen in this volume.

6 Ya (1991), p. 88.

7 Shakabpa (1976), 678–679.

8 Lopsang Trinle Gyaltsen, *Garland of Jewel Wonders*, 320-ba-5.

9 Details come from Shakabpa (1976), volume 2, 22–28; Rishikesh Shaha, *Modern Nepal: A Political History 1769–1955* (Riverdale, Maryland: Riverdale Company, 1990), volume 1, 244–245; and Michael C. van Walt van Praag, *The Status of Tibet: History, Rights, and Prospects in International Law* (Boulder, Col.: Westview, 1987), 291–295.

10 Shakabpa (1976), volume 2, 33–42. It had earlier been common for regents to bear the title "Desi," but in the 18th century the term had been replaced by "Gyeltsab" as the power of the office declined. The use of "Desi" in relation to Shedra was meant to indicate that he was a powerful regent.

THE THIRTEENTH DALAI LAMA
Tsering Shakya

1 Bell 1946: p. 91.

2 Phur lcog Thub bstan byams pa tshul khrims, 1984: p. 14.

3 Phur lcog Thub bstan byams pa tshul khrims, 1984: p. 26.

4 Phur lcog Thub bstan byams pa tshul khrims, 1984: p. 13.

5 Phur lcog Thub bstan byams pa tshul khrims, 1984: p. 8.

6 Phur-lcog thub-bstan byams-pa tshul khrims, 1984: p. 170.

7 Phur lcog thub bstan byams pa tshul khrims, 1984: p. 142.

8 Today, Terton Sönam Gyalpo is more commonly known by the shortened "Sögyal" [bsod-rgyal]

9 Phur lcog Thub bstan byams pa tshul khrims, 1984: pp. 240–42.

10 Another Buriyad who visited Lhasa was Tsybikoff, whose visit was also widely reported in the Russian press. Tsybikoff's journey to Lhasa was sponsored by Russian Geograhpical Society.

11 Kuleshov, 1996: p. 7.

12 Kuleshov, 1996: p. 38.

13 Damdinsüren, 1997: p. 37.

14 Rockhill, 1910: p. 18.

15 Rockhill Papers, Rockhill to Roosevelt, 8/11/1908.

16 Rockhill, 1910.

17 Phur lcog Thub bstan byams pa tshul khrims, 1984.

18 Zha skab pa dBang phyug bde ldan, 1976: p. 221.

19 Bell, 1946: p. 93.

20 Bell, 1946: p. 101.

21 Zha skab pa dbang phyug bde ldan, 1976: p. 221.

22 The relationship between the Dalai Lama and the Panchen Rinpoche is covered in Phur lcog thub bstan byams pa tshul–khrims, 1984: pp. 541–547.

23 The Political Testament of the 13th Dalai Lama, Kalimpong. 1958: pp. 7–8.

THE FOURTEENTH DALAI LAMA
Alexander Norman

1 From the interview with Martin Brauen, see Introduction and Interview.

FROM PROTECTIVE DEITIES TO INTERNATIONAL STARDOM
Georges Dreyfus

1 This term was coined by H. Bechert in his "Buddhist Revival in East and West," in H. Bechert and R. Gombrich, *The World of Buddhism* (London: Thames and Hudson, 1984), pp. 275–6.

2 This brief account of Buddhist modernism draws from Lopez' summary in *Prisoners of Shangrila* (Chicago: University of Chicago, 1998), 185, as well as H. Bechert, "Buddhist Revival in East and West," in H. Bechert and R. Gombrich, *The World of Buddhism* (London: Thames and Hudson, 1984). pp. 275–6.

3 The Dalai Lama, *Answers: Discussions with Western Buddhists* (Ithaca: Snow Lion, 2001), p. 24.

4 D. Lopez, *Prisoners of Shangrila* (Chicago: University of Chicago, 1998), p. 185.

5 The Dalai Lama, *A Policy of Kindness* (Ithaca: Snow Lion, 1990), p. 85.

6 For a detailed account of this controversy, see G. Dreyfus, "The Shuk-den Affair: History and Nature of a Quarrel," *Journal of International Association of Buddhist Studies* vol. 21, n. 2 1999): pp. 227–270.

7 See the Dalai Lama's collected speeches from 1978 to 1996 on the subject: *Gong sa skyabs mgon chen po mchog nas chos skyong bsten phyogs skor btsal ba'i bka' slob* (Dharamśālā: Religious Affairs, 1996)., pp. 17–9.

8 *Sa skyabs mgon chen po mchog nas chos skyong bsten phyogs skor btsal ba'i bka' slob*, pp. 36–41.

9 Interview with the Dalai Lama, October, 2000.

10 The Dalai Lama, *A Policy of Kindness*, p. 85.

11 The Dalai Lama, *Freedom in Exile* (New York: Harper, 1990), p. 25.

THE PANCHEN LAMAS AND THE DALAI LAMAS
Fabienne Fagou

1 Unlike the previous abbots of Tashilhünpo, Panchen Lopsang Chökyi Gyaltsen already belonged to a *tülku* lineage when he became abbot in 1601. In 1583, he was recognized as the incarnation of Ensapa Lopsang Döndrup [dben sa pa blo bzang don grub] (1505–1566), abbot of the small monastery of Ensa in Tsang, who was himself the incarnation of Sönam Chokkyi Langpo (1439–1504). Sönam Chokkyi Langpo was the incarnation of Kedrup Gelek Pelzang (1385–1438), who was a very close disciple of Tsongkhapa, the founder of the Geluk School. When Lopsang Chökyi Gyaltsen received the title Panchen Lama, the lineage of Ensa ended and a new one created. Although Panchen Lopsang Chökyi

Gyaltsen is the first to bear the title Panchen, he is also called the 4th Panchen Lama because he was the third incarnation of the Ensa tülku. We will adopt him as the 1st Panchen Lama in this article.

2 The history of Tashilhünpo, the fourth seat of the Geluk School (the others being Ganden, Sera and Drepung) and future seat of the Panchen Lama, is closely connected to the Dalai Lamas. The 2nd Dalai Lama, Gendün Gyatso, took his *getsul* and his *gelong* vows from Lungrik Gyatso, abbot of Tashilhünpo 1478–1487. He studied at Tashilhünpo and then left for Drepung, where he completed his Buddhist studies. He became the abbot of Tashilhünpo 1510–1517 after Yeshe Tsemo, abbot 1487–1510, invited him to do so. Later, Gendün Gyatso returned to Drepung as abbot. The 3rd Dalai Lama, Sönam Gyatso, recognized as the incarnation of Gendün Gyatso, also studied at Tashilhünpo but refused to become abbot as he was already in charge of Sera and Drepung.

3 According to the tradition, the Kālacakra initiation is linked to the kingdom of Śambhāla because its first king received the teaching directly from the Buddha.

4 Both hailed from Dakpo Province in southern Tibet. Rumors also spread that the 6th Panchen Lama and the 13th Dalai Lama were from the same family because the resemblance between them was striking.

5 Lhasa officials were afraid the 6th Panchen Lama would return with Chinese soldiers who would help him overthrow the Tibetan government.

6 When the Chinese divided Tibet into three regions, the 7th Panchen Lama became leader of Tsang region, the 14th Dalai Lama was put in charge of Central Tibet, while a committee ruled Amdo.

7 T. Schmid, Saviours of Mankind II, Panchen Lamas and Former Incarnations of Amitayus. VIII, Ethnography, 10, The Sven Hedin Foundation, Stockholm: Statens Etnografiska museum, 1964, p.10; *rdzong-rtse* Byams-pa Thub-bstan (1991), pp. 352–587.

THE PROTECTIVE DEITIES OF THE DALAI LAMAS
Amy Heller

1 This essay is based on readings of the Dalai Lamas' autobiographies (Dalai Lamas 2 and 5) and biographies (all other Dalai Lamas). Certain passages related to the 5th Dalai Lama were first published in my essay on protective deities in F. Pommaret (ed.), *Lhasa in the Seventeenth Century*, Brill, Leiden 2002. Full quotations in Tibetan of all passages cited on the protective deities in the biographies of the Dalai Lama are in my essay "Historic and Iconographic Aspects of the Protective Deities srung ma dmar nag," S. Ihara (ed.), *Tibetan Studies*, Narita, 1992: pp. 479–492.

2 In an interview with Martin Brauen, Dharaśālā, October 2004.

3 Dalai Lama 11, 1984, vol. 4: p. 299; Dalai Lama 9, 1984, vol.3: p. 656. All citations and pagination cited as 1984 hereafter are from an anthology of biographies of the Dalai Lamas (in 5 volumes) reprinted in Dharaśālā, 1984.

4 A. Macdonald, Annuaire de la 4e Section, l'Ecole Pratique des Hautes Etudes, Paris, 1975/1976: p. 981.

5 Dalai Lama 1, 1984: vol. 1: p. 214.

6 Ibid. Visions of Lhamo: pp. 222 (vision in 1410), 230 (vision of a richly decorated girl after *torma* offering to Lhamo Makzorma), 236, 244 for a vision in 1444. Visions of Mahākāla, p. 234 dream of Mahākāla and Yama, and vision of Mahākāla again ca. 1443, p. 243.

7 Dalai Lama 2, 1984: vol. 1: 386–388. (= Tibetan edition, fol. 28a–29a). I would like to thank Samten Karmay for his critical comments of my translation.

8 Dalai Lama 2, Collected Works, vol. Ma, 28a–30b and Ma, fol. 6a–26b, for Bektse as guardian assistant to Hayagriva, and Ma, fol. 65a–66a for the initiation ritual devoted solely to Bektse as *dharmapāla*.

9 Dalai Lama 3, fol. 15b.

10 Dalai Lama 3, fol. 60 b.

11 Dalai Lama 3, fol. 77b.

12 Dalai Lama 3, fol. 19b–20a.

13 Fourteenth Dalai Lama, *Essay on Protective Deities*, Dharaśālā, 1980, pp. 1–24.

14 Dalai Lama 3, fol. 23b.

15 Dalai Lama 3, fol. 39b.

16 Ibid, fol. 78b–79b.

17 Dalai Lama 3, fol. 43b.

18 Dalai Lama 3, fol. 84a.

19 Dalai Lama 3, 92a–93b.

20 Dalai Lama 5, Dukula vol. Ka 305a, 312 a, 335a–b; Vol. Kha. 154 a, 174a. 194a. 220a–b, 232 a–b, 257 b, 263 b.

21 The Funerary Stupa of the Fifth Dalai Lama, vol. 2, pp. 80–82

22 Dalai Lama 5, Chos rgyal chen po'i gsol kha, in the official Nechung monastery anthology of rituals, pp. 73–76, with the date of 1651 on p. 76.

23 For a summary of this book of his visions see Samten Karmay, *Secret Visions of the Fifth Dalai Lama*, London, 1988.

24 Adapted from Nebesky-Wojkowitz. *Oracles and Demons of Tibet*, pp. 25–26

25 According to the biography of the 1st Dalai Lama, which his personal disciple wrote in 1474, just after his death in 1471. In addition to the family line of teachings, the 1st Dalai Lama, who had received instruction from the Sakya teachers, initiated the 2nd Dalai Lama's father in teachings on Bektse. Thus the 2nd Dalai Lama's father passed on to his son rituals to Bektse from two traditions.

26 Dalai Lama 1, 1984: 235 and Dalai Lama 2, 1984: vol. 1: p. 341.

27 See Nebesky-Wojkowitz, pp. 94–133.

WESTERN VIEWS OF THE DALAI LAMAS
Martin Brauen

1 Due to the brevity of this essay, I can only address selected western depictions. I have omitted in particular superficial or implausible accounts or those that do not contain any additional pertinent information, in comparison to the ones I do discuss. I would like to thank Renate Koller for collecting so many articles and books, and Isrun Engelhardt for reading this essay critically and for her suggestions.

2 A term for the regency. Apparently, the regent at the time of the 5th Dalai Lama was called not *desi* [sde srid], but Skt. *deva* (Tib [sde pa]). S. Richardson, 1998 b.

3 de Filippi, 1932, p. 202, ff.

4 First phase: 1701–1722; second phase: 1716–1733; third phase: 1741–1745.

5 1724, 1741, and 1742. During the first phase, the Dalai Lama, born in 1708, was still quite young and not yet living in Lhasa; from 1728 to 1735 the Dalai Lama resided in exile. According to information from Isrun Engelhardt, there were apparently two short meetings in 1743.

6 There was no discussion with the Dalai Lama at this first meeting with the Capuchin missionaries.

7 There are only very brief notes available about the two audiences in 1743. At the final meeting, the Dalai Lama refused the presentation of Cardinal Belluga's letter and gifts from the Capuchin missionaries, according to Isrun Engelhardt.

8 Agostino Antonio Giorgi, who had never been to Tibet appropriated portions of the Capuchin reports, especially those of Orazio della Penna di Billi, in his Alphabetum Tibetanum. By doing so, he composed the first history of the Dalai Lamas ending with the Seventh. For a detailed report, see Petech, 1952–1953.

9 Manning, 1909, p. 436.

10 Huc, 1966, p. 266 ff. However, note Huc's reference to the "Nomekhan" (No-min-han), whom the Chinese called the spiritual emperor *Zangwang* 藏王 "King of Tibet" and who was said to have murdered the Dalai Lama. According to Huc, for years the Chinese had been using the fact that the Dalai Lama was still a minor to amass unheard-of rights for themselves. In Huc's opinion, the Nomekhan responsible for the death of not one Dalai Lama, but for that of three. The first was allegedly strangled, the second struck when his roof collapsed in on him, and the third poisoned along with many of his relatives. Viewed historically, one person could hardly be responsible for the death of three Dalai Lamas. Furthermore, when his book was published in 1850, Huc could have reported only the early demise of two Dalai Lamas (the 9th and 10th) since the 11th Dalai Lama died at eighteen, six years after publication. Perhaps Huc used the term "Nomekhan" as a synonym for "regent." In other words, he was arguing that regents had murdered the three Dalai Lamas, although how he came up with the number three remains unknown.

11 See also Engelhard, 1999, p. 191 ff.

12 Macdonald, 1932, p. 65.

13 In her article about encounters between Capuchin missionaries and Tibetans in the 18th century, Isrun Engelhardt concludes that matters of ceremony are often described in greater detail than the content of discussions. See for example Engelhardt, 1999, p 188.

14 "This was a very great honour indeed, for in Tibet only equals or the greatest of friends exchange scarves... The Dronyer Chhenmo informed me that the Dalai Lama had done me a very great honour by blessing me and my followers in the Durbar Hall." Macdonald, 1932, p. 235.

15 Gould, 1941 (2000), p. 218, ff.

16 Richardson, 1998, p. 674, p. 676, p. 677.

17 Bodleian MS, or Richardson 3, dated 11 October 1939, fol. 173. I am grateful to Isrun Engelhardt for pointing out these passages to me.

18 Gould, 1957, p. 229. Also in Richardson, 1998, p. 567, and in Gould, 1941 (2000), p. 95.

19 de Riencourt, 1951, p. 109.

20 For instance, Manning, Riencourt, Gould, Richardson, and Bell.

21 David-Néel, 1979, p. 72 ff.

22 David-Néel, 1979, p. 104.

23 I am grateful to Maybe Jehu, London, granddaughter of Thyra Weir, for making this text available to me.

24 Trimondi, 1999. For adulation of the Dalai Lama that later degenerated into superstition, see Brauen, 2000, p 91 (Antonin Artaud).

25 Harrer, 1952.

26 Xing Suzhi

27 Such portraits of the young 14th Dalai Lama are in the Newark Museum, with the widow and son of Sir Basil Gould and Ashis Krishna, the son of Kanwal Krishna.

28 Mannerheim, 1940, p. 694. See also Beranek, 1942, pp. 72–74.

29 Kozlov, according to Leonov, 1991, p. 119.

30 Leonov, 1991, p. 119.

31 For example, Bauer's book of photographs, 2005.

32 Harris, 1999, p. 82 ff.

THE NINTH DALAI LAMA'S SET OF SEVEN LINEAGE THANGKAS
Per Sørensen

1 The following essay must be regarded as preliminary; a proper inquiry would require access to and analysis of a number of contemporary written sources that will likely provide clues to its origins and to its anonymous creator or commissioners. An in-depth analysis would also allow a more detailed artistic appraisal in a wider context, and allowing comparison with similar sets in the future. I gratefully acknowledge the critical

comments and reference materials David Jackson and E. Gene Smith have provided.

2 See *Dad pa'i yid 'phrog* [*DL9*] (1b1–203a3) compiled by the 8th Demo Regent. *DL9* 69b2: *gser bum dkrug ma dgos*. See also the Qing Emperor Jiaqing's decree: *bum pa nas ming byang len mi dgos*; reproduced in Dölkar, *A Collection of Historical Archives in Tibet*. 1995: p. 53. For the many visions and recollections of his former incarnations, see *DL9* 18a1–2, 22a1–2, 23a2–4, 28a4–b3, 45a3–5, 70a3–4. One of the gifts, the Ninth Dalai Lama received in the wake of his enthronement included a priceless stitched silk brocade thangka of the 5th Dalai Lama (*rgyal ba lnga ba'i snang brnyan gos thang 'thags 'grub ma*).

3 See the official communication from June 1808 issued by amban Yu Ning which appointed Dechen Gyatso as steward, reproduced in Dölkar, *A Collection of Historical Archives in Tibet*. 1995: p. 52.

4 C.R. Markham, *The Mission of George Bogle to Tibet and the Journey of Thomas Manning to Lhasa* 1971: pp. 265–266.

5 *DL9* 175a1–195b3; Repgong 2000: 610–11; Lopsang Gyatso 1997: pp. 538–539.

6 See *bKa' gdams glegs bam* Vol. 2: pp. 97–205; also Sanggye Gyatso, *'Dzam gling rgyan gcig* 139, etc.

7 See the 5th Dalai Lama, *'Khrungs rabs* 4b3–5a4 (584.3–585.4); *Rwa sgreng dkar chag* 62–7; see also *5DL IV* in tr. Z. Ahmad, 1999: pp. 148–153.

8 A host of sources deal with the popular legend of the origin of the Tibetans from this union. Behind it towers Songtsen Gampo as father of the Tibetan state and as a manifestation of Avalokiteśvara. For other aspects related to aspects of Tibetan nationalism, see G. Dreyfus 1994.

9 *'Dzam gling rgyan gcig* 622, 634: *'khrung rabs gras*: Songtsen Gampo, Thrisong Deutsan, Nyangrel, Sachen, Lama Zhang, Khache Gönpapa, Gewabum, Padmavajra, 1st–4th Dalai Lama (all statues).

10 See his *'Khrung rabs* 6a4f.

11 *zla ba gcig la chu zla grangs med 'byung ba ltar*. See e.g. *5DL IV*: pp. 182–83. In his *Bla ma'i bstod tshogs* 117b5–18a4, 161a2–62a6, compiled by the 5th Dalai Lama in 1681: After listing a number of former incarnations, the 5th Dalai Lama responds to the critique that internal inconsistencies existed in the succession by stating that the Indian part of the succession lineage (i.e. until the Tibetan progenitor Nyakhri Tsenpo), there is no certainty in terms of the internal succession itself, but points out that since the nature of the individual incarnates is that of "one mind," i.e. that they are essentially identical, any inconsistency as to chronology in the rebirth succession is difficult to prove with reasoning or any logical arguments.

12 Among others, both canonical and apocryphal texts such as the pioneering *Kachen Kakholma* and *Mani Kabum: bKa' chems Ka khol ma and Mani bka' 'bum*.

13 See *5DL IV*: pp. 41–274.

14 He considered himself a manifestation of Avalokiteśvara and Songtsen Gampo; see Tsering Gyalbo *et al.* 2000.

15 Longdol here updated the Sanggye Gyatso's list; the deviating names were due in part to scribal errors that afflict Tibetan texts. See Longdol Lama, vol. *Za*, pp. 390–93 (of his *gSung 'bum*; Lhasa ed. 1991): his list similarly includes Indian (list nos. 1–37) and Tibetan (38–58) predecessors. Relevant for the present set, Lokeśvara is listed as no. 2, Indian King Könchog Bang (8), the Indian Devarāja (23), King Gewapal (37), Tibetan royal progenitor Nyathri Tsenpo (38; absent from Sangye Gyatso's list), Songtsen Gampo (40), Gewapal (repeated as 43), Khache Gönpapa (44), Domtön (45), Künga Nyingpo (46), Lama Zhang (47), Gewawum (49), Padmavajra (50), then in succession the 1st Dalai Lama Gendün

Drup (51) to the 8th Dalai Lama (58). Aside from the well-known sources composed by the 5th Dalai Lama and the regent, a number of currently still non-extant texts by the same masters deal with the variant Dalai Lama lineage succession (up to 78 figures are occasionally listed). A perusal and collation of such seminal lineage-prayer texts like the *rMad byung bskal pa ma*, *Blo bzang rgyal ba ma*, *'Gro la rjes brtse ma* and the influential *dByangs can rgyud mang ma* shall allow us to reconstruct more precisely the most authoritative lineage behind his lineage. See also the article by the present author in *Orientations* Sept. Issue 2005.

16 Such sets also consisted of images and sculptures. Entire sculptured sets of previous incarnations of the Dalai Lama have so far not surfaced in the West; cf. fn. 9 above.

17 The opposition right and left must be seen from the perspective of the central figure.

18 See *'Khrungs rabs* 9b5–10a4; *5DL IV*: pp. 214–221.

19 This mythic Bengali king is often listed as the thirty-six or -seventh Indian previous incarnation; see *5DL IV*: pp. 125–127.

20 See *'Khrungs rabs* 8a6–b4; *5DL IV*: pp. 154–59. For his role in compiling and disseminating the Avalokiteśvara and the Padmasambhava teaching cycles and the testamentary literature ascribed to Songtsen Gampo, see Per K. Sørensen, *Lhasa Diluvium* 2003.

21 See *'Khrungs rabs* 7b4–8a3; *5DL IV*: pp. 184–185.

22 See *'Khrungs rabs* 9a3–b1; *5DL IV*: pp. 197–202. For the 1st Dalai Lama, see Shen Weirong in this publication.

23 The sixth *jātaka* of Domtön; see *bKa' gdams glegs bam* vol. 206–303; *5DL IV*: pp. 65–71.

24 See *bKa' gdams glegs bam* vol. 2: 492; *'Khrungs rabs* 6a6–b4; *5DL IV*: pp. 142–146.

25 Jinaputra Lokeśvara, son of Amitābha; see *'Khrungs rabs* 2b5–3a6; *5DL IV*: pp. 43–47.

26 See 14 above; *bKa' gdams glegs bam* vol. 2: p. 491.

27 The portrait of Dalai Lama as middle-aged with a tiny mustache follows convention. The portrait and caption here seem to be copied from the mural of the Dalai Lama lineage done in the Potala in 1690–1694, and also from a stitched brocade *thangka* kept in the Potala, see Lading ed. 2000: 231; *Tibetan Thangkas* no. 76.

28 Cf. *'Khrungs rabs* 7a2–6, Cf. *5DL IV*: pp. 148–153.

29 See the depiction of Domtön executed 1690–94 in mural at Potala. From to the numerous correspondences, this mural may well have served as model for this painting. See Lading ed. 2000: 85.

30 Cf. *bKa' gdam glegs bam* vol. 2: pp. 479–536. The nineteenth *jātaka* in the collection; *5DL IV*: pp. 100–02.

31 See the nineteenth *jātaka* of Domtön (vol. 2: p. 481).

32 E.g. *'Khrungs rabs* 9b1–5; *5DL IV*: pp. 202–210.

33 See *5DL IV*: pp. 202–210.

34 See *'Khrungs rabs* 6b4–7a1, Cf. *5DL IV*: pp. 146–148.

35 See *'Khrungs rabs* 7a6–b3, Cf. *5DL IV*: p. 184. Khache Gönpapa, the Kaśmīrī hermit was pupil of Drokmi. See *thangka* in G-W. Essen & T.T. Thingo, *Die Götter des Himalaya* Pl. 72.

36 The biography maintains that starting in infancy he developed special spiritual bonds with Lama Zhang; cf. *DL9* 22a6–24a1, 61a5–62a6.

37 See also *'Khrungs rabs* 8a3–6; *5DL IV*: pp. 185–188. The monastic center Tshal Gungthang which Lama Zhang founded was later integrated into the Geluk monastic establishment. Zhang Yudrakpa as ruler of Lhasa Valley was considered a precursor of later Geluk rule. It was therefore part of the integrative politics of the same court to incorporate his legacy by ennobling him into the Dalai Lama lineage. For the history of this extraordinary person and his religious establishments, see Per K. Sørensen and G. Hazod, *Rulers on the Celestial Plain* (2006).

38 *'Khrungs rabs* 8b4–a4; *5DL IV*: pp. 190–192. For Gewabum's pioneering role in Lhasa; see Per K. Sørensen, *Lhasa Diluvium* 2003: pp. 105–07.

39 See *5DL IV*: pp. 182–183.

TIBETAN EPISTOLARY STYLE
Hanna Schneider

1 These are the five new Chinese ranks of nobility that were introduced in 1792. Petech 1972, p. 8 ff.; Tharchin, 1954, pp. 164–166.

2 Nornang, 1888, fol. 3 r/4 – 4v/1

3 This is the devotional form inserted after the salutation which expresses the respect of the sender for the recipient. This is set forth in three layers for letters to the Dalai Lama.

4 Nornang, 1888, Fol. 7r/4 – 7v/6

5 Epithet of Avalokiteśvara, whom the Dalai Lama embodies.

6 Rhetorical device to capture the good will of the audience.

7 "Lord of the Mountain" is a metaphor for the Mount Sumeru, center of Tibetan cosmology and navel of the world.

8 Here follows a list of the presents accompanying the letter and the *khatak* of good quality which must always be included.

9 See Nebesky-Wojkowitz, 1949, p. 77; Taring 1986 (2), p. 94; Grönbold, 1982, p. 378.

10 See Gassner, Jansen, Stehrenberger, 1991, p 86 ff.; an illustration of the *dayik* is on p. 87.

11 See Bell, 1987 (2).

ICONOGRAPHY OF THE DALAI LAMAS
Michael Henss

1 For dates of birth and death of the individual Dalai Lamas, I have referred to Lucian Petech 1959.

2 This does not preclude the existence of earlier likenesses of Sönam Gyatso, nor of pictorial representations of his predecessor Gedün Gyatso, posthumously named the 2nd Dalai Lama, that were done during his lifetime or shortly after his death.

3 Stoddard, 2003: p. 34.

4 London, private collection, see Rhie & Thurman 1991, no. 97; Tucci 1949, 392–399. Since this thangka does not show this significant trip of the 3rd Dalai Lama to Mongolia, it most likely was made between 1572 and 1577. My thanks to Prof. Karénina Kollmar-Paulenz for pointing this out.

5 See *Portraits of the Masters*, 2003: p. 309 (no.84; 16th century.)

6 See *Portraits of the Masters*, 2003: pp. 44 (no. 28a), 342, 346.

7 See *Portraits of the Masters*, 2003: pp. 175, 265

8 See *Portraits of the Masters*, 2003: pp. 38, 39, 42–44, and Weldon & Singer 1999: figs. 51, 53, 55, 56; plates 34, 35, 36, 39, 40, 41

9 See Selig Brown, 2004: plate 12.

10 Seckel 1997.

11 I argue that Heather Stoddard's assumption that this figure was made from life is not correct. See Stoddard 2003: 34: "Inscribed as being made from life in 1669–70." The inscription does not state this in any way. The statement that the material is stucco is also false; see Macdonald 1977: pp. 121–123

12 Macdonald 1977: p. 126

13 See Stoddard 2003: p. 18

14 On earlier textual references to lines of reincarnation, see Ishihama Yumiko 2003: 543 f. For a reference to the 5th Dalai Lama line beginning with Avalokiteśvara: *Khrungs rabs kyi zhing bskod 'dri tshul gyi rtogs brjod kha byang dang bcas pa gsal ba'i me long* (Tucci, 1949, p. 213); see also Per Soerensen in this volume.

15 5th Dalai Lama 1989–1991; see Ishihama Yumiko 2003: 546. For reproductions, see A Mirror 2000: 227–230; The Potala 1996: pp. 134–135. See also Fifth Dalai Lama 1989–1991: vol. 1, p. 286.

16 See Lange 1969: 209 ff.

17 Namgyal 2002, illustrations on pp. 137–149.

18 Gems of the Potala Palace, 1999 (Phodrang Marpo [pho brang dmar po] "Hall of the Superior Masters"), plates pp 104–107; Xizang Budala Gong 1996: plates 279, 280; The Potala 1996: illustrations on pp. 56–59.

19 Brussels Musées Royaux d'Art et d'Histoire, Songtsen Gampo, First Dalai Lama; Arnold Lieberman, Fourth Dalai Lama.

20 See Tucci 1949: pp. 410–436.

21 A direct print from the woodblock cannot be proven in the case of the Stockholm thangkas, according to Hakan Wahlquist in Febuary 2005. Schmid 1961 also does not provide any indication of the existence of a xylographed preliminary drawing for these paintings. A thangka of the 1st Dalai Lama in the Jucker Collection allegedly painted over a wood-block print should be reviewed again in regard to this allegation; see Kreijger 2001: no. 28. Schmid 1961: pp. 11–12 suspects that the Stockhom series originally included only eleven thangkas, with Avalokiteśvara in the middle, because of the aesthetically unsatisfactory and low quality of the last two images of the 6th and 7th Dalai Lama. Schmid also contends that it was supplemented only later under the 7th Dalai Lama with his image and that of his predecessor, yet the quality of the plates in Schmid does not permit any evaluation here.

22 Still, the size—approximately 72 x 46 cm—of individual pictures from at least six reincarnation series of similar iconography and composition are so closely concur that we can assume a common model or a wooden engraving used as a model. These six sets which generally survive only as fragments in similar published format (72–73 x 44–48 cm) are: Palace Museum Beijing; Tamashige Collection Tokyo; Christie's no. 95 (November 2001), Emil Mirzakhanian Milan 1998; Sotheby's no. 71 (September 1997); Musée Guimet nos. 324–326. The set at the Museum of Ethnology at the University of Zürich and Sotheby's no. 37 (September 2001) also have similar formats.

23 Qing Gong Zang Chuan Fo Jiao Tang Ka, 2003: pp. 10–23. Image format 72 x 46 cm each. On Rölpe Dorje, "vajra rebirth," and Chinese–Tibetan relations in art and religion under the Qianlong Emperor see Henss 2001. In the Palace Museum there are ten more Dalai Lama lineage thangkas of which at least three date to 1782 according to curator Luo Wenhua.

24 The presence of the west Tibetan lama Yeshe Ö "God-King Lama" (959–1036) in the Beijing set may indicate iconographic directions from Rölpe Dorje and thus an imperial commission since the highly educated and influential Janggyya Khutughtu had taken the Serkhang "maṇḍala" Temple as his model when he built the Qianglong Emperor's private temple of Qianlong in 1755 in the Beijing. For the five "woodcut thangkas" from the same series of Songtsen Gampo, Domtön, the 5th Dalai Lama, and what is probably the 7th Dalai Lama, see Tucci plates 225–229.

25 For instance, Sanggye Gyatso's fourth volume on the 5th Dalai Lama's autobiography. See Sanggye Gyatso 1999: 136 ff.

26 See V.L. Uspensky "Le texte des Visions secrètes du 5e Dalai Lama et sa diffusion dans l'espace du bouddhisme tibétain" in Bazin 2002: p. 27.

27 The idea of Avalokiteśvara being reborn in Songtsen Gampo must have already been present in Tibet in the 8th century. See Henss 2004: 129–137.

28 Karmay 1988: 54f; A. Heller, "Les nagthang (peintures sur fond noir) et les divinités protectrices", in Bazin 2002: p. 61.

29 See Schmid 1961: p. 20.

30 Mullin 2004, Biographie des Zweiten Dalai Lama: 37 f.; also according to Sumpa Khanpo (1702–88) in Schmid 1961: 22 or Sanggye Gyatso's fourth volume on the 5th Dalai Lama's autobiography, 148–153. On Domtön, see Ishihama Yumiko 2003: p. 552.

31 Sangs rGyas rGya mtsho, 1999, p. 184.

32 See also Lange 1969: p. 224. In a solo picture of the 5th Dalai Lama, Künga Nyingpo is the only previous existence as a lama shown among the figures on the upper margin of the picture (Tanaka 2003: no. 53).

33 Ishihama Yumiko 2003: p. 545; Sanggye Gyatso 1999: 179 f. We cannot determine whether the 5th Dalai Lama's comment that he was a rebirth of Phakpa was Sanggye Gyatso's invention or not, but it is probably true that Sakya clergy only found their way into later sets starting around 1700.

34 Schmid 1961: plate 11

35 Qing Gong 2003: no. 13

36 I am grateful to Luo Wenhua for pointing this out.

37 Tanaka 2003: no. 54; see also Chandra 1986.

38 See for example Tucci 1949: plates 225–229.

39 The image of the 1st Dalai Lama from the Zürich series, which most probably dates back to the first half of the 18th century, does not survive. If there were no previous existences—at least an Avalokiteśvara—as part of this set, we would suspect if only for the symmetrical arrangement, a frontally constructed thangka of the 7th Dalai Lama.

40 See Tanaka 2003: nos. 52–54. Interestingly, the central figure here, the 7th Dalai Lama, is not the chronological last one but rather the two smaller side figures in the picture of the 5th and 6th Dalai Lamas, who are probably the 8th and 9th Dalai Lamas, which makes it likely that these three thangkas date from after 1815.

41 Another thangka of the Great Fifth at the Leipzig Ethnology Museum portrays twenty-two of his previous incarnations from Avalokiteśvara to the 4th Dalai Lama. The printed lists of incarnation sets of the 7th and 8th Dalai Lamas contain fifty-seven sequentially numbered previous existences, as for example in a text by Longdol Lama Ngawang Lopsang (1719–94) in: L Chandra, ed The Collected Works of Longdol Lama, Delhi 1973: 1150–1214.

42 See Samphel & Tender 2000: pp. 13–14 for illustrations of the set at the Norbulingka Institute.

43 See Essen & Thingo 1989: pp. 1–92.

44 Rubin Museum of Art Catalogue, September 2002. Since neither the original nor detailed photographs of the picture were available, it was possible to read only a few inscriptions.

45 See [Bod kyi thang ka] 1985: plate 77.

46 See Priceless Treasures, 1999: no. 22 and Precious Deposits, 2000, vol.4 no.3.

47 See for example Tibetica 34, Schoettle Ostasiatica 1976: no. 9604.

48 See [Bod kyi thang ka] 1985, plate 77. According to H.Stoddard in Karmay 1988: 24, probably from a series of twenty-three thangkas on the life and visions of the 5th Dalai Lama, that Sanggye Gyatso commissioned in 1686.

49 Stoddard, in Karmay 1988: p. 17.

50 Thangka of the 3rd Dalai Lama, see Tibetica 32, Schoettle Ostasiatica 1976: no. 9267; see also H. Uhlig, Buddhistische Kunst aus dem Himalaya, Berlin 1976: 94. See also the thangkas of the 3rd and 7th Dalai Lamas in the Schleiper Collection, Belgium; see Neven 1978: nos. 19, 20. Unfortunately, it was not possible to read and evaluate the inscriptions on these pictures in time for this study.

51 On this topic see Selig Brown: 2004.

52 Thus for instance in the gold and red thangka of the 5th Dalai Lama in the Ford Collection, or the picture of the 3rd Dalai Lama painted from life that at the Hahn Cultural Foundation. See Tanaka 1999: no. 54; Selig Brown 2004; fig.18.

53 An original and barely recognizable handprint of the 7th Dalai Lama—as its inscription confirms—is on the back of a thangka of Dorje Dragden at the Rubin Museum of Art. See also Selig Brown 2004: p. 62.

54 The 7th Dalai Lama placed his double handprints and seal as consecration on the back of the center picture in a multi-part Tsongkhapa set. An inscription below confirms this: "The handprints of the Victorious Lopsang Gyatso, the Second Buddha." For a reproduction, see Tibetica 32, Schoettle Ostasiatica 1976: no. 9265. The present whereabouts of the thangka are unknown.

55 Apparently in the last years of his life the 12th Dalai Lama Trinle Gyatso placed his double handprints, seal and inscription on a thangka showing the 7th Dalai Lama at the Newark Museum. See Reynolds, Heller & Gyatso 1986: 200.

56 Another inscription, possibly alluding to the Indian Mahāyāna scholar monk, and which possibly goes back to the 6th Dalai Lama himself is discernible on the lower edge of the picture: "through a series of rebirths may all sentient beings find the path to enlightenment through my efforts towards enlightenment!"

57 Inscription: "Reverence to the omniscient Dalai Lama, Lopsang Tsangyang Gyatso," see Zhongguo Zangchuan Fojiao Jintong Zaoxiang Yishu 2001: no. 251.

58 For the picture in Basel, see Essen & Thingo 1989: II-269. Unfortunately the probable textual source for this representation was not available for this study.

59 The representation of the 7th Dalai Lama as a Tantric yogin seems even more unusual. In a thangka from the van der Wee Collection (Belgium), we see Kalsang Gyatso dressed like a Mahāsiddha in only tiger skins and bone jewelry, see van der Wee 1995: fig 35 and p. 81.

60 Of the fifty figures selected here, only eleven have an inscription that makes identification possible.

61 See Lhalungpa: 1983 for Bell's photo (not by "G.N.Roerich") on the dust jacket. According to Lhalungpa, this picture of the 13th Dalai Lama originated as a montage that was reworked with sketching which is now at the Eremitage Museum in St. Petersburg.

62 Bell 1946: 114 f, 214 and frontispiece. Also reproduced as a colorplate in Bell, Tibet – Past and Present, Oxford 1924: frontispiece and 55; and prior to that in Francis Younghusband, From India to Tibet. London 1910. One of these colored and signed photos was already framed in Lhasa, according to Bell, and is probably identical to the original photography published in Bell's books and kept today in the Ashmolean Museum Oxford. Translation of the dedication according to Bell, 1946: p. 115.

63 Today these drawings by N. Kozhevnikov are in the Eremitage Museum, St. Petersburg. See Leonov 1991: figs 1, 2.

64 Leonov, 1991: p. 117. The whereabouts of these drawings are not known.

65 Format: 87.6 x 63.5 cm, inv. no. 88.579; see Reynolds, 1999, plate 3. For the photo by Ilya Tolstoy that served as the basis, see Gould 1941 (2000): p. 50.

66 E.g. Stockholm thangka series (Schmid, 1961, Pl. VII) and Beijing (Qing Gong, 2003, Pl. 14), TTC (Tanaka, 2004, no. 22); also Jucker Collection (Kreijger, 2001, no. 28); Sotheby's Nov. 14, 1988, no. 23; Side figure on the thangka of the 8th Dalai Lama at VKM.

67 E.g. Paris–Brussels thangka series (Selig Brown, 2004, Pl. 18); thangka formerly at the Potala (Bod kyi thang

ka, 1985, Pl. 74); metal statue, Macieri Goralski Collection, Warsaw).

68 E.g. mural in the Great East Hall (built 1648) of the Potala Great East Hall (A Mirror, 2000, p. 227).

69 E.g. woodcut, Pantheon of Rölpe Dorje, Beijing, ca. 1800 (Lohia, 1994, p. 92).

70 E.g. painted wooden statuette, height: 14.5 cm, ca. 16th century, Beijing (exact location not known). Inscription on reverse: chos kun thams chad mkhyen pa dGe 'dun grub pa la na mo, "Reverence to the omniscient Gendün Druppa" (Precious Deposits, 2000, vol. 3, no. 64).

71 E.g. Stockholm and Beijing thangka series (Schmid, 1961, Pl. VIII; Qing Gong, 2003, Pl. 15); thangka of the 8th Dalai Lama at VKM (plate 25); M. Driesch Collection, Cologne; F.Meyer, Ed., *Tibet: Civilisation et Société*, Paris, 1990, jacket picture); Ford Collection, Baltimore (D.I. Lauf, *Verborgene Botschaft tibetischer Thangkas*. Freiburg, 1976, Pl. 42); E. Mirzakhanian Gallery (E.Lo Bue, A Tibetan Journey, Milano, 1998, no.11); SO (Tibetica 38, 1980, Nr. 3499); Sotheby's Sept. 24, 1997, no. 71; Christie's Amsterdam, Nov. 21, 2001, no. 95.5; MKB (Essen/Thingo, 1989, pp. I–92). For two metal statues, see plate 3 (Christie's, March 22, 2000, no.77, now Tibet House, New York), and *Portraits of the Masters*, 2003, Pl. 309.

72 E.g. thangka series at VKM; Sotheby's, Sept. 24, 1997, no. 85 (without Vajradhara), and Sept. 21, 2001, no. 37.4.

73 E.g. Gilded cooper figure at Rietbergmuseum, Zürich (H.Uhlig, *Auf dem Pfad zur Erleuchtung. Die Tibet-Sammlung der Berti Aschmann-Stiftung im Museum Rietberg*, Zürich 1995, No. 141, with inscription).

74 E.g. Mural at the Potala Palace, Great East Hall, 1648 (A Mirror, 2000, p. 228).

75 E.g. Stockholm und Beijing thangka series (Schmid, 1961, Pl. IX; Qing Gong, 2003, Pl. 16); K.D. Fuchsberger Collection; E.Mirzakhanian Gallery (E. Lo Bue, *Tibet. Arte e Spiritualita*. Milan 1988, no. 38); thangka of the 8th Dalai Lama at VKM .

76 E.g. VKM thangka series.

77 E.g. SO 1976 (Tibetica 32, no. 9267. The Dalai Lama here in frontal view); Schleiper Collection, Belgium (Neven, 1978, no. 20).

78 E.g. AMNH, inv. no. 70.2/872.

79 E.g. Mural at Potala Palace, Great East Hall, 1648 (A Mirror, 2000: 229).

80 E.g. thangka in a private collection, London; gilded metal statue, Musées Royaux des Arts et d'Histoire, Brussels.

81 For instance, a 32.7 cm high probably 17th century "Silver figure of third rebirth of the Dalai Lama," which was identified by the Second Janggya *Khutughtu* in the 44th year of rule [of the Qianlong Empire]" for exhibition again in a shrine completed in 1779. See also Qing Gong Zangchuan Fojiao Zaoxiang, 2003, no.192). Also a 15 cm high gilded metal statuette in the Xia Jingchun Collection, China (end of the 16th century?), which can be identified solely by the inscription on its pedestal: bSod nams rGya mtsho'i sde'i zhabs la na mo, "Reverence to the most worthy [Dalai Lama] Sönam Gyatso!: (Buddhist metal statues from Tibet in the Xia Jingchun Collection, Shenyang, 2000, fig. 52).

82 E.g. Metal statuette in the Eremitage Museum, St.Petersburg (A. Grünwedel, *Mythologie des Buddhismus in Tibet und in der Mongolei*. Leipzig, 1900, p. 68).

83 E.g. Stockholm and Beijing thangka series (Schmid, 1961, Pl. X; Qing Gong, 2003, Pl. 17); R.R.E. Collection (SO, 1969, Tibetica 3, no. 4216); Christie's Amsterdam, Nov. 21, 2001, no. 95.6; Solomon Collection, Paris; thangka of 8th Dalai Lama at VKM.

84 E.g. AMNH, inv. No.70.2/873.

85 E.g. VKM thangka series; Sotheby's, Sept. 21, 2001, no. 37.3. (without Sitātapatrā).

86 E.g. Mural at Potala Palace, Great East Hall, 1648 (A Mirror, 2000: p. 230.

87 Arnold Lieberman Collection, New York. The monks and masters on the upper and side margins of the picture have not been identified to date due to inadequate photographs.

88 RMA (Rhie & Thurman 1999: no.128)

89 A Tibetan text from around 1653, on the question of the relations between the Dalai Lama and temporal kings states, "As once in India there was a king who moved the wheel (of teaching) for each buddha, this applies precisely to the Dalai Lama." (according to Ishihama Yumiko, 2003, p. 540). Examples for this type: Potala Palace, statue in 'Khrung rab Lha khang (Namgyal, 2002, p. 135), Illus.12), and mural in the Great West Hall (A Mirror, 2000, p. 231); Lhasa, Jokhang (Tsering, 2000, p. 30); Stockholm, Beijing and VKM thangka series (Schmid, 1961, Pl. "VI"; Qing Gong, 2003, no. 18); Hahn Cultural Foundation (Tanaka, 2003, no.53); Sotheby's New York, Sept. 24, 1997, no. 85; AMNH 70.2/867; Rome, Museo Nazionale dell' Arte Orientale (Tucci, 1949, Pl. 80).

90 E.g. Galerie Koller thangkas 65/1987, No.19 and 109/1998, No. 67; Ford Collection (Selig Brown, 2004, Pl. 13); MG (Béguin, 1995, no. 318); Rom Museo Nazionale dell' Arte Orientale (Tucci, 1949, Pl. 227).; silk brocade thangka currently at Tibet House, New York (Christie's, March 20, 2002, no. 74). A good example for the difficult attribution of this iconographical type is the "Geluk Master" in the Oliver Hoare Collection, London (2nd Dalai Lama (?) late 16th century? See *Portraits of the Masters*, 2003, 308/309).

91 (only statues) e.g. in the possession of the 14th Dalai Lama (R.Steffan, *Tibetische Kunstschätze im Exil*. St.Gallen, 1989, No. 17); Boston, Museum of Fine Arts, inv. no. 50.3606, ca. 1669/70 (Macdonald, 1977, p. 119 ff.); Estournel Collection, Paris, ca. 1682/83. (Macdonald, 1977, p. 150 ff.; Bazin, 2002, no. 3, see here also no. 2 and 4);Cologne, Museum für Ostasiatische Kunst (Thingo, 1974, No. 36). On *phurbu* cult of the 5th Dalai Lama, see Macdonald, 1977, p.139 ff. and on his visions of the *phurbu* deity, Karmay, 1988, p. 67 ff.

92 E.g. RMA (according to Jeff Watt, the yogi on the lotus blossom to the right can be identified as Thangtong Gyalpo. Cf. the yogi on a thangka in the Potala—without the bridgebuilder's characteristic attribute! Gems, 1999, p. 234); Potala Palace Lhasa (now Tibet Museum, Lhasa? Bod kyi thang ka 1985, pl. 77). Also the Paris–Brussels series, here in a combination type of composition of the emblematic (hand- and footprints) and narrative (scene below the throne) pictorial elements and the otherwise typical figures and protective deities from the lines of descendent. (Bazin, 2002, no. 5; Selig Brown, 2004, pl. 19).

93 RMA (Rhie/Thurman 1999, no.129); thangka at Potala Palace (Gems 1999, p.234); silk brocade thangka at Potala Palace (Bod kyi thang ka 1985, Pl. 76).

94 (only statues) e.g. Beijing, Museum of Chinese History (Precious Deposits, 2000, III, no.3); Potala Palace, Lhasa (Zhongguo Zangchuan Fojiao Diaosu Quanji. *A Collection of Tibetan Buddhist Sculpture*, vol.3, Beijing 2001: 178); New York, Tibet House, formerly Rose Art Museum (Rhie/Thurman 1991, no. 98).

95 Macdonald, 1977, pp.137, 153, according to a text of the Regent Sanggye Gyatso.—As an example of iconographic type G: metal figure at the Jaques Marchais Museum of Tibetan Art, New York (Lipton, 1996, no. 27).

96 Solely as an example, Donation L.Fournier at MG (Karmay, 1988, fig. 7; Bazin, 2002, fig. 4). For two more examples of this Dalai Lama iconography, see here under the 1st Dalai Lama (wood statuette in Beijing, Illus.4) and the 7th Dalai Lama in the modern mural set at NID (TST, 2000, p. 13).

97 As example, one gilt cooper statue in Pelkhor Chöde monastery of Gyantse is known (U. von Schroeder, *Buddhist Sculpture in Tibet*, vol.II, Hong Kong, 2001, 280E).

98 E.g. Stockholm and Beijing thangka series (Schmid, 1961, Pl. XII; Qing Gong, 2003, no.19; TTC (Tanaka 2004, no. 22.4); thangka at Jokhang, Lhasa (Tsering, 2000, p.49); mural set at NID (TST 2000, p. 14); thangka of the 8th Dalai Lama at VKM (side figure); mural at Potala Palace (side figure; A Mirror, 2000, p. 232); statue at Potala Palace with lotus blossom, book and sword (Potala Palace, ed.by Shen Baichang, Beijing, 1988, Pl. 79).

99 VKM thangka series: Sotheby's, Sept. 21, 2001, no. 37.5.

100 RMA.

101 Silver statue at Potala Palace (Namgyal, 2002, p. 80).

102 Gilded metal statue in Beijing, exact location unknown (Zhongguo Zangchuan, 2001, vol.II, no. 251). See endnote 52.

103 E.g. Beijing thangka series (Qing Gong, 2003, no. 7) and the TTC series that is identical in its detail drawing (Tanaka, 2004, no. 22.5), and Stockholm (Schmid, 1961, Pl.XIII), whereby the picture of the latter series exhibits smaller iconographic deviations.

104 AMNH, inv. no. 70.2/863; Hahn Cultural Foundation, Seoul (Tanaka, 2003, no.52); MG (Béguin, 1995, no.364); Newark Museum (Reynolds et al. 1986, p. 42); Rölpe Dorje Pantheon (Lohia, 1994, p. 96); metal statue in Beijing (exact location unknown; Zhongguo Zangchuan, 2001, Pl. 253).

105 E.g. mural at Potala Palace, ca. 1757/58 (A Mirror, 2000, p. 233); Schleiper Collection thangka, Belgium (Neven, 1978), no.19).

106 E.g. mural at Samye, vestibule (sGo khang) in second story, ca 1770? Metal figure in China (location not known; China's Tibet, 4/2004, p. 44).

107 E.g. statue at the Potala Palace (Gems, 1999, p. 106); metal statuette in Beijing (exact location not known; Zhongguo Zangchuan, 2001, vol.II, no. 252); Jacques Marchais Museum of Tibetan Art, New York (Lipton 1996, no. 28).

108 Thangkas at VKM and MKB (as monk; Essen/Thingo, 1989, II–269; as Yogi, ibid., II–268); Van der Wee Collection, Belgium (as yogi; Van der Wee, 1995, fig. 35, p. 81)

109 E.g. at MKB (Essen/Thingo, 1989, II–270 ; an example of the "emblematic" pictorial type of such reincarnation series such as the picture at AMNH at type B); R.R.E. Collection, Winterthur (example of the narrative pictorial type); AMNH, inv. no. 70.2/871 (last picture of the serie, because only Avalokiteśvara is represented above the Dalai Lama, therefore can be dated to around or after 1804); statue at Potala Palace, mausoleum of the 8th Dalai Lama (Namgyal, 2002, p. 92).

110 Here as one example at VKM; see also the thangka at AMNH (Mullin, 2001, p.322), and the side figure of Maitreya, silk brocade thangka at the Norton Simon Museum, Los Angeles, M. 1975. 1.T (P. Pal, *Art from the Himalayas and China. Asian Art at the Norton Simon Museum*, vol. 2, New Haven, 2003, no. 135).

111 Mural at Potala Palace, ca. 1804/05? (A Mirror, 2000, p. 234).

112 See the thangka series in Fujita, 1984, and the mural set at the NID (TST, 2000, 13/14). No likenesses of the mural set at Kalachakra Tempel in Dharamsala were availabe for this study. Cf. also Chandra, 1986, fig. 1899–1912. Here the modern illustrations of the 9th and 12th Dalai Lamas are completely similar, with *vitarkamudrā*, lotus blossom and Poti book.

113 Side figure in the thangka of the 8th Dalai Lama, VKM; mural set at NID (TST, 2000, p.13). Se also Chandra, 1986, no.1907. The Speidel Collection metal statue that can be identified as the 9th Dalai Lama because of its inscription, the original Poti book has probably been lost.

114 Mural at Potala Palace (A Mirror, 2000: p. 235).

115 Mural at Potala Palace (lotus blossom with sword; A Mirror, 2000, p. 236); side figure in thangka of 8th Dalai Lama, VKM.

116 Mural at NID (TST, p. 14).

117 Mural at Potala (A Mirror, 2000, p. 237).

118 Mural at NID (TST: 14).

119 Mural at Potala Palace (A Mirror, 2000, p. 238).

120 Mural at NID (TST, p. 14).

121 E.g. Murals at Potala Palace (A Mirror, 2000, p. 239), Gyantse Tsuglagkhang (Zhal ras khang), Khamsun Sangak Ling Temple of Samye (painted 1936), Samye Utse (4th floor, 1989), and NID (without lotus blossom, TST, 13); the large metal statues in Lhasa Jokhang (Tsering, 2000, p.30) and at the Sera Monastery (Sera Thekchen Ling, Beijing, 1995, p. 49). On the distinctly different shape of the moustache of the 5th and 13th Dalai Lamas, see Gems, 1999, p.105, p. 107; Tsering, 2000, p.

30, p. 42; Sera Thekchen Ling, 1995, p. 49; the mural of the 14th Dalai Lama with the 5th and 13th Dalai Lamas in Samye (top floor) or photographs of the 13th Dalai Lama as well.

122 Silver statuette at the Museum for East Asian Art, Cologne (Thingo, 1974, no. 37).

123 Silver statuette with cold gilded and painted face, height 12.2 cm, private collection, Belgium (Jan van Alphen, Cast for Eternity. Bronze Masterworks from India and the Himalayas. Antwerpen, 2005, no.74). Cf. for example, the known photo of the 13th Dalai Lama by Charles Bell (1910), where the prayer chain and the particular collar shape of the robe worn underneath are discernible.

124 Representations of the 14th Dalai Lama in the sequence of the Norbulingka mural from 1955/56, two murals in the Sera Monastery, 1980s? (one of these portraying the 14th Dalai Lama wearing eyeglasses. Source: Tibet and Himalayan Digital Library); mural in the Samye Monastery (top floor), 1989, unusually, with the Padmasambhava cap of the Nyingmapa tradition so closely connected with Samye; mural set at the NID (TST, 2000, p. 13); thangka at the Musée d'Ethnographie, Geneva, MEG 53946 (painted by a Tibetan in Nepāl).

ENGLISH EDITORS' NOTES

A brief glance at the appearance of this edition will reveal our somewhat unusual use of language and scripts, and so we would like to explain how we have used diacritics and scripts to provide what we believe to be the best presentation of the languages related to Tibetan studies. Some of our work has also gone beyond the level of representation and into the actual text.

Readers who can compare the English-Language essays with their German versions, especially those from the European contributors, will no doubt notice great stylistic and rhetorical differences. English-language rhetoric, particularly the styles emerging in American academic circles, generally values concision and directness, whereas European rhetorical styles often place more emphasis on creating a lofty level of discourse that reflects a concern with erudition, "objectivity," and authority. Hence European writing often features more involved sentence structure, passive voice, and impersonal expressions than the English reader is accustomed to. Although the German-to-English translations are not our own, we nonetheless believe in naturalness over literalness: whereas in other genres, such as literature, a translation may try to convey the author's "style," in a more technical text such as this one, we found that a careful, literal preservation of style impeded understanding. We have thus tried to make many of the essays more concise and direct without changing the overall meaning the authors intended.

We acknowledge that this is in part a value judgement, although it is not meant to valorize our way of doing things—Americans have certainly never been known to impose their will unilaterally on others. Nor is this to say that we have in any way tried to "dumb down" the text, but rather to think very carefully about how the English is used and when certain kinds of language improve or inhibit the flow or readers' understanding. We would like to thank the non-native speakers who contributed essays for their patience and understanding in working with us to bring their texts in line with English-language readers' expectations.

Recent developments in technology have made it much easier to include non-Roman text in documents, and we have therefore supplied the Tibetan script for proper nouns and other words. We made use of Jskad, available online from the University of Virginia's Tibetan and Himalayan Digital Library (THDL). We have also included Chinese and Japanese in a few cases, although we could not provide the Mongolian. Representations of Mongolian remain a weak point—we do not yet have the expertise to include Mongolian text in either the traditional script or Cyrillic-based alphabet. While we have tried to choose only one system of transliterating Mongolian and use it consistently, there may prove to be lapses.

Similarly, for names and words from the Subcontinent, we have tried to provide all the correct diacritics. This seemed preferable to including only Devanāgari when there are after all myriad scripts in use in the Subcontinent. Anyone who has tried to take a Roman transliterations to search in a South Asian-language dictionary or other reference source can attest to the annoyances that non-technical spellings bring. We have also inserted the Sanskrit terms for many technical words for ease of reference—many of the originals provided only English translations of the *mudrā*, for example. Some may argue that we have gone too far in spelling place names following their representations in South Asian scripts, such as for Kalkattā "Calcutta," but we are in effect extending the principle by which Peking has become "Beijing" and Bombay "Mumbai."

We have tried to give three representations of Tibetan names and words—a romanization, a Wylie transliteration, and the Tibetan script itself. The Wylie and Tibetan script are basically the same, with the Wylie representing with Roman letters every part of a Tibetan syllable. We have erred on the side of caution, including more consonant than fewer. The romanization is more or less a representation of central Tibetan pronunciation, although we've broken with some of the conventions, especially in representing final stop sounds. Although used in Wylie, for a romanization we have found spellings such as "Gelug" or "Drub" less satisfactory than "Geluk" and "Drup." We are thinking not in terms of *English* phonology per se as much as a phonetic representation using the Roman alphabet, and so presenting the final Tibetan sounds as –g or –b is misleading because these sounds are not in fact voiced. For the same reasons, we have tried to use "h" only to indicate aspiration so that for example "cen" rather than "chen" represents Tibetan graphic CAN.

We could not, however, be entirely systematic. While most varieties of Tibetan share a common writing system and spellings, pronunciation varies widely across regions. Furthermore, certain spellings have become established and may prove less recognizable or confusing in a technically more correct version, such as "trülku" for "tülku," or "Trashi Lhünpo" for "Tashilhünpo."

Even if there is not sufficient demand for us to bring out a second edition of this volume, we would nevertheless value having corrections for use in other later projects. We would appreciate input from our readers. Our editors are not professional Tibetologists, Indologists, or Sanskritists. We have made a sincere effort, given the time restrictions, in order to make the text useful for many kinds of readers.

Patrick A. McCormick
Shane Suvikapakornkul
Editors

Serindia Publications
Chicago

ADDITIONAL PLATE DESCRIPTIONS

Text by Martin Brauen, unless otherwise stated.

6

Inscription:
Above all sources of needs and desires and fulfilling hopes of sentient beings
Chief of two-legged ones, depth of all good qualities, guide of gods and humans,
to the Shakya King I prostrate respectfully with body, speech, and mind.

In the deep darkness of obscurity in the distant land of Tibet,
They lit the great lamp of the holy Dharma,
Placed all sentient beings of Tibet in happiness
To the emanated kings and ministers I respectfully prostrate.

Only Protector for us wandering beings in the Land of Snows,
The supreme Ngawang Lopsang Tenzin Gyatso,
He who possesses the Three Secret Powers,
May [your life] be indestructible, eternal and without end,
And, seated immutably on the *Vajra*-essence throne,
May you live for a hundred eons,
May you be blessed
And your aspirations be fulfilled.

All siblings and relatives of the three provinces are of the same family and lineage,
By the large wave from the depths of our hearts with
This golden wheel of both Dharma and governance
Make effort in means to attain complete independence [for Tibet].

Tibetan year 2103 (1976) Fire Dragon.

15

Karma Pakṣī resided at the court of the Mongolian ruler for long periods and there met Phakpa (see plate 2) and Khubilai Khan, who became emperor of China in 1279. We can recognize a red deity in the upper right, a rare form of Four-Armed Ṣaḍakṣarī Avalokiteśvara. In the center foreground we see *dharmapāla* Damchen Garwa Nakpo riding a billy goat, a dark blacksmith with a *vajra* hammer and bellows in his hands, originally a shamanic deity.
Source: Essen/Thingo 1989: I-88; II-249.

18

Almost identical statues in the Jaques Marchais Museum in Staten Island, New York and at the Ivolginsky Monastery, in Buryatia, Russia. This style of Tsongkhapa statue is called *jetsong pon gelek* [je tsong pon geleg], based of a rich trader in the 14th century named Pon Gelek, a disciple of Tsongkhapa who commissioned a statue of his master without hat and with his hands in *vitarkamudrā*. A form was then produced that Tsongkhapa himself consecrated. All clay statues made with this form had Tsongkhapa's

blessing and so very prized. According to Joachim Baader of Munich this statue was probably made using that same form. As this book went to press, the owner said he intended to present to the 14th Dalai Lama as a gift at the "Dalai Lamas" exhibit at the Ethnographic Museum of the University of Zürich.

21

Inscription below central figure: "Panchen Gendün, Lord over Death, the Omniscient, Protector with a thousand eyes...on the throne, a manifestation of sublimity and sympathy."

27

Both depictions of the Jokhang (left and right) clearly show the chapel of the standing Eleven-Headed Avalokiteśvara and that of Jobo, the crowned golden Buddha. Legend says this statue of Jobo began to speak once while the 2nd Dalai Lama and some monks were making sacrificial offerings and it predicted his next reincarnation. The inscription on the thangka says that this occurred a second time.
Source: Essen/Thingo 1989: I-92; I-265.

29

Giuseppe Tucci, who purchased this scroll in Luk in western Tibet, assumes that the people shown on the textile hanging from the front of the throne are members of the Guge family, who were ruling western Tibet when the 3rd Dalai Lama visited there. Precise dating is not possible because the Dalai Lama visited western Tibet in both 1555 and 1577. Most of the scenes have to do with the visions, dreams, and teachings of the Dalai Lama. The upper left shows how the 3rd Dalai Lama arrived in tuṣita heaven in a "limbo" condition between the death of his second incarnation and rebirth of his third incarnation. There he saw the Buddha Maitreya and from there went to other regions of paradise. We can see other well-known monasteries that the Dalai Lama visited: to the left probably Johkang, main temple of Lhasa, with Golden Jobo and Thousand-Armed Avalokiteśvara. In front on a wagon is a statue of Maitreya being carried through Lhasa during an annual procession.
Source: Rhie/Thurman 1991: 268–271, Nr. 97; Tucci 1949: 392–399.

34

Of excellent craftsmanship assembled from different cast parts, this icon depicts a high hierarch garbed in a rich monk's robe seated on a traditional yet opulent lotus pedestal with chased floral pattern. His right hand is in the *bhūmisparśamudrā* "earth-witness" with the left in *dhyānamudrā* "contemplation" while holding a turquoise-set *triratna* emblem. Together with the finely carved flower towering behind his right shoulder, the hierarch's attributes and *mudrās* manifest his status as a Buddha in person. His physical features exude an air of majesty and natural dignity worthy of a ruling hierarch while also appearing as an imposing saint and master. The simple but evocative iconographic repertoire of this statue holding a lotus stalk over the right shoulder is found on other Dalai Lama icons.

The inscription on the socle reads: "eleventh [statue] counted from left: Glorious Dharmarāja of Dechen (*Mahā-sukha)." With some hesitation, we can identify the figure as the Mongol-born 4th Dalai Lama whose epithet in full is Yönten Gyatso Dechen Chökyi Gyalpo [yon tan rgya mtsho bde chen chos kyi rgyal po dpal bzang po]. Linking and furnishing each succeeding Dalai Lama with a prestigious background as Indian Buddhist kings was part of their legitimation. In Geluk circles, this royal epithet identifies a Dalai Lama in the overall lineage of the Dalai Lama.
Text: Per K. Sørensen

41

The Potala occupies the center of this scroll, painted as a karchak [dkar chag] "pilgrim card." Below the Potala are the residence and work areas of Shö (Zhol) built as was the palace itself between 1645 and 1695 on Marpori [dmar po ri] "Red Hill" in Lhasa. According to tradition, from the earliest royal period of 7th–8th centuries, Mount Potalaka in South India was the residence of the Bodhisattva Avalokiteśvara, who reincarnated as the Dalai Lamas. The Dalai Lamas in turn came to live in the Potala, named after Mount Potalaka, until 1959. To the right above in the middle of a small lake we see the Lukhang [klu khang] "Temple of the Naga Kings" built under the 6th Dalai Lama; left between Marpori and *Cakpori* [lcags po ri] Iron Mountain is the great *Bargo Kaling* [bar sgo bka gling] gate, western portal to ancient Lhasa. The *doring* [rdo ring] stone obelisk of 763 that still exists today has been drawn topographically correctly in front of the wall surrounding Shö district. Its inscription records the Tibetan conquest of Chang'an (modern Xi'an), capital of Tang China. On both sides are pavilions for the *doring* to commemorate the victory of Chinese troops in Tibet over the Mongolian Dzungars (Jün Ghar) in 1721 and the Gorkhas of Nepāl in 1792. The large complex to the lower right is the Jokhang, main temple of Lhasa, surrounded by Barkor Road. Also included are the *dorings* engraved in Chinese and Tibetan with the peace agreement between Tibet and China from 821-822, and the willow tree said to have been planted by the Chinese bride of Songsten Gampo. The shrine above is Ramoche Temple originally meant for the statue of Jobo Śākyamuni later installed in the Jokhang. To the left, far from Lhasa, is Samye Monastery with its characteristic three-story central building, square surrounding wall, and four-cornered stūpas of varying colors. As typical for pilgrimages guides to Lhasa, the state monasteries of the Geluk can be recognized at the upper edge of the picture: to the left, Drepung, built 1416 and in front, the small oracle monastery of Nechung, Sera (1418) and Ganden (1409), and probably Tashilhünpo near Shigatse. The identity of the other smaller buildings is not clear because of the schematic representation. The Devanāgarī labels on the monuments indicate a Nepalese artist or patron, presumably from the Newā community in Lhasa. Since the four gold roofs on the Potala are attributed to the Fifth, Seventh, Eighth, and Ninth Dalai Lamas, this picture must have been done after 1815 and came to the West around 1912.
Text: Michael Henss

45

Ritual implements used in the initiation to a special ritual cycle centered around Lokeśvara/Avalokiteśvara. In 1656 the 5th Dalai Lama received an empowerment initiation from Lokeśvara while he was mediating before an image of the deity at the behest of the Nechung Oracle. Among the implements are the ritual master's throne (upper middle), several *vajras*, vases, a *maṇḍala* in the center, a hat (left), skull dishes with special ingredients, torma offerings, etc.

Source: Karmay 1988.

47

Dating based on Rhie & Thurman, 1999. Noteworthy is that the title, "Demo Tülku," provides evidence that this thangka is almost a hundred years older than previously assumed. Based on its wording, it appears that the 5th Dalai Lama personally wrote the inscription along the left and right edges appears as a prayer for Demo Tülku's long life. The 5th Dalai Lama himself has been painted in to the main figure as a miniature icon, like an ānahaṭa or "heart cakra." The small images of Atiśa and Padmasambhava to the sides of the central Buddha Vajradhara along the upper edge of the picture represent the Geluk and Nyingma traditions, in both of which the 5th Dalai Lama practiced. Promising happiness and long life for the Dalai Lama upon taking office, the eight auspicious symbols, the ten sacrificial female deities symbolizing the senses of perception, and six of the seven jewels of the Cakravartin "enlightened ruler" are on the throne. The wheel of the seven jewels against the outer edge illustrates the precision with which this portrait was thought through, with its luxuriant aureole otherwise reserved for a Buddha or the highest hierarchs. This is meant to show the Dalai Lama as eternally present in time and space, rather than as having only the temporal power of the regents.

Text: Michael Henss

Source: Rhie/Thurman 1999: Nr. 133.

51

This monumental figure was brought to Sweden in the 1930s by Sven Hedin. It comes from a temple in Chahar, Inner Mongolia. Chahar became renowned after the 3rd Dalai Lama visited it in 1578.

Source: Rhie/Thurman 1991: 144–145.

56

This statue is thought to be of the regent Sanggye Gyatso. Julia Elikhina of Hermitage Museum has questioned this attribution and argues the portrait-like features point to the 5th Dalai Lama.

59

Inscription: "May Padmasambhava's rays from the sun of sympathy let the 1000-leafed lotus of all that is useful and helpful to Ngawang Sherap bloom. And may this light always shine without leaving him, in the center of his heart, to his advantage in this life and in all others. This was composed by the monk of Zahor [one of many names for the 5th Dalai Lama].

This statue of Zinon Zepartsal [zil gnon bzad pa rtsal], my primary lama and the most outstanding of all Jinas [epithet for the Buddha], contains hair and teeth, etc. from him personally, according to the inventory, instead of internal relics. This statue that satisfies wishes and needs was made as a symbol of the fervor of Ngawang Sherap, the master of offerings."

Ngawang Sherap commissioned this figure during the lifetime of the "Great Fifth." Sherap was responsible for sacrificial ceremonies and apparently used the figure as a personal reliquary or an object of veneration—probably on his own altar—and on trips as a "travel icon." The fact that

there is a *phurbu* "ritual dagger" in the Dalai Lama's belt, a ritual object characteristic of Nyingma monks, shows how the 5th Dalai Lama was connected with Nyingma teachings.

Source: MacDonald 1977.

60

Inscription: "Ngagi Wangchuk [the 5th Dalai Lama]. May the family and the descendants of the donor Ngödrup...achieve their desired goals and finally arrive at the highest state."

Source: Rhie/Thurman 1991: 272–273.

61

In this decree the 5th Dalai Lama describes in detail how the office of the regent was introduced and who the first regents were. He also explains that for a long time he attempted to convince Sanggye Gyatso of the necessity of assuming the office, which he always declined. Now, however, the time had clearly come when he must assume the office. Everyone must obey the orders of the regent without hesitation or contradiction. Whatever he does, it is as if he, the 5th Dalai Lama, has done it.

Source: Richardson 1980a.

63

Monastic rules of conduct from Ganden Rapgyeling, one of thirty monasteries the 5th Dalai Lama founded. In summary they state that these rules were composed upon the request of the monks of the monastery. After a general introduction to the teachings of Buddhism and mention of the close cooperation between the 5th Dalai Lama and Gushri Khan, the Mongolian ruler was an emanation of Vajrapāṇi [sic], the text focuses on monastic discipline, including conditions for accepting of monks; his activities (studies and rites); discipline when participating in ceremonies (not to come late, sleep, make noise, but to wear proper clothes and stand up straight); behavior in the kitchen and when eating, during leisure time, and working in the fields; general correct behavior (not to tell tales, play with arrows and rocks, jump around, fight or argue, or drink alcohol). The edict also includes rules about the surrounding areas and the people living there—no one may be forced to work in or for the monastery, but the monastery does have a right to wood and grazing in the area. No animals may be hunted in the immediate vicinity, and monks and laity may not fight during major festivals. The text closes with the demand to "follow these rules that say what one must do and from what one must refrain."

64

In his secret autobiography, the 5th Dalai Lama describes his mystical experiences and the visions he had between his sixth birthday and 1680. This text exists only in handwritten format. His red thumb appears on forty-three pages to authorize the text. Corrections on small slips have been glued in or added in red ink. Several copies of the text are known to exist, for example in the Bibliothèque Nationale in Paris, inv. no: Tibétain 538, and a magnificent copy with numerous miniatures at the Musée Guimet, Paris: see plate 45).

Source: Grönbold 2005.

65

The manuscript from which these pages were taken concerns the Tsokdag ritual. Tsokdag, the Lord of Collecting Merit, is similar to the Hindu god Gaṇeśa and is close to Vaiśravaṇa, who grants riches and with whom we see on the first two pages. On the next pages are images of cakras and a simple *maṇḍala*, below them diverse forms of torma and two mongoose spouting jewels.

Source: Himalayas: 266–268, 295.

68

Translation:

[Title] Speech of the Sixth Dalai Lama Vajradhara at the order of Altan Khan in the great kingdom of the Mongols.

[Recipients] Sent to all sentient beings in all four points of the compass in the world in general; in particular to all district commissioners of Ngari Korsum [Mnga ris skor gsum], more particularly in Taklakkar, as well as to the monastic administrative officers, the civil and military leadership of Hor and Sok, and to elders and the damsa of village and nomad communities.

[Narrative]: Because Paldzin...together with his son always fulfilled his duties as a loyal subject, they have been provided successively with confirmation documents bearing the seal of the Dalai Lama regarding their claims of ownership to their lands, farmsteads, and retinue, according to which [documents] they have lived unchallenged down to the present. I herewith confirm these [rights and privileges].

[Disposition]: Accordingly, in the future also demands shall not be made, such as of unjust forced sale, barter, or transportation by horse; nor unjust threats and hindrances regarding their grazing, water rights, and pasture boundaries; nor new encumbrances in the form of taxes. [This has been] arranged so can dispose of their documents in an agreeable manner.

[Closing]: Granted, from the Potala Palace, on the ....day of ..... month in the Year of the Wood Monkey (1704-1705).

Translation: Hanna Schneider

73

When Italian Capuchin missionaries returned to Lhasa in 1741 for the third time after an absence of eight years, they brought with them two letters from Pope Clemens XII dated 1738 and addressed to the 7th Dalai Lama and Regent Pholhane in which the Pope demanded unlimited approval for Capuchin missionary activity. To the extent that it is possible to reconstruct, it appears that the Capuchin prepared the same text in Tibetan for the Dalai Lama and the regent. In his reply (not shown here), the regent agreed to the Pope's demands and permitted not only the propagation and dissemination of their religion but even promised to support the free exercise of the Capuchin's missionary activity. The Dalai Lama's reply differs considerably, not only in being a third of the length of Pholhane's, but most especially in content.

While the present text begins the same, with a salutation to the recipients and a description of the "white-headed lamas," it then diverges significantly from the original and does not go beyond general formulas. It mentions only that the Pope has sent the Capuchin to do good for all people and that they should not be hindered in their work. The Pope's demands are consistently avoided and not mentioned and thus it contains an implicit rejection of the religious freedom demanded. Apparently the Dalai Lama had recognized much more clearly than the regent had just how unpredicatable the demands of the Pope and the Capuchins were for religious and missionary freedom.

Text: Isrun Engelhardt

Peter Lindegger's translation of the most important passage of the decree:

The Fathers of Europe ... obeying from the heart their own royal representative, the Lama named Summo Pontifice; the latter [the Pope] has sent them to do good to show their love for all people. Since that is the case, may they, each of them, wherever they go or stay, move in order to bring the greatest aid where it can be of use, without meeting in any form whatsoever hostile attitudes or resistance obstructing them, and may their work bring blessings upon them.

Source: [Petech, Luciano], Two Privileges of Religious Freedom Granted by the Dalai Lama on Yellow Silk, in: Sotheby's London: The Library of Philip Robinson, Part II, The Chinese Collection, November 22, 1988, Nr. 140, pp. 126–128; Peter Lindegger (Ed.), Dokumente zur sogenannten Christenverfolgung vom Mai 1742 in Lhasa, Rikon 2001, pp. 11–12.

77

Almost identical thangkas are at the Victoria and Albert Museum, London (R.L. 484) and at the Museum der Kulturen, Basel (S. Essen & Thingo, 1989, II-269). The main inscription on the counterpart at the V&A states: "The amazing secret signified by seven months of [Tantric] conduct, of manifestly arising as illusory body [united with realisation of] clear light." Essen & Thingo believe this is a description from the secret biography of the 7th Dalai Lama, that is, an earlier hermit-like existence and his achievement of siddha status.

78

The symbols on the lotus blossoms to the left and right of his shoulders are a sword and a book which identify Qianlong as the reincarnation of the Bodhisattva Mañjuśrī. Michael Henss believes such pictures represent the imperial protection of Tibetan Buddhism and thus also the regions where it is at home.

Source: Henss 2001.

79

Lama Janggya Khutughtu Rölpe Dorje [lCangs skya rol pa'i rdo rje] was the second "Great Lama" of Beijing and an important personage at the Chinese court in the mid-18th century. For his sake, the Emperor Qianlong had his father's old residence in the compound of Yonghe Gong Temple renovated. The emperor later built a refuge for Rölpe Dorje, Puleyuan on Wutaishan Mountain, dedicated to Bodhisattva Mañjuśrī. Rölpe Dorje was not only a capable diplomat who acted as an intermediary between the imperial court, Tibet, and Mongolia, but a major scholar and translator as well.

Source: Béguin 1995: 443 ff.

81

To the left of the central figure, we see the 8th Dalai Lama and at the same level is the 1st Dalai Lama, while on the other side is the 2nd Dalai Lama. Beneath them we see the Third to the left, across from the Fourth. On the lowest row are the Fifth to the left, the Sixth on the far right across from him, the Seventh in the middle, the Ninth between him and the Fifth; and the Tenth between the Seventh and Sixth.

Inscription on the reverse:

In the great place of the great Lo[psang Drakpa's] fortunate teachings,

Who with the seven precious jewels transforms method and wisdom,

And places in the state of having the Eight Powers [of the fully enlightened] all beings wandering in saṃsāra,

To Jampel Gyatso [the 8th Dalai Lama], I respectfully prostrate.

This captivating thangka, meaningful to behold [=image of a Buddha], Whose body is the center surrounded by desire-realm gods

Variegated like Indra's Bow [=rainbow], with the five aspects of a rainbow's colors,

As a holy object of the minds of an assembly of knowledge holders,

Well placed by Larong Ngakram Thrinle Lekzang,

[Sera] Jetsa[wa] Ngakram Lopsang Jinpa and

Serkong Ngakram Tsülthrim Drakpa,

Through the virtue of its being commissioned and offered, May all three together quickly attain Buddhahood for the sake of all wandering beings.

83

The first article is a criticism of the way reincarnated monks used to be confirmed that was said to occur solely "on the basis of personal interests." Instead, according to the decree, the correct reincarnation must be found by drawing of lots. After the candidates have been found through careful search and divination to the four protectors of Buddhist teaching has confirmed their identities, their names and dates of birth must be written on ivory lots and these placed in an urn from China, whereupon after a longer procedure the lots decide. Furthermore, the Qing Amban has the same political authority as the Dalai Lama for important decisions. Top positions in the Tibetan government are to be presented to the Qing emperor for his acceptance. The decree also forbids the exploitation of peasants and family members of the Dalai and Panchen Lamas are not allowed to hold public office during the lifetime of their powerful kinsman.

93

Agvan Dorjiev presented this dharmacakra to Tsar Nicholas II when he led the Tibetan missions to Russia in 1900 and 1901. In December 1901 the cakra was brought to the Winter Palace and given a very prominent position there, which reflects the value the Tsar placed on it. There was originally a ribbon around the cakra that has since been lost.

98

No date, no precise information about the recipient. Possibilities include the kings Prithvī Bīr Bikram (r. 1881–1911), Tribhuvan Bīr Bikram (r. 1911–1955) or the Rānā minister who directed government affairs, Chandra Shamsher (in office 1901—1929). (Periods of rule from M.C. Regmi: Land Tenure and Taxation in Nepal, Kāṭhmāṇḍū 1978, S. 447).

Translation:

At the present time as well, the elements of your youthful golden body, having matured in the lap of the earth through the accumulation of merit is in good health, and you rest in the radiance shining from your good works that you perform for the well-being of your governmental leadership and your subjects: this is indeed good.

Here I, too, the Dalai Lama, am in good health, and live in the sincere effort to promote the Buddhist teachings and bring about the well-being of all sentient beings.

As was usual in the past, I have recently sent letters and official gifts to the King and the Minister [the Rānā regent?] so that the sincere and good relations between Nepāl and Tibet do not end. I have had Pūjāmegha offerings performed at the two great Chörten [Svayambhunāth and Bodhnāth] for the best seat [of government] situated between them. As a supplement, I have also commissioned and directed [those knowledgeable about medication] to produce and to give away medications [and medicinal herbs] for the well-being of sentient beings.

In regard to our activities, we should direct our attention to all that achieves the greatest possible harmony and the greatest possible mutual usefulness. May you also in the future pay attention to your youthful body, to [ensure] that our sincere relatonship is without hindrance.

It would be correct if... you would continuously have letters sent to me.

Given together with a khatak, Chinese Sycee [xiyin?] silver bullion, silk cloth with four ornaments, ceden cloth, bricks

of tea, a set of chopsticks and a coffer made of mango wood as an additional gift. [this letter], on the ...day of .....month. [Seal]

Translation: Hanna Schneider

103 a–c

The current owner, Joachim Baader, believes this is a statue of the 13th Dalai Lama based on several inquiries he made in Mongolia, where this piece originated. Yet various details contradict this, including the bump on the head pointing to Rölpe Dorje, the form of the mustache, and the pointed goatee.

105

Disgraces that the 13th Dalai Lama could not tolerate occasioned this decree, which is directed generally against "deviant" behavior of people who ignore the collective well-being and subvert the policies of the spiritual and secular government of the 13th Dalai Lama. This is also a catalogue of diverse offenses, including taxation that unjustly exceeds the usual extent; using transportation without payment; egotistical leaders who break the law and take human life; melting down religious objects of gold; exploitative collection of money; and killing wild animals. The 13th Dalai Lama also calls on everyone to perform religious deeds including fasting on certain days, reading holy texts, and restoring old temples.

Source: Richardson 1980a/1998c.

123

This statue is one of very few statues of the 14th Dalai Lama. It was commissioned by the Ethnographic Museum of the University of Zürich and was made by Rajesh Awale with Basu Shresta of Hangrib Handicrafts, Kāṭhmāṇḍū, Nepāl, and given to the Museum by the Swiss-Tibetan Friendship Society.

130

This mural by Amdo Jampa (1911–2002), painted in 1955–1956, is a good example of a representation of the complete conquest of the three regions of Kham, Amdo and central Tibet. In the center is the fifteen-year-old Dalai Lama and Thupten Phala, his head treasurer, standing in front of him.

We can see to the left eight ministers on the top row, from right to left: Tenpa Jamyang, Ngabö Ngawang Jigme, Lehu Shar [sNe'u shar] Thupten Tharpa, Surkhang Wangchen Delei, Gadrang [dga brang]; in the second row: Shezur [bshad zur] Gyurme Topgye, an unknown person, Samdrup Phodrang?, Rakhashar Phüntshok Rapgye, the monk-minister Rampa Thupten Künkhen, and with the long beard, the abbot of the Dalai Lama's monk servants, Zimpön Khenpo. Below to the left are three higher officials in charge of finances, to the left, Namseling; to the right, Shukhüpa, and in the foreground, Tsoköpa. Below them are representatives of various countries, including Sikkim, Nepāl, Bhūtān, and Great Britain, as well as two Muslim traders in white turban and black cap. On the right side in the uppermost row are family members: the mother of the Dalai Lama, Sönam Tshomo, brothers Thupten Jikme Norbu and Gyalo Thöndrup; below them three higher monk officials and in the center foreground Lopsang Samten, another brother in monk's clothing. On the lowest level to the right of Thupten Phala are several monk officials. The figures shown did not all live at the same time, and several were already dead when the painting was made, including the two former regents Taktra Rinpoche in the far upper left and Reting Rinpoche in the far upper right. Below are the two subsequent principal teachers Ling Rinpoche to the left and Trijang Rinpoche to the right, both of whom were alive when the painting was done. The Dalai Lama himself wrote about the day he assumed power that "it was a particularly solemn event and the entire government took part, each in their best and most colorful garments, and the various foreign representatives who lived in Lhasa…during the ceremony I was given the Golden Wheel symbolizing the transfer of temporal power…when the ceremony was finally over, I was the undisputed head of six million defenseless Tibetans." (Dalai Lama 1990: 66 ff.) (Photomontage by Andreas Brodbeck of several photos, including Michael Henss, Corneille Jest, and Martin Brauen; our thanks to Corneille Jest, Boulogne, and Hugh Richardson for information on the various figures.).

200

The figures arranged around the 1st Panchen Lama are the three Thrichen ['khri chen] of Ganden Monastery in the upper left; the group of Atiśa (center), a disciple of Tsongkhapa (left), and the 10th Dalai Lama; four saints in four corners, namely Go Lotsāwa in the upper left, Abhayākaragupta, with snake, Sakya Paṇḍita in the lower left, and Yöntön Dorjephel of the Nyingma School known for his vision of Mahākāla and his mastery of the Kālacakra system. In the lowest register are three aspects of the Geluk protective deity, Dharmarāja Yama in his outer, inner, and secret aspects.

210

This painting represents an aspect of Mahākāla as protector of the Geluk School, indicated by the portrait of the 7th Dalai Lama surrounded by two Geluk monks in the upper register of the painting. At center, Black Mahākāla, in Tibetan Yeshe Gönpo Chakdruk [ye shes mgon po phyag drug] "Six-Armed Mahākāla of Wisdom," presides over his four ministers. Yeshe Gönpo has three eyes, a fierce expression, is crowned with five skulls, and is the 2nd Dalai Lama's family protective deity. This iconography originated in a vision an Indian hermit had in a cemetery, which was then transmitted to Chungpo Naljor [khyung po rnal 'byor], one of the main teachers of the 2nd Dalai Lama's ancestors. The Second eventually transmitted his teachings within the Geluk School. Yeshe Gönpo has a small *vajra* in his hair as a visual reminder of Buddha Akṣobhya, of whom he is a wrathful aspect. On the right, his hands clasp a *driguk* [gri gug] curved knife, a *ḍamaru* drum, and a crown of skulls, while his left hands hold a skull cup, a noose, and a small trident. He wears a tiger-skin dhoti and an elephant skin around his shoulders. Although he frequently wears a garland of fifty human skulls as a long necklace, instead he is here wearing gold chains. He is trampling on Gaṇeśa, symbolizing the triumph of Buddhism over Hindu deities. At the upper left is the dark red Ṭakkirāja holding a *ḍamaru* in his raised hand and a skull cup of offerings near his heart as he dances wildly. In the upper right is black Jinamitra, also holding a *ḍamaru* and skull cup. In the lower left, Zhingkyong [Zhing skyong] (Skt. Kṣetrapāla) "protector of the cemetery field" is the black deity with red hair riding a black bear and raising a skull cup towards Mahākāla. In the lower right corner riding a horse is Trakshe, also called Dügön Chenpo "Great Protector against Dü demons," dressed in flowing robes of silk. He holds a lance with which he appears to be piercing a demon beneath him.
Text: Amy Heller

211

In the Buddhist pantheon Vaiśravaṇa (Tib. Namse Serchen [rnam sras ser chen]) is the god of wealth and prosperity, but is also guardian of the northern direction and so is wearing armor as a defender of Buddhism. Here he is represented as Great Yellow Vaiśravaṇa, is "yellow like pure gold, radiating with the brilliance of a hundred thousand rising suns", and so crowned and adorned with gold jewelry and brocade silks. Beneath an assembly of illustrious Geluk monks and lamas, he sits on a glacier lion with dark turquoise mane adorned with jewels as befitting the mount of the lord of wealth. Here Vaiśravaṇa is holding a parasol of multi-col-

ored flags in his right hand, while in his left hand is a mongoose spouting jewels which fall nto the bowl of offerings placed in front of the lotus pedestal. Eight riders dressed in armor form Vaiśravaṇa's entourage and are called the "Eight Horsemasters." This depiction of Vaiśravaṇa emphasizes the prosperity and auspicious benefits that come from worshipping him.
Text: Amy Heller

213

This thangka shows only the attributes of Palden Lhamo. There are so many different weapons and auspicious offerings that it is almost impossible to determine which aspect of Lhamo is depicted, although it is certain that the thangka is for Lhamo because the horse in the center has the distinctive dice, flayed skins for saddle blanket, and an eye in its flank emblematic of Lhamo's mount, whether horse or mule. Numerous fantastic creatures surround the horse, including a quadruped with no fewer than twenty heads emerging from one very thick neck, lions, tigers, leopards, elephants, boars, jackals, and so many others all in homage to Lhamo. There are also many sorts of offering bowls, some containing blood and yoghurt, and elaborate torma cakes inside silver bowls and offerings of the five senses in skull cups.

We can imagine Lhamo herself above the horse from her crown of skulls and the bone ornaments of her necklaces and girdle. She is near skins of various animals and humans and has a scorpion-handled sword on the right side of her "phantom" body. This tells us she wields the scorpion sword with her right hand, which means that this aspect of Lhamo may be her as Kāmarūpa Lhamo, Powerful Goddess of the Land of Desires, in Tibetan Düsolma Dökham Wangchukma [dud sol ma 'dod khams dbang phyug ma]. Lhamo also holds the scorpion sword in her capacity as consort of Mahākāla, Lord of Time. It however seems more likely that here is not a consort but the principal deity. This is all the more likely from the presence of her two principal assistants, whose phantom bodies are depicted as is Lhamo's body, with the crown of skulls and the necklaces. These two may be Siṃhavaktra with a lion's head, and Makaravaktra, with the head of a makara sea-monster. The upper register of this painting is draped with numerous skins and garlands. Birds and flayed animal and human skins add to the ghoulish atmosphere of this painting.
Text: Amy Heller

214

This thangka was made as an offering for the funerary *chörten* (stūpa) of the 5th Dalai Lama's cousin, Paksam Wangpo [dPag bsam dbang po] (1593-1641), probably for his one year commemoration ceremony in 1642.
At that time the 5th Dalai Lama assumed power in Tibet. Since the thangka represents Lhamo, an important guardian of the Fifth, its creation was possibly linked with him. The 5th Dalai Lama was born in 1617 as the son of the governor of Chonggye. His cousin was also a scion of an influential family in the region and was himself a hierarch of the Kargyu School. Unfortunately, there are no inscriptions to give the names of the two lamas in the upper register. At center of the upper register is probably represented the *mahāsiddha* aspect of Padmasambhava, in Tibetan Nyima Öser "ray of light." In the center of the painting, we see the black Lhamo seated on the back of her mule in the midst of a sea of swirling crimson blood. She has four arms holding a flaming sword with scorpion handle, a trident, and a skull cup full of blood as well as a *phurbu* dagger with peacock feather plumes. Her three-eyed face is ferocious and grimacing as she chews on a small cadaver. She is adorned with various animal skins and bone jewelry. The sun and moon disk form her navel. Twenty ferocious attendants surround her, some with heads of birds, others with the head of a lion or a bear. Many are riding horses, yaks, or tigers, and hold a human

heart or skull cup. The entire scene is one of frenzy in the flames around Lhamo riding in the sea of blood.
Text: Amy Heller
Source: Essen/Thingo 1989.

216

In the center of the flag is the syllable "KYE" used in rituals to call the deity to pay attention and obey his promise to serve as protector of Buddhism. The syllable has been used for its graphic value, to represent the deity's body. Several of the attributes which are most associated with him surround the "body." At first when the 2nd Dalai Lama composed rituals for Bektse, Bektse held a flaming sword, a heart, and lungs of a defeated enemy, which we see in the center, in the middle of the letters. At left is a scorpion-handled sword. Then in 1672 the 5th Dalai Lama had a vision of Padmasambhava in which he mandated that Bektse be protector for the Dalai Lama. In his wrathful aspect, Padmasambhava wields a scorpion as his emblem, and so as his emissary, Bektse, acquires this visual reminder of Padmasambhava in his iconography. We also see rhinocerous horns, stylized earrings, round jewels and lingots, all auspicious symbols that show the benefits which Bektse's faithful protection bring.
Text: Amy Heller

218

This painting represents the protective deity Bektse as a red guardian wearing infallible armor, called *bektse*, which has given his most common name. He is also known as *Sokdak Marpo* [srog bdag dmar po] "Great Red Master of Vitality." Here he is depicted as protector of the Geluk School, as the illustrious Geluk teachers in the upper register evidence: Jetsünpa [rje btsun pa], Sera Jetsünpa [Se ra rje btsun pa]; to the left of the Buddha and right are the 2nd Dalai Lama Gendün Gyatso and the 3rd Dalai Lama Sönam Gyatso.

The 2nd Dalai Lama composed several rituals for Bektse describing his iconography precisely: wearing full armor, holding a sword in his right hand, holding a heart and lungs against his heart and brought towards his mouth, and a lance in the crook of his arm to crush obstacle-creating deities. We see here that Bektse's sword has a scorpion handle, which the 2nd Dalai Lama did not describe in the rituals he wrote around 1485, but which later became especially associated with Bektse after the Fifth had visions.

In this thangka to the left of Bektse is his dark red male attendant, also dressed in armor, holding a lance and blue noose while riding on a black jackal. To the right of Bektse is his sister Rikpe Lhamo Dongmarma [rig pa'i lha mo gdong dmar ma] "Red-Faced Black Goddess of Knowledge" wielding a long knife in her right hand and a *phurbu* in her left as she rides naked on a female brown bear holding a small human cadaver in her mouth. On the right border we also see a curious palace of skulls, thought to be Bektse's residence. At left a stream of pelting raindrops which generate waterfalls and rivers emerges from a cloud with a gruesome face. The 2nd Dalai Lama and his ancestors were renowned as rainmakers, and during his lifetime Bektse was invoked to save their region from a particularly dreadful drought. In front of Bektse is a large skull filled with offerings of the five senses and a black flag. Eight gyrating black men dressed in bone ornaments, flayed human skins, and animals pelts are dancing wildly and carry swords or knives in their right hands. These are the "Eight Knifeholders," Bektse's minor assistants.
Text: Amy Heller

219

According to the inscription at the bottom, this thangka represents the great *dharmapāla*, the minister Dorje Drakden [rDo rje grags ldan] and was formerly the principal thangka in his chapel at Kumbum Monastery in eastern Tibet. In the center is therefore Dorje Drakden, represented as a fierce deity with a breast-plate, holding a long-handled *vajra* club and noose in his right hand, bringing a heart and lungs to his mouth with his left hand while riding a black horse in a sea of flames. This iconography is unusual; other representations of Dorje Drakden portray him as a young monk (see plate 225) or as a riding warrior with noose. Usually he is depicted with a noose and red banner, wearing armor and helmet. Here however, it is particularly significant that he holds the heart and lungs to his mouth, for this is a gesture which Bektse usually makes. In the lower register is Pehar at center following his usual iconography with six arms riding a snow lion, with two additional emanations, whose precise identification remains elusive, flanking him.

At the center of the upper register is a very esoteric form of Hayagriva as the wrathful Tamdrin Yangsang [rta mgrin g.yang gsang]. Two lamas are beside him: at right we may tentatively identify the 5th Dalai Lama, his hands in the *vitarkamudrā* and *dharmacakramudrā*; at left, the lama holding the skull cup and vajra is probably an aspect of Padmasambhava. We propose these identifications because this painting apparently represents a special vision the 5th Dalai Lama had in 1672, in which he saw himself in this aspect of Hayagriva in discussion with Padmasambhava, who emanated the Bektse and reassigned to protect the 5th Dalai Lama through his emanations including Dorje Drakden. See S. Karmay 1988: 62 for a summary of this vision. Heller makes a detailed analysis of this vision (no date). Here the depiction amalgamates Dorje Drakden with the iconographic characteristics of Bektse.

Text: Amy Heller

223

In the center of this painting is a depiction of Pehar, one of the most important Tibetan protective deities, wearing a wide-brimmed yellow hat with a small skull over his three heads with a black and a red flanking the central white head. The expression on all three faces is ferocious, which the weapons he holds to wage war against the enemies of the Dharma reflect. In his upper right hand he holds an elephant goad, in his lower right a black sword with a gold *vajra* handle and gold tip, and in his middle right the tip of an arrow. In his upper left hand, he holds a knife with long black blade, in the middle left hand the bow in which is positioned an arrow, and in the lower left a small, thin stick. He wears in loose garments, a deep blue shirt with broad collar, white and green scarves, and over the center of his chest a circular emblem which forms a breast plate. Ritual descriptions of Pehar describe him as wearing armor, but this is not visible here except for the circular breast plate. He is also wearing green trousers and calf-high boots that tie around the top. He is riding a white lion with turqoise mane, considered to be the sacred Lion of the Glaciers.

Pehar's four principal emanations surround him, each responsible for a cardinal points. Pehar himself is guardian of the North. Shing Jacan "Great Wooden Bird" is "minister" of the South, his blue body draped in a tiger skin with serpent and bone ornaments, and is riding a horse and carrying a long-handled axe and a noose. Dralha [dgra lha] "Protector Against Enemies" is minister of the West, his red body dressed in clothing and armor similar to Pehar as he rides a long-eared mule and carries a stick and a spear. In the upper left corner is the minister of the Center, Gyajin "Great Brightness," his dark brown body in armor and carries a knife and noose while riding a white elephant. In the upper right corner is the minister of the East, Mönbu Putra "Boy of the Mön Area," who has a black body and holds a golden *vajra* and a lance. According to his ritual description, he ususally rides a bear, but here is mounted on a white lion similar to Pehar's.

In the center of the upper register appears to be a human figure, wearing a paṇḍita hat and monastic garments. He holds a skull cup bowl in his lap and raises a golden vajra in his right hand. This figure is probably Padmasambhava, the teacher said to have introduced Tantric Buddhism to Tibet, and who is traditionally believed to have tamed Pehar and entrusted him with the responsibility to protect the Buddhist teachings. While Padmasambhava has several different iconographic representations, here he is depicted as an Indian teacher.

Text: Amy Heller

225

This painting presents one of many variations on Geluk iconography for Pehar. At the center is Gyajin, Pehar's minister. He rides an elephant and holds a noose and a knife, and is dressed in silk scarves, animal skins and a loose brocade coat. His assistants surround him: two warriors in armor, one riding a tiger, the other a horse, and a young woman holding a conch shell and a long-handled spear. Padmasambhava asked Pehar and his ministers to protect Samye Monastery. Thus Padmasambhava is shown in the center of the upper register in his most typical iconography. Pehar is beside Padmasambhava, riding the white lion, recognizable with his six arms with bow and arrow in the central pair, and his characteristic white body. A young woman holding conch shell, and a monk, and a warrior surround Pehar. On the other side of Padmasambhava, the minister riding a horse is Dralha accompanied by the young woman, a warrior in armor, a lama whose hair stands on end, and his most illustrious attendant, Dorje Drakden in a monks robe of red silk, who looks as if he were a young monk mounted on a camel. (See plate 219 for a different iconography for Dorje Drakden.)

According to ritual descriptions, the deity to the right in the lower register is Shing Jacan, black in color and riding on a horse. However, the painter has chosen to represent him on a fabulous creature ressembling a giant elongated snail at variance with the other depictions. This may be linked to Shing Jacan's alternate name, as Luwang [klu dbang] "Great Nāga" (Nebesky: 131). In the left corner, there is another slight variation: the black Mönbu Putra, who is riding a lion and accompanied by a young woman, a young monk who has conquered all passions, and his own minister, should be depicted as riding naked on horseback and have only one eye and a snake turban. Yet here the artists have painted him with two eyes. These variations represent different ritual traditions and are perfectly orthodox.

Text: Amy Heller

226

Protective Deities in the lower register:
This thangka represents the Buddha with his hands in the *vitarkamudrā* surrounded by monks and lamas of the Geluk School. In front of him is a small table of offerings of with two snow lions and stylized earrings. In the lower left corner is Yama as Dharmarāja, with a black body and buffalo head, mounted on a bull, and waving his characteristic stick. Beside him on the bull is his sister Yami (also known as Yamunā). Beneath them is a large skull cup with offerings of the five senses.

Bektse sits on a lotus cushion in the midst of flames and tramples on obstacle demons represented with human and horse cadavers. Red Bektse here wears copper armor and boots, and on his head a crown of five skulls instead of a helmet. He waves a scorpion-handled sword with his right hand, brings a heart and lungs to his mouth, and grasps a lance with a victory banner in the crook of his arm. He would wave this lance in battle to show the victory of the Buddhist teachings.

Dorje Drakden has been here depicted as a wrathful warrior wearing armor and an elaborate helmet with banners. He carries a lance with victory in his right hand and a red noose in the outstretched left, and is also trampling cadavers of obstacle demons. In this aspect, Drakden is the oracle deity of the Dalai Lama lineage.

At the far right is depicted Palden Lhamo riding her mule with the eye in the flank. She raises a club with her right hand and holds a skull cup in her left and chews a small human cadaver. She is draped in scarves and bone ornaments and wears a five-skull crown and gold earrings. In her hair is a crescent moon with rising flames. If her midriff were more visible, we would see a disc of the sun.

Text: (partly after) Amy Heller

277

Translation:
A letter from the Dalai Lama: To the best Lönchen Bell, Political Officer in Sikkim.

You who are rich in knowledge, endowed with the high regard of the government of the great British empire, have always provided the Tibetan government with your support from the time the peace agreement was concluded, and otherwise in all matters according to the saying, "water is the friend of rain." Based on this fact, you have now been given the title of Commander of His Majesty's Government by the British Emperor in recognition of your services.

I am also extraordinarily happy about this. I have also recently days received with joy your *khatak* decorated with auspicious symbols...May we also in the future maintain our political [connection] with a view to the well-being of diplomatic relations between England and Tibet.

[Sent], together with a *khatak* of best quality, on the auspicious 9th day of the 12th month in the Year of the Wood-Tiger (early 1915) of the Tibetan calendar."

Translation: Hanna Schneider

289

In the upper left is the Panchen Lama Sönam Chökkyi Langpo [bSod nams phyogs kyi glang po] (1439–1504), teacher of Gendün Gyatso and abbot of Tashilhünpo, and below a smaller figure of Tsongkhapa. In the upper right is Cakrasaṃvara, while below is Palden Lhamo as Lhamo Makzorma [Lha mo dmag zor ma], who is connected with the 2nd Dalai Lama's visions at the oracle lake, Chökhorgyal. We also see Red Bektse and Dorje Drolö, an angry manifestation of Padmasambhava. To the left is part of Drepung Monastery of Ganden Phodrang, which the 2nd Dalai Lama built in 1517 as the Geluk hierarchs' residence until they moved to the Potala.

Text: Michael Henss

290

In the upper left is the Panchen Lama Sönam Drakpa [pa chen bsod nams grags pa] (1478-1554), the 2nd Dalai Lama's most important disciple, fifteenth occupant of the Ganden throne and main teacher of Sönam Gyatso, who initiated him in the Tantric rituals of Guhyasamāja, presumably represented by Yapyum in six-armed form resting on a lion in the upper right.

Below is Shinje Chökyi Gyelpo [gshin rje chos kyi rgyal po], the Dharmarāja Yama, so important to the Geluk School since the time of Tsongkhapa, with his Tantric companion Yami (also called Cāmuṇḍi). In the lower left riding a mule is Sethrapcan, a form of the national protective deity Pehar and special protector of one of the two high-ranking Geluk academies of Ganden Monastery; in the middle, the red

Chögyal Shinje Sangdrup [chos rgyal gshin rje gsang sgrub]
"Guhyasādhana Yamarāja" on a bull; and to the right, the
Mongol prince Altan Khan, who in 1578 gave Sönam Gyatso
the title "Dalai Lama." As is generally the case in such pictures, the monastery buildings on the right are represented
schematically; they could be from Kumbum in Amdo that
was built during Sönam Gyatso's journey to Mongolia. The
Tibetan inscription on the lower edge attests a reverence for
the 3rd Dalai Lama and includes a wish for the long life of
lama Gendün Tashi, presumably the donor of this thangka.
Text: Michael Henss

291

Upper left is the Tibetan teacher of the Dalai Lama Yönten
Gyatso, descendant in a princely Mongolian line who came
to Lhasa in 1602; the 1st Panchen Lama Lopsan Chökyi Gyaltsen (1570–1662). Below is Six-Armed Mahākāla. In the upper
right is buffalo-headed Yidam Bhairava Yapyum. Below is
the most common form of the Dharmapāla Yama, "Lord of
External Practices" or protector against external dangers as
well as lord of death and judge of souls at the gates of hell,
with Yami standing on a bull and holding a skull-shaped
bone club. On the left edge of the picture is Sera Monastery,
recognizable from the divided groups of buildings, Sera Je on
the left and Tsokchen main assembly hall to the right.
Text: Michael Henss

293

Upper left is the Red Vajrayoginī Dorje Neljorma [rDo rje rnal
'byor ma] to the left, probably the 1st or possibly 4th Panchen
Lama and teacher of the Great Fifth, Lopsang Chökyi Gyaltsen (1570-1662). In the round aureole is Phakpa Lokeśvara,
reborn as the 5th Dalai Lama and whose statue is still
revered today as the holiest image in the Potala, depicted at
the right. Lower left is Jikme Zhelcik ['jigs med zhal gcig] a
horrifying manifestation of Śiva manifestation. To the right
is probably Khubilai Khan, also considered a reincarnation
of a bodhisattva, and his religious mentor Phakpa, whose
concept of the "patron-spiritual teachers" anticipated the
theocracy the 5th Dalai Lama established. Thus the 5th Dalai
Lama is the first to be represented as a *cakravartin*, a "universal ruler" in religious and temporal realms, with a *cakra*
in his hand alluding to the Buddha.
Text: Michael Henss

294

Upper left, the 5th Panchen Lama Lopsang Yeshe (1663–1737),
who taught Tsangyang Gyatso in 1697 and who ordained
him during the year of his enthronement as Dalai Lama;
below, the red Vajrayoginī Dorje Neljorma, and upper right,
the red *ḍākinī* Rikjema [rig byed ma]. Below is the protective
deity Bektse. The fact that there are no images of a monastery is striking when compared with representations of
other Dalai Lamas. This painting is in the most common
style of depictions of the 6th Dalai Lama and is probably
related to his biography.
Text: Michael Henss

295

In the upper center, Tsongkhapa and his two primary dis-
ciples. Left is Vajrabhairava Yapyum, an especially important
Geluk deity, and to the right is White Tārā. Below are Yama,
Palden Lhamo, Vaiśravaṇa. In contrast to scrolls of previous
Dalai Lamas, all known thangka paintings of the 7th Dalai
Lama show him in frontal pose. Therefore this thangka, the
last chronologically, was the central image of the entire
series painted either during the 7th Dalai Lama's lifetime or
shortly after his death.
Text: Michael Henss

Ahmad, Zahiruddin, 1970: *Sino-Tibetan Relations in the Seventeenth Century*, Rome, pp. 108–145.

Ahmad, Zahiruddin, 1995: *A History of Tibet by the Fifth Dalai Lama of Tibet*, Bloomington.

Ahmad, Zahiruddin (Trans.), 1999: *Life of the Fifth Dalai Lama*, Vol. IV, Teil I, New Delhi.

Akester, Matthew, 2001: The 'Vajra temple' of gTer ston Zhig po gling pa and the politics of flood control in 16th century lHa sa, in: *The Tibet Journal*, Vol. XXVI, Nr. 1, Spring 2001, pp. 3–24.

Alphabetum Tibetanum: see Giorgi, Antonio Agostino.

Archives of the Tibet Autonomous Region, 1995: *A Collection of Historical Archives of Tibet, compiled by the Archives of the Tibet Autonomous Region*, Beijing.

Aris, Michael, 1989: *Hidden Treasures and Secret Lives, a study of Pemalingpa (1450–1521) and the Sixth Dalai Lama (1683–1706)*, London.

Art of Tibet, selected articles from Orientations 1981–1997, Hong Kong 1998.

Baker, Ian A., 2000: *Der geheime Tempel von Tibet, eine mystische Reise in die Welt des Tantra*, München.

Barks, Coleman (Trans.), 1992: *Stallion on a frozen lake, love songs of the Sixth Dalai Lama*, Athens (USA).

Barraux, Roland, 1995: *Die Geschichte der Dalai Lamas*, Frechen.

Bauer, Manuel, 2005: *Unterwegs für den Frieden*, München.

Bazin, Nathalie (Ed.), 2002: *Rituels Tibétains: visions secrètes du Ve Dalaï Lama*, Paris.

Béguin, Gilles, 1990: *Catalogue de la donation Lionel Fournier*, Paris.

Béguin, Gilles, 1995: *Les peintures du Bouddhisme Tibétain*, Paris.

Bell, Charles, 1924: The Dalai Lama: Lhasa, 1921, in: *The Journal of the Central Asian Society*, XI (1), 1924, pp. 36–50.

Bell, Charles, 1987 (1946): *Portrait of the Dalai Lama*, London.

Bell, Charles, 1992 (1928): *Religion of Tibet*, New Delhi.

Beranek, August, 1942: *Mannerheim*, Berlin.

Berger, Patricia, 2003a: Lineages of form, Buddhist portraiture in the Manchu Court, in: *The Tibet Journal*, Vol. 28, Nr. 1/2, pp. 109–146.

Berger, Patricia, 2003b: *Empire of Emptiness*, Honolulu.

Bernard, Theos, 1939: *Penthouse of the Gods, A pilgrimage into the Heart of Tibet and the Sacred City of Lhasa*, New York.

Bhadra Ratna Bajracharya, (1992): *Bahadur Shah, the Regent of Nepal (1785–1794 A.D.)*, New Delhi.

Bod kyi thang ka [Tibetan Thangkas], Beijing 1985.

Bogle, George, 1984: *Im Land der lebenden Buddhas, Entdeckungsreise in das verschlossene Tibet 1774–1775*, Stuttgart.

Boulnois, Lucette, (1989): Chinese maps and prints on the Tibet-Gorkha war of 1788–92, in: *Kailash*, XV, 1–2, 1989, pp. 85–112.

Brauen, Martin, 1998: *The Mandala: Sacred Circle in Tibetan Buddhism*, London.

Brauen, Martin, 2004 (2000): *Dreamworld Tibet: Western Illusions*, Bangkok.

Budalagong mibao/Gems of the Potala palace, Beijing 1994.

Chandler, Edmund, 1905: *The Unveiling of Lhasa*, London.

Chandra, Lokesh, 1986: *Buddhist Iconography of Tibet*, 2 Vols., Kyoto.

Chapman, F. Spencer, 1940: *Lhasa, the Holy City*, London.

Charleux, Isabelle u.a., 2004a: L'intronisation du IXe Dalaï Lama vue par un prince mongol, un rouleau peint concervé à la bibliothèque de l'Institut des Hautes Etudes Chinoises, in: *Arts Asiatiques*, Vol. 59, 2004, pp. 30–57.

Charleux, Isabelle, Marie-Dominique Even and Gaëlle Lacaze, 2004b: Un document mongol sur l'intronisation du IXe Dalaï lama, in: *Journal Asiatique*, 292 (1–2), 2004, pp. 151–222.

CPC: *Calendar of Persian Correspondance*, Vol. X, 1792–93, Delhi 1959.

Craig, Mary, 1998: *Kundun, une biographie du Dalaï Lama et de sa famille*, Paris.

Cüppers, Christoph, 2001: A letter written by the Fifth Dalai Lama to the King of Bhaktapur, in: *Journal of the Nepal Research Center*, 12, 2001, pp. 39–42.

Cutting, Suydam, 1940: *The fire ox and other Years*, New York.

Dalai Lama XIV.: see also Tenzin Gyatso.

Dalai Lama XIV., 1982: *Mein Leben und mein Volk, die Tragödie Tibets*, München.

Dalai Lama XIV., 1987: *Das Auge einer neuen Achtsamkeit*, München.

Dalai Lama XIV., 1989: *Logik der Liebe, aus den Lehren des Tibetischen Buddhismus*, München.

Dalai Lama XIV., 1990: *Das Buch der Freiheit*, Bergisch Gladbach.

Dalai Lama XIV., 1991a: *Der Schlüssel zum Mittleren Weg*, Hamburg.

Dalai Lama XIV., 1991b: *Die Vorträge in Harvard*, Grafing.

Dalai Lama XIV., 1991c: *Yoga des Geistes*, Hamburg.

Dalai Lama XIV. (and Glenn Mullin), 1993: *Gesang der inneren Erfahrung: die Stufen auf dem Pfad zur Erleuchtung*, Hamburg.

Damdinsüren, Ts., 1981: The Sixth Dalai Lama: Tsangs-Dbyangs Rgya-Mtso, in: *The Tibet Journal*, Vol. 6, Nr. 4, Winter 1981, pp. 32–36.

Damdinsüren, Ts., 1997: *Tales of An Old Lama*, Tring.

Dargye, Ngawang Lhungdrub, 1999: *La biografia segreta del Sesto Dalai Lama (1683–1706 [1746])*, Mailand.

Das, Sarat Chandra, 1904a: *Journey to Lhasa and Central Tibet*, edited by W.W. Rockhill, London.

Das, Sarat Chandra, 1904b: The hierarchy of the Dalai Lama (1406–1745), in: *Tibetan studies*, edited with an introduction by Alaka Chattopadhyaya, Kalkutta, 1984, pp. 247–261.

Das, Sarat Chandra, 1970 (1881): The Lives of the Panchen-Rinpoches or Tas'i Lamas, in: Sarat Chandra Das: *Contributions on the Religion and History of Tibet*, New Delhi, pp. 81–144.

David, Alexandra, 1912: Auprès du Dalaï-Lama, in: *Mercure de France*, I-X-1912, pp. 466–476.

David-Néel, Alexandra, 1928: *Arjopa, die erste Pilgerfahrt einer weißen Frau nach der verbotenen Stadt des Dalai Lama*, Leipzig.

David-Néel, Alexandra, 2000: *Wanderer mit dem Wind, Reisetagebücher in Briefen 1904–1917*, Stuttgart.

De Filippi, Filippo (Ed.), 1932: *An account of Tibet, the travels of Ippolito Desideri of Pistoia S.J., 1712–1727*, London.

Department of Information and International Relations, Central Tibetan Administration, 1996 (1995): *The Panchen Lama Lineage, How Reincarnation is Being Reinvented as a Political Tool*, Dharamśālā.

Desideri, Ippolito: see de Filippi, Filippo 1932.

Désiré-Marchand, Joelle, 1997: *Alexandra David-Néel, de Paris à Lhassa, de l'aventure à la sagesse*, Paris.

Dhondup, K., 1984: The Thirteenth Dalai Lama's experiment in modern education, in: *The Tibet Journal*, Vol. IX, Nr. 3, Herbst 1984, pp. 38–58.

Dinwiddie, Donald (Ed.), 2003: *Portraits of the Masters, Bronze Sculptures of the Tibetan Buddhist Lineages*, edited by Donald Dinwiddie, Chicago.

Diskalkar, D.B., (1933): Tibeto-Nepalese War, 1788–1793, in: *Journal of the Bihar and Orissa Research Society*, Vol. XIX (1933), pp. 355–398.

Dreyfus, Georges, 2003: Cherished memories, cherished communities: proto-nationalism in Tibet, in: *The history of Tibet*, Vol. 2, edited by Alex McKay, London, pp. 492–522.

Engelhardt, Isrun, 1999: Zur Ent-Fremdung des Europäers, Gastfreundschaft und Abbau von Fremdheit in den Beziehungen von Tibetern zu Europäern im 18. Jahrhundert, in: *Aneignung und Selbstbehauptung, Antworten auf die europäische Expansion*, edited by Dietmar Rothermund, München, pp. 184–202.

Engelhardt, Isrun, (2002): The closing of the gates: Tibetan-European relations at the end of the eighteenth century, in: *Tibet, Past and Present. Tibetan Studies I*, edited by Henk Blezer, Leiden, pp. 229–245.

Essen, Gerd Wolfgang and Tsering T. Thingo, 1989: *Die Götter des Himalaya, Buddhistische Kunst Tibets*, 2 Vols., München.

Farrer-Halls, Gill, 1998: *Die Welt des Dalai Lama, eine Innenansicht seines Lebens, seines Volkes und seiner Visionen*, Neuhausen am Rheinfall.

Foster, Barbara and Michael Foster, 1999: *Alexandra David-Néel – die Frau, die das verbotene Tibet entdeckte. Die Biographie*, Freiburg.

Fujita, Hiroki, 1984: *Tibetan Buddhist art*, Tokyo.

Giorgi (Georgii), Antonio Agostino, 1987 (1762/63): *Alphabetum Tibetanum missionum apostolicarum commodo editum*; unveränderter Nachdruck d. Ausg. Rome 1762/63, edited by Una Voce, Köln (deutsche Ausgabe: Georgi, Antonio, 2001: *Alphabetum Tibetanum, zum Nutzen der apostolischen Missionen im Druck erschienen bei der Heiligen Kongregation zur Verbreitung des Glaubens in Rom 1732*, aus dem Lateinischen übers. und mit Anmerkungen versehen von Peter Lindegger, 2 Teile, Rikon).

Goldstein, Melvyn C., 1989: The Dalai Lama, the army, and the monastic segment, in: *A History of modern Tibet, 1913–1951, the demise of the Lamaist state*, Berkeley, pp. 89–138.

Gould, Sir Basil J., 1957: *The Jewel in the lotus*, London.

Gould, Sir Basil J., 2000 (1941): Discovery, recognition and installation of the Fourteenth Dalai Lama, in: *Discovery, recognition and enthronement of the 14th Dalai Lama, a collection of accounts by Khemey Sonam Wangdu, Sir Basil J. Gould and Hugh Richardson*, Dharamśālā.

Grönbold, Günter, 1982: Die Schrift- und Buchkultur Tibets, in: *Der Weg zum Dach der Welt*, edited by C.C. Müller and W. Raunig, Innsbruck, 1982, pp. 363–380.

Grönbold, Günter, 2005: *Die Worte des Buddha in den Sprachen der Welt, The words of Buddha in the languages of the world*, Ausstellungskatalog, München.

Gruschke, Andreas, 2003: *Dalai Lama*, Kreuzlingen.

Hanzhang, Ya, 1991: *The Biographies of the Dalai Lamas*, Beijing.

Harrer, Heinrich, 1952: *Sieben Jahre in Tibet*, Wien.

Harrer, Heinrich, 1953: *Meine Tibet-Bilder*, mit Text von Heinz Woltereck, Zürich.

Harrer, Heinrich, 1983: *Wiedersehen mit Tibet*, Innsbruck.

Harrington, Laura (Ed.), 1999: *Kalacakra*, Text geschrieben von Namgyal Mönchen, Rome.

Harris, Clare, 1999: *In the Image of Tibet, Tibetan Painting after 1959*, London.

Harris, Clare and Tsering Shakya (Eds.) 2003: *Seeing Lhasa, British Depictions of the Tibetan capital 1936–1947*, Chicago.

Hayden, Henry and César Cosson, 1927: *Sport and travel in the highlands of Tibet*, London.

Heller, Amy, 1992: Historic and iconographic aspects of the protective deities Srung-ma dmar-nag, in: *Tibetan Studies*, Vol. 2, edited by Ihara Shoren and Yamaguchi Zuiho, Narita.

Heller, Amy, 1992: *On the development of the iconography and the cult of Begtse, a Tibetan protective deity, by translation of the Fifth Dalai Lama's vision* (Unpublished).

Heller, Amy, 1999: *Tibetan Art: Tracing the Development of Spiritual Ideals and Art in Tibet 600–2000 A. D.*, Woodbridge.

Henss, Michael, 2001: The Bodhisattva-emperor: Tibeto-Chinese portraits of sacred and secular rule in the Qing Dynasty in: *Oriental Art*, Vol. XL, Nr. 3, pp. 2–16, Vol. VIII, Nr. 5, pp. 71–83.

Henss, Michael, 2004: King Srong btsan sGam po revisited, the royal statues in the Potala Palace and in the Jokhang at Lhasa, problems of historical and stylistic evidence, in: *Essays on the International Conference on Tibetan Archaeology and Art*, Beijing, pp. 128–169.

Hofmann, Reik Alexander, 2002: *Zur Tibetpolitik der Qing-Regierung am Ende des 18. Jahrhunderts, das 29-Punkte-Dekret zur Reorganisation in Tibet (1793)*, Magisterarbeit, vorgelegt am Ostasiatischen Institut der Universität Leipzig.

Huc, Régis Evariste, 1850: *Reise durch die Mongolei nach Tibet und China 1844–1846*, Frankfurt am Main.

Hucker, Charles O., 1985: *A dictionary of official titles in Imperial China*, Taipei.

Hummel, Arthur W. (Eds.), 1991: *Eminent chinese of the Ch'ing Period (1644–1912)*, Vol. 1, Nachdruck, Taipei (Washington DC 1943).

Hyer, Paul, 1981: The Dalai Lamas and the Mongols, in: *The Tibet Journal*, Vol. 6, Nr. 4, Winter 1981, pp. 3–12.

Ishihama, Yumiko, 1992: A study of the seals and titles conferred by the Dalai Lamas, in: *Tibetan studies, proceedings of the 5th Seminar of the International Association for Tibetan Studies, Narita 1989*, Narita, Vol. 2, pp. 501–514, also in: *The history of Tibet*, Vol. 1, edited by Alex McKay, London 2003, pp. 90–98.

Ishihama, Yumiko, 1993: On the dissemination of the belief in the Dalai Lama as a manifestation of the Bodhisattva Avalokiteśvara, in: *Acta Asiatica*, Vol. 64, 1993, pp. 38–56.

Jackson, David, 1996: *A History of Tibetan Painting, the Great Tibetan Painters and Their Traditions*, Wien.

Kämpfe, Hans-Rainer, 1982: *Ni-ma'i od-zer/Naran-U Gerel: die Biographie des 2. Pekinger Lcan-skya Qutuqtu Rolpa'i rdo-rje 1717–1786*, St. Augustin.

Kapstein, Matthew, 1992: Remarks on the Mani bka'-bum and the cult of Avalokiteśvara in Tibet, in: *Tibetan Buddhism, reason and revelation*, edited by S. M. Goodman and R. M. Davidson, Albany, pp. 79–94, 163–169.

Karmay, Samten, 1988: *Secret Visions of the Fifth Dalai Lama, the Gold Manuscript in the Fournier Collection*, London.

Karmay, Samten, 2002: The Rituals and their origins in the visionary accounts of the 5th Dalai Lama, in: *Religion and secular culture. Tibetan Studies II*, Leiden, pp. 21–40.

Kaschewsky, Rudolf, 1971: *Das Leben des lamaistischen Heiligen Tsongkhapa Blo-Bzang-Grags-Pa (1357–1419)*, Wiesbaden.

Khemey Sonam Wangdu, Sir Basil J. Gould and Hugh E. Richardson, 2000: *Discovery, recognition and enthronement of the 14th Dalai Lama, a collection of accounts*, Dharamśālā.

Khetsun Sagpo Rinpoche, 1982: Life and times of the Eighth to Twelfth Dalai Lama, in: *The Tibet Journal*, Vol. VII, Nr. 1–2, Frühling/Sommer 1982, pp. 47–55.

Kirkpatrick, William J., (1969): *An Account of the Kingdom of Nepaul, being the substance of observations made during a mission to that country in the year 1793*, Nachdruck, New Delhi (London 1811).

Klieger, P. Christiaan, 1991: The Institution of the Dalai Lama as a symbolic matrix, in: *The Tibet Journal*, Vol. XVI, Nr. 1, 1991, pp. 96–107.

Kollmar-Paulenz, Karénina, 2001: *Erdeni tunumal neretü sudur, die Biographie des Altan qaghan der Tümed-Mongolen, ein Beitrag zur Geschichte der religionspolitischen Beziehungen zwischen der Mongolei und Tibet im ausgehenden 16. Jahrhundert*, Wiesbaden.

Kolmas, Josef 1994: The ambans and assistant ambans of Tibet (1727–1912), some statistical observations, in: *Tibetan studies, proceedings of the 6th International Seminar of the International Association for Tibetan studies, Fagernes 1992*, Vol. 1, Oslo, pp. 454–467.

Kossak, Steven M. and Jane Casey Singer,1999: *Geheime Visionen, frühe Malerei aus Zentraltibet*, Zürich.

Kreijger, H., 2001: *Tibetan Painting, The Jucker Collection*, London.

Kuleshov, Nikolai S., 1992: Agavan Dorjiev, the Dalai Lama's ambassador, in: *The history of Tibet*, Vol. 3, edited by Alex McKay, London 2003, pp. 57–68.

Kuleshov, Nikolai S., 1996: *Russia's Tibet File*, Dharamśālā.

Lange, Kristina, 1969: Über die Präexistenzen der Dalai-Lamas, Versuch einer kritischen Analyse tibetisch-buddhistischer Quellen, in: *Jahrbuch des Museums für Völkerkunde zu Leipzig*, Vol. XXVI, Berlin, pp. 205–228.

Lange, Kristina, 1976: *Die Werke des Regenten Sangs rgyas rgya mc'o (1653–1705), eine philologisch-historische Studie zum tibetischsprachigen Schrifttum*, Berlin.

Leonov, Gennady, 1991: Two portraits of the Thirteenth Dalai Lama, in: *Arts of Asia*, Juli–August 1991, pp. 108–121.

Levenson, Claude B., 1991: *Dalai Lama, die autorisierte Biographie des Nobelpreisträgers*, 2. Aufl., Zürich.

Lhalungpa, Lobsang P., 1983: *Tibet: The Sacred Realm, Photographs 1880–1950*, Philadelphia (deutsche Ausgabe: *Tibet, Heiliger Raum, Fotografien 1880–1950*, Frankfurt a.M. 1990).

Li, Ruohong (2002): *A Tibetan aristocratic family in eighteenth-century Tibet, a Study of Qing-Tibetan contact*, Cambridge/Massachusetts.

Lipton, Barbara and Nima Dorjee Ragnubs, 1996: *Treasures of Tibetan art, Collections of the Jacques Marchais Museum of Tibetan Art*, New York/Oxford.

Lohia, Sushama, 1994: *Lalitavajra's manual of Buddhist iconography*, New Delhi.

Macdonald, Ariane, 1977: Un portrait du cinquième Dalaï-Lama, in: *Essais sur l'art du Tibet*, edited by Ariane Macdonald and Yoshiro Imaeda, Paris, pp. 120–156.

Macdonald, David, 1929: *The Land of the Lama: A description of a country of contrasts and of its cheerful happy-go lucky people of hardy nature and curious customs, their religion, ways of living, trade and social life*, London (New Edition: New Delhi: 1978).

Macdonald, David, 1996: *Twenty Years in Tibet*, Delhi (London 1932).

MacGregor, John (1970): *Tibet: A Chronicle of Exploration*, London.

Mannerheim, C.G., 1940: *Across Asia from West to East in 1906–1908*, Helsinki.

Manning 1909: see Markham.

Markham, Clements R., 1909: *Aus dem Lande der lebenden Buddhas, die Erzählungen von der Mission George Bogle's nach Tibet und Thomas Manning's Reise nach Lhasa (1774 und 1812)*, translated from the English of Mr. Clements R. Markham and edited by M. v. Brandt, Vol. 3, Hamburg.

Martynov, A.S., 1978: On the status of the Fifth Dalai Lama, in: *Proceedings of the Csoma de Körös Memorial Symposium*, edited by Louis Ligeti, Budapest.

Mathews, R.H., (1969): *Chinese English dictionary*, Nachdruck, Cambridge/Massachusetts (Shanghai, 1931).

McGovern, William Montgomery, 1926: *Als Kuli nach Lhasa, eine heimliche Reise nach Tibet*, Berlin.

McKay, Alex, (Ed.), 2003: *The History of Tibet*, 3 Vols., London.

Meyer, Fernand, 1987: The Potala Palace of the Dalai Lamas in Lhasa, in: *Orientations*, 18/7, 1987, pp. 14–33

Michael, Franz, 1982: *Rule by Incarnation, Tibetan Buddhism and Its Role in Society and State*, Boulder/Colorado.

Mirror of the murals in the Potala: see *Pho brang pot a la*.

Mullin, Glenn H. and Andy Weber, 1996: *The Mystical Arts of Tibet: Featuring Personal Sacred Objects of H.H. the Dalai Lama*, Atlanta.

Mullin, Glenn H. (Eds.), 1985: *Selected Works of the Dalai Lama VII: songs of spiritual change*, Ithaca/NY.

Mullin, Glenn H., 1985: Kun-ga Gyal-Tsen's 'life of the Dalai Lama I, the twelve wondrous deeds of omniscient Gen-Dun Drub', in: *The Tibet Journal*, Vol. X, Nr. 4, Winter 1985, pp. 3–42.

Mullin, Glenn H., 1986a: De-Si Sang-Gye Gya-Tso's life of the second Dalai Lama, in: *The Tibet journal*, Vol. XI, Nr. 3, Herbst 1986, pp. 3–16.

Mullin, Glenn H., 1986b: Tse-Chok-Ling's biography of the Third Dalai Lama, in: *The Tibet Journal*, Vol. XI, Nr. 3, Herbst 1986, pp. 23–39.

Mullin, Glenn H., 1988: *Path of the Bodhisattva warrior, the life and teaching of the Thirteenth Dalai Lama*, Ithaca/NY.

Mullin, Glenn H., 1999a: *Gems of wisdom from the Seventh Dalai Lama*, Ithaca/NY.

Mullin, Glenn H., 1999b: *Meditations to transform the mind, by the Seventh Dalai Lama*, Ithaca/NY.

Mullin, Glenn H., 2001: *The Fourteen Dalai Lamas, a sacred legacy of reincarnation*, Santa Fe.

Mullin, Glenn H., 2004: *Der verrückte Weise auf Tibets Königsthron, mystische Verse und Visionen des Zweiten Dalai Lama*, Frankfurt.

Namgyal, Phuntsok (Ed.), 2002: *The Potala palace, splendour of Tibet*, Beijing.

National Museum of History (Organizer), 1994: *The Catalogue of Tibetan Artifacts Exhibition*, Taipei.

National Palace Museum, Taipei, Taiwan, 1971: *Masterpieces of Chinese Tibetan Buddhist altar fittings in the National Palace Museum*, Taipei.

Nebesky-Wojkowitz, René de, 1949: *Schriftwesen, Papierherstellung und Buchdruck bei den Tibetern*, Wien (Unpublished dissertation).

Nebesky-Wojkowitz, René de, 1975 (1956): *Oracles and Demons of Tibet: the Cult and Iconography of the Tibetan Protective Deities*, Graz.

Neven, Armand, 1978, *Etudes d'art lamaïque de l' Himalaya*, Brüssel.

Normanton, Simon, 1988: *Tibet: The Lost Civilisation*, London.

OIOC British Library, *Oriental and India Office Collections, proceedings and consultations of the Government of India.*

Olson, Eleanor, 1974: *Tantric Buddhist art*, New York.

Pal, Pratapaditya, 2003: *Himalayas: An Aesthetic Adventure*, Chicago.

Pardee, Thomas, 1999: *Karmapa: the Sacred Prophecy*, Wappingers Fall/NY.

Pereira, George, 1925: *Peking to Lhasa: the narrative of journeys in the Chinese empire made by the late brigadier-general George Pereira*, compiled by Sir Francis Younghusband from the notes and diaries of General Major Pereira, London.

Petech, Luciano, 1950: *China and Tibet in the early 18th Century: History of the Establishment of Chinese Protectorate in Tibet*, Leiden.

Petech, Luciano (Ed.), 1952–56: *I missionari Italiani nel Tibet e nel Nepal, i capuccini Marchigiani*, Vols. I–VII, Rome.

Petech, Luciano, 1959: The Dalai-Lamas and regents of Tibet, a chronological study, in: *T'oung Pao*, Vol. 47, 1949, Leiden, pp. 368–394.

Petech, Luciano, 1972: Lajang Khan, the last Qōśot ruler of Tibet (1705–1717), in: *The history of Tibet*, Vol. 2, edited by Alex McKay, London, 2003, pp. 362–370.

Petech, Luciano, 1973: *Aristocracy and Government in Tibet 1728–1959*, Rome.

Petech, Luciano, 1988: The Dalai Lamas, a chronological study, in: *Selected papers on Asian history*, Rome, pp. 125–148.

Petech, Luciano, 1990: The establishment of the Yünan-Sa-skya partnership, in: *The history of Tibet*, Vol. 2, edited by Alex McKay, London 2003, pp. 338–361.

Pho brang pot a la 'ildebs bris ri mo'l byung kungs lo rgyus gsal ba'ime long: A mirror of the murals in the Potala, Beijing 2000.

Pommaret, Françoise (Ed.), 1997: *Lhasa, lieu du divin*, Genf.

Pommaret, Françoise (Ed.), 2003: *Lhasa in the Seventeenth Century, the Capital of the Dalai Lamas*, Leiden.

Precious deposits, historical relics of Tibet, China, edited by Zhen Wenlei, 5 vols., Beijing 2000.

Priceless treasures, cultural relics and historical materials about the conferment of honorific titles upon the Dalai Lamas and Panchen Lamas of successive generations by the Central Governments through the ages, collections from gifts presented to the Central Governments by the Dalai Lamas and Panchen Lamas of successive generations, Beijing 1999.

Qing Gong Zang Chuan Fojiao Tangka, 2003a: *Thangkas Buddhist paintings of Tibet*, Hongkong.

Qing Gong Zang Chuan Fojiao Tangka, 2003b: *Buddhist statues of Tibet*, Hongkong.

Ray, Reginald A., 1986: Some aspects of the Tülku tradition in Tibet, in: *The Tibet Journal*, Vol. XI, Nr. 4, 1986, pp. 35–69.

Regmi, Delli R., 1975: *Modern Nepal*, Vol. I, Kalkutta.

Riencourt, Amaury de, 1951: *Tibet im Wandel Asiens*, Wiesbaden.

Reynolds, Valrae, 1978: *Tibet A Lost World, the Newark Museum collection of Tibetan art and ethnography*, New York.

Reynolds, Valrae, 1999: *From the Sacred Realm: Treasures of Tibetan Art from the Newark Museum*, München.

Reynolds, V., A. Heller and J. Gyatso, 1986: *Catalogue of the Newark Museum, Tibetan collection*, Vol. III: Sculpture and Painting, Newark/NY.

Rhie, Marylin M. and Robert A. F. Thurman, 1991: *Wisdom and compassion, the sacred art of Tibet*, San Francisco.

Rhie, Marilyn M. and Robert A. F. Thurman, 1999: *Worlds of Transformation, Tibetan art of Wisdom and Compassion*, New York.

Richardson, Hugh, 1958: The Karma-pa sect, a historical note, part 1, in: *Journal of the Royal Asiatic Society of Great Britain and Ireland*, Oktober, 1958, pp. 139–164.

Richardson, Hugh, 1959: The Karma-pa sect, a historical note, part 2, in: *Journal of the Royal Asiatic Society of Great Britain and Ireland*, April, 1959, pp. 1–18.

Richardson, Hugh, 1971: The Dalai Lamas, in: *Shambhala* 1, 1971, pp. 19–30.

Richardson, Hugh, 1976: The political role of the four sects in Tibetan history, in: *Tibetan Review*, 11/9, 1976, pp. 18–23, Nachdruck in: H.E. Richardson, *High peaks, pure earth, collected writings on Tibetan history and culture*, edited by Michael Aris, London 1998, pp. 420–430.

Richardson, Hugh, 1980a: The Fifth Dalai Lama's decree appointing Sangs-rgyas rgya-mtsho as regent, in: *Bulletin of the School of Oriental and African Studies*, 43, 1980, pp. 329–344.

Richardson, Hugh, 1980b: The Rwa-Sreng conspiracy of 1947, in: *Tibetan Studies in Honour of Hugh Richardson, proceedings of the International Association of Tibetan Studies*, edited by M. Aris and Aung San Suu Kyi, Warminster, pp. xvi–xx.

Richardson, Hugh, 1993: *Ceremonies of the Lhasa Year*, London.

Richardson, Hugh, 1998a: *High Peaks, Pure Earth: Collected Writings on Tibetan History and Culture*, edited by Michael Aris, London.

Richardson, Hugh, 1998b: Report on the arrival in Lhasa of the New Dalai Lama, in: *High Peaks, Pure Earth, Collected Writings on Tibetan History and Culture*, edited by Michael Aris, London, pp. 673–678.

Richardson, Hugh, 1998c: The Fifth Dalai Lama's decree appointing Sangs-rgyas-rgya-mtsho as regent, in: *High Peaks, Pure Earth, collected writings on Tibetan history and culture*, edited by Michael Aris, London, pp. 440–461.

Rituels tibétains, visions secrètes du 5e Dalaï Lama, Paris 2002.

Rockhill, William W., (1910): The Dalai Lamas of Lhasa and their relations with the Manchi Emperors of China 1644–1908, in: *T'oung Pao* II, ser. 2, pp. 1–104.

Rose, Leo E., 1971: *Nepal, strategy for survival*, Bombay.

Rossi, Anna Maria and Fabio Rossi, 2003: *Homage to the Holy: Portraits of Tibet's Spiritual Teachers*, London.

Ruegg, Seyfort D., 1991: Mcod yon, yon mchod and mchod gnas/yon gnas, on the historiography and semantics of a Tibetan religio-social and religio-political concept, in: *The history of Tibet*, Vol. 2, edited by Alex McKay, London 2003, pp. 362–370.

Samphel, Thubten and Tendar, 2000: *The Dalai Lamas of Tibet*, Torrance/CA.

Sangs rGyas rGya mtsho 1999: see Ahmad 1999.

Schaeffer, Kurtis R., [200?]: Ritual, Festival, and Authority under the 5th Dalai Lama, in: *Power, Politics, and the Reinvention of Tradition in Tibet, 1600–1800. Proceedings of the 10th Seminar of the International Association for Tibetan Studies, Oxford University 2003*, edited by Bryan J. Cuevas and Kurtis R. Schaeffer, Leiden, Forthcoming.

Schmid, Toni, 1961: *Saviours of mankind, Dalai Lamas and former incarnations of Avalokiteśvara*, 2 vols., Stockholm.

Schneider, Hanna, 2003: The Formation of the Tibetan official style of administrative correspondence (17th–19th century), in: *Tibet and her neighbours, a history*, edited by Alex McKay, London, pp. 117–125.

Schuh, Dieter, 1981: *Grundlagen tibetischer Siegelkunde, eine Untersuchung über tibetische Siegelaufschriften in 'Phags-pa-Schrift*, Sankt Augustin.

Schuh, Dieter and Loden Sherap Dagyab, 1978: *Urkunden, Erlasse und Sendschreiben aus dem Besitz sikkimesischer Adelshäuser und des Klosters Phodang*, Sankt Augustin.

Schulemann, Günther, 1958: *Geschichte der Dalai Lamas*, Leipzig.

Seckel, Dietrich, 1997: *Das Portrait in Ostasien*, Teil 1, Heidelberg.

Selig Brown, Kathryn, 2004: *Eternal Presence, Handprints and Footprints in Buddhist Art*, Katonah Museum of Art.

Shakabpa, Tsepon W.D.: Political history of Tibet, to be published under the title *One hundred thousand moons, an advanced political history of Tibet*, edited by Derek F. Maher.

Shakabpa, Tsepon W.D., 1967: *Tibet, a political history*, New Haven.

Shakya, Tsering, 1984: A biography of His Holiness the 16th Karmapa entitled "A droplet from the infinite Ocean-like outer Biography of Lokeshvara, the Great Sixteenth holder of the black crown", in: *Tibet Journal*, Vol. IX, Nr. 3, Herbst 1984, pp. 3–20.

Shakya, Tsering, 1986: Making of the great game players, Tibetan students in Britain between 1913 and 1917, in: *Tibetan Review*, Vol. XXI, Nr. 1, Januar 1986, pp. 9–14.

Shakya, Tsering, 1996: The 7th Panchen Lama: the man who wasn't allowed to tell the truth, in: *Lungta* 10: *The lives of the Panchen Lamas*, 1996, pp. 24–29.

Shen Weirong, 2002: *Leben und historische Bedeutung des ersten Dalai Lama dGe 'dun grub pa dpal bzang po (1391–1474), ein Beitrag zur Geschichte der dGe lugs pa-Schule und der Institution der Dalai Lamas*, Sankt Augustin.

Shiromany, A.A. (Ed.), 1998: *The Political Philosophy of His Holiness the XIV Dalai Lama: Selected Speeches and Writings*, New Delhi.

Sinha, Nirmal C., 1968: The Skyabs-mgon, in: *Bulletin of Tibetology*, Vol. V, Nr. 2, pp. 29–51.

Sis, Vladimir and Josef Vaniš, 1956: *Der Weg nach Lhasa*, Prague.

Sørensen, P.K., 1990: *Divinity Secularized: An inquiry into the Nature and Form of the Songs Ascribed to the Sixth Dalai Lama*, Wien.

Sørensen, P.K., 2003: Lhasa Diluvium, in *Lungta* 16: *Cosmonogy and the Origins*, pp. 85–134.

Spencer Chapman, Frederic, 1940: *Lhasa, the holy city*, London.

Stoddard, Heather, 1993: The death of the Thirteenth Dalai Lama, in: *Lungta* 7: *The institution of the Dalai Lamas*, 1993, pp. 2–7.

Stoddard, Heather, 2003: Fourteen centuries of Tibetan portraiture, in: *Portraits of the Masters, Bronze Sculptures of the Tibetan Buddhist Lineages*, edited by D. Dinwiddie, Chicago, pp. 16–61.

Surkhang, Wangchen Gelek, 1982: The Thirteenth Dalai Lama, Tibet the critical years, part 1, in: *The Tibet Journal*, Vol. VII, Nr. 4, Winter 1982, pp. 11–19.

Surkhang, Wangchen Gelek, 1983: The discovery of the XIVth Dalai Lama, Tibet the critical years, part IV, in: *The Tibet Journal*, Vol. VIII, Nr. 3, Herbst 1983, pp. 37–45.

Tada, Tokan, 1965: *The Thirteenth Dalai Lama*, Tokyo.

Tanaka, Kimiaki, 1999: *Art of Thangka from the Hahn Kwang-ho collection*, Vol. 2, Seoul.

Tanaka, Kimiaki, 2003: *Art of Thangka from the Hahn Kwang-ho collection*, Vol. 4, Seoul.

Tanaka, Kimiaki, 2004: *Gems of Thangka art from the Tamashige Tibet collection*, Tokyo.

Tangka-Buddhist painting of Tibet, the complete collections of treasures of the Potala palace, Hongkong 2003.

Taring, R.D., 1986 (1970): *Daughter of Tibet, the autobiography of Rinchen Dolma Taring*, London.

Tatz, Mark, 1981: Songs of the Sixth Dalai Lama, in: *The Tibet journal*, Vol. 6, Nr. 4, Winter 1981, pp. 13–31.

Tenzin Gyatso, 1991: *Freedom in exile, the autobiography of the Dalai Lama*, New York.

Tenzin Gyatso: see also Dalai Lama.

Thingo, Tsering Tashi, 1974: *Buddhistische Kunst aus dem Himalaya, Sammlung Werner Schulemann Bonn*, Köln.

Thomas, Lowell, Jr., 1951: *Tibet im Gewitter*, Berlin.

Thomas, Lowell, Jr., 1959: *The silent war in Tibet*, New York.

Thomas, Lowell, Jr., 1961: *The Dalai Lama*, New York.

Thurman, Robert A.F., 1983: The Dalai Lama of Tibet, living icons of a six-hundred-year millenium, in: *The Tibet Journal*, Vol. VIII, Nr. 4, Winter 1983, pp. 10–19.

Tibet Museum, zusammengestellt vom Tibet Museum, Beijing 2001.

Tibetan Administrative Office of the Potala, 1996: *The Potala, holy palace in the snow land*, Beijing.

Tibetan thangkas, Potala collection, [s. l], [198.].

Tolstoy, Ilja, 1946: Across Tibet from India to China, in: *National Geographic Magazine*, Juli 1946 , pp. 169–222.

Trimondi, Victor and Victoria, 1999: *Der Schatten des Dalai Lama*, Düsseldorf.

Tsai, Mei-fen, 1994: Art between Tibet and the Ch'ing court, Tibetan religious objects in the collection of the National Palace Museum (Taipei), in: *Tibetan Studies, Proceedings of the 6th Seminar of the International Association for Tibetan Studies*, Oslo.

Tse-chok-ling, Life of the Seventh Dalai Lama, from the Lam-rim-bla-brgyud, in: *The Tibet Journal*, Vol. VIII, Nr. 1, Frühling 1983, pp. 3–19.

Tsering, 2000: *Jokhang temple*, Beijing.

Tucci, Giuseppe, 1999 (1949): *Tibetan painted scrolls*, Rome.

Tung Jones, Rosemary, 1980: *A Portrait of Lost Tibet*, London.

Turner, Samuel, 1971: *An Account of an Embassy to the Court of the Teshoo Lama in Tibet, containing a narrative of a journey through Bootan and part of Tibet*, Nachdruck, New Delhi (London, 1800)

Tuttle, Gray, 200?: A Tibetan Buddhist mission to the east, The 5th Dalai Lama's journey to Beijing, 1652–1653, in: *Power, Politics, and the Reinvention of Tradition in Tibet, 1600–1800, Proceedings of the 10th Seminar of the International Association for Tibetan Studies*, Oxford University 2003, edited by Bryan J. Cuevas and Kurtis R. Schaeffer, Leiden, Forthcoming.

Uhlig, Helmut (Catalog Ed.), 1976: *Buddhistische Kunst aus dem Himalaya, Kaschmir – Ladakh – Tibet – Nepal – Bhutan*, Berlin.

Uhlig, Helmut, 1995: *Auf dem Pfad zur Erleuchtung, die Tibet-Sammlung der Berti Aschmann Stiftung*, Zürich.

Uspensky, Vladimir L., 1996: The illustrated manuscripts of the 5th Dalai Lama's 'The Secret Visionary Autobiography' preserved in the St. Petersburg Branch of the Institute of Oriental Studies, in *Manuscripta Orientalia* 2/1, 1996, pp. 54–65.

Van der Wee, Pia and Louis, 1988: *Symbolisme de l'art lamaïque*, Brüssel.

Van der Wee, Pia and Louis, 1995: *A Tale of Thangkas: living with a collection*, Gent.

Van Grassdorff, Gilles, 2003: *Le Dalaï-Lama, la biographie non autorisée*, Paris.

Vitali, Roberto, 2001: A note on the Third Dalai Lama bSod names rgya mtsho and his visionary thang ka of lHa mo'l bla mtsho, in: *The Tibet Journal*, Vol. XXVI, Nr. 3–4, Herbst-Winter 2001, pp. 91–102.

Waller, Derek, 1990: *The pundits, British exploration of Tibet and Central Asia*, Lexington.

Wang, Xiangyun, 2000: The Qing Court's Tibet Connections: Lcang skya Rol pa'i rdo rje and the Qianlong emperor, in: *Harvard Journal of Asiatic Studies*, 60/1, 2000, S.125–163.

Weldon, D. and J. Casey Singer, 1999: *The Sculptural Heritage of Tibet: Buddhist art in the Nyingjei Lam Collection*, London.

Wilson, H.H., 1997: *A glossary of judicial and revenue terms and of useful words occurring in Official Documents relating to the Administration of the Government of British India from the Arabic, Persian, Hindustáni, Sanskrit, Hindí, Bengálí, Uḍiya, Maráthi, Guzaráthi, Teluga, Karnáta, Tamil, Malayálam, and other languages*, New Delhi.

Winnington, Alan, 1957: *Tibet, record of a journey*, London.

Wylie, Turrell V., 1978: Reincarnation, a political innovation in Tibetan Buddhism, in: *Proceedings of the Csoma de Körös Memorial Symposium*, edited by Louis Ligeti, Budapest.

Wylie, Turrell V., 1980: Lama tribute in the Ming dynasty, in: *The history of Tibet*, Vol. 2, edited by Alex McKay, London, 2003, pp. 467–472.

Xia Jingchun, 2000: *Zang Jintong Faxiang* (Buddhistische Metallstatuen aus Tibet in der Sammlung Xia Jingchun), Shenyang.

Yang, He-chin, 1992: Autobiography of the Fifth Dalai Lama, quoted by Yang, he-chin, a study of the account of Dalai Lama's visit to Peking, in: *Proceedings of International Conference of Tibet in the Historical China Proper*, Taipei.

Younghusband, Francis Edward, 1910: *India and Tibet: a history of the relations which have subsisted between the two countries from the time of Warren Hastings to 1910*, London.

Zhongguo gudai jianju xizang budala gong, 1996: *Chinese ancient constructions Potala Palace*, 2 vols., Beijing.

Zhongguo Zangchuan (Ed.), 2001: *Zhongguo Zangchuan Fojiao Jintong Zaoxiang Yishu*, [Vergoldete Metallstatuen des tibetischen Buddhismus in China], 2 vols., Beijing.

Zuihō, Yamaguchi, 1995: The sovereign power of the Fifth Dalai Lama: sPrul sku gZims-khang-gong-ma and the removal of governor Nor-bu, in: *Memoirs of the research department of the Toyo Bunko*, Nr. 53, pp. 1–27.

WORKS IN TIBETAN LANGUAGE

THE SEVENTH DALAI LAMA

Archives of the Tibet Autonomous Region: *Bod-kyi yig-tshags gces-btus*, Beijing 1995.

Blo-bzang-chos-grags and Bsod-nams-rtse-mo (Ed.): *Gangs ljongs mkhas dbang rim byon gyi rtsom yig gser gyi sbram bu*, 3 Vols., Xining 1988.

The Collected Works (Gsung 'bum) of the Seventh Dalai Lama Blo-bzang-bskal-bzang-rgya-mtsho, Gangtok 1975–1983.

'Phags pa 'Jig rten dbang phyug gi rnam sprul rim byon gyi 'khrungs rabs deb ther nor bu'i 'phreng ba, Vol. 3., Dharamśālā 1977.

Thu'u-bkwan Chos-kyi nyi-ma, *Lcang skya Rol pa'i rdo rje'i rnam thar*, Lanzhou 1989.

THE THIRTEENTH DALAI LAMA

Phur-lcog thub-bstan byams-pa tshul-khrims: *lhar bcas srid zhi'i gtsug rgyan gong sa rgyal-ba'i dbang-po kha' drin mtshungs-med sku- phring bcu gsum pa chen-po'i rnam-par thar pa rgya mtsho lta-bu las-mdo tsam brjod pa ngo-mtshar rin-po che'i phreng-ba* [Biography of the 13th Dalai Lama], Dharamśālā 1984.

Gon sa skyab mgon gyal ba'l dbang po sku phring bcu gsum pa chen po mtshog gis bod rigs ser skya mi dmangs rnams la chu spril lor bstsal bo'l ma 'ongs lung bstan gyi zhal gtams slobs rnying gi nor bu zhes bya ba bzhugs so [The Political Legacy of the 13th Dalai Lama], Kalimpong 1958.

ICONOGRAPHY OF THE DALAI LAMAS

Fifth Dalai Lama (1989/91): *Za hor gyi ban de ngag dbang blo bzang rgya mtsho'i 'di snang 'khrul pa'i rol rtsed rtogs brjod kyi tshul du bskod pa du kū la'i gos bzang* [Autobiography of the Fifth Dalai Lama], 3 Vols., Lhasa (Indian reprint, Dolanji 1983).

TIBETAN EPISTOLARY STYLE

Nornang, W.T., 1888: *bKa' drung Nor rgyas nang pa dBang 'dus Tshe ring gis phyogs bsdebs zhu 'phrin yig bskur sogs kyi rnam gzhag nyer mkho smyug 'dzin dbang po'i yid gsos dpyid kyi pho nya'i glu dbyangs zhes bya ba bzhugs so.*

Tharchin, G., (Ed.), 1954: *Yig bskur rnam gzhag rgyas pa*, Kalimpong.

THE SET OF SEVEN LINEAGE THANGKAS

Primary sources

bKa' gdams glegs bam

Jo rje dpal ldan a ti sha'i rnam thar bka' gdams pha chos/ 'Brom ston rgyal ba'i 'byung gnas kyi skyes rabs bka gdams bu chos, Vol. 2, Xining 1993.

'Khrungs rabs

Ngag-dbang blo-bzang rgya-mtsho [1617–1682], *'Khrungs rabs kyi zhing bkod 'dri* [= 'bri] *tshul kyi rtogs brjod kha byang dang bcas pa gSal ba'i me long*, Xyl. 1b1–1345 [= 577–601]. In: Vol. BA of the *Collected Works of the Fifth Dalai Lama*. Lhasa Ed.

DL5 = Ngag dbang blo bzang rgya mtsho rnam thar

sDe-srid Sangs-rgyas rgya-mtsho: *Za hor gyi ban de ngag dbang blo bzang rgya mtsho'i 'di snang 'khrul pa'i rol brtsed rtogs brjod kyi tshul du bkod pa du kū la'i gos bzang, DL5 I, II, III.* In: Vol. CA-JA of the *Collected Works of the Fifth Dalai Lama*. Lhasa Ed. DL5 IV–VI *(kha skong)* Supplement Volumes. Lhasa Ed.

DL9 =Lung rtogs rgya mtsho rnam thar

De-mo Hu-thog-tu *dge slong* Blo-bzang thub-bstan 'jigs-med rgya-mtsho'i sde: *rGyal ba'i dbang po thams cad mkhyen pa Blo bzang bstan pa'i 'byung gnas ngag dbang Lung rtogs rgya mtsho dpal bzang po'i zhal snga nas kyi rnam par thar pa mdor mtshon Dad pa'i yid 'Ôphrog.* [A]: Ed. 1.1–405.3 based on dGa'-ldan pho-brang block prints. Ed. Dharamśālā 1979 [B] In: *'Khrungs rabs deb ther nor bu'i 'phreng ba III*: 627–759. [abridged biography, Ed. Dharamśālā 1984]. [A is used here].

Bla ma bstod tshogs

Ngag-dbang blo-bzang rgya-mtsho: *mKhas shing grub pa'i dbang phyug pa rnams gtso bor gyur ba'i bla ma'i bstod tshogs kyi rim pa*, Xyl. 1b1–180a4 [=217–575.4]. In: Vol. BA of the *Collected Works of the Fifth Dalai Lama*, Lhasa Ed.

'Dzam gling rgyan gcig

sDe-srid Sangs-rgyas rgya-mtsho: *mChod sdong 'dzam gling rgyan gcig rten gtsug lag khang dang bcas pa'i dkar chag Thar gling rgya mtshor bgrod pa'i gru rdzings byin rlabs kyi bang mdzod*, 1–1068, Lhasa.

Secondary sources

Reb gong pa 'Jigs med bsam grub: *Gong sa Tā la'i bla ma sku phreng rim byon gyi chos srid mdzad rnam*, Beijing 2000.

Blo bzang rgya mtsho: *Bod kyi lo rgyus gZhon nu dga' ba'i gtam phreng*, Ganzu 1997.

lHun grub chos 'phel: *Rva sgreng dkar chag = dPal gyi 'byung gnas rva sgreng rgyal ba'i dben gnas dang gtsug lag khang gi rten dang brten par bcas pa'i dkar chag mThong ba don ldan dge legs nor bu'i bang mdzod*] 1–209, Chengdu 1994.

CONTRIBUTORS

MARTIN BRAUEN, Ph.D., anthropologist, is Lecturer and Head of the Department of Tibet, Himalaya and Far East at the Ethnographic Museum of the University of Zürich. He is the author of several books about Tibet, Bhūṭān, Nepāl, Ladākh, and Japan. Among the books *The Mandala: Sacred Circle in Tibetan Buddhism* is the most widely known. His newest publication in English is *Dreamworld Tibet: Western Illusions*. He has curated many exhibitions, including the exhibition *The Dalai Lamas* at the Ethnographic Museum of the University of Zürich (August 2005–April 2006).

GEORGES DREYFUS was a Tibetan Buddhist monk for more than fifteen years and became the first Westerner to receive the degree of Geshe, the highest degree of Tibetan monastic universities. He received his Ph.D. at the University of Virginia in 1991 and since then has been teaching Buddhism in the Department of Religions at Williams College, Mass. His publications include: *The Svatantrika-Prasangika Distinction: What Difference does a Difference make?* (in collaboration with Sara McClintock), *The Sound of Two Hands Clapping: the Education of a Tibetan Buddhist Monk*, and *Recognizing Reality: Dharmakirti's Philosophy and its Tibetan Interpretations*.

AMY HELLER Doctorate in Tibetan history and philology at La Sorbonne, École Pratique des Hautes Études, Paris. Works as Tibetologist and art historian, affiliated with CNRS-Paris research team on Tibetan studies since 1986. She travelled twelve times to Tibet and Dolpo. Her trip to Tibet in 1995 as part of a team for evaluating restoration of monasteries of Grathang and Zhalu and subsequent research resulted in her book *Tibetan Art* (1999), published in English, French, Italian and Spanish. She is currently writing a cultural history of Dolpo and working as expert on architectural restoration in Tibet for the Swiss government. Cocurator of the exhibition *The Dalai Lamas* at the Ethnographic Museum of the University of Zürich (August 2005–April 2006).

MICHAEL HENSS studied European art history and archeology. Since 1978 he has been deeply involved with Tibetan culture, in particular its art and the study of historic monuments, initially in Ladākh, then in central, southern, and western Tibet. His book publications include: *Tibet - Die Kulturdenkmäler* (1981); Mustang (1993); *Kalachakra* (4th edition, 1996); and *The Cultural Monuments of Tibet: The Central Regions* (2006). Mr. Henss is cocurator of the exhibition *The Dalai Lamas* at the Ethnographic Museum of the University of Zürich (August 2005–April 2006).

FABIENNE JAGOU is Assistant Professor at the École française d'Extrême-Orient. Her researches are on the Sino-Tibetan political relations during the first half of the twentieth century, and in particular on the relations between borderland Tibetans and the Republican Chinese. She published *Le 9ᵉ Panchen Lama (1883-1937), enjeu des relations sino-tibétaines* (2004).

MATTHEW T. KAPSTEIN is Numata Visiting Professor of Buddhist Studies at the University of Chicago and Director of Tibetan Religious Studies at the École Pratique des Hautes Études, Paris. His recent publications include: *The Tibetan Assimilation of Buddhism: Conversion, Contestation, and Memory*; *Reason's Traces: Identity and Interpretation in Indian and Tibetan Buddhism Thought*; and *The Presence of Light: Divine Radiance and Religious Experience*.

KARÉNINA KOLLMAR-PAULENZ studied Tibetan studies, Mongolian language and literature, history of religion, and Indian studies in Bonn and New Delhi. Since 1999 she has been professor and director of the Institute for the Study of the History of Religion at the University of Bern. Her research focuses on Tibetan and Mongolian religious and cultural history and relations between Tibet and Mongolia in the 16th and 17th centuries. Her publications include: *Erdeni tunumal neretü sudur. Die Biographie des Altan Khan der Tümed-Mongolen. Ein Beitrag zur Geschichte der religionspolitischen Beziehungen zwischen der Mongolei und Tibet im ausgehenden 16. Jahrhundert*. Wiesbaden 2001; *Die Mythologie des tibetischen und mongolischen Buddhismus* (2002).

LEONARD W. J. VAN DER KUIJP is Professor of Tibetan and Himalayan Studies and Chair of the Department of Sanskrit and Indian Studies at Harvard University. His interests focus on Indo-Tibetan Buddhist intellectual history and early Sino-Mongol-Tibetan Relations. His recent publications include *A Treatise on Buddhist Epistemology and Logic Attributed to Klong chen Rab 'byams pa (1308-1364) and Its Place in Indo-Tibetan Intellectual History*, Journal of Indian Philosophy 31 (2003), 381-437.

ERBERTO LO BUE obtained a Ph.D. in Tibetan Studies at SOAS (University of London) in 1981 and is now Associate Professor at the University of Bologna. Most of his publications are related to Tibetan, Newar and Indian art history, but two of them reflect his special interest in the 6th Dalai Lama: *Vita e canti del VI Dalai Lama* (1993); and *Tsàn-yan-ghia-tsò, VI Dalai Lama, Canti d'amore* (1993).

DEREK F. MAHER received his Ph.D. in Tibetan Buddhist Studies under Jeffrey Hopkins at the University of Virginia. He specializes in Tibetan history, biography, and dGe lugs philosophy. His annotated translation of Tsepon W. D. Shakabpa's *One Hundred Thousand Moons: An Advanced Political History of Tibet* is forthcoming. He teaches in the Department of Philosophy at East Carolina University in Greenville, North Carolina.

ALEXANDER NORMAN has known and worked with the 14th Dalai Lama since 1988. He is presently working on a full-length history of the Dalai Lamas (to be published by Lubbe, 2006).

KURTIS R. SCHAEFFER is Associate Professor in the Department of Religious Studies at the University of Virginia. He is the author of *Himalayan Hermitess: The Life of a Tibetan Buddhist Nun* (2004) and *Dreaming the Great Brahmin: Tibetan Traditions of the Buddhist Poet-Saint Saraha* (2005).

HANNA SCHNEIDER is a Tibet specialist focusing on the fields of comparative legal history and Tibetan documentary research. She has served as the Chair of the German-Tibetan Cultural Society since April 2000. Her interests and work have also included the traditions of the Sakya School and the Rime movement in their historical, religious and intellectual context, as well as the history of Tibet, particularly the 19th and first half of the 20th centuries.

TSERING SHAKYA ཚེ་རིང་ཤཱཀྱ་དབང་འདུས་ is widely published on Tibetan affairs and in 1999 Shakya's history of modern Tibet, *The Dragon in the Land of Snows, A History of Modern Tibet Since 1947* was published. His publications include *Fire Under the Snow, The Testimony of a Tibetan Prisoner* which has been translated into nine languages. Shakya was also coeditor of the first anthology of modern Tibetan short stories and poems, *The Songs of Snow Lion, New Writings from Tibet*. Tsering Shakya is presently Canada Research Chair of Religion and Contemporary Society in Asia at the Institute of Asian Research, University of British Columbia.

SHEN WEIRONG 沈衛榮 Visiting Research Fellow, Research Institute for Humanity and Nature, Kyoto, Japan. Shen Weirong specializes in Tibetan history, religion, and relations between Tibet, China, Mongol and the Tanguts. Publication: *Leben und historische Bedeutung des ersten Dalai Lama dGe dun grub pa dpal bzang po* (2002).

PER K. SØRENSEN is Professor of Tibetology (Central Asian Studies) at the University of Leipzig (Germany). Author of numerous books and treatises dealing with the literature, history and culture of Tibet and Bhūṭān. His works include *Divinity Secularized* (1990), *The Mirror Illuminating the Royal Genealogies* (1994), *Civilization at the Foot of Mount Sham-po* (2000) and *Thundering Falcon* (2005).

ACKNOWLEDGMENTS

We would like to thank the many people and institutions who have helped us with their financial support, their goodwill, their cooperation, and by providing objects and photographs.

PATRONS
We have enjoy the support of significant financial resources provided by (in order of the amount donated):

Veena and Peter Schnell, Zürich
Volkart Foundation, Winterthur
Foundation for Scientific Research of the University of Zürich
Dr. Johannes Schindler (Founder of Sambhota Educational Society, Zürich)
Rosmarie Schwarzenbach, Muri bei Bern
Rahn & Bodmer Banquiers, Zürich
René Henri Bodmer, Zürich
Silvia and Roland Nyffeler, Dietlikon
Swiss-Tibetan Friendship Society, Zürich
Dr. Branco Weiss, Zürich
Peter Schafroth, M.D., Thun
Theres Riedweg, Männedorf
Lisina and Frank W. Hoch, New York
Harriet Széchényi, Zürich
Zürich University Alumni Association
Jubiläumsstiftung der Zürich Versicherungsgesellschaft
Zürcher Kantonalbank
Richard Dähler, Zürich
Otto Gamma-Stiftung, Zürich
Ruth Gonseth, Liestal
Prof. Dr. K.H. Henking, Winterthur
Doris and Thomas Hahnloser, Küsnach
Dr. Siegfried Fischer, Innsbruck
Sigrid Joss, Muri bei Bern
Gudrun Mathys, Bern
Prof. Christian Scharfetter, Zürich

We have received additional financial support from (in alphabetical order):

David Ackermann, Zürich; Dr. Michael Ensslin, Marbach; Jeannette Gubler, Horgen; Mary Gubser, Davos-Platz; Kurt and Ritzi Heinzelmann, Zürich; Dr. Martin A. Keller, Bad Ragaz; Hans and Christa Läng, Zürich; David Mück, Zürich; Marlene Nutt, Zürich; Doris Pfeiffer, Salzburg; Rotary Club, Zug; Astrid Schoch, Teufen; Peter Schwalm, Basel; Khando and Roland Siegrist, Suhr; Parfümerie Steinmann, Zürich; Dr. Robert Stupp, Küsnacht; Tibetan Women's Association, Association of Tibetan Youth in Europe and the Tibetan Community in Switzerland; Helene Vlasak, Zürich; Eugen Wehrli, Zürich; Konrad and Regina Witzig, Hombrechtikon; Tsezom Zatul, Volkertswil; Horst Zbinden, Hettlingen; Monika Zeindler, Spreitenbach.

LENDERS
We gratefully acknowledge the following people and institutions who have provided their materials to us for exhibition and publication:

His Holiness the 14th Dalai Lama, Dharamśālā; Ashmolean Museum (Andrew Topsfield), Oxford; Joachim Baader, München; Claus-Peter Bach, Memmingen; Bayerische Staatsbibliothek (Günter Grönbold), München; Harald Bechteler, Tutzing; Bibliothéque de l'institut des hautes études chinoises du Collège de France (Mme Delphine Spicq/Isabelle Charleux), Paris; Enrico Bonfanti, Locarno; The British Library (Burkhard Quessel), London; Roger Denis, Bagnéres de Bigorre; The State Hermitage Museum (Olga Ilmenkova/Julia Elikhina), St. Petersburg; Richard R. Ernst, Winterthur; Museum of Ethnography (Mr. Lars-Erik Barkman, Håkan Wahlquist), Stockholm; Karl-Dieter Fuchsberger, Kempten; Sandor P. Fuss, Denver; Maciej Góralski, Warschau; Hanamaki City Museum 花巻市博物館 (Terasawa Hisashi 寺澤尚), Hanamaki; Wolfgang Hellrigl, Bozen; Oliver Hoare, London; Thomas Isenberg, New York; Koninklijke Musea voor Kunst en Geschiedenis (M. Lambrecht), Brüssel; Dick and Erica Gould, Lymington; Musée Guimet (Jean-François Jarrige/Nathalie Bazin/Hélène Vassalle), Paris; Jean Lassale, Paris; Christian Lequindre, Paris; Jacques Marchais Museum of Tibetan Art (Sarah Johnson), Staten Island/NY; Aldo Mignucci, London; Musée d'Ethnographie (Jérôme Ducor), Genf; Museum der Kulturen (Clara Wilpert), Basel; Museum für Ostasiatische Kunst (Adele Schlombs/Christa Waschkau), Köln; Museum für Völkerkunde (Christian Schicklgruber), Wien; Museum of Fine Arts, Boston; Museum Rietberg (Albert Lutz), Zürich; Newark Museum (Valrae Reynolds/Amber W. Germano), Newark/NJ; Hanna and Dieter Paulmann, Darmstadt; Anna Maria and Fabio Rossi, London; Rijksmuseum voor Volkenkunde (S. Engelsman/Birgit Maas), Leiden; M. and Mme Eric Schleiper, Brüssel; Mr. and Mrs. Speelman, London; Rubin Museum of Art (Lisa Arcomano/Jeff Watt), New York; Veena and Peter Schnell, Zürich; Mrs. and Mr. Laurent Solomon, Paris; Carl Sommer, John Dimond and Hans Zogg, Zürich; Markus O. Speidel, Birmensdorf; Lambert Verhoeven, Gouda; Wereldmuseum (Sandra van den Broek, Stanley Bremer, Hugo Kreijger, Kees van den Meiracker), Rotterdam; The Royal Collection Trust (Mrs. Caroline de Guitaut), London; Victoria & Albert Museum (John Clarke), London; Aye Tulku and Jane Werner-Aye, New York; Jean-Pierre and Helga Yvergneaux, Sint-Martens-Latem.

PHOTOGRAPHS / ARCHIVES
Historical photographs were graciously provided to us by:

The Academy of Natural Sciences (Earle Spamer), Philadelphia; Bodleian Library, University of Oxford (Doris Nicholson), Oxford; British Library (Burkhard Quessel, John Falconer), London; British Museum (Richard Blurton, Lindsey Belcher), London; Cambridge University Museum of Archaeology and Anthropology (Wendy Brown), Cambridge; Roger Croston, Chester; Dick and Erica Gould, Lymington; Michael Henss, Zürich; James A. Cannavino Library, Archives and Special Collections, Marist College, Poughkeepsie, New York; Maybe Jehu, London; Thomas Laird, New Orleans; Library of Tibetan Works and Archives, Dharamśālā (Pema Yeschi, Tenzing Lhawang); Lowell Thomas, Achorage; Michael Marchant, Zürich; The Newark Museum (Amber W. Germano), Newark/NJ; The New York Times Photo Archives (Barbara Cox), New York; Nomad Picture Library (Dolma Beresford), London; Norbulingka Institute (Kim Yeshi, Thubten Tsewang, Ngawang Tharpa), Sidhpur/Dharamśālā; Pitt Rivers Museum (Jocelyne Dudding/Clare Harris), Oxford; Rose Art Museum, Brandeis University (Ben Thopson), Waltham, Massachusetts; Hansjörg Sahli, Solothurn; Sarah Central Archive (Ven. Lhakdor), Sarah/Dharamśālā; Anne Elisabeth Suter, Kilchberg; The Tibetan & Himalayan Digital Library (David Newman), Charlottesville, Virginia; Tibet Images (Ian Cumming), London; The Tibet Museum, DIIR (Dickyi, Thubten Samphel), Dharamśālā; Paljor Tsarong, Dharamśālā and Dadul Namgyal Tsarong, Dehradun; Josef Vaniš, Prague; Guido Vogliotti, Turin.

OTHER SUPPORT

In making this project a reality, assistance was also provided by: the Private Office of H.H. the Dalai Lama in Dharamśālā (Tenzin Geyche, Khuntsog Gyaltsen, Tenzing Takla); Dieter Kuhn, who translated English articles into German; Amy Heller, Nyon; Michael Henss, Zürich; Per K. Sørensen, Leipzig; Hanna Schneider, Bonn; Isrun Engelhardt, Icking; Ute Griesser, Cologne, the external restorer; Manuel Bauer, Winterthur; the exhibition service of the Zürcher Universitätsmuseen (Martin Kämpf, Andreas Brodbeck and Frank Lenz); from the publishing house: Dirk Allgaier, Julia Vogt, Karina Moschke and Silke Nalbach; at the Ethnographic Museum of the University of Zürich first and foremost: Dario Donati, Renate Koller, Kathrin Leuenberger, Silvia Luckner, Ina von Woyski Niedermann, Kathrin Kocher, Urs Wohlgemuth. It is not possible to mention by name all the people who have supported me in this project so this list must remain incomplete, unfortunately. I would like to mention the following people, however: Knud Larsen, Oslo; Simon Bosshart, Zürich; Martin Dällenbach, Zürich; Daniel Scheidegger, Bern; Herbert Schwabl, Zürich; Heather Stoddard, Paris; Susi Greuter, Binningen; Urs Haller, Bern; David Jackson, Hamburg; Christian Wehrlin, Bern and Dolma Roder.

My heartfelt thanks to all patrons, sponsors, lenders and those who worked with us for their friendly cooperation.

Martin Brauen
Ethnographic Museum of the University of Zürich

LADĀKH

• Rudok

• Dharamśālā

NGARI

INDIA

▲ Tise (Kailāśa)

NEPĀL

• Kyerc

Kāṭhmāṇḍū ●

T I B E T	Land
A M D O	Province
Dakpo	Region
• ● Gyantse	Town / City
• Tashilhünpo	Monastery
▲ *Tise (Kailāśa)*	Mountain
▢ *Lhamo Lhatso*	Lake
✳ **DL 14**	Birthplace of the Dalai Lamas

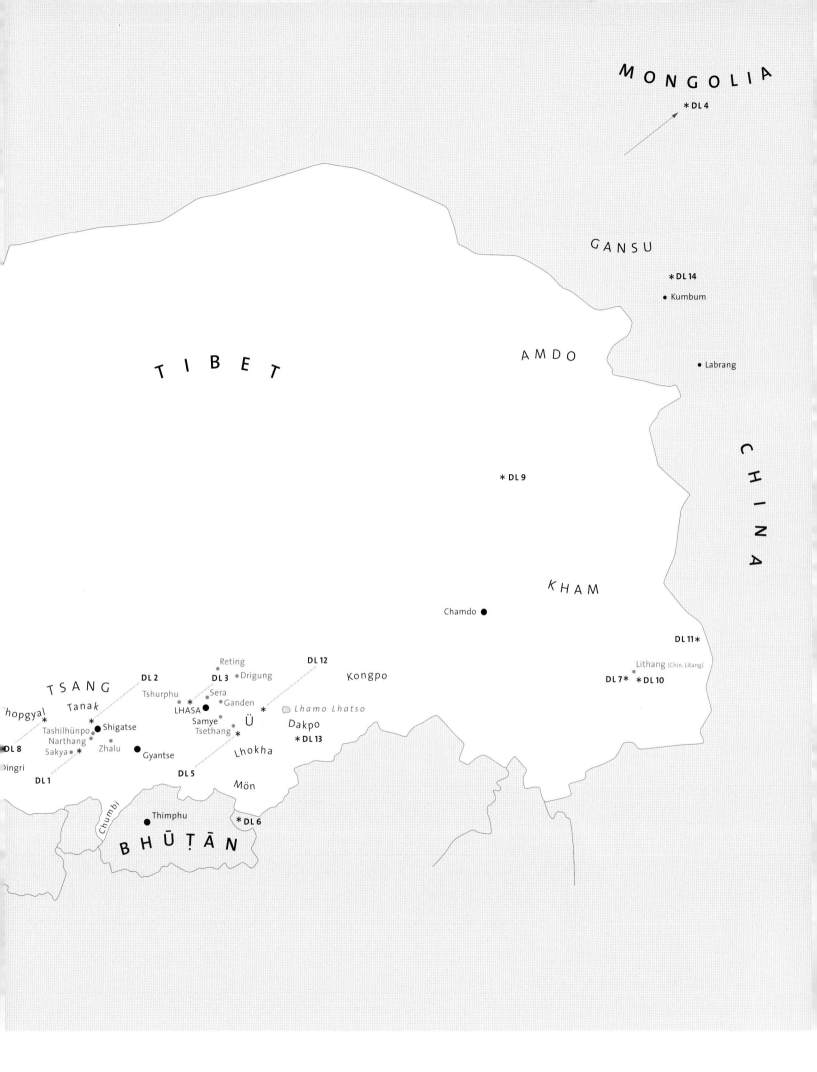

MONGOLIA

* DL 4

GANSU

* DL 14

• Kumbum

AMDO

TIBET

• Labrang

CHINA

* DL 9

KHAM

Chamdo ●

DL 11 *

Lithang (Chin. Litang)

Reting

DL 12

DL 7 * * DL 10

TSANG

DL 2

Tanak

• Drigung

Kongpo

Tshurphu

DL 3

Sera

hopgyal

*

* Ganden

Tashilhünpo ●

LHASA ●

Samye

Ü

Lhamo Lhatso

*

● Shigatse

Narthang

Tsethang

Dakpo

DL 8

Zhalu

*

* DL 13

Sakya ● *

Dingri

● Gyantse

Lhokha

DL 1

DL 5

Mön

Chumbi

● Thimphu

* DL 6

BHŪṬĀN

MAP   301

INDEX

ILLUSTRATION CREDITS

Archives of the Ethnographic Museum of the University of Zürich   162, 229, 230, 231

Archives of the Norbulingka Institute, Sidhpur, India   129, 132, 134, 140, 142, 143, 147, 157, 159, 160, 161, 163, 164, 165, 166, 167, 168, 169, 170, 171, 172, 176, 177, 181, 182, 183, 184, 185, 186, 187, 188, 190, 191, 192, 193, 194, 195, 196, 197, 206, 207

© Daniel Arnaudet, © Photo RMN   7, 42

© Manuel Bauer, AGENTUR FOCUS, Hamburg, 2005   135, 136, 137, 138, 139

Sir Charles Alfred Bell, in: Charles Bell, Tibet – Einst und Jetzt, Leipzig 1925, Frontispiece   110

© Brian Beresford / Nomad Pictures   126, 127, 246

John Bigelow Taylor   Frontispiece

Gérard Blot, © Photo RMN   199

Martin Brauen, Ethnographic Museum of the University of Zürich   189

© The British Museum   109

Andreas Brodbeck   105 (Photomontage assembled from two pictures from the Department of Central Asian Studies of the University of Bonn), 130 (Photomontage assembled from slides by Michael Henss and Martin Brauen), Chronology (folder)

Christopher Bruckner, London   78

Frederick Spencer Chapman, © Pitt Rivers Museum, University of Oxford, 2005   117, 119

Ian Cumming, © Tibet Images   122

D. James Dee   65

Brooke Dolan, The Academy of Natural Sciences of Philadelphia, Ewell Sale Stewart Library   146

Bernhard Drenowatz, Zürich   14a–c, 265

Collection of R.J. and E. Gould   107, 233

Collection of Lady Gould   232

Markus Gruber, Museum der Kulturen Basel, Sammlung Essen   15, 27, 218

Heinrich Harrer, Ethnographic Museum of the University of Zürich   149, 150, 151, 152, 154, 155, 178, 179

Michael Henss, Zürich   91

Erik Hesmerg, Sneek, Wereldmuseum Rotterdam © 2005   11, 20

Hopkinson Archive © The British Museum   180

Johnston and Hoffmann, 1910, Sir Charles Alfred Bell Collection © The British Library   237

Iza Kowalczyk, Warschau   23

Thomas Laird, New Orleans (Photo and ©)   125, 158, 212

Jean Lassale, Paris   227, 228

Kathrin Leuenberger, Ethnographic Museum of the University of Zürich   2, 5, 6, 8, 10, 12, 13, 19, 26, 30, 35, 36, 50, 53, 66, 77, 81, 88, 89, 92, 102, 123, 211, 215, 216, 221, 223, 281, 291, 297

Library of Tibetan Works and Archives, Dharamśālā   203

Francisco Little, Archives of the Norbulingka Institute, Sidhpur, Indien   131

Silvia Luckner, Ethnographic Museum of the University of Zürich   98

David Macdonald, 1912, Sir Charles Alfred Bell Collection © The British Library   234

© Michael Marchant (Photo and ©), Zürich   198

Hans Meyer-Veden, Museum der Kulturen Basel, Sammlung Essen   280

Musée national des arts asiatiques Guimet, Paris   43, 44, 45, 79

Musées Royaux d'Art et d'Histoire, Brüssel   21, 33, 225

Museum für Ostasiatische Kunst, Foto: Rheinisches Bildarchiv, Köln   101

Museum für Völkerkunde Wien   68

© Pitt Rivers Museum, University of Oxford, 2005, (Photographer probably Archibald Steele)   141a–c

© Pitt Rivers Museum, University of Oxford, 2005   175

© Ravaux, Photo RMN   210

Hugh Richardson, © Pitt Rivers Museum, University of Oxford, 2005   118

The Royal Collection © 2005, Her Majesty Queen Elizabeth II, RCIN: 74476. Cat. No.: V & A loan 485   71

Hansjörg Sahli, Solothurn   Seite 10

Sarah Central Archive   113, 133, 202, 204, 205

© Jean Schormans, © Photo RMN   41

Delphine Spicq, Bibliotèque de l'Institut des hautes études chinoises du Collège de France   84, 85, 86, 87

The State Hermitage Museum, St. Petersburg, 2005   32, 56, 58, 93, 94, 238, 239

Lowell Thomas (Photo and ©)   241

Lowell Thomas, James A. Cannavino Library, Archives and Special Collections, Marist College, Poughkeepsie, New York   144, 145, 287

The Tibet Museum / DIIR, Dharamśālā (Fotograf vermutlich Archibald Steele)   148

The Tibet Museum / DIIR, Dharamśālā   153, 173, 174

Ilya Tolstoy, © Collection of R.J. and E. Gould   120

Dadul Namgyal Tsarong, Dehradun   243

© Josef Vaniš, Prague   244

Ethnographic Museum of the University of Zürich   156, 245

Guido Vogliotti, Turin   67

Leslie Weir, Collection of Maybe Jehu, London   114, 115, 235

Sir Frederick Williamson, Sir Charles Alfred Bell Collection © The British Library   116

Sir Frederick Williamson, Cambridge University Museum of Archaeology and Anthropology, (P.97071.WIL)   108

Xing Suzhi, © The New York Times Photo Archives   242

CHAPTER OPENING FIGURES:

The Dalai Lamas and the Origins of Reincarnate Lamas: Details of 3, 7 and 21.

The First Dalai Lama Gendün Drup: Detail of 81.

The Second Dalai Lama Gendün Gyatso: Detail of 81.

The Third Dalai Lama Sönam Gyatso and the Fourth Dalai Lama Yönten Gyatso: Detail of 81.

The Fifth Dalai Lama Ngawang Lopsang Gyatso: Detail of 81.

The Sixth Dalai Lama Tsangyang Gyatso: Detail of 81.

The Seventh Dalai Lama Kalsang Gyatso: Detail of 81.

The Eighth Dalai Lama Jampel Gyatso: Detail of 81.

The Ninth to the Twelfth Dalai Lama: Detail from the temple mural at the Norbulingka Institute, Sidhpur/ Dharamśālā, India.

The Thirteenth Dalai Lama Thupten Gyatso: Detail from the temple mural at the Norbulingka Institute, Sidhpur/Dharamśālā, India.

The Fourteenth Dalai Lama Tenzin Gyatso: Detail from the temple mural at the Norbulingka Institute, Sidhpur/ Dharamśālā, India.